Interstate Relations in Classical Greece

In this book Dr Low explores the assumptions and principles which determined the conduct and representation of interstate politics in Greece during the fifth and fourth centuries BC. She employs a wide range of ancient evidence, both epigraphic and literary, as well as some contemporary theoretical approaches from the field of International Relations. Taking a thematic rather than a chronological approach, she addresses topics such as the nature of interstate society in the Greek world; the sources, scope and enforcement of 'international law'; the nature of interstate ethics and morality; interventionism and imperialism; and the question of change and stability. She argues that Classical Greece's reputation for unrestrained and unsophisticated diplomacy is undeserved, and shows that relations between Greek city-states were shaped by and judged according to a complex network of customs, beliefs and expectations which pervaded all areas of interstate behaviour.

POLLY LOW is Lecturer in Ancient History at the University of Manchester.

CAMBRIDGE CLASSICAL STUDIES

General editors

R. L. HUNTER, R. G. OSBORNE, M. D. REEVE,
P. D. A. GARNSEY, M. MILLETT, D. N. SEDLEY,
G. C. HORROCKS

INTERSTATE RELATIONS IN CLASSICAL GREECE

Morality and Power

POLLY LOW
University of Manchester

CAMBRIDGE
UNIVERSITY PRESS

CAMBRIDGE UNIVERSITY PRESS
Cambridge, New York, Melbourne, Madrid, Cape Town, Singapore, São Paulo

Cambridge University Press
The Edinburgh Building, Cambridge CB2 8RU, UK

Published in the United States of America by Cambridge University Press, New York

www.cambridge.org
Information on this title: www.cambridge.org/9780521872065

© Faculty of Classics, University of Cambridge 2007

First published 2007

Printed in the United Kingdom at the University Press, Cambridge

A catalogue record for this publication is available from the British Library

ISBN 978-0-521-87206-5 hardback

CONTENTS

PREFACE

This book is a study of the interstate politics of the classical Greek world. In it, I do not attempt to provide a diachronic narrative of the interstate relations of the period, nor do I offer detailed accounts of every significant event or action in interstate politics at this time. What I seek to do, instead, is to explain why these events and actions take the form that they do – that is, to explore the assumptions and principles which determine the conduct, and representation, of classical Greek interstate politics. In doing so, I make use of a wide range of ancient material, both epigraphic and literary, and of some contemporary theoretical approaches to international politics (which are discussed in Chapter 1). I tackle the subject thematically rather than chronologically, starting from (in Chapter 2) the most basic question of the structure and scope of the Greek interstate system (or society). Chapter 3 investigates the ways in which interactions between states in that system were regulated: that is, broadly, the question of 'international law'. A theme which emerges here is the degree of overlap between domestic and interstate activity, and this is the focus of the fourth chapter: to what extent are the ethics of interstate behaviour characterised in ancient writing as being distinct from those which apply within states? The fifth chapter looks at the practical combination of the various aspects which have been explored in the earlier chapters, focusing on approaches to intervention in Greek interstate relations, while the final chapter addresses the question of change (and the lack of it).

This book is a revised and expanded version of my 2002 Cambridge PhD thesis, 'Normative politics in Greek interstate relations'. Neither the thesis nor the book could have been written without the financial, academic and moral support of many institutions and people, all of whom I would like to thank here.

This project could not have been undertaken at all without the support of the Arts and Humanities Research Board (who funded my PhD) and of Christ's College, Cambridge (where I was a Junior Research Fellow from 2001 to 2003). Grants from the British Academy, the Faculty of Classics, Cambridge, the Kurt Hahn Trust, the Isaac Newton Trust and the University of Manchester enabled me to pursue parts of my research in Greece and Germany, and at various conferences in the UK and abroad. I am grateful, also, for the hospitality of the staff and members of the British School at Athens, an institution which provided inspiration in the middle stages of the project and a calm haven in which to complete it.

The thesis on which this book is based was supervised by Paul Cartledge, who has been a constant and sustaining source of information, advice, encouragement and good humour. I am also deeply indebted to my examiners, Robin Osborne and P. J. Rhodes, for their detailed comments on the original thesis and for their perceptive advice on how to develop it. Many other people have offered invaluable help, by reading some or all of the work as it has progressed through its various versions; by discussing and helping me to solve particular problems; or by allowing me access to their own unpublished material: Charles Crowther, Geoffrey Hawthorn, Peter Hunt, Liz Irwin, Alice König, J. E. Lendon, Peter Liddel, Paul Millett and Barry Strauss; students and colleagues at Manchester (who have borne their excessive exposure to the ideas in this book with unwarranted tolerance); and the editors of Cambridge Classical Studies.

I hope that my family and friends already know that none of this would have been possible without the unfailing support which they have provided. I suspect, though, that I may have forgotten – until now – to thank them for it.

ABBREVIATIONS

Abbreviations of classical periodicals follow those of *L'Année Philologique*; of authors and texts, those of LSJ⁹ and the *Oxford Latin Dictionary*; and of *corpora* of inscriptions, those of *SEG*. Exceptions from and additions to that rule are:

FGH F. Jacoby, *Die Fragmente der griechischen Historiker*, 3 vols., Berlin and Leiden 1923–58

HCP F. Walbank, *A Historical Commentary on Polybius*, 3 vols., Oxford 1957–79

HCT A. W. Gomme, A. Andrewes & K. J. Dover, *A Historical Commentary on Thucydides*, 5 vols., Oxford 1945–81

LSJ⁹ H. G. Liddell & R. Scott, *A Greek–English Lexicon*, rev. H. S. Jones & R. McKenzie, 9th edn with supplement, ed. E. A. Barber, Oxford 1968; revised supplement, ed. P. G. W. Glare, Oxford and New York 1996

ML R. Meiggs & D. M. Lewis, *A Selection of Greek Historical Inscriptions. To the end of the fifth century BC*, 2nd edn, Oxford 1988

RE G. Wissowa, W. Kroll, K. Mittelhaus & K. Ziegler edd., *Paulys Real-Encyclopädie der Classischen Altertumswissenschaft*, 83 vols., Munich and Stuttgart 1893–1978

RO P. J. Rhodes & R. G. Osborne, *Greek Historical Inscriptions 403–323 BC*, Oxford 2003

SV II H. Bengtson, *Die Staatsverträge des Altertums,* vol. II: *die Verträge der griechisch-römischen Welt von 700 bis 338 v. Chr.*, 2nd edn, Munich 1975

SV III   H. H. Schmitt, *Die Staatsverträge des Altertums,*
vol. III: *die Verträge der griechisch-römischen Welt
von 338 bis 200 v. Chr.*, Munich 1969

Tod   M. N. Tod, *A Selection of Greek Historical
Inscriptions,* vol. II: *from 403 to 323 BC*, Oxford 1948

INTRODUCTION

The classical Greek world has been admired for many things, but the way in which it conducted its interstate politics has rarely been one of them. Disparaging remarks start to appear early in the historical record: shortly before Xerxes' invasion of Greece in 480 (according to Herodotus), the Persian Mardonius observed that the Greeks,

ἀβουλότατα πολέμους ἵστασθαι ὑπό τε ἀγνωμοσύνης καὶ σκαιότητος· . . . τοὺς χρῆν, ἐόντας ὁμογλώσσους, κήρυξί τε διαχρεωμένους καὶ ἀγγέλοισι καταλαμβάνειν τὰς διαφορὰς καὶ παντὶ μᾶλλον ἢ μάχησι.

are accustomed to wage wars, and they do it most senselessly in their wrongheadedness and folly. . . . Since they speak the same language, they should end their disputes by means of heralds or messengers, or by any way rather than fighting. (Hdt. vii.9b)

Subsequent events might have revealed flaws in Mardonius' analysis of Greek military competence, but his damning assessment of their diplomatic capabilities has found consistent, and continuing, support. 'The foreign policy of the Greeks', wrote Adcock in 1924, 'was the foreign policy of the Kilkenny cats, and so the less said about it the better.'[1] In 1965, J. R. Grant discussed, and attempted to account for, the underdeveloped nature of Greek interstate interaction, and concluded that conventional definitions of diplomacy ('the application of intelligence and tact to the conduct of official relations between the government of independent states')[2] could hardly be applied to the classical Greek world, on the grounds that

the whole of Greek history testifies to the lack of restraint and political common sense . . . between these little states.[3]

---

[1] Adcock 1924: 93. (Adcock did go on in that work, and in later writings – esp. Adcock 1948 – to attempt to make the case for the existence of some sort of diplomatic art in ancient Greece.)

[2] Nicolson's definition, cited in Grant 1965: 261.

[3] Grant 1965: 262. MacMullen 1963 comes to similar concusions on the 'suicidally quarrelsome' (118) interstate relations of the Greek *poleis*.

Such dissatisfaction has persisted to the present. A recent textbook closes its account of Greek history (from the earliest times down to 146 BC) with the observation that the story is 'from start to finish . . . a tragedy of violence and blood shed in the name of liberty'.[4]

If the Greek practice of interstate relations has typically been regarded as defective, so too has their development of international theory: the consensus, at least among ancient historians, has been that the classical Greeks had no particular interest in, still less anything of great importance to say about, the practice of relations between states.

This attitude is not unreasonable: there is no evidence that the classical Greek world ever came up with any sustained theoretical account of interstate relations. This gap becomes particularly striking when it is seen alongside the distinguished corpus of political theory produced in the period: although interaction with other states – above all through war – is always present in the background of Platonic and Aristotelian writing, it is only rarely treated directly.[5] It is true that other genres – especially historiography and symbouleutic rhetoric – are more closely engaged with questions of interstate behaviour, but it is also the case that their analysis of this behaviour has often been regarded as distinctly sub-optimal: the failure to work out a developed theory of the causes of war is perhaps the most well-known complaint.[6] The only, and obvious, exception to that general pattern of ancient neglect and modern disdain is Thucydides. Even ancient historians would admit that this writer displays a close and critical interest in the nature and conduct of foreign relations, and many scholars – notably scholars working in the field of International Relations – would argue that he should be counted as the first practitioner of their discipline, and the first theorist of international politics.

It will already be apparent that I do not subscribe to this generally bleak assessment of the potential interest or value of the subject of Greek interstate politics, and an overarching aim of this book is to demonstrate that the absence of an explicit theory of interstate

---

[4] Orrieux & Schmitt Pantel 1999: 368.

[5] See Forde 1992: 74–5; similar observations appear in Sinclair 1952: 105; Ryder 1965: 116.

[6] Momigliano 1966c. See also Finley 1985c; Shipley 1993: 8–13.

politics does not entail an absence of complex thinking about the subject, and, moreover, that the search for that complex thinking does not have to begin and end with Thucydides. I hope to show that it is possible to discover and to describe a developed normative framework, visible in a range of ancient sources, which shapes both the conduct and the representation of interstate relations in this period. The subject of this book is not, therefore, the events of classical Greek interstate politics, but the underlying motivations for those events: the conventions and customs which surround the behaviour of states and individuals, the role of moral criteria and moral judgements, the demands of power and self-interest and, most importantly, the interaction between these different factors.

Although the aim of this study is historical, its method might be characterised as primarily literary: that is, it is through reading and analysis of written texts and documents – epigraphic texts as well as those normally classed as 'literary' – that it seeks to develop a rounded picture of the beliefs, principles, conflicts and inconsistencies that make up the Greek approach to interstate politics. This choice of method has imposed certain constraints (I have, for example, made very little use of archaeological material) but allows for considerable breadth in other important respects – notably, the chronological and geographical scope of the enquiry.

The range of the former is, broadly speaking, the classical period – approximately 479 to 322 BC. (The questions of periodisation and of diachronic change which the choice of these conventional boundaries begs are addressed in Chapter 6.) Within these limits, the bulk of the evidence, both literary and epigraphic, comes from the first half of the fourth century, but it is complemented and supplemented by important material from other parts of the period: oratory and philosophy from the third quarter of the fourth century, for example, and the great wealth of material produced by and associated with the Delian League and Peloponnesian War (including, but not limited to, Thucydides' account of those things).

The geographic boundaries are similarly flexible: the cities and states which will feature in this work are scattered round the Aegean, and beyond – westwards towards Italy and Sicily, and north and east to and beyond the margins of what is traditionally counted the Greek world. It must be admitted, however, that this assertion of broad geographical scope is to some extent misleading: almost all of the literary evidence considered here, and a significant majority of the epigraphic material, has some connection with Athens. Most usually, Athens is the site of production, and often consumption, of a particular piece of evidence; sometimes, more rarely, it features as a participant in activities recorded by some other state (as a recipient of honours, for example); material in which Athens plays absolutely no part forms a tiny minority of the evidence used. The potential distortions which can arise from this unavoidable weighting of the material do not need to be itemised, but the fact that they exist must be emphasised (and will surface again as a more specific problem at certain points in the discussion).

This broad focus has been adopted for a specific reason: namely, that past approaches to this subject have often been constrained by the narrowness of their concerns. One egregious example of this – the amount of attention paid to Thucydides' analysis of foreign relations – has already been mentioned, and deserves brief further comment at this point. My objection to Thucydides, or to the work done on Thucydides, is not that it is unimportant or uninteresting. Rather, the reverse seems to be the case: the compelling problems of Thucydidean interpretation have tended to act as a sponge for the enthusiasm and attention of those with an interest in Greek conceptions of interstate politics – a (somewhat stifling) fascination which has affected not only ancient historians but also, and often to a much greater extent, international theorists.

Meanwhile, other parts of the field have focused on different, but equally restricted, subjects. Work within Ancient History on non-Thucydidean approaches to ancient interstate relations has typically tackled specific aspects of the subject (diplomacy, treaties, federalism and so on);[7] or, and particularly in the case of fourth-century studies, has been absorbed by the problems of trying to reconstruct coherent diachronic accounts of interstate

---

[7] For example, Mosley 1973; Adcock and Mosley 1975; Piccirilli 2002 (all on diplomacy); Baltrusch 1994 (on treaties); Beck 1997 (on federalism); Mitchell 1997a (on friendship and reciprocity); Van Wees 2004 (on warfare and its uses).

politics;[8] or, finally, has concentrated on the approaches of individual authors.[9]

The result of this widespread particularism is, I would suggest, a failure to exploit fully the possibilities either of modern theories of interstate behaviour, or of the ancient Greek evidence for that behaviour: the great majority of theoretical attention is directed at a very small proportion of the ancient evidence. Conversely, the majority of ancient material describing and discussing interstate politics is rarely subjected to the sort of close, critical scrutiny which is devoted to the elucidation of Thucydides' views on the subject. It is this damaging narrowness – damaging to studies of International Relations as well as Ancient History – that the inclusive approach adopted here is intended to overcome.

One further aspect of this attempted inclusiveness should also, finally, be mentioned. It has already been observed that the interstate politics of classical Greece are not of interest only to ancient historians – scholars working in the field of International Relations have also regularly turned their attention to this part of the ancient world. The engagement between the two disciplines has, as has already been suggested, taken place on a narrow – largely Thucydidean – front; but it should also be noted that the interaction has been overwhelmingly one-sided: international theorists have made repeated, if limited, appeals to Greek history, but Greek historians have often paid little attention to the results of this work.[10] And they have paid even less attention to larger theoretical and methodological developments in the discipline of International Relations,

---

[8] For example: Accame 1951 or Hamilton 1979 on the Corinthian War; Heskel 1997 on the 'North Aegean Wars'. Other diachronic accounts of post-Thucydidean interstate politics have tackled longer periods, but focused on individual states: important examples are Cloché 1934 or Badian 1995 on Athens; Cartledge 1987 on Sparta; Buckler 1980 on Thebes; Ellis 1976 or Ashley 1998 on Macedon. Harding 1995 is an important exception, which deliberately adopts a 'lumping' approach to the subject (106), but is more interested in questions of policy and strategy than wider principles and structures.

[9] For example: Missiou 1992 on Andocides; E. M. Harris 1995 on Aeschines; Pickard-Cambridge 1914; Jaeger 1938; Luccioni 1961; Sealey 1993 on Demosthenes; Cloché 1963; Bringmann 1965; Grieser-Schmitz 1999 on Isocrates; Tuplin 1993 on Xenophon. Constantineau 1998 looks at international theory in a range of Greek authors, but treats each author separately.

[10] There are some exceptions to this general pattern: note especially Lebow & Strauss edd. 1991; Crane 1998.

even though debates in that field have increasingly tackled problems which are far from irrelevant to the study of Greek interstate politics. A debate which has been at the heart of the discipline since its early years – that concerning the roles (individual and relative) of morality and power in interstate politics – is still important (and has if anything become more prominent in recent years), and Thucydides still regularly plays a significant part in arguments on this subject. But that debate – which is also central to the concerns of this book – is now being conducted in the context of a much richer set of theoretical questions: what is the nature of interstate society?; how do these societies create and sustain norms of interstate behaviour?; what are the relative roles and duties of individuals, groups and states, and how rigid are the boundaries between these different actors in interstate politics?

It is by asking questions of this sort that this book approaches the problem of morality and power in Greek interstate politics. But in order to get a clearer sense of the reasons why these questions are being asked by international theorists, and why and how ancient historians might want to try to answer them, it is worth starting with a brief exploration of the intellectual and ideological history of International Relations, and of its (sometimes troubled) relationship with Ancient History.

INTERNATIONAL RELATIONS AND
ANCIENT HISTORY

1.1 A case study: Professor Sir Alfred Zimmern

In April 1919, in a small town on the coast of Wales, academic history was made. The first chair of International Politics at the University College of Wales, Aberystwyth, took up his post, and in doing so became the world's first professor of that subject – the first official representative of a newly constituted discipline.[1] The holder of this new position was Alfred Zimmern: a classicist by training; an ancient historian in his early career; and, now, given the responsibility for shaping the substantive and theoretical agenda of this new subject.

The extent to which Zimmern succeeded in this task is questionable. His stay at Aberystwyth was both short-lived and scandalous,[2] and his wider contribution to the discipline of International Relations has also traditionally been thought to be generally underwhelming. A recent assessment of his work concludes that Zimmern

---

[1] 1919 is not universally accepted as the year of the discipline's birth. The term 'international' was coined by Bentham in 1780 (see 83 n. 28); the phrase 'international relations' starts to appear from the mid-nineteenth century (see, for example, the original title of Laurent 1862; Mackay 1880; Stephen 1884): see Der Derian 1989: 3–4. Academic study of aspects of the subject certainly precedes the invention of a name for it: the creation in Oxford of the Chichele Chair of International Law and Diplomacy in 1859 is an important indication of that; see also Schmidt 1998 on the study of the subject in the US in the nineteenth century. The case for 1919 as a turning point is restated by Dunne 1998a; Brown 2001b: 20.

[2] Zimmern was forced to resign two years after his appointment, although this was more for personal than for academic reasons: on Zimmern's favourable reaction to the academic side of his job, see Zimmern 1921a; for other aspects of his Welsh interlude (including his marriage to the wife of another professor – the catalyst for his resignation), see Porter ed. 1972: 362. Departure from Wales did not mark the end of Zimmern's academic career: he was elected as Oxford's first professor of International Relations in 1930. The standard biography is now Markwell 2004; other details appear in Miller 1979/80; Markwell 1986; Calder 1989.

is a key thinker in International Relations not because he is a great thinker, but because his work imparts important lessons in how *not* to think about international law and international organisation.[3]

Zimmern will, nevertheless, make regular appearances in this chapter. This is not because I have any strong wish to attempt to salvage his battered academic reputation, but rather because his career, and subsequent reactions to it, can usefully serve to illustrate the three themes which will form the focus of discussion here: first, and perhaps most obviously, the disciplinary history of International Relations;[4] second, the relationship between International Relations and Ancient History; and finally, the approaches which international theorists have made to questions of ethics and norms. These three themes are, as will be apparent, somewhat diverse, and my reasons for discussing them in this chapter are similarly varied. One general aim is to provide a small amount of academic orientation in a discipline with which many ancient historians are relatively unfamiliar, but whose research questions underpin much of this book. More specifically, I hope to illustrate the particular methodological and ideological problems which have surrounded, and continue to surround, the study of interstate norms and interstate morality in International Relations, and to explore the role which classical Greek material can play in that exercise.

1.2 Traditions of International Relations: the history of the discipline

The chair to which Zimmern was appointed at Aberystwyth had been established on the initiative, and with the financial support, of local philanthropist and Liberal MP David Davies, together with his two sisters, 'in memory of the fallen students of our university'.[5]

---

[3] Griffiths 1999: 100 (emphasis original). Miller 1979/80 and Markwell 1986 come to similar conclusions. Manning 1962: 205f., has a more positive view (although Manning, too, does not have the best reputation among international theorists: see Suganami 2001). The most sympathetic recent assessment of Zimmern's work in International Relations can be found in Rich 1995.

[4] In what follows, references with upper case ('International Relations', etc.) denote the discipline, those with lower case the activities studied by that discipline.

[5] John, Wright & Garnett 1972: 86.

The post-war climate is reflected, too, in the chair's stipulated aims and objectives:

> the study of those related problems of law and politics, of ethics and economics, which are raised by the project of a League of Nations, and for the encouragement of a truer understanding of civilisation other than our own . . . Political Science in its application to International Relations with special reference to the best means of promoting peace between nations.[6]

The fact that this disciplinary agenda has undergone considerable change since 1919 is not, in itself, particularly unexpected or unusual. What does deserve further comment, though, is the extent to which the reformulations of the scope and purposes of the subject – and, more specifically, the diachronic narrative of those developments – have become central to the structures and self-image of the discipline.[7] The story is worth relating, not only for the light it can shed on the changing theoretical and ideological concerns of International Relations, but also because it can help provide a better understanding of the way in which the discipline is connected (or sees itself as being connected) to the wider world of academic and political practice.

The ideological starting point of International Relations was liberalism, and the liberal agenda which drove the discipline's foundation is also prominent in the early years of its history. Early liberal theorists – more usually labelled 'Idealists' – believed, broadly, that moral judgement could be applied to the practice of international relations and that moral considerations could and did influence that practice. Their claims extended, therefore, to the assertion of the possibility of progress in international relations: it could be possible to develop a stable world order, based on moral considerations rather than pure power, in which international law could become an alternative to warfare as the driving force of international politics.[8] Zimmern's work illustrates these concerns clearly, and, in

---

[6] Quoted in Herbert 1928: 185.

[7] For a standard version of this narrative – the story of the 'Great Debates' – see Banks 1985; see also Olson 1972; Olson & Onuf 1985; Vasquez 1998: ch. 2; Brown 2001b: chs. 2 and 3. More critical versions can be found in Smith 1989; Hollis & Smith 1990: ch. 2; Smith 1995; Kahler 1997; Wæver 1997; Linklater 2000; and see further below: 22–8.

[8] On the Idealist thinkers of the inter-war period, see esp. Long & Wilson edd. 1995; other discussions can be found in Osiander 1998; Ashworth 1999: esp. ch. 5.

particular, shows a recurring interest in the possibility of change in international politics: how should the west respond to the increasing power of Japan?; what should succeed the British Empire?; how could the League of Nations encourage the development of a 'rule of law' in international relations?[9] Zimmern's programme was not a radical one – his concern was to introduce reform and progress into the existing international system rather than to create a revolutionary new world order[10] – but it was, fundamentally, moral: he believed that future international stability could come from a state of mind rather than from military power,[11] and saw his task as being, above all, to create that moral state of mind among those involved in international relations.[12] It is the reactions to, and against, this approach to international relations (and International Relations) which has set the agenda of the discipline for much of the rest of its existence.

As the conventional story is told, the first, and most significant, reaction to the Idealist approach was mounted by the 'Realists'. This group – whose leading figures in the middle of the century were E. H. Carr and Hans Morgenthau – represented, more or less, the opposite of the Idealist world-view. Moral judgements had no place in international relations – power was what determined and directed the behaviour of states.[13] Such a situation was, moreover, fundamentally unchangeable: human nature, and

[9] On the rise of Japan – exemplified by the Japanese success against Russia in the war of 1904/5 – see Zimmern 1926b: 82. On the Empire and the Commonwealth, see esp. Zimmern 1926a, 1926b. On the League of Nations, see Zimmern 1936 (his most famous work).

[10] See Rich 1995: 88–9. This approach to International Relations is most clearly visible in Zimmern's inaugural lecture at Oxford (Zimmern 1931); see also below: 12–13.

[11] Zimmern 1926a: 21–2.   [12] Rich 1995: 81.

[13] See, e.g., Carr 1946: vii: 'The Twenty Years' Crisis was written with the deliberate aim of counteracting the glaring and dangerous defect of nearly all thinking, both academic and popular, about international politics in English-speaking countries from 1919–1939 – the almost total neglect of the factor of power.' Or, Morgenthau 1985: 29: 'international politics, like all politics, is a struggle for power. Whatever the ultimate aims of international politics, power is always the immediate aim. Statesmen and peoples may ultimately seek freedom, prosperity, or power itself. They may define their goals in terms of a religious, philosophic, economic, or social ideal . . . But whenever they strive to realize their goal by means of international politics, they do so by striving for power.' On treatments of power in IR, see Buzan 2000. Generally on the history of Realism, see Guzzini 1998.

more specifically the human urge to maximise power and security, would ensure that the behaviour of states remained basically constant.[14]

This methodological confrontation became known as the 'First Great Debate', and was a contest in which the Realists claimed (and, often, still claim) outright victory. By the late 1950s, therefore, the field was clear for the 'Second Great Debate'. This time, the issues were not primarily ideological – the debate took place within the broad framework of Realist assumptions about international relations[15] – but methodological. The academic background of International Relations lay in the humanities, and in history and law in particular: once more, the choice of Zimmern as the first chair of the subject illustrates the point. These 'traditionalist' approaches were now challenged by theorists who argued for the application of 'behaviouralist' social-scientific methods to the study of the subject. Legitimate theories of international relations, it was argued, could not be based on assumptions about unobservable elements of human nature and behaviour. Instead, international theorists should adopt the methods of natural science, and base their theories solely on objective analysis of observable and quantifiable phenomena.[16] The outcome of this Debate was perhaps less absolutely clear-cut than that of the first, but the behaviouralists undoubtedly came out of the contest in the stronger position, particularly in the United States.[17]

But while the dust was still settling on the aftermath of that struggle, a Third Debate was developing, which turned attention back from methodology towards more fundamental questions of theory and ideology. Also known as the 'inter-paradigm debate', this was a more complex set of arguments, with (at least) three parties:

---

[14] See sec. 4 below.   [15] Hollis & Smith 1990: 32.

[16] The two sides of the debate are set out by Kaplan 1966 (behaviouralist) and Bull 1966a (traditionalist). See Hollis & Smith 1990: 28–32; Wæver 1997: 11–12. For a thorough examination of these two approaches to International Relations, and their implications, see Hollis & Smith 1990.

[17] The classic analysis of International Relations as 'an American Social Science' is Hoffman 1977. The strong behaviouralist bias of American IR is illustrated by Alker & Biersteker 1984: see esp. fig. 3. The social-scientific turn was, however, never as enthusiastically embraced in British IR (see the discussion of the English School: 26–8 below).

realism (or neorealism)[18] versus structuralism (or neo-Marxism) versus pluralism (or liberalism, or globalism).[19] Finally, and most recently, the development of critical and postmodern approaches to International Theory has sparked discussion which can be depicted as either a continuation of the inter-paradigm debate, or the beginnings of another – Fourth – Great Debate.[20]

If (for now, at least) such a story of disciplinary development is accepted, a secondary question immediately arises: how is that story to be explained? And here, too, there is more than one theory from which to choose.

Given the concerns of the subject, it is not, perhaps, too surprising to find a tendency to connect changes within International Relations to movements in the real world of international politics. This is a view which appears early on in the history of writing about the discipline – Carr, for example, emphasised the possible historical contingency of international (and other) theories[21] – and which still has strong advocates.[22] An explanation of this sort does have its attractions. International Relations was 'born' in the aftermath of World War One, and as a direct response to that conflict. A war which seemed so senseless – both in its causes and in the nature of the fighting which characterised it – should never be allowed to happen again, and the way to prevent its recurrence was to study the international system, and to hope that better understanding of that system would make it more humane. As was noted above, this motivation is explicitly present in the foundation of the

---

[18] On neorealism, see below: 25–6.

[19] The idea of the 'inter-paradigm' debate was promoted most influentially by Holsti 1985. It is discussed (and challenged) in Wæver 1996, 1997: 12–15.

[20] Wæver 1997: 15–25; Smith 1995: 24–6. Vasquez 1995 and Smith 1996 are good surveys of 'post-positivist' approaches to International Relations, and the essays in Smith, Booth & Zalewski edd. 1996 and in Doyle & Ikenberry edd. 1997 provide thorough coverage of contemporary meta-theoretical concerns in the discipline. On critical theory in International Relations, see especially Linklater 1996. On postmodernism & IR, the work of Der Derian is central: see, for example, Der Derian 1997, and the assessment of his writing in Huysmans 1997; for (generally critical) accounts of postmodernism and IR, see Jarvis 2000; Nicholson 2000.

[21] Carr 1946: 69–70, quoting Hobhouse's dictum that 'philosophers . . . suffer as much from toothache as other mortals, and are, like others, open to the impression of near and striking events and to the seductions of intellectual fashion'. (See also Bull 1972b: 32.)

[22] Recently, Ashworth 1999.

Aberystwyth chair. The holder of the post was not only expected to increase the understanding of international relations; it was also hoped that he would change them for the better.[23] Such beliefs are reflected in other writings of the interwar period. Zimmern's inaugural lecture at Oxford, for example, refers both to his memories of students who died in the war and his feelings of responsibility towards them,[24] and to the moral goals of International Relations: its function is to make the world a better place.[25]

The historical origins of International Relations seem, therefore, to explain its early theoretical emphasis, and they can also be argued to be influential in its later development. The Realist turn of the late 1930s makes good sense in the context of the failure of Idealist thinkers to bring about any improvements in international behaviour. The conspicuous lack of success of the League of Nations – with which many Idealist thinkers had been closely associated – seemed to provide the best evidence of this.[26] The post-war international situation was similarly conducive to Realist thought. Many of the scholars who were most prominent in the discipline after the Second World War were exiles from Eastern Europe and were well aware of the 'realities' of power politics, while the Cold War provided an environment in which theories which promoted the idea of perpetual conflict and mistrust between states would always be likely to flourish.[27] In the post-war period, US scholars came to dominate the discipline as much as the US dominated the international scene,[28] and the interests and assumptions of those scholars largely reflected the international situation with which they were most familiar: 'the US study of International Relations is within traditions whose core assumptions are most

[23] John, Wright & Garnett 1972: 88–9 (who suggest that the prescriptive task was seen as more important than the explanatory).
[24] Zimmern 1931: 26.   [25] Zimmern 1931: 22–7.
[26] The Abyssinia crisis (1935/6) is the most notorious example. See Carr 1946: 9: 'the course of events after 1931 clearly revealed the inadequacy of pure aspiration as the basis for a science of international politics, and made it possible for the first time to embark on serious critical and analytical thought about international problems'.
[27] Smith 1989: 10.
[28] The phenomenon is not unpredictable. See Crawford 2000: 118: International Relations 'is a subject of sustained interest only in countries reasonably placed to make some impact on the processes and interactions that constitute its subject matter'.

appropriate to the policies of a hegemon'.[29] Cold War International Relations theory can often seem to be 'nothing but a rationalization of cold war policies'.[30]

The events of 1989, and their consequences, can be seen to mark the final stage in this story of disciplinary development. The end of the Cold War and the collapse of the communist regimes of Eastern Europe provoked something of a crisis of self-confidence in International Relations. The discipline had, notoriously, failed to predict that anything of this sort would happen, and it was also at something of a loss to explain it. How, then, could it continue to claim its place as one of the practical social sciences?[31] The more diverse theoretical approaches which have been visible in International Relations over the last decade could, therefore, be understood as attempts to deal with that crisis, as well as to analyse and understand the post-1989 international situation: an increased concern with smaller states, rather than superpowers; further investigation of ideas of statehood, ethnicity and identity; and, above all, the increasing prominence of normative issues in the International Relations agenda.[32]

International Theory did not, therefore, develop in a historical vacuum. Indeed, its inevitable engagement with contemporary events is strengthened still further – again, especially in the US – by the willingness of foreign policy makers to take advice from international theorists: international theory and international practice, that is, can become mutually reinforcing activities.[33] The

---

[29] Smith 1989: 19. On US dominance of International Relations, see also Hoffman 1977; Krippendorf 1989; Windsor 1989; Crawford 2000: ch. 4; and on the continued tendency in IR to ignore (continental) European work in IR, see Jørgensen 2000. For some statistical analyses of the phenomenon, see Holsti 1995: ch. 6; Alker & Biersteker 1995; Wæver 1999 (who demonstrate both the leading position of American scholars as 'producers' of work in International Relations, and the reluctance of those scholars to engage with work which is produced outside the US: Holsti, for example, calculates that *c.* 75 per cent of work cited by American scholars is produced by American scholars (Holsti 1985: ch. 6)).

[30] Hoffman 1977: 48.

[31] Gaddis 1992/3; Vasquez 1998: ch. 13; Donnelly 2000: 31. For a survey of post-Cold War approaches, see George 1996. On change as a problem for Realism, see below: 24 and n. 72.

[32] For more practically oriented examples of this concern, see Elfstrom 1998; Harbour 1999. On theoretical developments, see below: 28–30.

[33] Smith 1989: 11; see also Webb 1994. There is further consideration of (and attempts to validate) the connection between theoreticians and practitioners in Nincic & Lepgold

historical contingency of many modern theories of international politics needs, therefore, constantly to be borne in mind, particularly when those theories are being applied to different historical situations.

It should also, however, be noted that a model of disciplinary development which represents International Relations as simply responding to and replicating political changes in the wider world would be misleading – particularly in the impression of academic isolation which it might create. Although intimately and necessarily connected to the 'real' world, International Relations is also part of the academic world, and subject to the influence of changes within that environment. Many of the explanations for the course of the discipline's history which were offered above can be supplemented or amended by reference to that broader academic context. The early form of the discipline, for example, makes sense not only as part of a reaction to the Great War, but also as a natural development from the liberal intellectual concerns of the preceding century.[34] It is clear, too, that the social-scientific turn which underlies the 'Second Great Debate' is paralleled in many other areas of the humanities.[35] The increasing interest in critical, postmodern, feminist and other theoretical approaches in the last decades of the twentieth century is also, of course, a phenomenon which is not restricted to International Relations.

This point is not particularly surprising, but it is worth making because the fact that International Relations is, at heart, an academic discipline like any other is something which its practitioners have often been strangely reluctant to accept. In spite of – perhaps even in part because of – its multi-disciplinary origins, for much of its history IR has deliberately represented itself as a subject apart, to the extent of becoming 'a sort of disciplinary

edd. 2000. For opposition to this connection – 'the academic international relations specialist . . . should not be a servant or agent of his government' – see Bull 1972a: 264.

34 Ashworth 1999: esp. ch. 1; Schmidt 1998 (concentrating on British and American examples respectively). On liberal responses to international relations, and in particular to the problem of war, see Howard 1989.

35 The discipline of History provides a good example, on which see, briefly, Evans 1997: ch. 2.

Albania'.[36] In many ways, of course, this is not a problem about which ancient historians need worry. One particular aspect of it, however, is relevant, and that is the impact that this approach to disciplinary identity has had on the relationship between International Relations and Ancient History.

1.3 International Relations and Ancient History

The possibility of a strong and productive link between International Relations and Ancient History is visible in the earliest years of the newer discipline. As was noted earlier, Zimmern began his academic life as an ancient historian: he studied Classics at New College, Oxford, and, for the first seven years of his career, remained in the same place, as lecturer and then fellow in Ancient History.[37] But, according to his own reminiscences, he recognised the importance of maintaining an interest in contemporary politics even before his official move away from the ancient world:

Well do I remember, as though it were yesterday, the impression made upon my mind when, as a young lecturer in Ancient History at Oxford, I read of the first great victory of the Japanese over the Russians. I went into my class and told them that I was going to lay aside Greek history for that morning, 'because,' I said, 'I feel I must speak to you about the most important historical event which has happened, or is likely to happen, in our lifetime, the victory of a non-white people over a white people.'[38]

This dual interest in ancient and modern politics continues to manifest itself in Zimmern's subsequent career, albeit usually in less dramatic ways. A good example can be found in his treatment, in *The Greek Commonwealth*, of the fifth-century Athenian Empire: this is described – and justified – in terms which are strikingly similar to those which Zimmern elsewhere uses to characterise the British Empire and Commonwealth. For Zimmern, the Athenian

---

[36] Crawford 2000: 28; see also Buzan & Little 2001: 19. IR's relationship to History is discussed in the next section. Its lack of dialogue with Politics can seem perverse, given its general insistence on the centrality of the sovereign state, but is based on the equally widespread conviction that international politics is entirely distinct from internal politics (see below: 25): what goes on inside the state need not, therefore, concern international theorists (see Bethke Elshtain 1995). This view has been increasingly challenged, most notably in Onuf 1989, introduction; Walker 1993; see also Boucher 1998: ch. 1.

[37] Markwell 2004.   [38] Zimmern 1926b: 82.

Empire is distinguished above all by Liberty, and the Athenian mission was to spread that liberty throughout the Greek world.[39] Fifteen years later, he can be found identifying that same liberty as the key to the longevity of the British Empire.[40]

This fairly non-specific sort of intellectual cross-fertilisation is more characteristic of Zimmern's work than any attempt at focused comparisons or analogies. Zimmern in fact can be found arguing strongly against the 'misunderstanding and shallow thinking [of] attempts to apply Greek ideas and maxims too literally to modern life'.[41] 'Thucydides and Plato give us no help for the League of Nations',[42] and it is for their general insights into the nature of political action and human motivation, rather than for any particular guidance, he argues, that Greek writings should be used by modern theorists.

Zimmern's enthusiasm for the usefulness of historical writing and historical examples has persisted in the later history of International Relations, but the caution which runs alongside that enthusiasm has not always been so visible. As has been seen, the disciplinary divisions between International Relations and other subjects, including Ancient (and Modern) History, became less permeable in the course of the twentieth century. Although, therefore, several figures in interwar International Relations – not just Zimmern, but also Gilbert Murray, Goldsworthy Lowes Dickinson and E. H. Carr – had strong ancient or modern historical links,[43] by

---

[39] The title of the chapter (7) which deals with the subject is 'Liberty, or the Rule of Empire'. An explicit analogy with British rule of India appears at 189. The perception of such parallels is not, of course, unique: see Cromer 1910; Cramb 1915 for Athens as a positive model for Britain's 'democratic empire'; or, for its use as a negative parallel, Murray 1900; Tillyard 1914.

[40] Zimmern 1926b: 2. P. C. Millett, in an unpublished conference paper of 1999 ('Alfred Zimmern's *The Greek Commonwealth* revisited'), suggests that Zimmern's work in modern international politics influenced his assessment of the Athenian Empire; Rich 1995: 89, writing from the perspective of an international theorist, argues that the flow of intellectual influence operated in the other direction. It is interesting to note that the Athenian Empire is characterised in very similar terms by Woodrow Wilson (in his notes for lectures on Greek history, delivered in 1885: Wilson 1968: 32–4; his book (Wilson 1889: 86–7) is more critical of Athens).

[41] Zimmern 1921b: 325.

[42] Zimmern 1921b: 327. Contrast England 1921 on Plato *Laws* 684b9: 'here we have the principle of our "League of Nations"'.

[43] On Murray and the League of Nations, see Cecil 1936; D. Wilson 1987: chs. 18, 21, 22, 26; on Dickinson's work in international politics, see Schmidt 1998: 160 (who, however,

the latter part of the century, the international theorist's relationship with History was typically rather more detached.

One characteristic later approach to the use of history was outlined by Hedley Bull:

historical study is the essential companion of theoretical study itself . . . because history is the laboratory of the social sciences, the source of the material by which general propositions may be verified or falsified.[44]

Work informed by this approach does contain much which can be of great value – to historians as well as international theorists[45] – but the method does have its dangers. Above all, the idea that history provides an unproblematic repository of facts, ready to be marshalled for (or against) grand theories of international behaviour, is one to which there are many and legitimate objections, among both historians and, increasingly, international theorists.[46] Even when historical material is used more sensitively, there remains a problem of selection. The relative popularity of some areas and periods of history among international theorists is often a reflection of the extent to which they can be made to seem relevant to contemporary theoretical concerns.[47] The emphasis on continuity rather than change which dominated International Relations for most of

finds his move away from ancient history 'difficult to explain'). Connections between International Relations and History remained stronger in British IR than in the US: Martin Wight is a notable post-war British theorist with a strong historical background (on Wight in general, see sec. 4 below; on Wight and history, Epp 1996: 123–9; on the close links between History and British IR, Hill 1985: 130–1; and on the English School and the Greek city-states, see Little 1995: 22–3). For an argument that modern IR should make more, and better, use of history, see Buzan & Little 2001.

[44] Bull 1972b: 32.

[45] See Hill 1985: 124. Wight 1977 (on systems of states, and including extensive analysis of the Greek world) is one good example: see ch. 2 for further discussion.

[46] The subjectivity of historical analysis was, indeed, emphasised by Zimmern: history is 'not the last word of science, but a work of subjective imagination' (Zimmern 1928: 54). For objections from international theorists, see Hall & Kratochwil 1993 (with the response of Fischer 1993); Schroeder 1994. On IR's tendency to 'strip history of its thorny dilemmas' (11), see Smith 1999.

[47] See Buzan & Little 1994: 234: 'the few historical times and places that resemble the international anarchy of modern Europe get a disproportionate amount of attention, most notably classical Greece, Renaissance Italy, the "warring states" period in China during several hundred years of the first millennium BC, and to a lesser extent, "warring states" periods in South Asia'; see also Smith 1999: 106. Attempts to overcome this problem can be seen in the move to produce (temporally and spatially) universal histories of international relations: for example, Frank & Gills edd. 1993; Denemark 1999; Buzan & Little 2000.

the twentieth century further strengthened the tendency to emphasise similarities rather than differences between past and present: the focus is on structures rather than processes, and the attempt to identify the 'permanent essence'[48] of interstate behaviour forces the possible historical specificity of that behaviour to recede into the background.

This tendency is even more apparent in the other major way in which international theorists have made use of the past – which is also the most prominent way in which they have made use of ancient history – as a source of 'great writings', in which eternal truths of international relations can be found:

> just as America needs its Columbus and 'founding fathers' to mythicize and legitimize the best and worst of its history, IR needs its seminal (they never seem to be 'embryonic') fathers (and never 'mothers') like Thucydides, Machiavelli, Hobbes, Weber, and so on.[49]

The names which are included in such lists of founding fathers do vary – Grotius, for example, makes an occasional appearance – but the inclusion of Thucydides is a strikingly consistent feature,[50] and has been since the early days of the discipline. One of the first manuals for the subject – Heatley's *Diplomacy and the Study of International Relations* (1919) – includes in its list of 'supplementary reading' the advice that

> a reading of Thucydides and of Tacitus may be substituted for Machiavelli and Guicciardini. For an understanding of policy, of democracy (howsoever defined) and of empire, the pages of Thucydides are still unsurpassed.[51]

The appearance of such advice in the context of early twentieth-century British scholarship is not particularly surprising. The place of Thucydides at the centre of the classical curriculum was still assured; and the status of a classical education as a background to a career in public service was – for the moment – equally secure.[52]

---

[48] Walker 1993: 91.   [49] Der Derian 1995b: 382.

[50] An interesting exception is Thompson 1994 which includes sections on Plato and Aristotle, but not on Thucydides.

[51] Heatley 1919: 150.

[52] On Thucydides' place in the curriculum, especially in Oxford Greats, see Ogilvie 1964: 98–107; Bowen 1989. On classical education and the empire, see Symonds 1991: 31–5. The First World War marks something of a turning point, bringing increasing challenges to the status of Classics: see, in general, Stray 1998: ch. 9.

What is more surprising is the persistence of the appeal to Thucydides, and indeed the increasingly widespread appearance of such appeals. In part this must be simply a matter of habit – of turning to the same models used by one's predecessors. But the use of Thucydides by theorists – and in particular by Realist theorists – is not only an indication of continuing familiarity with the author; it is also symptomatic of one of the basic theoretical assumptions of Realism. If human nature is constant throughout time, and, as Realist theory supposes, a central determinant of the character of international politics, then an author like Thucydides – who can be argued to share that belief in the continuity of human nature[53] – is an entirely legitimate source for analysis of the international relations of any period. Thucydides, like the other 'founding fathers' is not to be seen, therefore, as representing part of a process of developing, or even evolving, thought about international relations,[54] but as a purveyor of eternal theoretical truths:

Thucydides, Machiavelli, Hobbes, Rousseau and the rest appear to us as quite unproblematic figures, often in disguises that make them quite unrecognisable to anyone who examines the textual evidence we have of them. That each of these figures is open to sharply differing interpretations has mattered little. The history of political thought turns into an ahistorical repetition, in which the struggles of these thinkers to make sense of the historical transformations in which they were caught are erased in favour of assertions about how they all articulate essential truths about the same unchanging and usually tragic reality: the eternal game of relations between states.[55]

Once this basic point is understood, the theoretical 'battle over Thucydides' shroud'[56] becomes easier to understand. It is not enough simply to claim Thucydides as a general intellectual ancestor. The struggle is to establish which specific theoretical position Thucydides exemplifies. Is he a classical realist; a neo-realist;

---

[53] Th. 1.22.4: the interpretation of the passage is disputed (see de Ste. Croix 1972: 29–33).

[54] For the non-chronological nature of the 'tradition' of Realism, see Forde 1992, where – in the discussion of 'founding fathers' – Thucydides is preceded by Machiavelli. Some writers do take a more evolutionary view: see, for example, Banks 1984 – who nevertheless performs the usual leaps from Thucydides to Machiavelli (who is, in fact, very little influenced by Thucydides: Walker 1993: 35–6) to Hobbes. For more historically sensitive studies of the development of international theory, see Knutsen 1997; Boucher 1998.

[55] Walker 1993: 92. Similar observations in Alker 1996: ch. 1; Beer & Hariman 1996: 7–8. See Ober 2001 for an argument for caution from a classicist's perspective.

[56] Der Derian 1995b: 383.

a minimalist realist; a hedged realist?[57] What particular theory of hegemonic warfare or systemic leadership succession does he support?[58] And, once Thucydides had become so closely involved in theoretical debates within the field of Realist approaches, it was almost inevitable that he would also be invoked in attempts to undermine the Realist world-view: Thucydides becomes the moralist, the 'humanitarian', the anti-realist.[59] Therefore, although a survey of monographs and articles in International Relations might give an impression of widespread interest in classical, and especially fifth-century, Greece among international theorists, such an impression would be quite misleading. There is certainly widespread interest in Thucydides, but the primary concern is not that any international theory should illuminate the world of Thucydides, but that Thucydides' writing should illuminate, and often more importantly justify, that theory.

Even the rapid survey of the last two sections might, however, have suggested that this minimalist, and one-sided, version of interaction between the two disciplines need not be the only type of relationship which is possible. The concerns of International Relations are not entirely alien to those of the historian of Greek interstate politics, and the debate in which Thucydides has become embroiled – a debate which revolves around questions of power, morality and

---

[57] Generally on the use of Thucydides in International Relations, see Der Derian 1995b: 382–5; introduction to Blanco & Roberts edd. 1998; Bagby 2000; and, on his 'pernicious' influence, Welch 2003. On Thucydides' brand of realism, see Garst 1989 (attacking the view that Thucydides is a neorealist); Doyle 1990, 1991 (Thucydides as a minimalist realist); Bagby 1994 (a realist, but a 'Thucydidean realist'); Forde 1992: 69–75, Donnelly 2000: ch. 6 (a hedged realist); Doyle 1997: ch. 1 (a 'complex realist'); Lebow 2003: chs. 3 and 4 (part realist, part constructivist).

[58] The central work on Thucydides and hegemonic warfare was done by Gilpin 1986 and esp. 1988; see also Lebow 1996, and the essays in Lebow & Strauss edd. 1991 (an extremely rare example of co-operation between international theorists and ancient historians). On Thucydides and 'systemic leadership succession', see Thompson 1995.

[59] Walzer 2000 (originally published 1977) uses Thucydides as a negative example in his attack on Realism. Johnson 1993 questions the Realist interpretation of Thucydides, and he is used in argument against Realist approaches by Orwin 1994; Rahe 1995/6; Crane 1998; Monoson & Loriaux 1998; Bedford & Workman 2001. For his conscription in the service of still more diverse theoretical approaches, see, for example, Jansson 1997 (Thucydides on 'identity-defining practices'); Kokaz 2001 (Thucydides as post-structuralist); and the essays in Gustafson ed. 2000. A parallel, but related, tradition of the use of Thucydides can be found in more practical areas: his work becomes a source for guidance in military (see, for example, Strauss & Ober 1990) and diplomatic (see Neustadt & May 1986: ch. 13; Chittick & Freyberg-Inan 2001) activities.

the relevance of norms – is one which is closely relevant to the overall subject of this book.

1.4 Idealism, Realism and the problem of norms

There is a gentle paradox in the fact that International Relations, a discipline which was founded with an explicitly normative agenda, appears to have spent so much of its history denying the validity of such a project. Such a paradox needs closer examination, and the obvious place from which to start is the point at which the question of morality was – allegedly – expelled from the discipline: the 'First Great Debate'.

The flaw in the logic of the story of the First Great Debate, as it is conventionally told, is not hard to spot: if the publication of Carr's *The Twenty Years' Crisis* in 1939 not only marked the resurgence of Realist thought in International Relations, but also struck the fatal blow against the claims of the Idealists, where is the room for any (small or great) Debate? Carr's work, it would seem, not only started the debate, but also finished it off. It provoked not so much a discussion as a 'Kuhnian-style paradigm shift'.[60] In fact, neither a distinct paradigm shift nor a neat bipolar debate is the most appropriate model to use, since both impose an unrealistic amount of clarity on a less than clear-cut situation.[61] The idea of a strict Realist/Idealist divide seems to have developed not at the time when that divide was alleged to have existed, but in the 1950s and later,[62] when Realist thought was firmly established as the dominant force in International Relations, and the discipline was gearing up for its Second – methodological – Debate. 'As a statement of historical fact', it has been argued, 'it [the notion of the Realist/Idealist debate] is highly misleading.'[63] Nevertheless, its appearance is not hard to explain. In an academic context in which Realism was left as a sole and unopposed power, the development of the idea of a heroic feud against the misguided

[60] Wilson 1998: 1.   [61] See Smith 1995: 16.

[62] Ashworth 1999: 126. Wilson 1998: 8, puts the date even later, in the early 1970s (pointing to the publication of Porter ed. 1972 as the start of 'disciplinary self-consciousness').

[63] Wilson 1998: 1.

forces of Idealism begins to look like a classic case of 'Other' construction. Such a construction inevitably increases the apparent solidity of the boundaries between the two approaches – boundaries which may in fact be more permeable. It can also create artificial impressions of unity within those competing schools of thought.

On the one hand: 'Idealism'. It has been suggested that,

> in the sense of a cohesive, and certainly self-conscious, school of thought, an 'idealist' or 'utopian' paradigm never actually existed . . . It is a realist category of abuse.[64]

More detailed study of the various international thinkers of the interwar period does, indeed, reveal that they are far from being a unified group.[65] Nor can individuals so easily be made to conform to the stereotype of the naïve idealist. Zimmern is as good an example as any: although his belief in progress, and in the possible civilising effects of international institutions, laws and – above all – education are hallmarks of the paradigmatic, 'utopian' idealist, he was always careful, too, to take account of the realities of the situation – at least as he perceived them.[66] In the post-war period, some of his pre-war beliefs persisted, but they appear to have co-existed with a less than utopian cold-warrior attitude to US–Soviet conflict.[67]

If Idealism should be seen as a more complex phenomenon than it is often allowed to be, then this is even more true of Realism. Although Realism is sometimes characterised as a unified 'theory' of international relations, it is more accurate to regard it as a style of approach, or even as a general attitude towards the world and its inhabitants. 'Realism' comes in many forms and with many qualifying prefixes:

---

[64] Wilson 1998: 1; Hutchings 1999: 7, also notes that Idealism was 'identified as a substantive tradition very much in hindsight'.

[65] Wilson 1998: 13–14, provides an outline of the range of approaches which have been subsumed under the 'Idealist' label; on the 'Realist' aspects of some 'Idealist' thought, see Osiander 1998: esp. 412–15.

[66] Rich 1995: 82–4.

[67] Of the pre-war beliefs, most prominent is Zimmern's continuing commitment to education, visible in his work for UNESCO after the Second World War (see Markwell 1986: 282). On Zimmern as 'cold warrior', see Griffiths 1999: 104.

Realism . . . Machiavellian, Hobbesian, Rousseauian, Hegelian, Kissingerian realism . . . Classical and scientific realism. Minimalist, maximalist, fundamentalist, potentialist realism. Positivist, post-positivist, liberal, neoliberal, institutionalist, radical, radical interpretivist realism.[68]

The broadness of the Realist approach becomes apparent once an attempt is made to define it in any terms more exact, or positive, than 'not Idealism'. A recent survey of eleven scholars' attempts to define Realism revealed eleven different definitions.[69] But it also showed that, although none of these definitions shared identical elements, there was a strong 'family resemblance'[70] between them: Realism may be a big tent, but its adherents are, nevertheless, sheltering under a single canvas, and the diverse forms of Realism do include some distinctive elements. The two most important of these are, as was mentioned above, a belief in the importance of 'human nature' and an emphasis on the significance of the structure of the international system. A satisfactory, though minimal, definition of Realism might then be that

Realism emphasizes the constraints on politics imposed by human nature and the absence of international government. Together, they make international relations largely a realm of power and interest.[71]

Belief in the importance of human nature in determining the character of international relations, although common to all species of Realism, is traditionally strongest among 'biological' or 'classical' Realists. Human nature is constant: it 'has not changed since the days of classical antiquity'.[72] More importantly for the Realist

[68] Der Derian 1995a: 1.
[69] Tabulated in Donnelly 2000: box 1.1 (7–8). (The discussion which follows is heavily indebted to Donnelly's analysis.)
[70] Donnelly 2000: 9.
[71] Donnelly 2000: 9. It is important to remember that, in spite of the Behaviouralist objection to dealing with normative issues, Realism is, in its origins, as much a distinctive ethical outlook on international relations as any other approach. It should be seen as not so much an amoral approach to international affairs, as one which argues that moral judgements have little or no force in that context (Nardin 1992: 15–16; Dyer 1997: 35).
[72] Thompson 1985, quoted in Donnelly 2000: 57; see also Donnelly 2000: ch. 2. On the importance of an (unchanging) human nature in determining international relations, see esp. Morgenthau 1946; Waltz 1959: chs. 2 and 3. See Stevenson & Haberman 1998 for an analysis of various theories of human nature. This attitude does, however, make it extremely difficult for Realist approaches to explain change: for criticisms based on this weakness, see Buzan & Barry Jones edd. 1981; Kratochwil 1993; Rosenau 1997: esp. ch. 2; Vasquez 1998: esp. chs. 13 and 14.

argument, human nature is constantly egotistical and inclined to immorality:

> to an alarming degree, the history of international relations is a history of selfishness and brutality. It is a story in which spying, deceit, bribery, disloyalty, ingratitude, betrayal, exploitation, plunder, repression, subjection, and genocide are all too conspicuous.[73]

Such a history may be alarming, but it is not a result of chance. While even Realists may admit that, from time to time, human nature may aspire to higher things (morality, or justice), they are convinced that its core remains self-interested. Control of those 'egoistical passions'[74] is the central problem of international politics.

The absence of that control, and the inevitability of its absence, form the basis of the second fundamental Realist belief. The structure of the international system – specifically its anarchic structure[75] – allows and encourages the egotistical aspects of human nature to run riot. In domestic systems, political authority enables the control of the worst aspects of human nature; in the international system, such authority is missing, and it is this which is crucial in determining the nature of international politics. An insistence on the strict division of domestic and international politics, and of the inapplicability of domestic standards of behaviour to international affairs is, therefore, central to the Realist view of international relations.

While 'classical' Realists typically regard this structural element as being subordinate to the constraints of human nature, it is given greater prominence by other groups of Realist theorists, and in particular by those labelled neorealists. The strongest form of this view was developed by Kenneth Waltz in his *Theory of International Politics*.[76] Like the classical Realists, Waltz perceives an element of continuity in international relations throughout history,

---

[73] Cohen 1984: 299.   [74] Donnelly 2000: 10.

[75] 'Anarchic' is typically used in International Relations to imply lack of leadership rather than disorder: the latter may follow from the former, but is not a necessary characteristic of an anarchic system.

[76] Waltz 1979. For discussion and criticism of Waltz's views, see Ashley 1984; Keohane ed. 1986; Hollis & Smith 1990: ch. 5; Linklater 1995; Guzzini 1998: ch. 9; Donnelly 2000: ch. 3; Hobson 2000: ch. 2. For a recent defence, Waltz 1997.

but he sees the primary reason for this as lying not so much in an unchanging human nature, as in the unchangingly anarchic structure of the international system. The basic unit of that system is the sovereign state, and although these states may vary in capability, all share the same functions and aspirations: to maximise their relative power, and to ensure their survival.[77]

In the US, neorealism dominated International Relations for much of the latter part of the twentieth century. But on the other side of the Atlantic the discipline took a slightly different turn. The approach which has come to be seen as most typical of British International Relations in the second half of the twentieth century is that of the 'English School'. The School developed in the late 1950s, growing out of the work of the British Committee for the Study of International Politics (founded in 1958), and produced the work for which it is most famous in the 1960s and 1970s.[78]

The English School has often been categorised as a variant on Realism.[79] In part, such a categorisation might seem to be simply a default assumption: how could any theoretical work in the post-war period not be Realist in orientation? But it also rests on a more detailed interpretation of their writings, and, in particular, of Martin Wight's famous essay, 'Why is there no International Theory?'[80] Wight's argument in that paper is based on the existence of a strict division between domestic and international politics: the tradition of political theory cannot, therefore, be applied to international relations. International Relations lacks its own tradition of theory for two reasons: because the focus, since the Renaissance, on the sovereign state as the 'consummation of political experience and activity' led to international relations being seen as the 'untidy fringe of domestic politics';[81] and because international relations,

[77] Waltz 1979: 93–7.
[78] The standard history of the English School is Dunne 1998b; see also de Almeida 2003; Little 2000; and the comprehensive bibliographic survey in Buzan 2001, which is the best guide to the scope of the School's membership and interests. On the British Committee, see Watson 1998. On the applicability of the School's ideas to contemporary problems in international politics, see Bellamy ed. 2004. The most notable criticism (from the US) of the School's activities comes in Jones 1981. The figures most closely associated with the school are Martin Wight and Hedley Bull: on Wight's career and writings, see Nicholson 1981, Bull 1991, Epp 1996, Dunne 1998b: ch. 1; on Bull, Miller & Vincent edd. 1990, Alderson & Hurrell 2000: esp. 1–53.
[79] For discussion of these views, see de Almeida 2003.
[80] Wight 1966b.   [81] Wight 1966b: 21.

being a 'realm of recurrence and repetition'[82] was not open to the type of progressivist interpretations which characterise political theory.

This emphasis on the centrality of the sovereign state and on the lack of progress in international behaviour does indeed seem to be impeccably Realist. However, this essay was not Wight's – let alone the English School's – last word on the subject of international theory. In a later work – called, in fact, *International Theory*[83] – Wight formulated a tripartite model of international theories: Realist, Rationalist (or Grotian, emphasising co-operation between states) and Revolutionist (or Kantian, emphasising the unity of mankind). These three traditions are not consecutive or mutually exclusive, but co-existent and constantly able to 'influence and cross-fertilise one another'.[84] Such a model not only underlies the School's assessment of the work of other international theorists, it also applies to their own. While some aspects of the English School's work may seem characteristically 'Realist', therefore, others are closer to other traditions.

This is especially true of the area of research with which the School is most closely associated: the study of international society.[85] Such a study immediately complicates the basic Realist assumption of unchanging and inevitable international anarchy, not, necessarily, by denying that such anarchy exists, but by exploring how systems and societies of states could operate within that anarchic environment. And this interest in international society led the English School to investigate things still further removed from traditional Realist concerns: the question of inclusion in society led, unsurprisingly, to the issue of exclusion, and the School's work is notable for its early interest in non-Western states and the

---

[82] Wight 1966b: 26.   [83] Wight 1991.

[84] Wight 1991: 260; see Dunne 1998b: 54–63; Bull & Holbraad 1979: 19. On Wight's 'dialogic' approach to the study of international relations, see Epp 1996: 132–5.

[85] Wight 1977 is the classic contribution to the subject; other major works are Bull 1966b; Watson 1992; Bull 1995. For recent responses to the English School's work in this area, see the essays collected in Roberson ed. 1998. 'Constructivism' – the approach to IR which sees interstate behaviour as socially constructed – can be seen to owe much to the views of international society proposed by the English School. (Important contributions to the constructivist approach can be found in Onuf 1989; Wendt 1992; and especially Wendt 1999. For the link between constructivism and the English School, see Dunne 1995; Barry Jones 1998; Suganami 2001.)

'Third World' – those excluded from the society of international relations.[86] The attempt to analyse life within international societies drew attention to the question of common interests and shared practices among states – back, that is, to questions of international norms and international ethics.[87]

The attitudes of international theorists to the question of norms and of normative theory are, however, conditioned not only by ideology but also by methodology. The study of norms, in any context, is hampered by substantial practical problems. Take, for example, the case of the driver who stops at a red light at a deserted junction in the small hours of the morning. Is this action determined by an ethical decision – a commitment to obey the law at all times simply because it is the right thing to do – or is it more pragmatic – there just might be a police car round the corner? Obtaining a reliable answer from an individual driver would be difficult enough. Trying to apply such reasoning to states, let alone historical states, must be all but impossible.[88] Given the dominant methodological orientation of International Relations for much of the post-war period, a reluctance to engage with unobservable, unquantifiable, issues of this sort is not surprising.[89] And, for the same reason, it is not surprising to find that the majority of work in this area in this period took place in an academic context less dominated by Behaviouralism – that is, in British international theory.[90] Similarly, the post-positivist turn of the end of the twentieth century must be held at least partially responsible for a new willingness to engage with the problems of international norms, and has provided a new – and arguably more useful – set of interpretative tools with which to approach them: increased sensitivity to the language of interstate politics, and an acknowledgement that the representation(s) of international relations can

[86] See, for example, Bull 1984. For a discussion of this aspect of the School's work, see Epp 1998: esp. 56–9.
[87] See esp. Wight 1979: ch. 24. On the importance of ethics to the English School, see Dunne 1998b: 9–11; Epp 1996: 129–32; Little 2000.
[88] The analogy is provided by Goertz 1994: 241.   [89] Frost 1998: 123.
[90] Brown 1992: 4. Especially significant is the English School's acknowledgement of the inevitability of approaching international relations through language, and of the importance of paying attention to the language of international activity (very prominent in Manning 1962; on the tendency, see Epp 1996: 122; Epp 1998: 55; Little 2000).

be just as, if not more, significant than the facts underlying that behaviour.[91]

The study of international norms is, of course, related, and often a precursor, to the development of normative theories of international relations, and it is possible to find evidence of the same methodological objections to this area of research.[92] But there are more fundamental problems associated with normative theory: above all, the relationship of morals to power. It has already been suggested that the narratives of disciplinary history which attempt to impose strict divisions between theoretical approaches dominated by either power or ethics are likely to be misleading. Attempting to separate the two concepts themselves is an equally difficult, if not impossible, activity. This is something which Carr, in spite of his objections to 'utopianism', made quite clear:

> If, however, it is utopian to ignore the element of power, it is an unreal kind of realism which ignores the element of morality in any world order . . . The fatal dualism of politics will always keep considerations of morality entangled with considerations of power.[93]

However, it was the impossibility of disentangling morality from power, and the apparent failure of the inter-war Idealists to appreciate this, which formed an important part of Carr's objections to their views. The problem was, at heart, one of the relativity of moral judgements: what appeared to be a morally justified action to one state was in fact likely to be an action which preserved their own conception of the proper order of things – a conception which might not be shared by other nations.[94] Even if the extreme view

---

[91] On critical theory and international ethics, see Linklater 1992; Frost 1996: esp. ch. 1. On postmodernism, see Cochran 1995; Der Derian 1997. See also, in general, Welch 1994; Dyer 1997; Raymond 1997; Hutchings 1999.

[92] On the positivist objection to normative theory as an unscientific – 'soft' – subject, see Hollis & Smith 1990: 29; Frost 1996: 32, 41. Neufeld 1995 argues that it is the positivist bias of International Relations which has hampered the development of normative theory in the discipline.

[93] Carr 1946: 235–6. On Carr's position on this subject – which is more nuanced than it is often represented as being – see Jones 1998: esp. ch. 7. Compare Howard 1983 on the impossibility of separating power from morality. On the problem of the relativity of norms in the construction of an 'ethical foreign policy', see, for example, Walzer 1994; more recently, see Barry 1998, for a series of case-studies of the interaction of ethical and coercive actions in US foreign policy.

[94] Carr 1946: esp. chs. 4 and 5.

that power creates its own morality is not accepted,[95] it is hard to escape from the suspicion that 'so-called normative theories are themselves practices of power'.[96]

The dispute between 'Realism' and 'Idealism' was not, therefore, definitively settled in 1939, and the interaction of power and morality remains a major problem for those who wish to develop normative theories of international relations.[97] But the scale and complexity of the problem should also make it a central point of interest for those concerned with the history of international normative thought.

1.5 Conclusion: the *Ecclesia* and the League of Nations

In his inaugural lecture as Oxford's first Professor of International Relations, Zimmern imagined a possible objection to the introduction into the University of this, dangerously modern, subject:

Is there not a certain incongruity, almost an element of profanation, in the thought that an Oxford man in the future may be as familiar with the League of Nations Assembly as with the Ecclesia or the Areopagus?[98]

It has been seen, however, that Zimmern's own writings demonstrate how hard it is for any ancient historian to avoid that double familiarity. The case of Zimmern might be unusually clear, but it is far from unique: this connection between ancient and modern also emerges, with varying degrees of clarity, from the writing of many other commentators on Greek interstate politics. Ancient historians are, inevitably, prompted by their understandings of the inherent nature of international relations – understandings equally inevitably derived from their own historical circumstances – to analyse and evaluate ancient behaviour in those terms. And, since a broadly 'Realist' agenda dominated both International Theory and international practice for so much of the twentieth century, it is not surprising that it is this conception of the basic nature of interstate politics which pervades some of the most important work on the subject in the field of Greek history. Some anachronisms

---

[95] Carr 1946: 236.   [96] Frost 1996: 42.
[97] A point emphasised by Crawford 2000.   [98] Zimmern 1931: 20.

are, now, fairly easy to spot: the belief, prominent in the 1960s, for example, that the Greek quest for stability was doomed by their failure to develop any source of Mutually Assured Destruction.[99] But others are more embedded in works which are still, properly, influential: particularly notable is G. E. M. de Ste. Croix's assessment of the nature of fifth-century Greek interstate politics: this was a world in which moral justification was appropriate only for the defeated and the naïve.[100]

It is Zimmern's solution to this perennial dilemma that has informed this chapter, and will inform the rest of this book: ancient historians should not attempt to ignore the politics of the modern world, but should rather try to make themselves better informed about it, and about the theories which are used to explain it.

Some of the advantages of such an approach are, relatively, general. One – negative, but nevertheless important – conclusion which should emerge from the material discussed here is that if all history is contemporary, so too is all theory. International theory, also, is intimately linked to its historical as well as its academic context, and it is not possible to turn to International Relations for statements of eternal truths about the character of interstate politics. The use of international theory in writing history does not, that is, provide a means of escape from the concerns of the contemporary world towards an untainted, objective, scientific analysis.

But more positive conclusions can also be drawn. First of all, a fuller understanding of this theory and its history forces the explicit formulation of some implicit assumptions about the way in which interstate relations function (and have functioned in the past). As a consequence, by encouraging a fuller understanding of what is peculiar to the contemporary world of international politics, it allows a properly comparative approach to the interstate relations of classical Greece. Familiarity with the League of Nations (or the UN, or NATO . . .) will always colour the assessment of the policies

---

[99] See esp. Grant 1965: 265. Note also the assessment of Larsen 1962: 234: 'since the Greeks had no atomic bomb, there could be no lasting peace'.

[100] De Ste. Croix 1972: 5–34; de Ste. Croix notes (24) that 'the morality of the Cold War has imposed itself to an extent which scarcely anyone has altogether escaped' – a point he makes in relation to the moral relativism of many Cold War commentators, but which is not irrelevant to his own interpretation of Greek interstate politics. Compare also Woodhead 1970 (on the centrality of power to Greek – and all – foreign politics).

of the *ecclesia*; but a better understanding of the beliefs and theories which underlie contemporary international politics might help in avoiding accidentally judging the interstate activities of the ancient world in terms more appropriate to the international relations of the early twenty-first century.

Finally, and most importantly for what follows, what should have emerged from this chapter is that it is possible to find in International Theory – and particularly in its more recent forms – an extremely valuable set of tools with which to think about ancient interstate relations, and a range of important new questions to put to, often very familiar, material. These questions do not exclude the traditional subjects of power and morality, but they are not confined to them either: what this chapter has revealed is that, in order to think properly about the relationship between power and morality in Greek interstate politics, it is also necessary to consider questions of norms, society and political authority.

A better understanding of the richness of International Theory – a realisation that its debates do not simply revolve around a straightforward contest between 'Realism' and 'Idealism' – can therefore stimulate a more wide-ranging approach to the study of Greek interstate politics. But, as was noted in the Introduction, the benefits of an inclusive approach can apply in more than one direction. The potential breadth of International Theory has been investigated; what remains to be done is to explore the consequences of applying this fuller range of questions to a more extensive range of ancient Greek evidence. It is this task which is the focus of the next five chapters of this book.

STRUCTURING INTERSTATE RELATIONS

2.1 Introduction: society, system and anarchy

The problem of international society is often considered to be central to the whole discipline of International Relations. Any consideration of the specific problems of the subject must start, it could be argued, by defining the scope and nature of the object of its study.[1] This definition can be based on a variety of criteria: the types of political community which make up the society; forms of interaction between them; the overall structure of the society; the rules of conduct which apply within it; the environment(s) in which interactions occur.[2] And this potential complexity is one reason why this question is also one which can be, and has been, addressed as an end in itself. Much of this study, especially that produced in the context of the Cold War, has aimed at answering practical questions of power-politics: which grouping of states is most likely to achieve lasting stability? How is hegemony best achieved and retained? How can a bipolar system avoid the risks of war? And so on.[3] The ethical dimension has not, though, been entirely obscured. In fact, it was this dimension which provided the stimulus for some of the first systematic discussions of the question, as sixteenth- and seventeenth-century writers attempted to clarify the proper relationship between the 'old' world of European states and their new conquests in the Americas: were all these peoples – even those not sharing in the Christian community of states – to be

---

[1] Mayall 1990: 7, who also points out the necessity of facing the question: at some point, discussions of international relations need to use a collective noun for the objects of their study, and the choice of noun is inevitably a loaded one.

[2] Stern 1995: 46; compare the list of methods of analysis provided by Holsti 1995: 24–5: boundaries, character of members, structure, stratification, interaction, regulation. For a sustained example of the analysis of international societies using these criteria, see Luard 1976.

[3] See, for example, Bull 1995: pt 3.

thought of as part of one society, and entitled to the same treatment as those within that Christian community?[4]

Although such writers as Grotius and Vitoria were prepared to base their arguments on the notion that some ethical criteria should apply in relations between (at least some) states, modern students of International Relations have, in general, been less happy to accept this as a starting point, and the appropriateness of introducing the concept of 'society' into discussions of interstate relations has been strongly challenged. The argument against such an approach runs along the following lines. If there were to be such a thing as an international society, it would be 'practical' not 'purposive.'[5] That is, it would not come into existence in order to achieve some shared purpose (unlike, for example, some non-state international organisations), but would be created, and discernible, through common practices and shared rules:

> international society is distinguished from a state of extreme conflict not so much by the degree to which its members are moved to cooperate in the pursuit of common interests as by the degree to which they understand themselves to be members of a society defined by common rules.[6]

While this may seem uncontroversial, it is not entirely unproblematic. The largest problem surrounds one question: in the absence of any overall sovereign power, how could such rules either come into existence or have any serious force?

That problem will be addressed at length in the next chapter. Here, it will simply be noted that, even among international theorists, it is not universally seen as an insurmountable difficulty. It has been argued that equal, if not greater, importance should be given to other factors:

---

[4] A trend which prompted the first attempts to characterise international relations as driven by 'natural law', especially in the writings of Vitoria and Grotius. See Bull 1995: 26–44, for these (and later) developments (or, at greater length, Nardin 1983: ch. 3); for a more detailed study of Vitoria's work and its historical and ideological context, see Pagden 1982: esp. ch. 4; on Grotius, see Tuck 1999: ch. 3. On various ethical approaches to international society, see Mapel & Nardin edd. 1998. On the study of international society in International Relations, see Roberson ed. 1998; Alderson & Hurrell 2000: 20–73.

[5] The terms, and the argument which follows, are from Nardin 1983: ch. 1; see also Nardin 1998: 20–2.

[6] Nardin 1983: 24.

it would seem, however, that 'social' relations among people could exist on other foundations, such as custom, conventions, a common morality, or religious faith . . . Society could also rest on repeated economic transactions or simply on voluntary association expressed otherwise than economically, religiously, or legally.[7]

In other words, the presence of anarchy (in the technical sense) can be thought to be compatible with the existence of a society: an international society can arise, not as a result of externally imposed or enforced rules, but from the presence of some form of common culture or civilisation.[8]

But that solution immediately raises another question: how is that common 'culture' to be identified and defined? It is in this context that the example of Greece – particularly classical Greece – becomes increasingly prominent. Where some precedent is sought for the possible co-existence of international society and international anarchy, it is the Greek example which is frequently cited. The clearest formulation of that example appears, notoriously, in the words which Herodotus puts into the mouth of the Athenians, as they soothe Spartan fears of a unilateral peace between Athens and Persia: Athenian loyalty is guaranteed, at least in part, by

τὸ Ἑλληνικόν, ἐὸν ὅμαιμόν τε καὶ ὁμόγλωσσον, καὶ θεῶν ἱδρύματά τε κοινὰ καὶ θυσίαι ἤθεά τε ὁμότροπα, τῶν προδότας γενέσθαι Ἀθηναίους οὐκ ἂν εὖ ἔχοι.

the kinship of all Greeks in blood and speech, and the shrines of gods and the sacrifices that we have in common, and the likeness of our way of life, to all of which it would not be right for the Athenians to be false.[9] (VIII.144.2)

It has even been claimed that 'ancient Greece . . . occupies a more central position in the evolution of modern international society than any other system'.[10] This claim to centrality is based on the perceived innovations of the Greek model, as well as on its direct influence on modern statesmen, from the seventeenth century

---

[7] Whelan 1998: 39.
[8] Bull 1995: 13. See also Watson 1990: 101; Stern 1995: 46. For an extended discussion of the varieties of definitions possible, see Wight 1977: ch. 1.
[9] For use of the passage by international theorists, see Bozeman 1960: 85; Wight 1966a: 126; Wight 1977: 46. Other discussions of the passage in Cartledge 1995: 81–2; or (concentrating on the religious aspect) Parker 1998: 10–11. Compare the range of factors appealed to as unifying the members of a *polis* at X. *HG* II.iv.20–1: there is some difference (education, military service) but also considerable overlap (religion, kinship).
[10] Watson 1992: 47.

onwards.[11] It has also been argued, probably with some justification, that the preference for the Greek example relies largely on its apparent similarity to the contemporary world, and on the ease of transferring conclusions drawn from an ancient model to modern situations.[12] Even among those who are happy to use the Greek example, however, there is little consensus on what conclusions should be drawn from it. The extent of the society is disputed: does it include just the states of the Greek 'heartland', or those of Asia Minor and Western Greece too? Should Persia be included as part of the same society, or as a neighbouring society (perhaps sharing a system with the Greek society of states)?[13] And – whatever the boundaries of the system – how should relations within it be defined and described: as dominated by ideology,[14] or by state loyalty,[15] or by panhellenic sentiment?[16] As characterised by hegemony, or diarchy, or something else entirely?[17]

This multiplicity of definitive answers is not coincidental: contemporary sources provide us with a multiplicity of views on this question. What I aim to do in what follows, therefore, is to examine some of these sources and attempt not necessarily to provide the answer to the question of the existence and nature of an interstate society in the classical Greek world, but rather to sketch the range of possible answers. Although Herodotus may have had the first word on the subject, it is not to be assumed that he also had the last.

2.2 No such thing as society? A system of reciprocal relationships

Is there even any need to introduce the idea of a 'society' of states? It might be argued that the dominant ordering principle

---

[11] Watson 1992: 47.   [12] Buzan & Little 1994: 234; see also ch. 1, sec. 3.

[13] On Greek–Persian relations in this context, see esp. Wight 1977: ch. 3; Martin 1940: 19–20 (arguing for two discrete societies). Cf. Buzan & Little 1994: 240.

[14] Claimed by Bozeman 1960: 73; Luard 1976: 74–9; denied by Wight 1977: 37.

[15] Claimed by Wight 1977: 37; denied by Luard 1976: 76.

[16] Claimed by Bozeman 1960: 77; denied by Luard 1976: 77.

[17] Hegemony, Gilpin 1988; diarchy, Wight 1977: 60–1; Greek system as 'antihegemonial', Watson 1992: 51–2; as a 'diffused society', Luard 1976: 366. For an analysis of the problem from an ancient historical perspective, see Van Wees 2001, 2004: ch. 1.

of the interstate interactions of the classical period is, in fact, much simpler: a system of, often intersecting or overlapping, bilateral relations between individual states and, in particular, bilateral relations formed on a basis of reciprocity. This concept – 'the principle and practice of voluntary requital of benefit for benefit . . . or harm for harm'[18] – is much used by both international theorists and ancient historians, although it will become clear that it can imply rather different things to each group.

In writing on international relations, reciprocity is most frequently appealed to in the construction and explanation of models of interstate behaviour based on a particular type of game theory, the model of the 'Prisoner's Dilemma'.[19] In the second half of the twentieth century, game theory became a popular method of formalising and predicting the behaviour of actors in international politics: the games reproduce a situation – which fits well with the Realist perception of interstate politics – in which there is no controlling authority, no sense of community, and in which each player's primary objective is to maximise its own success. The model of the Prisoner's Dilemma – which is a non-zero-sum game – can also show how, when played in some ways, independent actions which should increase the success of one player could, in fact, combine with the actions of the other player to produce a worse result for both. Attempts to show how this outcome could be avoided have led to a more influential contribution, in the form of the theory arguing that, if the game is played according to a particular strategy, and played over an infinite series of moves (the 'Iterated Prisoner's Dilemma'), it could bring about a situation in which co-operation could start to develop.[20] The strategy – developed

[18] Definition of Seaford 1998: 1. For an overview of the development of theories of reciprocity, see Van Wees 1998.
[19] On the Prisoner's Dilemma, see Parfit 1979; Axelrod 1984: 7–9; Leng 1993: chs. 7 and 8. For an attempt to apply the model to domestic politics in classical Athens, see Herman 1998; for an analysis of classical and hellenistic ethical philosophy in these terms, see Denyer 1983. The other model which is often used to characterise interstate behaviour – especially arms races – is the 'Chicken' game (on which see Hollis & Smith 1990: 126–8). More generally, on the application of game theory to IR, see Quandt 1961; Hollis & Smith 1990: chs. 6 and 8, who list (135–41) the main advantages and disadvantages of the use of such theories, for both theorists and statesmen (noting, in the latter case, the insight of former US Secretary of State Dean Rusk that, 'there are real dangers for world peace if leaders treat crises as games of Chicken' (140)).
[20] Axelrod 1984: 4.

through computer models – is the so-called 'Tit-for-Tat' approach, which relies heavily on the use of reciprocal behaviour: never being the first to start a quarrel, but, once it has been started, responding in kind to the actions of the opposition.[21]

Although the strategy was developed in the abstract, it has been claimed that it can be seen in operation: for example, the 'live-and-let-live' system which occasionally appears to have operated in trench warfare during the First World War fits the model reasonably well, and would be a striking example of co-operation arising not only in the absence of overall control, but even in the presence (in theory at least) of outright hostility.[22] It has been argued, too, in a number of studies of modern international affairs, that this model of reciprocal behaviour between states is a powerful tool not just for guiding and predicting future policies, but also for explaining the development of past events.[23] And, perhaps unsurprisingly, the makers of such claims can be found claiming the authority of a classical tradition:

> reciprocity has featured as a norm in human relations since ancient times, and in the interstate system, where there exists no established central authority . . . reciprocity provides the guiding norm for cooperation.[24]

This claim for the universality of reciprocity, and specifically for its applicability to the ancient world, may seem to be relatively uncontroversial: the norm of reciprocity has, increasingly, been identified as the key to a whole range of problems in Greek history and culture.[25] This trend has spread even to discussions of Greek foreign relations, where both the relationships of reciprocity and exchange which are visible within domestic society, and the principles which underlie those relationships – helping friends, harming enemies – have been shown to operate outside and between *poleis*

---

[21] On the strategy, and the history of its development, see Axelrod 1984; Hollis & Smith 1990: 132–4.

[22] Axelrod 1984: ch. 4.

[23] Goldstein & Freeman 1990; Leng 1993, with further bibliography at 7.

[24] Leng 1993: 70.

[25] On the tendency to see reciprocity as 'the fashionable solution to all our problems as ancient historians', see Millett 1998: 203, n. For recent examples of the application of the concept of reciprocity to those problems, see, in general, the papers in Gill, Postlethwaite & Seaford edd. 1998, and in Cartledge, Millett & von Reden edd. 1998.

too.[26] Attention has, however, tended to focus on the positive manifestations, and consequences, of reciprocity. Research has also, for the most part, concentrated on the existence and effects of reciprocal ties at an interpersonal level: the potential influence on interstate politics of reciprocal ties of friendship between individuals belonging to different states; or the adoption of relationships based on these ties into the formal framework of interstate politics. The institution of *proxenia* is the clearest and most discussed example of the second case.[27] The first could be demonstrated through numerous examples, whether detected by modern scholars on the basis of accumulated evidence,[28] or explicitly discussed by contemporary writers – the most famous example of the latter sort being the encounter between Agesilaus and Pharnabazus, described by Xenophon at *Hellenica* IV.i.29–41, a meeting which illustrates both the potential and the limitations of such connections:

ἀκούσας ταῦτα ὁ Ἀγησίλαος ἐλάβετο τῆς χειρὸς αὐτοῦ καὶ εἶπεν· εἴθ᾽, ὦ λῷστε σύ, τοιοῦτος ὢν φίλος ἡμῖν γένοιο. ἐν δ᾽ οὖν, ἔφη, ἐπίστω, ὅτι νῦν τε ἄπειμι ὡς ἂν δύνωμαι τάχιστα ἐκ τῆς σῆς χώρας, τοῦ τε λοιποῦ, κἂν πόλεμος ᾖ, ἕως ἂν ἐπ᾽ ἄλλον ἔχωμεν στρατεύεσθαι, σοῦ τε καὶ τῶν σῶν ἀφεξόμεθα.

On hearing this, Agesilaus took Pharnabazus' hand and said: 'Would that you, sir, a man of such a spirit, come to be our friend. But at least,' he said, 'be assured of one thing, that now I am going away from your land as quickly as I can, and in the future, even if war continues, we shall hold off from you and yours so long as we can turn our attack against another.'[29] (X. *HG* IV.i.38)

---

[26] See, above all, Mitchell 1997a; also Karavites 1980; Herman 1987, 1990; Mitchell 1997b; Missiou 1998; Van Wees 2004: 10–12 (usefully connecting the concept to the idea of the society of states).

[27] On proxeny in general, see Monceaux 1886; Phillipson 1911, vol. I: 147–56; Gschnitzer 1973; Walbank 1978: ch. 1; Marek 1984; see also the review article of Virgilio 1969. On the origins of the custom, see Wallace 1970. For accounts of its operation in (broad) terms of reciprocity, see Herman 1987: 130–42; Mitchell 1997a: 28–37. Wight 1977: 53–6, notes that the institutionalisation of this interpersonal element to diplomacy marks a significant difference from modern practice. Even in this case, however, the distinction between interpersonal and interstate is not absolute: RO 55 – admittedly an extreme example – shows Mausolus awarding the status of *proxenia* to the entire population of Knossos.

[28] A good example being the career of Iphicrates, whose well-documented northern connections (Aeschin. 2.28; Dem. 23.129; Nep. *Iph.* 3) coincide neatly with his repeated commands in Thrace and Macedon (see Mitchell 1997a: 102–3, 141–2; Archibald 1998: 218–22; Heskel 1997). For a catalogue of similar cases, see Mitchell 1997a: chs. 4 (Spartan appointments) and 5 (Athenian).

[29] Discussions of the episode in Cartledge 1987: 192–3; Mitchell 1997a: 13–14; Krentz 1995 *ad loc.*; Konstan 1997: 83–6.

But the idea of reciprocity can also be applied to relations between states themselves.[30] It is possible, too, to characterise at least some of these relations as operating in accordance with the kind of 'systemic' reciprocity which forms the basis for the modern theories just discussed: that is, a rigidly bilateral pattern of positive – helping friends – and negative – harming enemies – behaviour.[31] The theme is particularly strong in Xenophon's writing. In the *Hellenica*, for example, the Phliasian Procles, trying to win Athenian support for Sparta in the aftermath of Leuctra, argues that if Athens were to help Sparta on this occasion, Sparta would be bound to offer help in return, if Athens were to need it:

ὑμῖν δὲ νῦν ἐκ θεῶν τινος καιρὸς παραγεγένηται, ἐὰν δεομένοις βοηθήσητε Λακεδαιμονίοις, κτήσασθαι τούτους εἰς τὸν ἅπαντα χρόνον φίλους ἀπροφασίστους.

So to you has now been offered by some god the opportunity, if you help the Lacedaemonians when they are in need, of acquiring them for all time as unhesitating friends. (*HG* VI.v.41)

Another example, found earlier in the same work, suggests that Procles' arguments, although perhaps put with exaggerated forcefulness, were not wholly implausible. Xenophon describes Cyrus (the Younger), in asking for Spartan help, basing his request on a claim that a favour should be reciprocated:

ἐκ δὲ τούτου πέμψας Κῦρος ἀγγέλους εἰς Λακεδαίμονα ἠξίου, οἷόσπερ αὐτὸς Λακεδιμονίοις ἦν ἐν τῷ πρὸς Ἀθηναίους πολέμῳ, τοιούτους καὶ Λακεδαιμονίους αὐτῷ γίγνεσθαι.

After this, Cyrus sent messengers to Sparta and asked that the Lacedaemonians should show themselves as good friends to him as he was to them in the war against the Athenians.[32] (*HG* III.i.1)

The influence of the idea of harming enemies or, more strictly, reciprocating past wrongs (whether actual or perceived) is, if

---

[30] Although the distinction between the two categories may not always be entirely clear-cut: see Herman 1990.

[31] Mitchell 1997a: 15; Blundell 1989: 26 (who claims, in passing, that the model can be projected forward into contemporary international relations).

[32] It also suggests that, in Xenophon's view at least, reciprocal claims of this sort were not restricted to relations between Greeks. A commitment to reciprocity is attributed to Persians elsewhere in his writing: see, for example, *An.* I.ix.10–11 (of Cyrus the Younger); *Cyr.* I.vi.11 (of Cyrus the Great). On the practical problems which could arise from such assumptions, see Mitchell 1997a: esp. chs. 6–9.

anything, even more prominent. Athenian unease at the end of the Peloponnesian War was, according to Xenophon, increased by the belief that they would now suffer revenge for their actions against Melos, Histiaea, Scione, Torone, Aegina, and so on (*HG* II.ii.3). One of Sparta's alleged motives for starting the war against Elis in *c.* 402 was desire for revenge for past Eleian offences against them (πάλαι ὀργιζόμενοι τοῖς Ἠλείοις . . ., 'they had been getting angry with the Eleans for a long time . . .'; III.ii.21).[33] Similarly, one of Agesilaus' declared motives for his invasion of Asia Minor in 396 was revenge for the Persian invasions of Greece a century earlier (*Ages.* I.8). The same motive could apparently persist still longer, appearing, for example, as Alexander's justification for the burning of Persepolis:

ὁ δὲ τιμωρήσασθαι ἐθέλειν Πέρσας ἔφασκεν, ἀνθ' ὧν ἐπὶ τὴν Ἑλλάδα ἐλάσαντες τάς τε Ἀθήνας κατέσκαψαν καὶ τὰ ἱερὰ ἐνέπρησαν, καὶ ὅσα ἄλλα κακὰ τοὺς Ἕλληνας εἰργάσαντο, ὑπὲρ τούτων δίκας λαβεῖν.

He said that he wanted to punish the Persians for sacking Athens and burning the temples when they invaded Greece, and to take retribution for all the other injuries they had done to the Greeks.[34] (Arrian, *An.* III.18.12)

It is this last example, however, which might arouse some suspicion – not necessarily because of the long delay between action and counteraction, but because the claim to negative reciprocity seems to have been transferred away from those who had suffered the original wrong (the Athenians, or – at most – the Greeks who fought against Persia) to their new, and self-proclaimed, representative, in the form of Alexander.[35] The sincerity of Alexander's claim cannot

---

33 The date is disputed (Diodorus (14.17.4–5) has 402; Xenophon, 399), but it is generally accepted that Xenophon's version – which makes the outbreak of war synchronous with Dercylidas' campaigns in Asia Minor – is either an inadvertent (Cawkwell 1979 *ad loc.*) or a deliberate (Tuplin 1993: 54–5) misrepresentation. For an analysis of the build-up to the war, see Alonso Troncoso 1995: 232–5; specifically on vengeance as a motive for the war, see Falkner 1996; Lendon 2000: 18–22. On vengeance in Greek foreign relations in general, see Lendon 2000: 13–21; on vengeance in domestic conflict, Fisher 2000. A similar motive of festering anger is alleged for Sparta's decision to fight Thebes (X. *HG* III.v.5).

34 The revenge motive is one of the (few) consistent themes in the various accounts of the burning of Persepolis: cf. D.S. 17.72.2–3; Curt. 5.7.3–4; Plut. *Al.* 38.2–4; and Bosworth 1980 on *An.* III.18.11.

35 Alexander I of Macedon was a vassal of Persia by 480 (Hdt. VIII.136). On Macedon's role in the Persian Wars, see Hammond 1989: 42–8. A desire to repay the wrongs of the Persian War on behalf of the Greeks had already been expressed by Philip in the aftermath of Chaeroneia, according to Diodorus (16.89.1–2).

be tested – although its propaganda value is self-evident – but what it does highlight is the possible manipulability of claims to reciprocity in the context of Greek interstate relations. This can be seen, too, in the many cases where an allusion to a reciprocal relationship (whether positive or negative) is accompanied by a claim that reciprocity has not, in this case, had any effect. In *Against Aristocrates*, for example, Demosthenes represents his opponents as putting forward the argument that:

ὁ Κερσοβλέπτες καὶ Χαρίδημος ἴσως ἐναντί᾽ ἔπραττον τῇ πόλει τόθ᾽ ὅτ᾽ ἦσαν ἐχθροί, νῦν δὲ φίλοι καὶ χρησίμους παρέξουσιν ἑαυτούς. οὐ δὴ δεῖ μνησικακεῖν· οὐδὲ γὰρ Λακεδαιμονίους ὅτ᾽ ἐσῴζομεν, οὐκ ἀνεμιμνησκόμεθ᾽ εἴ τι κακῶς ἐποίη- σαν ἡμᾶς ὄντες ἐχθροί, οὐδὲ Θηβαίους, οὐδ᾽ Εὐβοέας τὰ τελευταῖα νυνί.

Cersobleptes and Charidemus did perhaps oppose Athens at a time when they were unfriendly; but now they are our friends, and wish to be useful friends. We must not bear grudges. When we were saving the Lacedaemonians, we did not recall the wrongs they had done to us when they were our enemies; nor did we do so with the Thebans, nor, most recently, with the Euboeans. (23.191)

Demosthenes' objection to this argument focuses not so much on its general validity, as on his specific reluctance to trust Cersobleptes. Withholding from an act of negative reciprocity can also be repre- sented as a positive characteristic, as it is by, for example, Lysias in his account of Athenian help for her former enemies in the Corinthian war (2.67).[36]

It is, however, true that such negative approaches to reciprocal relationships are, more usually, a subject for criticism. Isocrates, in his *To Philip*, constructs an argument for the possibility of reconcil- iation, and for the poor standards of behaviour of Greek city-states, based on a whole series of cases where Greek cities have decided to help rather than harm their enemies (5.42–5). Aeschines' account

---

[36] Such claims of the refusal of vengeance should perhaps be considered in the gen- eral context of Athenian domestic politics of the period, specifically the post-403 amnesty: see Bearzot 1998: esp. 144 for the connection between domestic and inter- state vengeance/reconciliation. As the Demosthenic example shows, however, the phe- nomenon is not restricted to the early fourth century; see also Aeschin. 3.85, for the claim that Athens went to help Chalcis and Eretria in spite of having been wronged by them, οὐχ ἡγούμενοι δίκαιον εἶναι τὴν ὀργὴν ἀπομνημονεύειν ('not thinking it right to bear their anger in mind'). For the argument that the refusal of vengeance is a notable characteristic of Athenian domestic society, see Herman 1993, 1994, 1995, 1996, 1998, 2000.

of his attempt to persuade Philip II to make some concessions to Athens emphasises the use which he made of arguments based on positive reciprocity: an account of the history of services carried out by Athens for Macedon (and in particular for Philip's ancestors) formed the opening point of his argument (2.26–9); but he went on to make it clear that, in spite of these services, the Athenians had received few favours from Macedon. Failure to maintain a reciprocal system of behaviour is, therefore, a potential source of criticism; but what these examples nevertheless suggest is that reciprocal actions in Greek interstate relations are perhaps best characterised not as systemic, quasi-mechanic reflexes, but as reflections of a more structured, formalised – even societal – approach to the construction of connections and relations between states. A consideration of the appearance in these contexts of some of the language and ideology of reciprocity (in the sense in which it is most frequently used by classical scholars) may make this clearer.

2.3 Reciprocity as the basis for a society

While international theorists have tended to focus on the types of action, and their motivations, which distinguish systems of reciprocal behaviour, classicists have paid more attention to the relationships which can result from those actions, and in particular to the networks which can develop from various sorts of (positive) reciprocity. Under that general heading, three broad (though overlapping) categories can be established: *philia* (φιλία) as a general, all-encompassing term – coming closest to 'friendship' – for those bound by reciprocal ties; the reciprocity between citizens; and that which applies between kin.[37]

The use of the language of reciprocity, and in particular of *philia*, to characterise and reinforce the positive ties between two states is widespread. It appears as a, relatively informal, way of describing friendly relations between states (the same metaphor, of course, also applies in English), appearing in both epigraphic and literary

---

[37] Blundell 1989: 39–49; Mitchell 1997a: ch. 2. These categories, of course, replicate those which apply in domestic and interpersonal relationships (for a proper consideration of other aspects of this phenomenon, see ch. 4).

texts. A *dēmos* (probably of Sinope) is praised (in *IG* ii² 409, lines 19–22) ὅτι διατελοῦσιν φ]|ίλοι ὄ[ντες αἰεὶ τοῦ δήμου τοῦ Ἀθηναίω]|ν, 'because they continue to be constant friends to the Athenian people'.[38] A similar usage appears in the *Antidosis*, in Isocrates' description of Timotheus' approach to the establishment of good relations between Athens and other Greek cities:

τοῦτ' ἐφιλοσόφει καὶ τοῦτ' ἔπραττεν, ὅπως μηδεμία τῶν πόλεων αὐτὸν φοβήσεται τῶν Ἑλληνίδων, ἀλλὰ πᾶσαι θαρρήσουσι πλὴν τῶν ἀδικουσῶν. ἠπίστατο γὰρ τούς τε δεδιότας ὅτι μισοῦσι δι' οὓς ἂν τοῦτο πεπονθότες τυγχάνωσι, τήν τε πόλιν διὰ μὲν τὴν φιλίαν τὴν τῶν ἄλλων εὐδαιμονεστάτην καὶ μεγίστην γενομένην, διὰ δὲ τὸ μῖσος μικρὸν ἀπολιποῦσαν τοῦ μὴ ταῖς ἐσχάταις συμφοραῖς περιπεσεῖν.

He made it the object of his theory and of his actions to see to it that no Greek city should be afraid of him, but that all should feel secure, apart from those which did wrong; for he realized that men who are afraid hate those who inspire this feeling in them, and that it was through the friendship of other cities that the city had become prosperous and powerful, and through their hatred that she barely escaped suffering the worst disasters.[39] (15.121–2)

The concept can also, and more frequently, be found as part of a more formal vocabulary, associated in particular with the creation of alliances and other peace agreements.[40] The treaty of alliance made between Athens and Chios in 384, for example, refers to the Peace of Antalcidas as τὴν ε[ἰρήνην καὶ τὴν φιλίαν | κ]αὶ τὸς ὅρκ[ο]ς κα[ὶ τὰς οὔσας συνθήκας, 'the peace and the friendship and the oaths and the existing agreements' (*IG* ii² 34, fr.a, lines 5–6).[41] The idea can then be extended, in clauses requiring the participants

[38] The supplements (as well as the suggestion that the *dēmos* is Sinope) were suggested by Wilhelm 1942: 150–2, and accepted by Veligianni-Terzi 1997: no. A151. References to *philoi* and *philia* in interstate documents (in a non-technical sense) are more usually found applied to individuals than to *poleis*: for examples and discussion, see Veligianni-Terzi 1997: 202–3, 254–5.

[39] See also, e.g., Isoc. 5.32; 8.134; 12.54; Dem. 2.7; 6.26; 15.18; and Mitchell 1997b: esp. 42–4.

[40] The distinction is emphasised (probably too strongly) by Bauslaugh 1991: 62: '*philia* was an official relationship, not a state of mind'. On the development of the formal diplomatic concept, see Bauslaugh 1991: 56–64; Panessa 1999: xv–xxxiii.

[41] See also RO 12, line 20 (alliance of Amyntas and Chalcidians, *c.* 393); *IG* ii² 127 (= RO 53), lines 39–40 (alliance of Athens and Thracian, Paeonian and Illyrian kings, 356); RO 50, lines 12–13 (alliance between Philip II and the Chalcideans, 356); *IG* ii² 213 (= Tod 168), lines 9–10 (alliance of Athens and Mytilene, 346). Again, the association of *philia* and *summachia* (συμμαχία, 'alliance') is also found in literary sources: e.g., X. *HG* III.v.4 (Thebes and Locris); Isoc. 12.103 (Sparta and Persia). For a catalogue of examples (from the archaic period to the end of the fifth century), see Panessa 1999.

in alliances to 'have the same friends and enemies' as each other – τοὺς αὐτοὺς ἐχθροὺς καὶ φίλους νομίζειν – a formula which is found, for example, in the description of the tie which links Cyrus to the 10,000 (X. *An.* II.v.39).[42]

A different manifestation of this association of *philia* with the establishment of good relations between states can be seen in the iconography of the reliefs which accompany decrees establishing such relations, and, in particular, by the appearance on those reliefs of the motif of *dexiosis*.[43] This gesture is closely associated with the formal establishment of friendship, marking not simply greeting, but trust and absence of hostility or fear.[44] Although only one extant example (from the ten which survive on Athenian decrees) can securely be connected with an actual decree of alliance (*IG* i[3] 86: the alliance of Athens and Argos in 416),[45] almost all of those which remain, and for which the content of the inscription can be identified, relate to decrees which commemorate or reinforce the close tie between Athens and another state.[46] And the reliefs, by depicting the divine representatives of the states concerned joined by that gesture of trust and friendship, act as powerful illustrations

---

[42] For discussion of the formula's various forms, and its varying implications – it can be used in both equal and unequal, subordinating, alliances – see de Ste. Croix 1972, appendix 5; Pistorius 1985: ch. 3.

[43] It should be noted that references to *philia* or *philoi* do not appear in any of the decrees associated with these reliefs; it might, therefore, be better to think of the relationship between language and image not as one of simple repetition and reinforcement, but as alternative ways of representing a (broadly) similar idea. The fragmentary state of many of the decrees makes certainty difficult, however. The relevant inscriptions are: *IG* i[3] 61 (= Lawton 1995: no. 2; Athens and Methone, 423); *IG* i[3] 86 (= Lawton 1995: no. 5; alliance of Athens and Argos, 416); *IG* i[3] 101 (= Lawton 1995: no. 7; honours for Neapolis, 409); *IG* i[3] 124 (= Lawton 1995: no. 9; Athens and Cius, 406/5); *IG* i[3] 127/ii[2] 1 (= Lawton 1995: no. 12; Athens honours Samians); *IG* ii[2] 18 (= Lawton 1995: no. 16; Athens honours Dionysius I of Syracuse, 393); *IG* ii[2] 128 (= Lawton 1995: no. 28; Athens and Neapolis, 355); *IG* i[3] 190 (= Lawton 1995: no. 82; unidentified); *IG* ii[2] 167 (= Lawton 1995: no. 110; unidentified).

[44] The symbolism of the gesture lies in the joining of two – potentially weapon-carrying – hands in unarmed friendship: see Herman 1987: 50–3. On the appearance of *dexiosis* in document reliefs, Meyer 1989: 140–5; Lawton 1995: 36–7.

[45] Lawton 1995: no. 5 and plate 3: the relief shows Athena and Hera, with Zeus looking on. Lawton suggests that reliefs nos. 82 (*IG* i[3] 190) and 110 (*IG* ii[2] 167) might also have been associated with treaties.

[46] The exception is *IG* ii[2] 1374 (= Lawton 1995: no. 13) – an inventory of the treasurers of Athena and the Other Gods – which seems to be a copy of the relief which accompanies the decree honouring Samos, and which shows Athena and Hera. The use of the motif of *dexiosis* might be intended to refer to the unification (in *c.* 406/5) of the boards of treasurers of Athena and of the Other Gods (Lawton 1995: 89).

45

of such links, symbolising not only the reciprocal nature of the relationship (usually, services to Athens are rewarded by honours), but also, in theory at least, its equality. The conspicuously loyal people of Thracian Neapolis, for example, are honoured twice by the Athenians for their services to the city, once for their loyalty at the end of the Peloponnesian War (*IG* i³ 101), and again during the Social War (*IG* ii² 128). On both occasions, the decree is accompanied by a relief showing the *dexiosis* of Athena and the Parthenos of Neapolis.[47] The document recording the sequence of decrees voting honours to the Samians at the end of the Peloponnesian War (*IG* i³ 127/ii² 1) is, similarly, accompanied by a relief showing the *dexiosis* of Athena and Hera.[48] The relief could, moreover, serve not only to reinforce the message of the decree with which it was linked, but also to widen its scope: *IG* ii² 18, recording honours voted to Dionysius I of Syracuse (along with his two brothers and his brother-in-law), contains a relief showing Athena with a female figure, representing either Syracuse or Sicily.[49] The focus of the monument as a whole is thus widened from Athens' relations with a small group of individuals – albeit rulers of their state – to the whole Syracusan community.

The adoption of the language and images of *philia* in these cases suggests that the two states involved were interacting on a basis of equality. Even in these instances that impression may, of course, be quite misleading.[50] But in cases where other types of reciprocal concepts are used the potential for inequality is made more obvious.

The first of these is citizenship. Grants of citizenship to individuals were, in the fifth and (increasingly) in the fourth centuries, used as a tool of Athenian foreign policy, with the aim of bringing the non-Athenian into the 'network of duties and obligations that one owed to one's fellow countrymen and to one's *polis*'.[51] And this was a practice which (again, more frequently in the fourth century)

[47] Lawton 1995: nos. 7 (plate 4) and 28 (plate 15) respectively.

[48] Lawton 1995: no. 12 (plate 7).

[49] Lawton 1995: no. 16 (plate 9): the figure is usually identified as either Demeter or (perhaps more plausibly) Persephone (whose head appears on Syracusan coinage).

[50] On the potentially oppressive use of *philia* in interstate relations, see Mitchell 1997b: 42. Generally on the inequality of reciprocal relationships, see Arist. *EN* 1124b10–16 (who supports his claim with reference to the arguments used in interstate relations).

[51] Mitchell 1997a: 38. See, for example, And. 2.23 on the benefits which come to Athens as a result of making grants of citizenship: καὶ ταῦτα μέντοι ὀρθῶς ὑμεῖς φρονοῦντες

could be extended to apply to whole states.[52] The same principle of the extension of reciprocal obligation must also apply when the grant is being made to a whole community, although there are also differences between the two practices. The quantitative difference is self-evident. The more important difference, however, is qualitative, and lies in the fact that the offer of mass citizenship was, in most cases, not expected to be taken up *en masse*.[53] Its primary significance was, therefore, symbolic – a strong assertion of the links between two cities. In some cases, this link does seem to be based on an assumption of equality: this is most obvious in reciprocal isopolity agreements, such as that made between Ceos and Eretria in the first quarter of the fourth century (*SV* II.232): Ceans are granted the right to be listed as Eretrian citizens; Eretrians are offered exactly equivalent rights in Ceos.

Elsewhere, however, and particularly where the grant of citizenship operates in only one direction, these agreements have greater potential for inequality. This can be seen in the use which is made

δίδοτε· οὕτω γὰρ ἂν ὑπὸ πλείστων ἀνθρώπων εὖ πάσχοιτε ('you are thinking sensibly when you give these things out: for in this way you will be well-treated by most men'). For complaints of the excessive use of the honour (and its consequent debasement), see, e.g., Dem. 23.200; [Dem.] 13.24–5.

[52] Many of these mass grants could be labelled *isopoliteia* agreements (on which, see Gawantka 1975), but it is important not to impose too firm a distinction between these and grants of *politeia*: cases such as the grants of Athenian citizenship to the Samians (*IG* i³ 127/ii² 1) or to the Plataeans ([Dem.] 59.104; D.S. 15.46.6) demonstrate the close connection between the two categories (see Osborne 1981–3, vol. IV: 181, 202–4.) For a list of examples, see Gawantka 1975: ch. 7.2; to this can be added the Athenian grants to the people of Elaious (341/0: *IG* ii² 228; they are possibly being given only the status of Athenian cleruchs: Osborne 1981–3, vol. IV: 202); and (perhaps) the people of Troezen (338/7: Hyp. 3.32). Although such grants might be prompted by a particular cataclysm in the recipient state (especially obvious in the case of Plataea), they can also reflect an extended sequence of exchanges between the two states: Elaious, for example – a loyal member of the Second Athenian League – had been the subject of an Athenian honorific decree in 357/6 (*Agora* XVI: no. 53), and had, in turn, voted a gold crown to Athens in 346/5 (*IG* ii² 1443, lines 93–5; Dem. 18.92).

[53] This is suggested, for example, by the language of the inscription (*IG* ii² 1 = RO 2) recording various decrees in honour of the Samians (including the decree of citizenship): the δεῖπνον ('dinner') referred to in lines 51 (restored) and 54 (which usually implies that the recipient of the meal is a citizen) has reverted by lines 63 (where it is restored) and 74 to a ξένια (*xenia*) – the form of entertainment usually granted to non-citizens (Gawantka 1975: 57–8). However, some people clearly did take up the offer. See, e.g., Lysias 23 *passim* for Plataean residents at Athens. Similarly, in the grant of citizenship to the Samians (*IG* ii² 1), the original decree is amended (lines 32–4) to allow Samians actually resident in Athens to be enrolled in a tribe, and a funerary inscription recording Athenian citizens with a Samian father (*IG* ii² 6417) shows that this did happen. For full discussion of the inscriptions, see Osborne 1981–3, vol. II: 25–6, vol. III: 38–9.

of the paradigmatic case, the granting of Athenian citizenship to the surviving citizens of Plataea in 427. For Isocrates' Plataeans, arguing (in theory) in the aftermath of the destruction of their city in 373, this grant is evidence of a tradition of Athenian commitment to the protection of their state, and, in turn, a strong argument in favour of continuing Athenian concern for their fate:

καὶ γὰρ ἂν πάντων εἴη δεινότατον, εἰ πρότερον μὲν ἡμῖν μετέδοτε τῆς πατρίδος τῆς ὑμετέρας αὐτῶν, νῦν δὲ μηδὲ τὴν ἡμετέραν ἀποδοῦναι δόξειεν ὑμῖν.

For it would be the worst thing of all, if you first of all granted us the right of common citizenship with yourselves, but now decide not even to restore to us our own. (14.52)

Some years later, the same grant provides Apollodorus with proof of the pre-eminent devotion of the Athenians to the Plataean cause ([Dem.] 59.104).[54] And it is this use of the episode – placing the achievement of Athens at the centre of the story – which highlights a characteristic which is implicit in the Isocratean version too. The Athenian self-image as helpers of other states necessarily places those other – smaller, weaker (cf. Isoc. 14.1, 34) – states in the subordinate position. Offering Athenian citizenship to the citizens of another state is a still more tangible way of tightening the link between the two communities while simultaneously demonstrating which holds the dominant position.

The third general category is that of kinship.[55] Such relationships could, of course – in interstate as in interpersonal relations – take a variety of forms, and could also be used in the construction of more widespread groups.[56] Their use as a means of emphasising connections, as well as obligations, between pairs of states is widely visible. Thucydides' Corinthians represent themselves as kinsmen to the Spartans, in the speech in which they attempt to encourage Spartan intervention in their struggle over Potidaea (1.71.4);[57]

---

[54] On the role of the example in Apollodorus' argument, see Trevett 1992: 105; on the accuracy of Apollodorus' version of the decree granting citizenship, id.: 188–9 (suggesting that this is a compressed, but basically reliable, version). For a more general account of the decree and its motivations, see Kapparis 1995.

[55] For an overview of the role of kinship in interstate relations in the ancient world, see Jones 1999. Lücke 2000 concentrates on the Hellenistic period, but some of his conclusions have a wider relevance.

[56] See Curty 1995; Mitchell 1997a: 23–8; and the discussion at 56–7 below.

[57] On Thucydides' use of the theme of kinship, see Curty 1994; Hornblower 1996: 61–80; Crane 1996: ch. 5; Van Wees 2004: 9.

Aristophanes' Lysistrata argues that the *sungeneia* (συγγενεία) of Athens and Sparta should propel them towards peace (*Lys.* 1128–32); Demosthenes claims that Athens should feel obliged to defend Thebes since οὐδὲ ἀλλότριον ἡγεῖται εἶναι ὁ Ἀθηναίων δῆμος τὸν Θηβαίων δῆμον οὔτε τῇ συγγενείᾳ οὔτε τῷ ὁμοφύλῳ, 'the Athenian people is not considered foreign to the Thebans, in kinship or in shared race' (18.186). Again, such ties could be argued to extend beyond the Greek world: the Thracian Seuthes suggests to Xenophon that he is usually inclined to trust Athenians ὅτι συγγενεῖς εἶεν εἰδέναι, 'because he knows that they are kin' (X. *An.* VII.ii.31).[58] And, again, they were no less subject to construction and manipulation than other types of reciprocal relationship.

A good example of this manipulation can be found in an inscription from Paros, dated to 373/2.[59] The precise context of the inscription is unclear. It has frequently been seen as an early example of Athenian recidivism to her old imperial ways, forcing the Parians to rejoin the Second Athenian League after a revolt.[60] But a recent reinterpretation has suggested that the inscription refers not to a conflict between the Parians and the League, but to *stasis* on Paros, which had been settled by the arbitration of the League.[61] The point which is most significant here, however, is the statement with which the (extant part of the) inscription opens:

[——————————] ηρηι κατὰ τὰ πά-
[τρια καὶ εἰς Παναθήν]αια βōν καὶ πανο-
[πλίαν καὶ εἰς Διονύ]σια βōν καὶ φαλλὸ-
[ν] ἀ[π]ά[γεν μνημεῖο]ν ἐπειδὴ τυγχάνοσ-
[ι] ἄποικοι ὄ[ντες τ]οῦ δήμο τō Ἀθηναίων·

---

[58] Possibly a reference to the alleged marriage between the Thracian Tere(u)s and the Athenian Procne. The truth of the story is denied by Thucydides (II.29), but the very fact that he felt the need to do so suggests that the story was felt, by some, to have some validity (see Archibald 1998: 99, n. 25).

[59] RO 29. See also Wilhelm 1940: 3–12; Accame 1941: 229–44; *SEG* XXXI.67; *SV* II.268; Dreher 1995: 110–11.

[60] So, e.g., Accame 1941: 236–44; Cargill 1981: 121 – although Cargill also insists that the terms of readmission to the league were 'mild and unvindictive' (163).

[61] Dreher 1995: 113–31. The argument rests, primarily, on the phrase τὰς διαλλαγὰς ἃς ἐψηφ[ί]σαντο οἱ σύμμαχοι τοῖ[ς] Παρίο[ι]ς ('the reconciliation which the allies have decreed for the Parians'; lines 7–9), which, Dreher argues, implies a settlement between Parians (since διαλλαγὴ is used only of internal agreements) arranged by the allies of the Second Athenian League on behalf of the Parians, rather than an agreement between the Parians (as a whole) and the League.

. . . in accordance with tradition, and to send to the Panathenaea a cow and a panoply, to the Dionysia a cow and a phallus as a commemoration, since they happen to be colonists of the Athenian people. (lines 2–6)

It is not at all clear that Paros was in fact a colony of Athens,[62] but the use of the connection between colony and mother-city as a powerful weapon in arguments over interstate behaviour is well attested: the most famous example is, perhaps, the dispute between Corcyra and Corinth which precipitates the Peloponnesian War.[63] That the manipulation of such connections could sometimes – as here – extend to their invention should make their usefulness still clearer.[64] The assertion of this bond in this particular context may also be significant, and suggests that the existence of such ties could be used not only to argue in favour of mutual obligations between states but also to validate the behaviour of one (or both) parties after the event. There are no other (recorded) examples of an arbitration of this sort, by an external power in an internal dispute.[65] If this is what is being recorded in this document, it might well require or provoke the assertion of a close tie of kinship between Athens and Paros, transforming what could be seen as meddling into the justifiable concern of a mother-city (and, by extension, the allies of the mother-city) for her colonists, and – again – firmly establishing Athens as the dominant partner in the relationship.

The example of kinship, however, brings into sharper focus another fundamental difference between reciprocity, as envisaged

---

[62] Claims that they were colonists of Athens are found only in the scholion to Dion.Per. 525 and in Vell. 1.4.3 – both of which are likely to be influenced either by this inscription or by a general assumption that all Aegean island states are Athenian foundations. Arist. fg. 611.25 makes Paros an Arcadian colony (Dreher 1995: 130–1).

[63] On Corinth and Corcyra, see Curty 1994; Crane 1996: ch. 5. On obligations between mother-city and colony, see Phillipson 1911, vol. II: 118–24; Graham 1983: esp. pt 2.

[64] There is some precedent in the treatment of the members of Athens' first empire, who were required to send offerings to the Panathenaea (IG i³ 71 (= ML 69), lines 55–60), although only 'as if' (καθάπερ – line 58 (restored)) colonists, not as actual colonists. It is not clear whether the custom is being newly instituted in this decree (of 425/4), or whether it should be seen as clarifying an existing practice. For discussion and bibliography, see ML: pages 198–9. On Athenian 'colonisation propaganda' in the fifth century, see Barron 1964: 46–8; Smarczyk 1990: pt 2; Hall 1997: 55. In the fourth century, compare I.Priene 5 (= Curty 1995: no. 49), in which Priene both decrees the sending of πομπὴν καὶ πανοπλίαν ('procession and panoply') to Athens for the Great Panathanaea (lines 4–5), and claims to be doing so μνημεῖον τῆς ἐξ ἀρχῆς συγγενείας καὶ φιλίας ('as a memorial of their longstanding kinship and friendship'; lines 5–6).

[65] No comparable example is recorded in Piccirilli 1973, Ager 1996 or Magnetto 1997. On sungeneia as a possible reason for selecting an arbitrator, see Piccirilli 1973: no. 1.

in descriptions of contemporary international relations, and reciprocity as a feature of Greek interstate relations, namely the fact that, in the latter case, reciprocal relations could be thought of as being transitive. Kinship is perhaps the clearest example of a network of bilateral ties combining to form a wider 'family', and this extension can be seen in the application of the concept to external relations. Agesilaus, for example, can claim to the Paphlagonian Otys that the formation of a marriage tie with the family of Spithridates will result in the creation of a long chain of interconnected links: through Spithridates to Sparta, and through Sparta to the rest of Greece (X. *HG* iv.i.8). A similar argument is used by Isocrates, arguing for Philip's connections to the rest of Greece: Philip is linked through kinship (a shared descent from Heracles) with Athens, Thebes, Sparta and Argos; these states, in turn, have networks of connections with other smaller Greek cities (5.30–4).[66]

The impression that bilateral ties could become the basis of more extended groups does not always have to be expressed so formally. This can be seen most clearly in the use which is made in this period of the concept of *eunoia* (εὔνοια, 'goodwill'). This is, fundamentally, a bilateral relationship,[67] which can be claimed to exist between individuals, or groups, or a mixture of the two, and which can also – like *philia* – seem to operate in interpersonal, domestic political, and external contexts. *Eunoia* can be a preliminary to, or perhaps a part of, personal friendships.[68] As one of the characteristics displayed by the recipients of honorific decrees, it also becomes part of the standard vocabulary of praise in domestic and, particularly, interstate politics.[69]

But *eunoia* can also be claimed to be the best basis for the formation of networks of relationships in external politics. This

[66] The idea of transferable ties of reciprocity can also, of course, be applied to the example of Alexander at Persepolis quoted above (41–2).

[67] Wight 1977: 71.

[68] The nature of the distinction between *eunoia* and *philia* is not, it seems, rigidly defined: while Aristotle (e.g. at *EN* 1167a3–4, *EE* 1241a11; followed by Konstan 1997: 74) wants to treat *eunoia* as the (non-reciprocal) preliminary stage to 'proper' *philia*, other writers seem to operate with a less rigid distinction between the two concepts. On this, see Mitchell 1997b: 33–4.

[69] Whitehead 1993: 52–4; Veligianni-Terzi 1997: 200–2, 218–19 (general); 256–62, 274–5 (external politics); 294–5 (domestic politics); see also ch. 4, sec. 2.

approach to the structuring of interstate relations is perhaps most closely associated with Isocrates. It forms, for example, a prominent part of his praise in the *Antidosis* for the policies of the general Timotheus: it is Timotheus' recognition of the importance of *eunoia* which has enabled him to be so successful in enhancing Athenian power and prestige (15.122). It also appears as part of Isocrates' advice to Philip II:

καίτοι πῶς οὐ χρὴ προθύμως ὀρέγεσθαι τῆς τοιαύτης εὐνοίας, δι' ἣν οὐ μόνον τὴν ὑπάρχουσαν ἀρχὴν ἀσφαλῶς καθέξεις, ἀλλὰ καὶ πολλὴν ἑτέραν ἀκινδύνως προσκτήσει; . . . πολὺ γὰρ κάλλιόν ἐστι τὰς εὐνοίας τὰς τῶν πόλεων αἱρεῖν ἢ τὰ τείχη. τὰ μὲν γὰρ τοιαῦτα τῶν ἔργων οὐ μόνον ἔχει φθόνον, ἀλλὰ καὶ τῶν τοιούτων τὴν αἰτίαν τοῖς στρατοπέδοις ἀνατιθέασιν· ἢν δὲ τὰς οἰκειότητας καὶ τὰς εὐνοίας κτήσασθαι δυνηθῇς, ἅπαντες τὴν σὴν διάνοιαν ἐπαινέσονται.

Yet is there any reason why you should not eagerly reach for such goodwill, through which you will not only hold securely your present empire, but also without risk acquire another great one? . . . For it is much better to capture the goodwill of cities than their walls; for achievements like the latter not only bring ill-will, but people attribute the credit for them to your armies; yet if you are able to win friendships and goodwill, all will praise your wisdom.[70] (*Ep.* 2.18, 21)

The appearance of such claims is not, however, purely an Isocratean phenomenon. In the *2nd Olynthiac*, for example, Demosthenes makes a very similar point. Again, his claim is directed at Philip, although in this case it is not a suggestion but an accusation (Philip's failure to cultivate *eunoia* will lead to his downfall):

ὅταν μὲν γὰρ ὑπ'εὐνοίας τὰ πράγματα συστῇ καὶ πᾶσι ταὐτὰ συμφέρῃ τοῖς μετέχουσι τοῦ πολέμου, καὶ συμπονεῖν καὶ φέρειν τὰς συμφορὰς καὶ μένειν ἐθέλουσιν ἄνθρωποι· ὅταν δ' ἐκ πλεονεξίας καὶ πονηρίας τις ὥσπερ οὗτος ἰσχύσῃ, ἡ πρώτη πρόφασις καὶ μικρὸν πταῖσμα ἅπαντ' ἀνεχαίτισε καὶ διέλυσεν.

For when a league is held together by goodwill, when all the allies have the same interests, then men are willing to remain steadfast, sharing the toil and enduring the hardships; but when a man has gained power, as Philip has, by greed and crime, then the first pretext, some tiny slip, overthrows and destroys everything.[71] (2.9)

---

[70] On *eunoia* in Isocrates, see especially de Romilly 1958.
[71] Similar argument in [Dem.] 11.7. Generally on *eunoia* in interstate politics, see Perlman 1991; Mitchell 1997b.

Perhaps most surprisingly of all, a similar idea appears in Thucydides, in an argument attributed to Alcibiades: the best way for the Spartans to establish their security, and become leaders of Greece, is to rely not on force, but on the acquisition and cultivation of goodwill (VI.92.5: οὐ βίᾳ, κατ᾿ εὔνοιαν δὲ ἡγῆσθε, 'you will lead not through force but by goodwill').

A similar process of extension, from reciprocal relationship to wider network, can be detected (although it is less prominent, and less coherently argued) in negative characterisations of interstate relationships – of the sort perhaps more typically associated with Thucydidean characterisations of empire – phrased in terms of connections between tyrant and subject, or between master and slave.[72] Such relationships are, of course, radically different in tone from those which arise from the cultivation of *eunoia*; in fact, in Cleon's famous description of the nature of Athens' empire, an explicit contrast is drawn between the two models of relationship:

οὐ σκοποῦντες ὅτι τυραννίδα ἔχετε τὴν ἀρχὴν καὶ πρὸς ἐπιβουλεύοντας αὐτοὺς καὶ ἄκοντας ἀρχομένους, οἳ οὐκ ἐξ ὧν ἂν χαρίζησθε βλαπτόμενοι αὐτοὶ ἀκροῶνται ὑμῶν, ἀλλ᾿ ἐξ ὧν ἂν ἰσχύι μᾶλλον ἢ τῇ ἐκείνων εὐνοίᾳ περιγένησθε.

You fail to notice that you hold your empire as a tyranny, in the face of unwilling and conspiratorial subjects, whose obedience is not ensured by your suicidal concessions; rather, your superiority derives more from your strength than from their goodwill. (III.37.2)

But while the inequality of the reciprocal relationship which operates between tyrant and subject is more obviously marked, the basic nature of the connection, and of its wider implications, is fundamentally similar: a state's position in a more extensive system is represented in terms of a network of bilateral relationships, of which the leading state is the focus.

All of these concepts – *eunoia*, tyranny, slavery – are, of course, closely associated with 'empire', in its various forms. And it is, I think, in this context of essentially bilateral relationships that it is most appropriate to place much of the 'imperialistic' discourse of this period, particularly that of the fourth century: *hegemonia* and *archē* are created, and to a great extent sustained, not so much

---

[72] See Tuplin 1985, and, for Isocrates' use of the language of tyranny: ch. 4, sec. 3.

through the creation of one single, encompassing, unit, as through the careful utilisation of bilateral, often reciprocal, interactions.[73]

2.4 Multilateral societies and panhellenic communities

One could, then, create a picture of a society of states developed almost entirely on the basis of a network of reciprocal relationships, and certainly much of the characterisation of interstate relations in classical texts can be interpreted in this way. But not all of it. Running alongside – sometimes overlapping with, and sometimes contradicting – the picture just discussed is a pattern which requires a different sort of framework: one which allows for multilateral groupings, and one which does not always make the *polis* the basic unit of interaction.

Some of these structures are more easily perceived in a fifth-century – and especially in a Thucydidean – context. The suggestion of the existence of two parallel interstate societies, whose membership is determined by political ideology – democratic versus oligarchic – is a recurring motif of Thucydides' account of the Peloponnesian War. A striking characteristic of the boundaries of those two groups is that they need not, necessarily, align with the boundaries of *poleis* – a point which emerges most clearly during Thucydides' account of the Corcyrean stasis: the Greek world is divided, within cities as well as between them, into democrats (who favour Athens), and oligarchs (who favour Sparta):

τοῖς τε τῶν δήμων προστάταις τοὺς Ἀθηναίους ἐπάγεσθαι καὶ τοῖς ὀλίγοις τοὺς Λακεδαιμονίους.

the leaders of the people were struggling to bring in the Athenians, and the oligarchs the Lacedaemonians.[74] (III.82.1)

This sort of representation of interstate societies does recur in the less obviously ideologically polarised world of the fourth century. It is, for example, an important part of Demosthenes' argument in

---

[73] For a more detailed account of this process, see ch. 5, esp. sec. 4; on the particular case of the Athenian Empire, see ch. 6, sec. 4.

[74] On the possibility of ideological commitments overcoming *polis*-loyalty, see de Ste. Croix 1954/5: 29–30 (against Ehrenberg 1947: 48).

For the Liberty of the Rhodians,[75] and its (regrettable) persistence is also noted by Isocrates:

τῶν γὰρ Ἑλλήνων οἱ μὲν ὑφ' ἡμῖν οἱ δ' ὑπὸ Λακεδαιμονίοις εἰσίν· αἱ γὰρ πολιτεῖαι, δι' ὧν οἰκοῦσι τὰς πόλεις, οὕτω τοὺς πλείστους αὐτῶν διειλήφασιν.

For the Greeks are subject, some to us, others to the Lacedaemonians, the constitutions by which they govern their states having thus divided most of them. (4.16)

But although the ideological approach to the construction of interstate societies does not disappear at the end of the Peloponnesian War (and although the ideological element is not absent, either, from other aspects of interstate relations),[76] the impression of a Greek world definitively divided into parties of democrats and oligarchs emerges much more weakly from fourth-century writing than it does from Thucydides' account.

A second Thucydidean theme – of divisions within the Greek world based on ethnicity – is, if anything, even less prominent in the fourth century,[77] although, again, some traces of such approaches can be seen. The *Anabasis*, for example, although often perceived to be a prime panhellenist text,[78] does reveal in places the tensions – between Lacedaemonians, Arcadians, Dardanians, and so on – which lurk beneath the surface of the harmonious community of the 10,000.[79] Ethnic divisions within the 'Greek' world are significant factors in interstate politics in general: the increasing prominence of (ethnically based) leagues and federations is the best evidence for that.[80] But, as with democracy and oligarchy, smaller-scale

---

[75] For discussion of this speech, see below: 72–4.

[76] Particularly civil war, and associated interventions: see Fuks 1984; Gehrke 1985; and ch. 5, esp. sec. 3, for more discussion.

[77] The Thucydidean divide is between Dorian and Ionian, although the existence, nature and significance of this distinction in the fifth century have been the subject of extended debate: in particular, attention has focused on the reliability of the Thucydidean picture of these groups as being essentially artificial – created by the requirements of political expediency and equally subject to destruction by the same forces (see, notoriously, Thucydides' comments in the catalogue before the battle at Syracuse, VII.57–8). On this, see especially Will 1956; Alty 1982; Hornblower 1992a. On the historiography of the question, see Hall 1997: ch. 1.

[78] Dillery 1995: ch. 3, has a statement of the case; Rood 2004 argues for a more nuanced reading.

[79] See, for example, the dispute over the selection of leaders described at VI.i.25–32 (esp. VI.i.32).

[80] See, for example, Nielsen 1997 on the ethnic basis for the Triphylian League. It is important not to insist on *polis*-identity and ethnic identity as two distinct, or mutually

ethnic divisions are not widely appealed to as important structuring factors in interstate politics. The focus of attention has shifted from groups within the Greek society of states to that society as a whole.

It is this 'Panhellenic' discourse which, as mentioned above,[81] is usually responsible for drawing the attention of international theorists to the Greek example, and which is undoubtedly extremely prominent in Greek sources, particularly in the fourth century.[82] Often, the criteria by which Greekness might be determined are not explored in any great detail, but, where they are, two broad categories – already familiar from Herodotus – recur: namely, kinship and religion.

Kinship remains a central factor – as it had been in establishing connections on a much smaller scale – in arguing for the unity of the Greeks.[83] References to the Ionians are relatively infrequent after the end of the fifth century, but assertions of a broader, Hellenic, kinship are correspondingly more common. Isocrates, for example, whose description (at 12.164f.) of Athens' noble tradition of helping those states τῆς αὐτῆς συγγενείας μετεχούσας ('sharing in the same kinship') might seem to be a reference to the Athenian role as metropolis of the Ionian colonies,[84] goes on to speak as if it was not just the Ionians but all of Greece which was aided by

exclusive, categories: see Archibald 2000 (on Macedonia, Thessaly and Thrace); Cohen 2000: 22–30 (on Athens); Davies 2000 (on the Molossians). In this context, however, it is equally important to note that such groupings, once formally constituted, can function not so much as ordering principles of interstate society, but as discrete units within that society: see generally Beck 1997: 212–49. Such groupings are, of course, contestable, and constantly liable to (forced or voluntary) reformulation, but the points which must be emphasised are that the *polis* cannot be counted as the inevitable basic unit of interstate society (see Rhodes 1993; Rhodes 1994: 587; Davies 1994: 64–5), and that the line between 'foreign' relations and 'domestic' is one which is not as stable as we would sometimes like to believe.

[81] 35–6.

[82] On panhellenism see, in general, Martin 1940: 585–9; Dobesch 1968: 3–28; Perlman 1976; Green 1996; Cartledge 1997: ch. 3; Constantineau 1998: ch. 6; Flower 2000a. In particular: on Demosthenes, Luccioni 1961; on Isocrates, Bringmann 1965: ch. 1; on Xenophon, Dillery 1995: esp. chs. 2–4; on Plato, Schütrumpf 1972. Although the fourth century can seem to be the 'golden age' of panhellenism, it should not be seen as a purely fourth-century phenomenon, let alone invention: Herodotus' contribution has already been noted; on Aristophanes, see Hugill 1936; for an analysis of Thucydides' work in this context, see Price 2001: ch. 7; generally on pre-fourth-century panhellenism, see Flower 2000b.

[83] On the determination of Greekness by kinship, see Diller 1937: esp. ch. 1.

[84] The interpretation suggested by Norlin 1929, *ad loc.*

Athens.[85] Plato's well-known comments describing war between Greeks as *stasis* develop from an argument for Greek unity which also has a basis in shared kinship:

φημὶ γὰρ τὸ μὲν Ἑλληνικὸν γένος αὐτὸ αὑτῷ οἰκεῖον εἶναι καὶ ξυγγενές, τῷ δὲ βαρβαρικῷ ὀθνεῖόν τε καὶ ἀλλότριον.

I say that the Greek race is friendly and kin to itself, and foreign and alien to the barbarian.[86] (*R.* 470c1–2)

The potential of such ideas to exclude as well as include can be seen in arguments adopted by Demosthenes in attempting to prove the inadmissibility of Philip's claims to a share in the Greek community:

καὶ μὴν κἀκεῖνό γ' ἴστε, ὅτι ὅσα μὲν ὑπὸ Λακεδαιμονίων ἢ ὑφ' ἡμῶν ἔπασχον οἱ Ἕλληνες, ἀλλ' οὖν ὑπὸ γνησίων γ' ὄντων τῆς Ἑλλάδος ἠδικοῦντο, καὶ τὸν αὐτὸν τρόπον ἄν τις ὑπέλαβεν τοῦτο, ὥσπερ ἂν εἰ υἱὸς ἐν οὐσίᾳ πολλῇ γεγονὼς γνήσιος διῴκει τι μὴ καλῶς μηδ' ὀρθῶς, κατ' αὐτὸ μὲν τοῦτ' ἄξιον μέμψεως εἶναι καὶ κατηγορίας, ὡς δ' οὐ προσῆκον ἢ ὡς οὐ κληρονόμος τούτων ὢν ταῦτ' ἐποίει, οὐκ ἐνεῖναι λέγειν. εἰ δέ γε δοῦλος ἢ ὑποβολιμαῖος τὰ μὴ προσήκοντ' ἀπώλλυε καὶ ἐλυμαίνετο, Ἡράκλεις ὅσῳ μᾶλλον δεινὸν καὶ ὀργῆς ἄξιον πάντες ἂν ἔφησαν εἶναι.

And you know this also, that the wrongs which the Greeks suffered from the Lacedaemonians or from us, they at least suffered at the hands of true-born sons of Greece, and they might have been regarded as the acts of a legitimate son, born to great possessions, who behaved wrongly or rashly; in this respect he would deserve blame and reproach, yet it could not be said that it was not a relative or not the lawful heir who was acting in this way. But if some slave or suppositious bastard had wasted and squandered what he had no right to, by Hercules, how much more terrible and infuriating all would have called it! (9.30–1)

The other central Herodotean criterion – a shared religion – also recurs in characterisations of the basis of the panhellenic

[85] See, for example, 12.166: τοὺς μάλιστα βίου δεομένους τῶν Ἑλλήνων κατῴκιζον ('they [the Athenians] settled those of the Greeks who were most in need of the necessities of life'). A similar expansion of the Athenian role – from leader of Ionians to leader of the Greeks – occurs when these events are discussed elsewhere in this speech (at 12.42–4; 190), as well as in the *Panegyricus* (at 4.36–7). On the possible range of motivations for emphasising (or de-emphasising) Athens' Ionianism, see Hall 1997: 51–6; see also Dušanić 1999: 9–13, who finds evidence for extensive 'Ionianism' in Plato's writing, and argues that this should be seen as an elite trait, opposed to 'egalitarian autochthony propaganda' (11).

[86] Again, these comments are foreshadowed in Herodotus' characterisation of conflict within Greece as στάσις ἔμφυλος ('inter-tribal conflict'; Hdt. VIII.3.1).

society,[87] although it would be impossible to establish a rigid division between this and kinship. Isocrates can claim that a major function of the panhellenic religious festivals is to make participants ἀναμνησθῆναι ... τῆς συγγενείας ('remember their kinship'; 4.43). Lysias, with a slightly different emphasis, argues that such gatherings should demonstrate the mutual *philia* of the Greeks in the face of outsiders (33.2).[88] Again, the criterion can be used as an argument for exclusion from the society: for Demosthenes (9.32), the encroachment of Philip into the Pythian Games is an outstanding example of the Macedonian's outrageous behaviour, forcing his way into an arena to which he should not be allowed access.[89]

It is possible, too, to see such claims to shared inheritance and shared (religious) culture becoming the basis for arguments of common norms of behaviour. Some of these can be quite closely tied to religious activities. An Athenian decree of 367 (*Agora* XVI.48; RO 35) orders that a herald be sent to the Aetolian League to protest against the arrest by a member of the league of a group of ambassadors which had been sent out to announce the sacred truce of the Eleusinian Mysteries. Such an act, according to the decree, contravened τοὺς νόμους τ|[ο]ὺς κοι[ν]οὺς τῶν Ἑλλήνων, 'the common *nomoi* of the Greeks' (lines 13–14).[90] Claims to a shared code of behaviour among Greeks can also be found in less obviously religious contexts. A striking example is the reported outrage of Sparta and her allies, in the aftermath of Aegospotami, at Athenian (actual or planned) contraventions of such codes (εἰς Ἕλληνας παρανομεῖν, 'to transgress against Greek *nomoi*': X. *HG* II.i.32):

---

[87] On religion as a panhellenic phenomenon, see Price 1999: 3–6; on panhellenic cults, Bruit Zaidman & Schmitt Pantel 1992: ch. 11. For a more detailed consideration of religion as a source of 'group identity' (both inclusive and exclusive) in the Greek world, see Parker 1998.

[88] Note, again, the overlap of the language of reciprocity and that of panhellenism.

[89] See Golden 1998: 4–5, on the use of athletic competitions at festivals as a means of fostering unity and marking rejection.

[90] The decree – usually noted as providing the earliest evidence for the existence of the Aetolian League (see Beck 1997: 51, n. 43) – is also an unusual example of the inscription and public display of a short-term resolution (whereas such treatment would usually be given only to decrees concerning 'matters of long-lasting consequence or deserving of enduring commemoration' – Woodhead *ad Agora* XVI.48). The anomaly should perhaps, as Woodhead suggests, be explained by the perceived sacrilege of the act, and by the location (near the Eleusinion) in which the fragments of the inscription were found. On the inviolability of heralds, see Mosley 1973: 84–7; on the status of the *nomos*, see ch. 3, sec. 3.

killing the crews of captured triremes, and planning (allegedly) to cut off the right hands of any prisoners captured after the battle.[91]

The phrasing of these last examples illustrates, again, a point which has already been made in the discussion of democratic and oligarchic groupings: that interstate societies need not be conceived of as being built up purely from states. In some contexts, it is the individual which forms the basic unit. The members of the panhellenic society may, that is, sometimes best be thought of as οἱ Ἕλληνες – the Greeks – rather than αἱ Ἑλληνίδες πόλεις, the Greek cities. Slippage between representations of individuals and states as actors in interstate politics is, generally, a prominent feature of discussions of Greek interstate relations – much more so than in accounts of contemporary international politics, where the use of the state as the basic unit of analysis is more firmly established.[92] And it is a feature which is particularly marked in discussions of panhellenism.[93] The phenomenon is perhaps most easily visible in cases where one individual is represented as belonging to the panhellenic society, while others from the same state are excluded: the differentiation between Philip (and Alexander) and the rest of the Macedonians is an obvious example.[94] But more general manifestations of this approach to the panhellenic society can also be found – an approach which, while not strictly cosmopolitan, does come close to a characterisation of the Greeks as members of a single *polis*. The clearest example can be found in Plato's remarks on the unacceptability of *stasis* among Greeks:

Ἕλληνας μὲν ἄρα βαρβάροις καὶ βαρβάρους Ἕλησι πολεμεῖν μαχομένους τε φήσομεν καὶ πολεμίους φύσει εἶναι, καὶ πόλεμον τὴν ἔχθραν ταύτην κλητέον·

[91] The historicity of the event has been doubted (Krentz 1989 *ad loc.*); nevertheless, it is, at least, evidence for a Xenophontic version of what the accepted norms of behaviour were, and it is significant that these norms are represented as applying only among Greeks, not among all combatants. (See also the comments of Plato, *R.* 469b8 ff.)

[92] For a reassertion of the centrality of the state to analyses of international politics, see Wendt 1999: esp. chs. 1 and 5 (with the response of Smith 2000: 161–2). For a cosmopolitan approach, see, for example, Rawls 1999. Generally on this subject and the history of approaches to it, see Linklater 1990. The distinction between state and individuals can, however, be over-emphasised, especially in the context of the classical Greek *polis*, where the divisibility of the state from its citizens is questionable. See the further discussion of this problem in ch. 4.

[93] Again, perhaps not purely a fourth-century phenomenon: on 'political content' as a notable omission from Herodotus' list at VIII.144, see Finley 1975a: 120–1.

[94] Badian 1982: 38–43. The example of Seuthes (above: 49) could be categorised similarly.

῞Ελληνας δὲ ῞Ελλησιν, ὅταν τι τοιοῦτον δρῶσιν, φύσει μὲν φίλους εἶναι, νοσεῖν δ᾽ ἐν τῷ τοιούτῳ τὴν Ἑλλάδα καὶ στασιάζειν, καὶ στάσιν τὴν τοιαύτην ἔχθραν κλητέον.

We shall then say that Greeks fight and wage war with barbarians, and barbarians with Greeks, and are enemies by nature, and this enmity should be called war. Greeks, however, we shall say, are by nature the friends of Greeks even when they act in this way, but that Greece is sick in that case and divided by *stasis*, and *stasis* is the name we must give to that enmity. (*R.* 470c5–d1)

Isocrates' exhortation – made both to the Athenians and to Philip II – to see Greece as a κοινὴν ... πατρίδα, a 'shared homeland' (4.81; compare 5.127), seems to rely on a similar idea: Greece is one *polis*, in which all Greeks (however they are defined) have a share, and to which all Greeks should feel a responsibility.

But although these claims for the existence of a society of Greeks based on shared culture are widespread, arguments for panhellenism depend not only on the qualities of the members of that society, but also on their relationship to those outside: the stability of the society of Greeks, that is, is intimately connected with its opposition (practical as well as theoretical) to non-Greeks. The operation of this connection can perhaps be seen most clearly in the use made of the concept of *homonoia* (ὁμόνοια, 'fellow-thinking'). Although evidence for the development of a formal cult of *Homonoia* cannot be found until the late 300s,[95] it becomes a theme in political vocabulary – in interstate as well as domestic politics – from the early years of that century.[96] *Homonoia* is not, however, purely an abstract ideal, but is closely connected with – both as a prerequisite for and as a consequence of – campaigns against the barbarian. This connection can be seen in more than one writer (and with more than one target as barbarian opponent). Demosthenes, for example (9.38), makes *homonoia* (for him, an

[95] Thériault 1996: 180.
[96] On *homonoia* in all its aspects, see Thériault 1996. On its use in internal politics in the early fourth century, see Funke 1980, and on its representation as a particular quality of Spartan domestic life, see Cartledge 2001b: 150. On the earliest appearances of the word, see de Romilly 1972. The word is not always used in discussions of interstate relations to imply unity of all the Greeks: at X. *HG* vi.v.35, for example, it appears in a discussion of a coalition against the Thebans. (Although even here the context is an exhortation to recreate the unity of the Persian Wars, and the use of the word may well be intended to emphasise the exclusion of the Thebans from the legitimate society of (anti-Persian) fellow-thinking Greeks.)

unfulfilled objective) parallel with the equally desirable quality of Greek ἀπιστία towards τοὺς τυράννους καὶ τοὺς βαρβάρους ('mistrust' of 'tyrants and barbarians'). It is, though, in the writings of Isocrates that the two ideas of Greek unity and a campaign against the barbarian (in this case, Persia) become firmly conjoined, to the extent that it is hard to find a mention of *homonoia* (in the context of interstate relations) without a parallel reference to a Persian expedition.[97] This applies to Isocrates' version of the myth-historical past: the Greek expedition to Troy is described, in the *Helen*, as an occasion when τοὺς Ἕλληνας . . . ὁμονοήσαντας καὶ κοινὴν στρατείαν ἐπὶ τοὺς βαρβάρους ποιησαμένους ('the Greeks . . . thought as one and made a shared expedition against the barbarians'; 10.67).[98] It also applies to his visions of future policy: it is picked out, for example, in the *Antidosis* as one of the central themes of his political arguments:

ἔτι δὲ τίς ἂν περὶ καλλιόνων καὶ μειζόνων πραγμάτων τοῦ τοὺς Ἕλληνας ἐπί τε τὴν τῶν βαρβάρων στρατείαν παρακαλοῦντος καὶ περὶ τῆς πρὸς ἀλλήλους ὁμονοίας συμβουλεύοντος;

And, finally, what could be a nobler or a greater theme than to call on the Greeks to make an expedition against the barbarians and to advise them to be of one mind among themselves?[99] (15.77)

In Isocrates' writings at least, therefore, it seems to be possible to detect a picture of an interstate society which is not only practical, but also purposive.

Once more, however, the problem arises that the unqualified acceptance of this picture requires a certain amount of exclusion, and the (artificial) stabilisation of much which remains uncertain. An obvious problem is one of boundaries: if we accept the existence of a panhellenic society, where are its edges to be placed? This is not a dilemma which is restricted to the case of classical Greece. As Martin Wight has pointed out:

[97] The creation of *homonoia* within cities is also a major Isocratean preoccupation (see, for example, 3.41; 8.19; 18.44; 18.68). The two aspects of the ideal are not unconnected: the unity which will be brought about by a panhellenic crusade will apply not only within Greece, but also within the *polis*: see, for example, 7.51.
[98] On the *Helen* as a panhellenic text, see Kennedy 1958. Compare Isoc. 12.76–82 on Agamemnon's creation of *homonoia* among the divided Greeks before the Trojan expedition.
[99] The combination appears again in, for example, Isoc. 4.173; 5.16; 12.13; 12.42.

a historic states-system may seem a tolerably clear and distinct kind of community, or set of relationships and practices, when we study its internal structure and organic life. But when we examine its penumbra, look at its connections with what lies beyond it, explore the scarcely definable gradations by which it shades into its cultural and diplomatic background, it begins to lose its coherence and identity.[100]

But it was the example of Greece in particular which prompted this claim from Wight, and it is not hard to see why.

Although the construction of the community of Greeks relies heavily on the existence of others (or Others) against which the community could be defined,[101] the question of exactly who those others are, of where Greece stops and the barbarians begin, is one to which there are a number of apparently authoritative answers, between which there is considerable variation.[102] There is a tendency among modern commentators to characterise the shifting of the boundaries of the Greek world as being, in essence, a process of expansion over time: the barbarian Macedonians acquire 'Greekness' over the course of the fifth and fourth centuries; by the end of Alexander's reign, even the Persians can, in some senses, be counted a part of Greek international society.[103]

There is, of course, some truth in this picture, which is supported perhaps above all by Isocrates' striking claim that Greekness could become a matter of nurture rather than nature (4.50).[104] But this appearance of diachronic development can mask an equally strong synchronic instability. The shifting position of Macedon, or of Philip II, is a good example of this fluidity.[105] For Demosthenes

---

[100] Wight 1977: 105.   [101] See esp. Cartledge 1997: ch. 3.

[102] On the perennial difficulty of establishing the boundaries of the Greek world, see Hall 1989: ch. 4, sec. 2. For the specific case of Macedon, see Green 1996.

[103] For such approaches, see, for example, Jüthner 1923: 28–33; Baldry 1962: 177. On Alexander's (alleged) cosmopolitanism, see Badian 1958; Baldry 1965.

[104] See Jaeger 1945: ch. 3; Baldry 1965: 69–70; Masaracchia 1995: 74–7; Hartog 1996: 105–7; Usher 1994: 142–3. (It should be emphasised that the basis of this Greek culture is, for Isocrates here, Athenian: the individual *polis* is an intrinsic part of Isocrates' panhellenic vision in this speech; to characterise this passage as 'a remarkable change' (Linklater 1990: 22) in Greek attitudes to the relative importance of the *polis* and the broader society of Greeks is, therefore, somewhat misleading.) Note also Isoc. *Ep.* 9.8 for the suggestion that the reverse process is also possible: bad behaviour – τῷ τρόπῳ τῷ τῶν βαρβάρων χρωμένος, 'using the custom of the barbarian' – can make those who are Greek by culture 'un-Greek'.

[105] The 'Greekness' of the (ancient) Macedonians still, of course, provokes considerable debate, and extensive bibliography: for a survey of this, and on the history of the question

(9.30), Philip has no legitimate claim to share in a Greek inheritance. But for Isocrates, his descent from Heracles gives him a central role in that world, subject to both rights and obligations in his dealings with the major powers of Greece, and, by extension, the rest of Greece too (5.30–4). Similarly, Philip's participation in Greek religious organisations could be represented not (as it is by Demosthenes) as an unacceptable act by a non-Greek, but as proving Macedonian – or at least Philip's – legitimate inclusion in the Greek community of states. By making himself the defender of the shrine at Delphi, through his intervention in the Third Sacred War, Philip not only – practically – took his place among the Greeks of the Delphic Amphictiony (D.S. 16.60.1), but also symbolically asserted his commitment to Greek religion and so, by extension, to Greece.[106]

The existence of such clear statements of both sides of the argument makes the example of Philip an unusually good one, but comparable traces of uncertainty are detectable elsewhere too. The treatment of the Greeks of Asia Minor, for example, suggests that they occupied a similarly unstable position, slipping in and out of the Greek community, their cause either championed or abandoned according to circumstances.[107] Such an impression is, however, hard to confirm from the literary sources, which tend to be interested in these Greeks only when they want to assert their true Greekness (or protest at their maltreatment).[108]

What the example of the Asian Greeks also illustrates, however, is another aspect which undermines the concept of an egalitarian 'community' of Greeks: that is, the constant tendency for distinctions within that community to resurface in even the most

in the modern era, see Borza 1990: ch. 1. For an account of the arguments on both sides, see Badian 1982; Borza 1999: ch. 2. Arguing in favour of Greek nationality, Daskalakes 1965 (who also claims (pt v) that no Greek – including Demosthenes – suggests that Macedonians are not Greek); Hammond 1972: 269–76.

[106] On the importance of the Third Sacred War to Philip, see Buckler 1989: esp. 78–9, 145–7. Isocrates' *To Philip*, written with the Sacred War as its background (Hammond 1994: 89), suggests that Philip's intentions had some success (on the speech, see Perlman 1969).

[107] See Seager & Tuplin 1980. On the difficulty of fitting the Greeks of Asia Minor into the range of national polarities which characterise the Funeral Orations (and on their omission from those orations), see Ziolkowski 1993.

[108] See, for example, X. *HG* III.i.3; Isoc. *Ep.* 9.8.

panhellenic of contexts, and for those distinctions to carry some implications of inequality. For example, Demosthenes' argument in *Against Aristocrates* (23.140), that, after criticising Sparta for abandoning the Greeks of Asia Minor, it would be 'shameful' (αἰσχρόν) for the Athenians to fail to protect the Greeks of Europe, seems to suggest an escalating scale of betrayal: the Greeks of Europe are even more worthy of defence than those of Asia.

Sometimes, as with the distinction between Asian and European Greeks, this inequality operates between larger, apolitical, groups. More frequently, however, it is the reintroduction of the *polis* to panhellenic debate which makes the tension between community and hierarchy most obvious. And it is the frequent presence of this tension which might help to clarify (if not resolve) the problem which so often surfaces in discussions of panhellenism – the (quite understandable, and probably quite legitimate too) sensation that all this talk of community and unanimity is simply a façade, con-cealing the old-style imperialist ambitions of individual states.[109] Depictions of the ordering of bilateral relations between states are, as has been seen, often marked by a clear sense of inequality. And since, as has also been seen, there is no firm division between the two broad approaches to the characterisation of the interstate sys-tem, it is not too surprising to find these same hierarchical ideas sliding into depictions of the panhellenic society. The result is that the inequality in this society applies not only between it and the outside world (that is, between Greeks and barbarians: see, for example, Dem. 3.24), but also within the Greek society of states:

καὶ γὰρ αὐτοὶ προέχετε καὶ διαφέρετε τῶν ἄλλων οὐ ταῖς περὶ τὸν πόλεμον ἐπιμελείαις, οὐδ' ὅτι κάλλιστα πολιτεύεσθε καὶ μάλιστα φυλάττετε τοὺς νόμους, οὓς ὑμῖν οἱ πρόγονοι κατέλιπον, ἀλλὰ τούτοις, οἷς περ ἡ φύσις ἡ τῶν ἀνθρώπων τῶν ἄλλων ζῴων καὶ τὸ γένος τὸ τῶν Ἑλλήνων τῶν βαρβάρων, τῷ καὶ πρὸς τὴν φρόνησιν καὶ πρὸς τοὺς λόγους ἄμεινον πεπαιδεῦσθαι τῶν ἄλλων.

For you [Athenians], are pre-eminent and superior to the rest of the world, not in your preparations for war, nor because you govern yourselves most excellently or preserve the laws handed down to you by your ancestors most punctiliously, but in those qualities by which the nature of man excels the other animals, and the race of the Greeks the barbarians, namely, in the fact that you have been better educated than the others in wisdom and in speech. (Isoc. 15.293)

[109] See esp. Perlman 1976.

The focus here on rhetoric and education as the factors which make Athens the most Greek, and the most important, of the Greek states is a typically Isocratean twist.[110] A more usual connection, however, between panhellenism and hegemony comes with representations of the 'purposive' manifestation of that society. The panhellenic community is to be defined and maintained, at least in part, by campaigns against those outside the community; and these actions will require leaders. Isocrates, in the *Panegyricus*, suggests, briefly, that this leadership could be exercised by more than one *polis*: the best way forward is shared hegemony between Athens and Sparta (4.17, 185, 188).[111] But even in this speech, Isocrates is also eager to assert the superiority of the Athenians (4.18–20, 99), and the idea that a panhellenic crusade requires a single champion is even less ambiguously present elsewhere. As Demosthenes reminds (or attempts to remind) the Athenians:

εἰ δ' οἴεσθε Χαλκιδέας τὴν Ἑλλάδα σώσειν ἢ Μεγαρέας, ὑμεῖς δ' ἀποδράσεσθαι τὰ πράγματα, οὐκ ὀρθῶς οἴεσθε· ἀγαπητὸν γὰρ ἐὰν αὐτοὶ σώζωνται τούτων ἑκάστοις. ἀλλ' ὑμῖν τοῦτο πρακτέον· ὑμῖν οἱ πρόγονοι τοῦτο τὸ γέρας ἐκτήσαντο καὶ κατέλιπον μετὰ πολλῶν καὶ μεγάλων κινδύνων.

If you imagine that the Chalcideans will save Greece, or the Megarians, while you run away from the task, you are wrong. For it will be a miracle if they can save themselves separately. But it is you who have to do this. Your ancestors won this privilege for you and bequeathed it to you at great and manifold risk.[112] (Dem. 9.74)

The panhellenic society needs a leader, and that leadership will be both an indication of current status among the Greeks, and a guarantee of continued primacy.

This combination of community and hierarchy is most strikingly visible in these panhellenic contexts, but it can be perceived – in various manifestations – in other types of multilateral structure, including ones which are more formally constructed.[113] The

---

[110] On Isocrates and education, see Jaeger 1945: chs. 2–6; Too 1995: chs. 5 and 6; on culture as a route to hellenism, Hall 2002: 205–20.

[111] On the idea of shared hegemony in Isocrates, see Flower 2000b: 94–5.

[112] Compare Dem. 1.25: Thebes and Phocis cannot be expected to help in fighting Philip; this responsibility must fall on Athens.

[113] A notable exception to this pattern is the (relatively limited forum of the) Delphic Amphictiony, in which the distribution of votes to members of the Amphictionic Council

Common Peaces of the fourth century, for example, are essentially multilateral agreements, and – in their imposition of certain obligations on those who take part in them – result in the creation of a type of multilateral interstate structure. Yet they also rely on the sponsorship of single *poleis* or rulers: the Persian King, Athens, Sparta, Thebes. The peaces are, therefore, multilateral, but they are far from being egalitarian.[114]

In the rather different structural environment of the Boeotian federation, a similar stretching of the principle of equality can be perceived. To a much more formal degree than the system created by the Common Peaces, this organisation forms a multilateral structure. That structure can be seen as creating a community which is not only coherent but also reasonably egalitarian: the representative system of government within the pre-386 version of that federation did provide equality in one ('geometric', or proportionate) sense. But this was a type of equality which allowed the majority of practical power to lie with the Thebans.[115] And it is not a coincidence that it is this, hierarchical, element to the Boeotian federation which is most prominent at the moment of its downfall: it is the desire of the Thebans to swear to the Common Peace on behalf of the Boeotians which provides the excuse for the dissolution of the League (X. *HG* v.i.32–3).

Finally, briefly, it is worth mentioning in this context the constitution of the Second Athenian League. Here too, I think, the combination of bilateral and multilateral, of community and

---

is strikingly non-hierarchical (on the structure and operation of the Council, see Lefèvre 1998: pt 2, sec. 2).

[114] That it was thought possible to 'win' a Common Peace is most clearly visible in the Athenian response to the Peace of 375: a statue of Nike was set up on the Acropolis (*IG* ii² 1425, lines 45–6); if Vatin's reading is correct, Timotheus, the Athenian general most closely associated with the Peace, set up a statue at Delphi, claiming that he was ν[έ]ον συν]οι[κ]ισμὸν ποι[ῶ]ν Ν[ι]κῆ[ς | καὶ τοῦ Δή]μ[ο]υ τοῦ Ἀθηναίω[ν], 'making a new union of Victory and the Athenian people' (Vatin 1983: 33). See also Accame 1941: 248–51; Tuplin 1993: 160.

[115] For the structure of the Boeotian Federation, see esp. *Hell.Oxy.* 19; Th. v.37.4–38.3. Thebes provided 240 out of 660 councillors, and 4 out of 11 Boeotarchs; the administrative machinery of the federation was also located in Thebes. On the varieties of equality (and inequality) in the Boeotian Federation of this period, see Cartledge 2000a. The change from a representative system to a direct assembly in the revived federation appears to have made this inequality still more marked; it has been suggested (Rhodes 1993: 172–3) that this increased sense of inequality should be connected with the increased evidence for unrest within the federation.

hierarchy can be seen – and it is a combination which seems even more firmly embedded in the formal arrangements which surround the organisation. The creation of a differentiated community is, at one level, obvious and straightforward: although the various members of the League combine to form a body of *summachoi*, united both in formal institutions (the *synedrion*, above all) and in shared obligations to other members of that group, those *summachoi* are consistently distinguished from the Athenians.[116] What is created is, in one sense, a bilateral relationship between Athens on the one hand and a multilateral community on the other – but a multilateral community which exists only as a result of the connection of its members to Athens. What is interesting, however, is the combination of this, limited, multilateral approach with a continued use of bilateral arrangements between Athens and individual *poleis*, even those which are also members of the Second Athenian League. The alliance between Athens and Chalcis, for example (*IG* ii² 44), made in the same year as the creation of the Second Athenian League, appears to be a straightforward bilateral agreement between the two parties: the only hint at the existence of the League in the extant portion of the document is the reference to the δόγματ[α τῶ|ν συμμάχων ('proposals of the allies') in lines 25–6. But it is also clear from the 'charter' of the League (*IG* ii² 43, line 80) that the Chalcideans were enrolled as members of it. The case of Corcyra is more controversial, but can, I think, be interpreted in the same way: *IG* ii² 96 shows that Corcyra became a member of the Second Athenian League; *IG* ii² 97 records a bilateral alliance between Athens and Corcyra; and the two documents should be seen not as inherently contradictory, but as an (admittedly unusually obvious) manifestation of a theme which has pervaded this chapter: the inseparability of these two different approaches – multilateral and bilateral – to the structuring of interstate politics.[117]

---

[116] The distinction is especially clear in *IG* ii² 97, lines 31–3. On the structure of the *synedrion*, and Athens' relation to it, see Accame 1941: 107–42; Cargill 1981: ch. 7; Cawkwell 1981: 48–51.

[117] Such an interpretation would, therefore, support the view of Fauber 1998 that Corcyra was a member of the Second Athenian League, and remove the need for arguments such as Cargill's (1981: ch. 4) which create special categories of alliance to cope with cases

2.5 Conclusion: some examples

International Relations is a discipline which, for much of its history, has directed its activities towards the discovery of definitive answers. The difficulty with this approach, however, is that so much of international relations takes place not at any tangible, easily defined, level, but 'inside our heads':[118] 'our' heads being those of the people who take part in international relations, as well as of those who study it. The Greek example provides an excellent illustration of this point. The existence of these various competing versions of the international system – of which at least two have considerable explanatory and emotional power – increases the temptation to reject some as inaccurate, or as insincere propaganda, and elevate one to the status of absolute truth.[119] But it should, I hope, be obvious that the temptation should be resisted, and, indeed, that the divisions which have been adopted above are to a great extent artificial: the categories can overlap, confirm, or contradict each other. So, ideas of reciprocal ties – *philia, sungeneia* – which can be used as a mechanism for extending the network of interstate relations in one context – become arguments for exclusivity in another. The panhellenic community is, at the same time, a strongly hierarchical system of states. Units which make perfect sense in isolation begin to seem less coherent when placed in their broader context. The members of the Delphic Amphictiony, for example, may relate to each other on terms of formalised equality; but those same members, outside that setting, behave very differently towards each other.[120] The Greeks who are depicted in one breath as being unworthy even of the description of being κοινοὺς ἀλλήλοις φίλους, 'shared and mutual friends' (Dem. 14.3), can be

such as that of Corcyra, and have to construct reasons why the decree which appears to admit Corcyra to the League (*IG* ii² 96) did not come into effect. It would also support Dreher's conclusion (1995: 287) that the nature of the Second Athenian League '*zwischen* "empire" und "free alliance" liegt und nicht bei einem dieser Extreme'. A similar combination of bilateral and multilateral alliances can be perceived in the Peloponnesian and Delian Leagues (see de Ste. Croix 1972: 101–24), but in this case it is much harder to detect precisely how the relationship between the different forms of alliance operated.

[118] Manning 1962: 13.   [119] On the temptation and its dangers, see Walbank 1985b.

[120] Compare the formal relationship between Athens and Phocis within the Amphictiony with that implied by Demosthenes at 1.25 (above: n. 112).

described in (almost) the next as being united by the fundamental ties of χώρας καὶ βίου καὶ ἐθῶν καὶ ἐλευθερίας, 'territory and life and customs and freedom' (Dem. 14.32).

This is not to claim that there is no logic to the system at all: certain ideas do recur, and it is clear that there is an established repertoire of concepts and categories from which to choose. The selection of items from that repertoire depends, however, on the aims of the selector and the demands of the situation.[121] In place of a conclusion, therefore, and also to demonstrate how misleading it would be to propose a single, universally applicable, conclusion, some examples of the manifold ways in which the inter-state system (or society) could be depicted will, very briefly, be considered.

Xenophon Hellenica *III.v.3–17*

Xenophon's account of the origins of the Corinthian War presents a notorious historiographical problem: whose version – Xenophon's or the Oxyrhynchus Historian's (found at §21) – is to be preferred?[122] Here it is Xenophon's particular presentation of events which is of interest, although the contrast between his version and that found in *Hell.Oxy.* will sometimes be instructive. There is, as always, some difficulty in knowing where the chain of causal events should be thought to finish and the war itself be claimed to have started: in this case, the obvious candidates for (immediate) catalysts are the bribes – whether Persian of Greeks, or Theban of Locrians – and the dispute between Locris and Phocis.[123]

---

[121] See Crane 2001 for a discussion (based on the example of Plataea in the Peloponnesian War) of the tensions which can arise when a state is forced to privilege one network of relationships over another.

[122] The two accounts differ on a range of details – which Locrians are involved (Xenophon has the eastern (Opuntian) Locrians; *Hell.Oxy.* the western); which side is bribed by the Thebans (Xenophon – the Locrians; *Hell.Oxy.* – the Phocians) – and on the broader presentation of events: the version given in *Hell.Oxy.* is notably kinder to the Spartans than that of Xenophon. On the question, and on the more general problem of the war's origins, see esp. Accame 1951: chs. 1 and 2; McKay 1953; Bruce 1960; Perlman 1964; Hamilton 1979: 182–208; Lehmann 1978a, 1978b; Cartledge 1987: 290–1. On Xenophon's account of the war's preliminaries, see Tuplin 1993: 60–4.

[123] On the difficulty of defining the beginnings and ends of wars in classical Greece, see Alonso Troncoso 1999.

It is, however, clear that this last event is qualitatively different from those which precede it, and it is also striking that the Thebans can apparently be confident that, once the Locrians have been bribed to set the chain of events in motion, the ultimate result will be widespread war in Greece. This aspect of Xenophon's account of the opening moves of the war has often been perceived as being basically implausible: how could the Thebans be sure that all the parties involved would behave as required by their master-plan? One answer which has been suggested is that Thebes had simply bribed all the interested parties and that Xenophon neglected to mention this.[124] This may, of course, be correct, but Xenophon's account could make sense in its own terms, if it is assumed that the regular pattern of interstate behaviour was believed by him to be sufficiently predictable to allow for the formation, and successful completion, of such clockwork-like schemes.[125]

The opening stages of the war, as Xenophon describes them (III.v.3), would fit quite neatly into a model of tit-for-tat reciprocity: Locrian incursion into Phocian territory is met with Phocian reprisal in the form of an invasion of Locris.[126] Reciprocal behaviour continues to be important in the next sequence of events, but the form which it takes is closer to the societal model than the systemic. Its effects, however, are perhaps no less predictable. The Locrian appeal to Thebes, and Thebes' positive response to it, are explained by the fact that Locris is ὁμολογουμένην φίλην τε καὶ σύμμαχον, 'an avowed friend and ally' (III.v.4). The next stage of escalation – the intervention of Sparta – is explained, again, through reciprocity: either positive, in the response to the Phocian appeal for help which forms the *prophasis* for Spartan action;[127] or negative (and in Xenophon's version more significant), in the

---

[124] McKay 1953: 7; similar suggestion in Krentz 1995 *ad loc.*

[125] An interpretation which might be supported by the rapidity (εὐθὺς . . . ταχὺ . . . εὐθὺς, 'immediately . . . swiftly . . . immediately'; III.v.3–4) with which the chain of events unfolds in Xenophon's narrative (which can be contrasted with the more measured pace of events – including an attempt at arbitration – in the *Hell.Oxy.* version).

[126] *Hell.Oxy*'s version – which includes some more stages of escalation – also fits the pattern quite well.

[127] Probably used here in the sense of 'official justification'. On the many shades of meaning of the word, see Pearson 1952.

form of Spartan anger at a string of acts of *hubris* committed by Thebes against them (III.v.5).[128]

The final stage of Xenophon's account of the war's preliminaries – the appeal of the Theban ambassadors to the Athenians – makes explicit many of the assumptions which have been implicit in the earlier narrative. The Thebans attempt to show first why Athens has no legitimate claim to retribution against Thebes, then why at least some Athenians do have such a claim against Sparta (III.v.8). And the Athenian response to the Theban request is, again, phrased in terms of the paying and repaying of favours (although emphasising that Athens now holds the superior position in the sequence of exchanges):

Θρασύβουλος δὲ ἀποκρινάμενος τὸ ψήφισμα καὶ τοῦτο ἐνεδείκνυτο, ὅτι ἀτειχίστου τοῦ Πειραιῶς ὄντος ὅμως παρακινδυνεύσοιεν χάριτα αὐτοῖς ἀποδοῦναι μείζονα ἢ ἔλαβον. ὑμεῖς μὲν γάρ, ἔφη, οὐ συνεστρατεύσατε ἐφ᾽ ἡμᾶς, ἡμεῖς δέ γε μεθ᾽ ὑμῶν μαχούμεθα ἐκείνοις, ἂν ἴωσιν ἐφ᾽ ὑμᾶς.

Thrasybulus, in reply, gave the ambassadors the decree, and pointed out that, although Piraeus was without walls, they would nevertheless brave the danger of repaying to the Thebans a greater favour than they had received. 'For you,' he said, 'did not join in the campaign against us, but we are going to fight with you against them, in case they march upon you.' (III.v.16)

The Theban speech at Athens also, however, makes more obvious a number of other factors which must be allowed for in explaining the actions of the states involved. Apart from the practical considerations of Spartan weakness (III.v.10, 15), the ambassadors also emphasise the possible broader implications of Athenian involvement. Athens can, they suggest, use the war as a stepping-stone to empire (III.v.10); fighting Sparta will establish the Athenians as leaders of Greece – πολὺ ἤδη μεγίστους τῶν πώποτε, 'more powerful than anyone yet' (III.v.14). Nevertheless, the basis of this argument too is, fundamentally, one of reciprocity: the Greeks will be grateful to Athens for liberation from the Spartan yoke. (It is worth noting that the network of gratitude is envisaged as extending even to the Persian king.) For Xenophon then, here as elsewhere

---

[128] *Hell.Oxy.* has a similar line on the Locrian appeal to Thebes (διάκειν[τ]αι δὲ πρὸς αὐτοὺς ἀεί ποτε φιλίως, 'they were always friendly towards them'; 21.4), but a slightly less jaundiced version of Spartan behaviour: only after an attempt at arbitration has failed do the Spartans send out a military force.

in the *Hellenica*, it is this pattern of reciprocal behaviour which is the dominant factor in determining the nature of relations between states.

Demosthenes 15, For the Liberty of the Rhodians[129]

Demosthenes' speech in support of the Rhodian democrats is, perhaps, most well known for its apparently classically Thucydidean claim that justice in interstate relations is created by the powerful (15.29).[130] But it is also a good example of how such an assertion can co-exist with more 'Idealistic' characterisations of reciprocal obligations and interstate communities, both of which play a major part in Demosthenes' arguments.[131]

The picture of reciprocal connections which emerges from the speech is, however, rather more complicated than that which appeared in the Xenophontic passage. Arguments based on reciprocity are still found, and the language of reciprocal relationships is still used (e.g., at §§4, 20), but reciprocity is not characterised as the absolute determinant of behaviour. In fact, Demosthenes argues against the enforcement of a strict policy of reciprocal behaviour: although the Rhodians have harmed Athens, and although the Athenians might therefore be expected to make a claim for revenge, they should be prepared to forgo this claim:

φημὶ δὴ χρῆναι πειρᾶσθαι σώζειν τοὺς ἄνδρας καὶ μὴ μνησικακεῖν, ἐνθυμουμένους ὅτι πολλὰ καὶ ὑμεῖς ὑπὸ τῶν ἐπιβουλευσάντων ἐξηπάτησθε, ὧν οὐδενὸς αὐτοὶ δοῦναι δίκην δίκαιον ἂν εἶναι φήσαιτε.

I say that it is your duty to try to save these men and not to bear grudges, remembering that you too have in many cases been led by plotters into errors, for none of which you would yourselves admit that you ought to pay the penalty.[132] (§16)

---

[129] For the best general discussion of the speech, see the introductions in Radicke 1995. Other versions in Pickard-Cambridge 1914: 135–7; Jaeger 1938: ch. 4; Sealey 1993: 133–4. On the situation in Rhodes and Asia Minor in the period, Hornblower 1982: ch. 5. On the problem of the speech's date, Lane Fox 1997: 187–91 (arguing for a date of 352).

[130] See esp. de Ste. Croix 1972: 16–17; further discussion of this passage in ch. 4, sec. 4.

[131] Supporting, perhaps, Seaford's (1998) claim (5) that the rigid distinction between self-interest and justice 'may obstruct our understanding of a system of ethics pervaded by reciprocity, for reciprocity transcends the distinction'.

[132] The example Demosthenes has in mind may be the events of 404/3; this would fit, too, with the broader theme of oligarchic/democratic discord.

And the specific reason for this is that the Rhodians are members of two larger communities, to both of which Athens owes particular obligations: that of democrats (in opposition to oligarchs), and that of Greeks (in opposition to Persians).

The community of democrats is, in fact, characterised in part as being built up through ties of *eunoia* (§4), united by common antipathy to oligarchy (εἰς ὀλιγαρχίαν κοινοὺς ἐχθρούς: §20), and operating with expectations of mutual help:

ἔπειτα καὶ δίκαιον, ὦ ἄνδρες Ἀθηναῖοι, δημοκρατουμένους αὐτοὺς τοιαῦτα φρονοῦντας φαίνεσθαι περὶ τῶν ἀτυχούντων δήμων, οἷάπερ ἂν τοὺς ἄλλους ἀξιώσαιτε φρονεῖν περὶ ὑμῶν, εἴ ποτε, ὃ μὴ γένοιτο, τοιοῦτό τι συμβαίη.

Then again, Athenians, it is right that you, living under a democracy, should show the same sympathy for democracies in distress as you would expect others to show for you, if ever – God forbid! – you were in the same situation. (§21)

But it is also a community which can be seen to transcend such claims to friendship and enmity, at least according to Demosthenes' striking (and deliberately paradoxical)[133] claim that:

μᾶλλον [. . .] συμφέρειν δημοκρατουμένους τοὺς Ἕλληνας ἅπαντας πολεμεῖν ὑμῖν ἢ ὀλιγαρχουμένους φίλους εἶναι.

it would be more beneficial for all the Greeks to be your enemies under democracy than your friends under oligarchy. (§18)

The other main strand of Demosthenes' argument rests on the Athenian obligation to the Rhodians as part of the Greek community: it would be perverse, he suggests, for Athens to give support to Egyptians – who are properly part of the Persian sphere of influence – but to refuse help to the Rhodians:

θαυμάζω δ᾽ ὅτι τοὺς αὐτοὺς ὁρῶ ὑπὲρ μὲν Αἰγυπτίων τἀναντία πράττειν βασιλεῖ τὴν πόλιν πείθοντας, ὑπὲρ δὲ τοῦ Ῥοδίων δήμου φοβουμένους τὸν ἄνδρα τοῦτον. καίτοι τοὺς μὲν Ἕλληνας ὄντας ἅπαντες ἴσασι, τοὺς δ᾽ ἐν τῇ ἀρχῇ τῇ ᾽κείνου μεμερισμένους.

I am surprised to see the same men urging the city, in the interests of the Egyptians, to oppose the King of Persia, but dreading him where the Rhodian democracy is concerned. Yet everyone knows that the Rhodians are Greeks, while Egypt is a division of the Persian Empire. (§5)

---

[133] Radicke 1995, *ad loc.*

The two arguments are not entirely separate, just as the precise villains of the piece – oligarchs or Persians (both enemies to *eleutheria*) – are not quite distinguished from each other. In both cases, moreover, it is possible to detect a less harmonious and egalitarian aspect to the imagined communities. The logic of Demosthenes' argument at §5 would suggest that Athens' relationship to the other Greeks is analogous to that of the Persian King to his subjects, and this assumption is made explicit later in the speech. Although the Athenians allowed their allies in the Second Athenian League, including Rhodes, an equal alliance (ἐξ ἴσου συμμαχεῖν) they remained their superiors (βελτίοσιν αὐτῶν) (§15). And, in revolting from the League, the Rhodians not only removed themselves from the community of Greeks, but placed themselves in an even lower position in the hierarchy of states – βαρβάροις καὶ δούλοις... δουλεύουσιν, 'slaves of barbarians and of slaves' (§15). The common aim for democrats, and/or Greeks, may be the preservation of ἐλευθερία (*eleutheria*), but it is the Athenians who hold the position of προστάται τῆς πάντων ἐλευθερίας, 'champions of the freedom of all' (§30). The combination of arguments in the speech demonstrates quite neatly, therefore, how ideas of reciprocity and community, equality and hierarchy could be woven together to form an apparently plausible (if objectively illogical) picture of the situation.

Isocrates 14, Plataicus

A similar combination of arguments can be seen in Isocrates' *Plataicus*, a speech placed in the mouth of Plataean ambassadors at Athens, seeking refuge in the city after the Theban destruction of their native town.[134]

Arguments from negative reciprocity are used, both to explain past actions (the Thebans are alleged to have attacked Plataea out of revenge – μνησικακεῖν – §14), and to encourage future ones:

---

[134] The dramatic date of the speech is, therefore, *c*. 373. Its relationship to the politics of the period is, as always with Isocratean speeches, a controversial subject. The fullest discussion (arguing for a connection with the Common Peace of 371) is that of Momigliano 1936. See also Mathieu 1925: 85–9; Cloché 1963: 49–54. On the history of Plataea's relations with Thebes and (to a lesser extent) Athens, see Amit 1973: pt 2, esp. chs. 6 and 7.

the Athenians are reminded of past Theban wrongs against them (§27). Claims of positive reciprocity are, however, far more prominent, and appear in a variety of forms. The Plataeans remind the Athenians of their φιλία (*philia*) (§26), and also, at rather greater length, insist on the importance of strong ties of shared citizenship and (as a consequence of this) common kinship:

καὶ γὰρ οὐδ᾽ ἀλλότριοι τυγχάνομεν ὑμῖν ὄντες, ἀλλὰ ταῖς μὲν εὐνοίαις ἅπαντες οἰκεῖοι, τῇ δὲ συγγενείᾳ τὸ πλῆθος ἡμῶν· διὰ γὰρ τὰς ἐπιγαμίας τὰς δοθείσας ἐκ πολιτίδων ὑμετέρων γεγόναμεν· ὥστ᾽ οὐχ οἷόν θ᾽ ὑμῖν ἀμελῆσαι περὶ ὧν ἐληλύθαμεν δεησόμενοι.

For indeed we are not strangers to you; on the contrary, all of us are kin to you in our loyalty and most of us in blood also; for by the right of intermarriage granted to us we are born of mothers who were of your city. You cannot, therefore, be indifferent to the pleas we have come to make. (§51)

But although great emphasis is placed on the mutual obligations imposed by these ties, the Plataean self-presentation also stresses their role as the inferior partner in the encounter. At the same time as asserting their absolute right to Athenian help, in exchange for Plataean loyalty in the Persian Wars, the Plataeans also characterise themselves as suppliants – that is, as being, in theory, excluded from any pre-existing network of obligation with the Athenians (§§1, 56). The manoeuvre – which can be paralleled in the appeal of the Epidamnians to (their mother-city) Corcyra (Th. 1.24)[135] – seems to be used here to highlight the extreme weakness of the Plataean position: the insecurity of their status forces them to reach for all available arguments; in doing so, they place themselves still further away from the privileged circle of interstate relationships.

This simultaneous assertion of inclusion and exclusion can be seen, too, in the uses of panhellenic arguments in the speech. In many ways, the panhellenic significance of the incident is implicit: Plataea's role as one of the main *loci* of the panhellenic ideal needs no emphasis.[136] But the Plataeans, unsurprisingly, do not restrain themselves from labouring the point, in, for example, the references to the monuments in their home city, set up ὑπὲρ ἁπάσης τῆς Ἑλλάδος πρὸς ὅλην τὴν ἐκ τῆς Ἀσίας δύναμιν, 'on behalf

---

[135] See Mitchell 1997a: 24, n. 9.   [136] Thériault 1996: 130.

of the whole of Greece, in the face of all the power of Asia' (§59).[137] Again, however, this claim to be central to the panhellenic vision must be contrasted with the picture, established in the Plataeans' opening remarks, of a people who have been so badly treated that the result is exclusion from the (equal) community of Greeks:

πολὺ δὲ μάλιστ' ἀγανακτοῦμεν ὅτι τοσούτου δέομεν τῶν ἴσων ἀξιοῦσθαι τοῖς ἄλλοις Ἕλλησιν, ὥστ' εἰρήνης οὔσης καὶ συνθηκῶν γεγενημένων οὐχ ὅπως τῆς κοινῆς ἐλευθερίας μετέχομεν, ἀλλ' οὐδὲ δουλείας μετρίας τυχεῖν ἠξιώθημεν.

The chief cause of our annoyance is that we are so far from being judged worthy of equality with the rest of the Greeks that, although we are at peace and although treaties exist, we not only have no share in the liberty which all the rest enjoy, but that we are not considered worthy of even a moderate condition of slavery. (§5)

What should be a community has become a hierarchy. But the fundamental paradox remains in the fact that it is only through an appeal to Athens as leader of the Greeks, and defender of *autonomia* that the Plataean place among the equals can be restored.

[137] Except, of course, Thebes.

AN ANARCHIC SOCIETY? INTERNATIONAL LAW AND INTERNATIONAL CUSTOM

3.1 Introduction: law and society

The claim for the existence of a close, and necessary, connection between law and society is one which is well established in the study of contemporary domestic, as well as international, law. The link is typically summed up in the motto *ubi societas, ibi ius*, and is expressed at somewhat greater length in one of the standard works on international law: 'law can only exist in a society . . . there can be no society without a system of law'.[1] This claim has important implications for the interpretation of interstate relations: it was seen in the last chapter that the question of the existence of a 'society' of states is disputed among international theorists,[2] and, as will be suggested below, the question of the existence of international law is equally problematic. Many of these assertions of a relationship between international law and international society must, however, be seen as part of a long tradition. Like many other aspects of the discipline of International Relations, the origins of this question lie in the seventeenth and eighteenth centuries, and in the problems raised by Western European conquests of the Americas. In that political and intellectual context, arguments that a 'society' of states could be defined through shared (western) culture or through 'natural' (or Christian) law became increasingly hard to sustain. The idea developed, therefore, that membership of the society of states required the positive acceptance of 'diplomatic, military, and other international usages'.[3] Acceptance of these rules and (occasionally) laws became a state's passport into international society.

---

[1] Brierly 1963: 41. For recent explorations of the connection, see Arend 1999: esp. ch. 4; Müllerson 2000.

[2] See ch. 2, sec. 1.

[3] Nardin 1983: 115. For a full discussion of the development of these arguments, and for their culmination in the creation of international institutions in the late-nineteenth and twentieth centuries, see Nardin 1983: chs. 2–5.

International society, it is argued, is not only controlled by these rules, but also constructed and defined by their presence.

The appeal to the centrality of the connection between law and society is also familiar to students of Greek history. Its tradition is less long-lived, but in recent years its importance has nevertheless been clearly demonstrated, in work which has highlighted both how aspects of Greek law must be understood in a specific societal context, and how law and legal procedures contributed to the creation and operation of those societies.[4] Such work has, however, concentrated on domestic law and domestic society. What I intend to do in what follows, therefore, is to look at the question of laws in Greek interstate relations – not so much the details of their content, as the principles underlying their creation, scope and enforcement – and to consider whether (and if so how) such laws affect our understanding of the operation of Greek interstate relations.

3.2 Greek law, international law and Greek international law[5]

Greek law and international law are two subjects, or sub-disciplines, which have, traditionally, struggled to establish their claim to be deserving of serious attention by students of ancient Greek history and of modern law respectively. Greek law was once described by Finley as 'notoriously a stepchild in modern study'.[6] His claim has more recently been amplified: 'it is not simply a stepchild, but a stepchild overawed by several overbearing (not to say ugly) sisters'[7] – the ugliest of the sisters being the study of Roman law, a subject which has been favoured in particular because of its more obviously direct relevance to the study of modern civil

---

[4] See, for example, Osborne 1985; Garner 1987; Cartledge, Millett & Todd edd. 1990; Cohen 1995; and the review article of Golden 2000.

[5] The term 'international law' will be used in what follows with reference to Greek practices, partly in line with convention (see, for the most recent example, the title of Bederman 2001; and note also his justification (14) for that title), and primarily for convenience: the straightforward application of the concepts of 'international' and of 'law' to the Greek world are, as will become clear, problematic; but although it is an imperfect label, any (short) alternative is likely to be equally inaccurate.

[6] Finley 1985a: 99.   [7] Todd & Millett 1990: 1.

law.[8] Moreover, it is argued, ancient historians' traditional focus on fifth-century Greek history and consequent neglect of the chief source of evidence for Greek (or at least Athenian) law, the fourth-century Attic orators, pushed the study of Greek law still further towards the margins of the discipline. The increasingly common expression of these complaints in the last decades of the twentieth century was also, however, a symptom of a change in the attitudes against which they were protesting. Since the 1980s, and especially in the 1990s, Greek (and especially Athenian) law has been brought back into the limelight and, more importantly, approached in ways which are more sympathetic to its peculiar contexts and concerns. The revival of interest in the connection between law and society, mentioned above, is perhaps the most obvious general trend. More specific foci of attention have included, for example, investigations into the role of rhetoric in the construction, as well as the operation, of Athenian law,[9] or the study of the connection between written law, literacy and political ideology.[10]

The study of international law has also been a growth area in recent years, although the impetus for this has come not so much from theoretical advances as from practical developments. The growth of international institutions – the United Nations, the European Union, and so on – and the regulations associated with them has provided a definite area for practical study. At a more abstract level, however, the theoretical problems of the nature and status of international law have not yet been fully resolved. Austin's belief that there could be no law without a sovereign power to enforce it, and his consequent assertion that 'the admitted maxims for the conduct of international transactions are not Law, but Ethics'[11] may no longer be widely accepted, but some residual uncertainty

---

[8] On the absence of a direct 'legacy' of Greek law, see Todd 1993: 3–4, and note also the absence of Greek law from works, such as Livingstone ed. 1921, promoting the 'legacy' of ancient Greece to the modern world. Indirect influence on the legal tradition comes not so much from Greek legal practice as from philosophical theories of natural and written law, which were read and used by Roman legal theorists interested in problems of distinguishing between Roman civil law and the *ius gentium* (see, briefly, Jolowicz & Nicholson 1972: 104–5; on other aspects of Greek influence on Roman legal practice and institutions, *ibid.*: 406–8, 469–73).

[9] See, for example, Johnstone 1999; Todd 2000.

[10] For example, Hölkeskamp 1992; Thomas 1995; Whitley 1997.

[11] Austin 1885, vol. II: 575.

over the status of the subject, and more specifically over the best ways to approach it, can still be detected.[12]

Although, therefore, there are many obvious differences between the traditions of the study of Greek law and international law, some fundamental similarities can nevertheless be identified: namely, that both disciplines are felt to occupy a subordinate position relative to another branch of study; are often studied in terms of standards established in that dominant branch; and sometimes, too, are judged according to their success or failure in achieving those standards.[13]

Given the problematic status of its two constituent parts, it is not, perhaps, surprising that the study of international law in ancient Greece has never been a particularly vibrant field. In the work of ancient historians, the subject is, in general, notable by its absence. Even when it does appear it is in a rather limited form,[14] and, for more comprehensive treatments of the subject – treating both public and private law, and general concepts rather than specific areas or cases, it is usually necessary to return to works written in the nineteenth and the early years of the twentieth centuries.[15] More strikingly, these works are, almost exclusively,[16] produced not by classicists, but by lawyers. The author of what was, for most of the last century, the standard work on Greek and Roman international law – Coleman Phillipson – described himself as being 'of the Inner Temple, Barrister-at-Law';[17] the majority of his other works

---

[12] For an impression of these uncertainties, see Kratochwil 1983; Nardin 1983: ch. 6; Loriaux 2000; Watts 2000.

[13] See, for example, Todd & Millett 1990: 1, on the problems arising from the study of Greek law by Roman lawyers, 'constrained by inappropriate categories of thought'. Compare Kratochwil 1989: 2: 'we understand the international order largely negatively, i.e., in terms of the "lack" of binding legal norms, of central institutions, of a sovereign will, etc'. See also Bederman 2001: 11–15, on the 'double blight' (12) of ancient international law, as seen by lawyers: both ancient law and international law are generally regarded as defective.

[14] As, for example, in Todd's (1993: ch. 15) study of private international law.

[15] Interstate arbitration is the one area of international law which has received substantial attention from classicists: the classic work in English is Tod 1913; more recent studies can be found in Piccirilli 1973 (continued in Magnetto 1997) and Ager 1996. Again, the situation has become less bleak in recent years, and some general studies are appearing: Baltrusch 1994 and Sheets 1994 are two notable examples, although both focus on the earlier classical period; the work of Gauthier 1972 and Cataldi 1983 on *symbola* agreements should also be noted.

[16] The most obvious exception is Busolt & Swoboda 1926.

[17] Phillipson 1911, vols. I and II, title pages.

were studies of modern international law.[18] Its putative replace-
ment (Bederman 2001) has also been written by an expert on contemporary law (and is published in a series of legal, not classical,
texts).

The study of Greek international law by modern international
lawyers has a predictable consequence: namely, a marked tendency
to attempt to interpret the features of Greek international life in
terms of modern concepts of international law.[19] That is, the problems (described above) which have dogged the study of Greek law
and international law recur here. In this case, however, another level
of dependence must be added: if modern international law is often
judged according to criteria derived from domestic law, so Greek
international law is then judged according to its similarity to or difference from modern international law. In other words, the terms
of the debate are those which have been established in a field twice
removed from that of Greek international law. Moreover, in an academic context in which the status of international law constantly
requires justification, the value of the Greek case as a legitimating
example is obvious: Hosack, for example, opens his study of the
subject with the claim that the Greek example exemplifies the point
that 'throughout all periods of authentic history we find that certain international obligations have been regarded as binding upon
mankind'.[20] The fact that Greek international law has traditionally been studied by those whose main interest is modern law has
also encouraged a strongly teleological approach,[21] and, with it, an
inclination to emphasise those features of the Greek system which
seem to foreshadow contemporary practice. The Delphic Amphictiony, for example, was paid particular attention in the first decades
of the twentieth century because it seemed to provide a precedent

---

[18] E.g. Phillipson 1908, 1915 and 1916. Although Phillipson's book was well received in
some classical circles (see Blake Reed 1912), he is described by Rostovtseff (1922: 31)
as an excellent lawyer, 'but a dilettante in the domain of ancient history'.

[19] Bederman 2001 marks a notable, and explicit, departure from that tradition, adopting a
comparative rather than a teleological approach. Nevertheless, he makes it clear that 'the
organising principle of this book will be to examine whether an ancient law of nations
had the paradigmatic attributes of modern international law' (6).

[20] Hosack 1882: 1.

[21] Noted by Schwarzenburger 1980: 228. The practice is a long-standing one: see, for
example, the title of Maine 1861, and the remarks of Leech 1877: 4; Leech 1883a:
262.

for the League of Nations.[22] This tendency has also affected the work of ancient historians. It is, presumably, no coincidence that the development, in the Hague Conferences of the beginning of the twentieth century, of a modern system of international arbitration was closely followed by two major works on that subject by classical scholars.[23]

Not all historians of international law accept that the subject can legitimately claim that its history extends back to classical Greece. Other proposed starting points range from the Peace of Westphalia, through the Congress of Vienna and the establishment of the League of Nations, to the foundation of the United Nations in the aftermath of the Second World War. Nevertheless, most are prepared to concede that 'some system of rules, however rudimentary'[24] can be found in earlier periods too, and a surprisingly large number choose to start their discussions of the history of the subject with classical Greece.[25] Although there is little consensus on how far the ancient Greeks had travelled along the road towards a developed system of international law,[26] there seems to be a widespread perception that they had, at least, made a start on the journey.

---

[22] See Vinogradoff 1922: 163, for example. Note also, however, Zimmern's strong reaction against such interpretations: 'the League of Nations is not a patent method of interstate co-operation applicable to all states at any moment of history. It is a particular method which is being attempted at a particular moment of history' (Zimmern 1936: 5–6); see also Boak 1921 and Ténékidès 1931 for more detailed arguments against those who seek to find precedents for the League of Nations in classical Greece.

[23] Raeder 1912 and Tod 1913. (For discussion of the Hague Conferences and their impact on the study of arbitration, see Ager 1993: 3–5.)

[24] Brierly 1963: 1.

[25] This is not only true of the 'classic' histories of international law (many of which have been cited above; other examples are Redslob 1923 (ch. 1); Wegner 1936 (ch. 2)). For a more recent example of the same tendency, see Ziegler 1994. On the phenomenon, see Verzijl 1968: ch. 10, esp. 403 on the 'rare charm' of ancient civilisations for legal historians.

[26] Judgement of the extent of the development of the Greek system of international law is often heavily moralising. For Hosack (1882: 15), for example, the lack of a developed international law is a stain on Greek culture: 'it is sufficient for our purpose to admit – and the admission is a painful one – that in their international transactions the most enlightened people of antiquity appear to have been the most regardless of the rights of humanity'. (Laurent 1862: 125–7 has a similar, if slightly less harsh, view.) Walker (1899: 43) praises Greek international law as being 'an improving law'. (Compare Hershey 1911: 914.) For Tod, on the other hand (1913: 189), the lack of a developed international law is a sign of Greek moral probity: their example serves as 'a mute protest against the cynical doctrine that all international relations are governed by the law'.

This perception is, I would suggest, basically correct. The difficulty, however, lies in finding a suitable way of approaching the subject. First, there is an immediate problem of definition and of scope. 'Greek international law' could be understood in more than one way: the laws which are common to all Greek states, and are international in that sense (although their scope might be purely domestic);[27] or laws which regulate the ways in which states interact with each other.[28] There is, of course, some overlap between the two, but the focus in what follows will be on 'international law' in the second sense. Even with this restriction, Greek international law is not easy to locate in the surviving sources; it is harder still to classify and describe in its own terms. It is impossible, of course, to divorce this subject (any more than any other aspect of the ancient world) from its, claimed or actual, heritage. But approaching the subject through this heritage is, I think, unlikely to be helpful. What is more useful is to look at the subject in its own context – the Greek world – and, specifically, to attempt to assess its relationship to other contemporary forms of law – most obviously, domestic law. The enquiry falls most naturally into two general sections: first, the sources and scope of international law; second, its application and enforcement.

3.3 The sources and scope of Greek international law

The search for the sources of Greek international law – like that for domestic law[29] – could be understood in two ways: either as a quest for suitable historical evidence for the existence, and nature, of international law; or as a legal enquiry: how, and by whom, is international law created? The two types of enquiry are, of course, closely connected, and consideration of the second question will

---

[27] As, for example, the common Greek *nomos* regulating the treatment of slaves, which Demosthenes claims to exist (21.48). On the question of the unity of Greek law, see Finley 1975b.

[28] The problem has also affected modern international law: the term 'international law' was coined by Bentham 1996 (1780): 296, n. x, who felt that its predecessor, 'law of nations', implied law applying to all nations, rather than laws regulating the behaviour of nations towards each other (see Janis 1984). The French and German terms for the subject – *droit des gens, Völkerrecht* – remain closer to the form rejected by Bentham.

[29] Todd 1993: chs. 3 and 4 (and esp. 30).

inevitably be conditioned by the answer given to the first. Nevertheless, it is worth pausing very briefly to consider the first question separately.

Discussions of Greek international law often assert that there exists no formally defined, authoritative, published 'code' of the international law of classical Greece.[30] This is, undoubtedly, true; and there is, moreover, no evidence to suggest that such a thing ever existed. It might be added that there is no 'lawgiver' – no Lycurgus or Solon – of Greek international law. Nor – to change the terms of the comparison – is there any Grotius, any dedicated theoretician or philosopher of international law.[31] These factors (which are, of course, of more than methodological relevance) make the attempt to study Greek international law harder; they do not, however, make it impossible. There is a wide range of evidence which is relevant to this subject, and which can be found in both literary and epigraphic material. All of the literary evidence, and the great majority of the epigraphic, has its origins in Athens. What will be under discussion in what follows, therefore, is largely an Athenian conception of international law. This description may seem self-contradictory, but might make more sense when the evidence has been considered in more detail.

What, then, do these historical sources reveal about the sources (in a legal sense) of Greek international law? It seems best to start from the most widely held position on the subject, which is neatly expressed by Gomme:

the only form of international law in Greece (as opposed to custom, like the reception of foreign suppliants – οἱ Ἑλλήνων νόμοι [the *nomoi* of the Greeks] of [Th. 1.]41.1) was that contained in treaties between states – not a general convention agreed to by all or most states, but a series of separate treaties between states.[32]

Gomme's assertion is made with specific reference to a comment concerning foreign judges, but seems intended to have a much broader scope, and it expresses a view whose various aspects are generally accepted: the central importance of treaties; the unique importance of treaties; the strict distinction between law and

[30] See, for example, Plescia 1970: 58; Adcock & Mosley 1975: 121; Ostwald 1986: 119.
[31] See Wight 1966a: 127.   [32] *HCT ad* 1.37.3.

custom.[33] It is, of course, quite true that interstate treaties (whether bilateral or multilateral) establish specific obligations between states, which we could, in theory, choose to describe as 'laws'. But this does not reveal very much about classical Greek perceptions of these agreements and of their relationship to other forms of law. A more systematic way into the problem, and the one I adopt in what follows, would be to start from something about whose status we have relative confidence – namely domestic law – and work outwards from there into the world of interstate agreements. The examples which follow have therefore been chosen precisely because they demonstrate, in various ways, how law, as understood in a domestic sense, could be extended to the international sphere. (This choice of examples does not, that is, imply a belief that other interstate agreements are not necessarily a source of international 'law'. But starting from this more restricted set of evidence will, I hope, provide easier access to the larger picture.)

Some of the language of interstate agreements – of *summachiai* and *spondai* – is quite distinct from that associated with law in the domestic sphere,[34] but there is some overlap. *Sunthēkē*, for example (or more usually the plural *sunthēkai*) is most usually associated with interstate agreements, but is also used to describe domestic contracts.[35] The area of overlap on which I want to focus here, however, is concerned not just with language, but also with procedure. The evidence for many Greek states is uncertain,[36] but in Athens the procedure is clear: interstate agreements, once formulated, are drawn up in the form of a resolution, proposed, and, if all goes according to plan, passed by the assembly.[37] In Athens at least, therefore, interstate agreements are, often, formally identical to domestic, and can be described as *nomoi* or (more frequently)

---

[33] For examples of similar views on the importance of treaties, see Baltrusch 1994: 191; on law and custom, Busolt & Swoboda 1926: 1259–64; Ostwald 1986: 119.

[34] On Greek terminology for treaties (and its relationship to the formulae found in Near Eastern documents) see Weinfeld 1990. More generally, Bickerman 1950: 99–116; Adcock & Mosley 1975: 122.

[35] As, for example, in Finley 1985b: no.17. On συνθῆκαι in general, see Schultheß 1935.

[36] There are some non-Athenian examples which seem to mirror the Athenian system (and which are discussed below), but, since the Athenians are involved in these cases, it is hard to judge how far they represent local practice and how far they are influenced by Athenian procedure.

[37] See de Ste. Croix 1963: esp. 114; Adcock & Mosley 1975: 215–16.

psēphismata.[38] One consequence of this similarity in procedure, however, is the introduction of a certain fuzziness: these laws, or decrees, may be international in substance, or have implications which extend beyond the boundaries of the *polis*, but they are domestic in origin and, often, in application and enforcement.[39] The boundaries between internal and international law may not, in other words, be as absolute as is sometimes assumed.

Nevertheless, in some places it is easier to define than others, and this is the case in the context in which references to *nomoi* or, more precisely, to proceeding κατὰ τὸν νόμον, 'in accordance with the *nomos*', most frequently appear in Athenian texts connected with external relations. The phrase appears as part of the formula dealing with the grants of *enktēsis* which often form a part of Athenian decrees honouring individual or groups of foreigners.[40] A typical example can be seen in *IG* ii² 343, a decree (of the third quarter of the fourth century)[41] honouring Apollonides of Sidon. After listing some of his services to the city, and voting him a crown, the decree continues:

---

[38] The post-403/2 Athenian distinction between *nomos* and *psēphisma* (on which see, generally, Hansen 1983c) is obviously relevant here. All Athenian treaties are *psēphismata*, not *nomoi* (Hansen 1983b: 183): for a good example, see *IG* ii² 43 (= RO 22), lines 51–4: ἐὰν δέ τ|ις εἴπηι ἢ ἐπιψηφίσηι . . . | παρὰ τόδε τὸ ψήφισμα ὡς λύειν τι δεῖ τ|ῶν ἐν τῶιδε τῶι ψηφίσματι εἰρημέν[ων, 'if anyone proposes or puts to the vote . . . contrary to this *psēphisma* that any of the things stated in this *psēphisma* ought to be undone'. Hansen interprets this as an indication of a firm distinction between treaties and laws, citing in support of this view the likely opinion of a 'modern jurist' that 'treaties come within the law of nations and cannot be classified as legislation in the proper sense', as well as the distinction made by Aristotle (*Pol.* 1298a3–7) between decisions concerning πολέμου καὶ εἰρήνης, καὶ συμμαχίας καὶ διαλύσεως, 'war and peace and alliance and truce', and those concerning *nomoi*. For Hansen, therefore (1983b: 184), treaties should not be seen as comparable to other areas of Athenian law. However, the classification of treaties as *psēphismata* could also be explained without the need to imagine such a rigidly defined distinction, if (as suggested by Rhodes 1987: 14–15) their continued treatment as *psēphismata* after 403/2 reflects not so much a logically considered position on their (non-permanent, non-general) status, as the more practical fact that no treaties were included in the code of *nomoi*, and therefore no subsequent decisions on foreign policy had to be expressed as *nomoi*. It is less clear that the *nomos/psēphisma* distinction always applies elsewhere in the Greek world: for a discussion of the (fairly sparse) evidence, see Rhodes with Lewis 1997: 498–9.

[39] For a fuller discussion of sanctions, see sec. 4 below.

[40] On the practice, and the formula, see Lambrechts 1958: 89–93 and, especially, Pečírka 1966 (which includes a catalogue of all decrees which include the formula or a variant of it).

[41] Kirchner (*IG, ad loc.*) dates the decree to *c.* 333/2; Lambrechts (1958: 157) and Pečírka (1966: 63–7) to 323/2 (on the basis of Schweigert's (1940: 342–3) restoration of the preamble of the inscription, with the archon name Cephisodorus).

καὶ εἶναι αὐ[τὸν]
[π]ρόξενον καὶ εὐεργέτην τοῦ δήμου τοῦ Ἀθ[ηναί]-
[ων] αὐτὸν καὶ ἐκγόνους· εἶναι δὲ αὐτῶι καὶ [γῆς]
[κ]αὶ οἰκίας ἔγκτησιν κατὰ τὸν νόμον.

and he is to be a proxenos and benefactor of the Athenian people, him and his descendants; he is to be granted the right of owning land and a house, in accordance with the *nomos*. (lines 10–13)

The reference to a *nomos* is, in fact, one of the least consistent elements of this formula. This probably reflects a genuine inconsistency of practice in the phrasing of these decrees, rather than a chronological development, although it does seem to be more common from the second half of the century onwards.[42] But even if it is not possible to identify the specific law which is being referred to here, still less the point at which it was introduced, the instinct of those who have commented on this formula to interpret *nomos* here in a strong sense, as referring to some definite piece of legislation, seems likely to be correct. More importantly, this example – and those like it[43] – show clearly how domestic *nomoi* could influence, even at a very trivial level, the behaviour of the *polis* towards outsiders, and this is something which should be borne in mind when considering less straightforward examples.

One such example comes from a well-known document: the Athenian imposition of a monopoly on the export of Cean ruddle.[44] The inscription, which was erected in Athens, consists of a 'dossier' of (at least) three decrees, each from a different Cean city. It is probable that there was originally also an Athenian decree

---

[42] Pečírka 1966: 140–2. The difficulty of dating some of the decrees involved makes the task of establishing chronological development (or lack of it) harder: the relevant documents are *IG* ii² 425 (possibly 2nd/3rd quarter of the fourth century); *IG* ii² 342 (?330s/320s); *IG* ii² 360 (325/4); *IG* ii² 343 (?323/2); possibly *IG* ii²⁺285 (mid-fourth century; but the phrase is restored). Throughout this period, decrees continue to be published which contain a version of the formula, but make no reference to the *nomos*.

[43] Such as the references to a *nomos* in the context of regulations concerning the payment for the erection of a stele recording a proxeny decree (*IG* ii² 240, lines 24–5 (= Tod 181)); or to the *nomos* regulating enrolment into a deme and a phratry in an honorific citizenship decree (*IG* ii² 374, lines 14–17).

[44] *IG* ii² 1128 (= RO 40). The precise date is unclear (and not vital for the argument here): RO juxtaposes the text with another Athenian intervention in the island, securely dated to 362, but does not explicitly reject the 350s date suggested by Tod (162; following Koehler, *IG* ii 546). On Cean ruddle, see Photos-Jones, Cottier, Hall & Mendoni 1997. For this decree in the context of Cean relations with Athens, see Brun 1989; Osborne 2000b: 86–9.

inscribed on the stone, and possible that a decree of the fourth city of Ceos, Poeessa, was also included.[45] The two best-preserved decrees – those of Coresus and of Iulis – record, in similar terms, a decision by their respective assemblies to allow export of ruddle only on Athenian-approved ships (lines 12–13 (Coresus)) and only to Athens (lines 10–11 (Coresus); 26–7 (Iulis)).

The combination of state and interstate activity in this example is quite clear. The decrees are passed, as *psephismata*, by individual states, with individual variations in details of form and of content. This is also, in fact, one of the rare occasions when such a regulation is explicitly referred to as a *nomos*:

[ἀ]ναγράψαι δὲ τόδε τὸ ψήφισμα ἐς στήληι λιθίνηι κα[ὶ καταθεῖναι --------- τ]-
[ο]ῦ Ἀπόλλωνος, καὶ τὸν νόμον καθάπερ πρότερον εἶχ[ε κύριον εἶναι].

This decree is to be written up on a stone stele and placed [in the temple/enclosure] of Apollo, and the *nomos* shall be valid as before. (lines 15–16, from the Coresian decree)[46]

But these decrees are also inextricably connected with interstate behaviour, and, in this case, the connection is based not only in the subject matter of the law – although this is, of course, a fundamental aspect – but also in its origins: the initiative for the implementation of the law comes, explicitly, from outside the Cean city which enacts it. Again, the Coresian decree illustrates this nicely: it opens with a reference to earlier Athenian and Coresian decrees on the subject of the export of ruddle (lines 10–12), but, towards the end of the decree, gives a more precise indication of where the initiative for these, and future, decisions is likely to originate:

[ἐὰν δέ τι ἄλλο ψηφίζωντα]-
ι Ἀθηναῖοι περὶ φυλακῆς τῆς μίλτου, κύρια εἶναι κατακομι[σθέντα τὰ
ἐψηφισμένα.

If the Athenians make any other decree concerning the protection of ruddle, what the Athenians decree is to be valid. (lines 21–2; similar provision in the decree of Iulis at lines 31–3)

A similar division of authority can be seen, too, in the provisions for the control of the law, which will be shared between Athens

---

[45] The argument against this is based on the fact that Poeessa is not listed on *IG* ii² 43 with the other Cean cities as a member of the Second Athenian League.

[46] A reference to the agreement as a *nomos* is restored in the decree of Iulis (line 36).

and the Cean city involved. The law will be enforced by the local authorities in the first instance, with the possibility of appeal to Athens (lines 16–21 (Coresus); 35–6 (Iulis)).

It might be argued that the interstate element of this law is compromised, even negated, by the obvious Athenian input into its creation and concern for its application – that there is less sense of an international community here, and more sense of the imposition of Athenian will on a subservient partner.[47] It could, indeed, be claimed that the process illustrated here is less one of the creation of an international legal space, and more one of the extension of Athenian (domestic) legal space to incorporate that of another *polis*. Such an argument cannot quite, however, account for the impression (which, even if it is only a façade, is surely a deliberately created one) that the Cean city does have a role in the creation and operation of the law. There is an important sense, therefore, in which this document, or group of documents, does represent a piece of international law, even though the international element is inseparable from the domestic.

A different perspective on a similar process can be found in another Athenian document of (roughly) the middle of the fourth century.[48] The document – the decree of Hegesippus – is, however, not entirely straightforward. The decree itself is quite poorly preserved; in addition its historical context – the history of Athenian relations with the Euboean cities in the middle of the century – is very poorly understood.[49] The decree lays out penalties against some party which has carried out an attack against Eretria. The date of that attack and that of the decree are uncertain. Worse still, the identity (or origin) of the attacker is not specified. It has been convincingly argued that the culprit is most likely to be Athenian. This fits with what is known of the historical circumstances: no other state is likely to have had the motive, or the ability, to have intervened in Euboea in the middle of the fourth century,[50] and there is evidence of one Athenian intervention in this period – the

---

[47] An interpretation emphasised by Osborne 2000b: esp. 88–9.

[48] RO 69 (a more recent text than *IG* ii² 125).

[49] The best attempt to understand them is Brunt 1969. See also Tritle 1993; and, for an account focusing on the epigraphic evidence, Knoepfler 1995: esp. 338–46.

[50] Knoepfler 1984: 154–5.

expedition of Phocion in 349/8.[51] Certainly, the regulations laid out for the trial and punishment of the offender seem very Athenocentric. It is the Athenian *boulē* and the Athenian assembly which is to be involved (lines 7–9), and the penalty for the attack which has already happened is to be determined by the Athenian assembly, κατὰ [τοὺς νόμους], 'according to the laws' (line 9).[52] Given the context of the proposed trial and punishment, it seems most likely that this is a reference to Athenian laws. (It has been noted that the whole process seems very similar to the Athenian procedure of *eisangelia*.)[53]

However, the focus of this decree is not solely Athenian. Hegesippus' proposal is concerned to control the behaviour not only of Athenians, but also of their allies. This becomes apparent in the decree's opening clause:

[ἔδοξεν τῶι δ]ήμωι· Ἡγήσ[ι]ππ[ος Ἡγησίου Σουν(ιεὺς) εἶπεν·]
[ὅπως ἂν τῶ]ν συμμάχων μηδεὶς [-------16-------]
[---7---]ν μηδείς, μήτε ξένος μή[τε ἀστός, ἀδικῆι (?)τ-]
[ὧν συμ]μάχων μ[η]δένα, ὁρμώμενος [-------14-------]
[τῶν π]όλεων τῶν σ[υ]μμαχίδων μηδ[---6 or 7---, δεδόχθαι / ἐψηφίσθα-]
[ι τ]ῶι δήμωι.

The people decreed; Hegesippus son of Hegesius, of Sounion, proposed: so that no-one of the Athenian allies . . . no-one, neither foreigner nor townsman, shall injure (?) anyone of the allies, setting out . . . any of the allied cities, let it be resolved/decreed by the people. (lines 1–6)

What seems to be happening here, therefore, is that an Athenian, in the Athenian assembly (not the *synedrion* of the Second Athenian League), is creating regulations which are intended to be binding on a much wider community – that of Athens' allies. (And also,

---

[51] Plut. *Phoc.* 12; Aeschin. 3.86; Dem. 9.57. The date is not entirely certain: for the arguments, see Dreher 1995: 156, n. 4. The question of how long after the expedition this decree was passed is even less clear: Dreher 1995: 167–73, suggests 348; Knoepfler 1984: 159–60, 343 (a suggestion repeated in Knoepfler 1995). A date closer to the event seems more plausible, although a firm commitment to that date seems both unwise and (for the purposes of the argument here) unnecessary.

[52] The restoration of νόμους here is Knoepfler's (1984: 155) suggestion (accepted by Dreher and RO), returning to the original supplement made by Koehler (*IG* ii 65). Tod's text (154), following Kirchner, in his *IG* ii² text, has κατὰ τοὺς σπονδάς ('according to the agreements'), which is taken to be a reference to the Decree of Aristoteles. But such a use of σπονδάς to describe an alliance of that sort would be unusual. (For more detailed arguments, see Knoepfler 1984: 155.)

[53] The action is listed in Hansen's catalogue of *eisangeliai* (Hansen 1975: no. 99).

to take a more positive view, attempting to ensure the protection of that wider community.) Although, as has been seen, the response to the attack which has taken place is fixed in Athenian procedure, the proposals relating to future offences broaden the scope once again:

ἐὰν]
δέ τις τοῦ λοιποῦ χρόνου ἐπιστρατ[εύσηι ἐπὶ Ἐρέ-]
τριαν ἢ ἐπ᾽ ἄλλην τινὰ τῶν συμμαχίδ[ων πόλεων, Ἀθη-]
ναίων ἢ τῶν συμμάχων τῶν Ἀθηνα[ίων, ἀτιμίαν αὐτοῦ]
κατεγνῶσθαι καὶ τὰ χρήματα δ[ημόσια εἶναι καὶ τ-]
ῆς Θεοῦ τὸ ἐπιδέκατον· καὶ εἶν[αι τὰ χρήματα αὐτοῦ]
ἀγώγιμα ἐξ ἁπασῶν τῶν πόλεω[ν τῶν συμμαχίδων· ἐὰν]
δέ τις ἀφέληται πόλις, ὀφείλε[ιν τῶι συνεδρίωι (?) τῶι τ-]
ῶν συμμάχων.

If, in the future, anyone marches against Eretria or against any other of the allied cities, whether one of the Athenians or of the Athenian allies, let him be condemned to loss of rights, and let his possessions be confiscated to the state, and a tenth part to the Goddess [Athena]. And his possessions shall be liable to seizure from all the allied cities. If any city refuses, the debt shall be owed to the *synedrion* (?) of the allies. (lines 9–17)

The place of trial is not specified. It has been suggested that, following the pattern laid out in the Decree of Aristoteles, the trial would be conducted by the allied *synedrion*,[54] but there is no positive evidence for this. The role of the allies is, however, made clear in the regulations for the distribution of confiscated property: if property is not surrendered, it is the συνεδρίωι τῶι τῶν συμμάχων ('the *synedrion* of the allies') to which the debt is owed, not the Athenians alone. As in the Cean decrees, therefore (although perhaps rather less strikingly),[55] there is a combination of domestic legislation with a wider concern. The Athenian input into, and control of, the legislation is more obvious here. But the scope of the decree is much wider: rather than representing a set of bilateral agreements, as the Cean decrees do, this document is intended to create regulations which will dictate the relations of a whole group of *poleis*. There is, in fact, an interesting tension represented here.

---

54 Cargill 1981: 121–2.
55 It is, of course, possible that this is due simply to an accident of survival: Cargill (1981: 122) suggests that this decree would have had a parallel in a *dogma* of the allied *synedrion*. Again, however, there is no way of proving this claim.

The content of the decree is intended to safeguard the territorial inviolability of the members of the Second Athenian League – to outlaw military intervention;[56] but the fact that the decree is passed at all represents a striking piece of legal intervention by Athens into the actions of those member states.

In these examples it is possible to see how laws, or decrees, though created by a single *polis*, could have implications beyond the boundary of that *polis*. But there are also cases where the inter-state nature of *nomoi* and *psēphismata* is more closely tied to their origins, as well as (or sometimes instead of) their content: that is, where the body which creates the legislation is not a single *polis*, but a unit encompassing several *poleis*. However, such examples are, it must be admitted, extremely rare. One instance concerns, again, the Second Athenian League, and is the decree of the allied *synedrion* – the only such decree extant – concerning settlement of *stasis* on Paros.[57] If this inscription is interpreted, as I think it must be, as a decree (rather than a proposal) of the *synedrion*,[58] then it provides an excellent example of an interstate organisation legislating as a unit. The decree is passed by the *summachoi*:

ἐπὶ Ἀστ[ε]ίο ἄρχοντος, Σκιροφο-
[ρίω]νος ἕνηι καὶ [νέ]αι, ἐ[πιψηφί]ζοντος
[.] υ [. . . Θ]ηβαίο, ἔδοξεν το[ῖ]ς [συ]μμάχοις·
[ὅ]π[ως ἂ]ν οἰκῶσι Πάρ[ιο]ι [ὁμονό]ως καὶ μηδὲν [?αὐτ]όθι βίαο[ν] γίγ[νηται]· ἐ[ά]ν τις ἀ-
ποκ[τείν]ηι [τινὰ ἀδίκως ?], τ[ο]ὺς αἰτίος τ-
ō θα[νάτ]ο [----8---- ?διδόνα]ι [δίκ]ην κατ-
ὰ το[ὺς ν]ό[μ]ος [----12----] ε[. .]ηι ἢ φυ-
γαδε[ύ]ηι [τιν]ὰ παρὰ [το]ὺ[ς ν]ό[μ]ος καὶ τὸ [ψ-
[ή]φισ[μα τ]όδε, [----13----] ιανεστ [.]

In the archonship of Asteius; on the last day of Scirophorion; with . . . of Thebes putting to the vote. Resolved by the allies: So that the Parians shall live in agree-ment and nothing violent shall happen there (?). If anyone kills anyone unjustly (?) he shall be put to death, and those responsible for the death shall pay the penalty (?) in accordance with the laws . . . or exiles anyone contrary to the *nomoi* and this decree. (lines 14–23)

---

[56] Noted by Dreher 1995: 283.   [57] RO 29. For further bibliography, see ch. 2, n. 59.

[58] The *synedrion* more usually seems to operate as a probouleutic body, producing *dog-mata* rather than *psēphismata* (see Rhodes 1985: 60–1, and compare Wilhelm's (1940) characterisation of this text as a *dogma*); this text provides the only evidence for a more fluid system, in which the *synedrion* could complete as well as suggest legislation (for this view, see Cargill 1981: 117–18; Cawkwell 1981: 49–50; Dreher 1995: 117–18).

It should be noted that the scope of this decree is much narrower than those discussed above, and that only a single *polis* – Paros – is to be affected by these regulations. It is also worth noting that, again, there is some overlap between domestic and interstate legislation, in more than one respect. If the restorations in lines 21–3 are correct, then it seems that this decree will operate alongside pre-existing *nomoi* – presumably Parian *nomoi* – in regulating Parian behaviour in the future. In addition, the Athenian input into the decree should not be forgotten. Although the decree's immediate setting is the allied *synedrion*, its broader context remains entirely Athenian: it is preceded on the stone by an Athenian resolution on the same subject; even the allied decree is formulated (and dated) in an Athenian style; and the stele itself was to be erected on the Acropolis.[59]

A second example provides less direct evidence for the existence of *nomoi* created by an interstate organisation. An Athenian decree (dated to 362)[60] votes honours to an official of Delphi, Astycrates, and his colleagues. These Delphians had been exiled by the Amphictions, and their property had been confiscated. The decree claims that these actions were παρὰ τοὺς νόμους τῶν Ἀ[μ]φ[ικτιόνων], 'contrary to the *nomoi* of the Amphictions'.[61] It is difficult to establish precisely which *nomoi* the Athenians may have had in mind here, but it is quite easy to accept the suggestion that there will have existed *nomoi* – in a 'strong' sense of (positive) laws – created by and applicable to the Delphic Amphictiony.[62] But this is not always the case, and at this point a fundamental problem – the one which is relegated by Gomme to the parenthesis – needs to be considered: what is the relationship between 'law' and 'custom'? Are they, in fact, two discrete entities, suitable to be 'opposed' to one another?

In the standard definitions of international law, the distinction is not as sharp as might be expected. This is true, for example, of Brierly's version:

---

[59] The Standort is specified in lines 9–10. (The stone was found on the South Slope of the Acropolis.)

[60] *IG* ii[2] 109, line 17 (although the most recent text is in Osborne 1981–3, vol. I: no. D11).

[61] On the context for this decree see Buckler 1989: 9–13.

[62] On Amphictionic legislation see Lefèvre 1998: pt 2, sec. 1, ch. 2.

the Law of Nations, or International Law, may be defined as the body of rules and principles of action which are binding upon civilised states in their relations with one another.[63]

For Brierly, it seems, vaguer concepts – rules, principles – are not only part of the world of international law, but basic to its content, and to its creation. This picture of a more fluid system, where customs can form the basis of laws, is one which is rejected by some commentators on international law,[64] but which is quite appropriate to the Greek world. The reason for this lies, first of all, in language, and, specifically, in the problem of the meaning (or meanings) of *nomos*. LSJ lists definitions for the word which range from 'usage' and 'custom', via 'statute', through to 'musical melody'.[65] The word does, arguably, undergo a diachronic development in its meaning;[66] but it also shows enormous synchronic variation: Ostwald identifies thirteen different senses in which *nomos* is used in classical Greek,[67] and even if some of his categorisations and divisions might be thought to be somewhat arbitrary, the emphasis on the word's semantic range is both valid and important. More important still for the subject under discussion here is the fact that this range of meanings encompasses, and thus sometimes obscures, the contrast between normative and positive law.[68]

Such uncertainty can, again, be seen in the epigraphic record of interstate agreements. A number of Athenian agreements, with different rulers or states, contain a reference to the swearing of νόμιμα ὅρκα ('*nomima* oaths').[69] How, though, is *nomima* to be

---

[63] Brierly 1963: 1. This is probably the most widely accepted 'standard' definition among international lawyers, and most other versions follow similar lines: compare, for example, the definition in Sheets 1994: 52: international law is the 'rules, doctrines and policy goals which exert a regulatory effect on international relations'.

[64] Notably by Austin 1995 (1832): 123, 171.   [65] LSJ[9] *s.v.* νόμος.

[66] This is the thesis of Ostwald 1969, who suggests that the development of the meaning of νόμος as statute is a consequence of the Cleisthenic reforms. (Against this view, see Todd & Millett 1990: 12, n. 23.)

[67] Ostwald 1969: 54 for the quantification, ch. 2 for description and discussion.

[68] See de Romilly 1971: 24.

[69] All the examples from this period are Athenian, although the other state involved varies. The relevant inscriptions are: *IG* ii[2] 16, fr.b, lines 8–9 (= Tod 103; alliance with Eretria, 394); 105, lines 37–8 (= RO 34; treaty with Dionysius of Syracuse, 367); 116, line 20 (= RO 44; alliance with Thessalians, 361/0); 230, fr.a, line 11 (alliance with Eretria, 341/0). The phrase also appears in a domestic context in Athens (e.g., *IG* ii[2] 204, line 9). It is interesting to note that *IG* ii[2] 116 and 230 contain both details of oaths to be sworn

interpreted here? Like *nomos*, the word has a considerable range of meanings, relating both to customs and to legal rights and processes,[70] and it is not immediately clear which shade of meaning is required here. The religious element might encourage the suspicion that such oaths might, like other aspects of religious practice, be (or be thought to be) defined and regulated through tradition and custom rather than through positive legislation.[71] To this suspicion could be added the negative evidence of the absence of any decree or document in which the form of these *nomima* oaths is explicitly laid out. However, arguments from silence have obvious dangers, and the first argument, too, is made harder to sustain by two factors. First, that the majority of treaties do specify the form of the oaths which are to be sworn by each party; second, and more importantly, that there is considerable variation between these oaths. There is, in other words, little sign of a straightforward 'custom' which could regulate this practice, and to which *nomimon* could definitively refer.[72]

In other cases, however, it is easier to be certain that the *nomoi* have little to do with positive law. This is illustrated in (yet) another Athenian decree: the decree (RO 35), of 367/6, records the sending of a protest by Athens to the Aetolian League in response to the breaking of a sacred truce by a member of the League (consisting of the arrest of the heralds who had been sent to announce the truce). Such an act was, according to the decree, παρὰ τοὺς νόμους τ|[ο]ὺς κοι[ν]οὺς τῶν Ἑλλήνων, 'contrary to the common *nomoi* of the Greeks'(lines 13f.).[73] Two things – one linguistic, one practical – suggest that *nomoi* should here be interpreted in a general sense. The linguistic point rests on the qualification of *nomos* by *koinos*, a usage which – in a domestic context – usually implies not just

and a reference to the swearing of *nomima* oaths. See Martin 1886: ch. 3, for general discussion and list of examples.

[70] LSJ[9] *s.v.* νόμιμος. (There is a brief discussion of the word in the context of interstate relations in Paradisi 1957: 242–6.)

[71] On the relationship between religion and tradition, see Price 1999: 78–9.

[72] Adcock & Mosley 1975: 217–19. For more detailed discussion of oaths in interstate documents, see Martin 1886; Heuß 1934: 20–5; Plescia 1970: ch. 4; Lonis 1980; Pistorius 1985; Bederman 2001: 67–71; see also the discussion below: 118–26. On oaths in Athenian domestic law, see Thür 1996.

[73] The incident is included by Mosley 1973: 84–5, in his discussion of the rules relating to the treatment of envoys; see also de Romilly 1971: 40–3.

95

shared, but also 'unwritten' laws.[74] The practical point is obvious: there existed no legislative body which could create positive *nomoi* on behalf of the Greeks. If there did exist some piece of positive legislation relating to the treatment of heralds, it could only, strictly, be claimed to apply to some smaller group of *poleis*. Whether or not there was such a piece of legislation, therefore (and I would be inclined to believe that there was not), this particular claim for the existence of a *Greek nomos* cannot be dependent on it.

This does not, however, mean that the *nomos* invoked by the Athenians is necessarily less authoritative, or less likely to command respect, than the examples of positive *nomoi* discussed earlier. Formally created *nomoi* in fact form a minority of laws attested in interstate contexts in this period, and it is in the less formal, customary, sense that the majority of the references to international law or custom (usually under the description of *nomos* or *nomimos*), and (more frequently) to breaches of law or custom (*paranomia*),[75] have to be understood. Some of these references are connected with particular aspects of relations between states, the majority of which, perhaps unsurprisingly, concern practices related to war. The *nomoi* connected with the treatment of war dead are frequently invoked, both in cases where they are conspicuously upheld and when they are conspicuously (or allegedly) broken. (See, for example, Dem. 60.8; Isoc. 12.170, 14.53; Lysias 2.9.)[76] The treatment and maltreatment of prisoners of war are also characterised in terms of *nomoi* and of *paranomia* (for example, at X. *HG* II.i.32, III.ii.22).[77] So too is the treatment of ambassadors and heralds, where the literary sources confirm, and amplify, the claim made in the decree mentioned above: in [Dem.] 12.3, for

---

[74] Triantaphyllopoulos 1985: 14–16.

[75] *Paranomia* (and its related forms) is, again, a term whose meanings range from the very general to the specific and technical (most obviously, in the latter sense, in the charge of *graphē paranomōn*: see Todd 1993: 108).

[76] On the *nomoi* associated with the burial of war-dead, see Pritchett 1971–91, vol. IV: ch. 2; Vaughn 1991.

[77] Compare Polybius II.58.6–7, describing the massacre by the Mantineans of some Achaean prisoners as a violation of τοὺς κοινοὺς τῶν ἀνθρώπων νόμους ('the common laws of mankind'); the crime is compounded by the fact that the Achaeans had become prisoners as a result of Mantinean treachery (on Polybius' inconsistent approach to the 'laws' of war, see Walbank *HCP ad loc.*). On the treatment of prisoners of war see Ducrey 1968 and (with special reference to the Peloponnesian War) Panagopoulos 1978: pt I.

example, the arrest of an ambassador is described as the τέλος . . . παρανομίας, the 'utmost illegality'.[78]

The same vocabulary can also be applied to more general patterns of interstate behaviour. The adverb *nomimōs* (νομίμως) is used by Isocrates to describe expansionist, or hegemonic, activity which is, in his view, acceptable, and even admirable. So, in the *Panegyricus*, Athens' (past) approach to foreign relations is contrasted with that of Sparta:

καὶ τότε μὲν ἠγανάκτουν, ὅθ' ἡμεῖς νομίμως ἐπάρχειν τινῶν ἠξιοῦμεν· νῦν δ' εἰς τοιαύτην δουλείαν καθεστώτων οὐδὲν φροντίζουσιν αὐτῶν, οἷς οὐκ ἐξαρκεῖ δασμολογεῖσθαι καὶ τὰς ἀκροπόλεις ὁρᾶν ὑπὸ τῶν ἐχθρῶν κατεχομένας, ἀλλὰ πρὸς ταῖς κοιναῖς συμφοραῖς καὶ τοῖς σώμασι δεινότερα πάσχουσι τῶν παρ' ἡμῖν ἀργυρωνήτων.

At that time the Spartans were annoyed because we thought it right to extend our rule over certain people by legitimate means. But now they feel no concern, when these peoples are reduced to such abject servitude that it is not enough that they should be forced to hand over money and see their citadels occupied by their enemies, but, in addition to these public calamities, must also in their own persons submit to greater indignities than those which are suffered in our world by purchased slaves. (4.123)

It is worth noting the range of behaviour covered in this claim – all of which, the logic of the argument suggests, should be regarded as not *nomimos*. This includes not only actions which might possibly be ruled out by some specific agreement (payment of tribute, attacks on citadels), but also much more loosely defined 'outrages' or 'indignities' (δεινότερα). This broad conception can be seen elsewhere in Isocrates' work. Imperial expansion is, in theory, subject to certain *nomoi*. The Spartans know that

κατὰ μὲν τοὺς νόμους τάς τε πόλεις καὶ τὰς χώρας τούτων εἶναι δοκούσας, τῶν ὀρθῶς καὶ νομίμως κτησαμένων.

according to the *nomoi*, states and territories are deemed to belong to those who have duly and lawfully acquired them. (12.46)

They also know, however, that such *nomoi* do not always hold in practice (κατὰ . . . τὴν ἀλήθειαν). The one person, who, in Isocrates' opinion, demonstrates such standards of behaviour in the

---

[78] Cf. Dem. 19.234 for a positive example of the *nomimon* treatment of envoys. In general, see Mosley 1973; Bederman 2001: ch. 4.

contemporary world of interstate relations is the paradigm of generalship (and pupil of Isocrates), Timotheus, who behaves *nomimōs* not only towards his allies but also his enemies:

πρὸς δε τούτοις τὰς δοριαλώτους τῶν πόλεων οὕτω πράως διῴκει καὶ νομίμως ὡς οὐδεὶς ἄλλος τὰς συμμαχίδας, ἡγούμενος, εἰ τοιοῦτος ὢν φαίνοιτο περὶ τοὺς πολεμήσαντας, τὴν μεγίστην πίστιν ἔσεσθαι δεδωκώς, ὡς οὐδέποτ' ἂν περί γε τοὺς ἄλλους ἐξαμαρτεῖν τολμήσειεν.

In addition, when cities had been taken by him in battle, he would treat them with a mildness and a consideration for their rights which no one else has ever shown to allies; for he thought that if he showed such an attitude toward those who fought against him, this would serve as the most secure guarantee that he would never dare to wrong the others. (15.125)

Again, general characterisations of interstate behaviour of this sort can also be found in a negative form: a good example is the *paranomia* of Alcibiades in his dealings with foreign states (alleged by And. 4.30).[79]

There is one other field of activity to which this language is regularly applied in the literary sources, namely, the making and breaking of treaties and truces. And this area is, I think, worth considering in rather more detail, since it can help both to illustrate how these positive and customary *nomoi* relate to each other and to highlight the closeness of the connection between them. As was noted above (n. 38), treaties (in Athens, at least) are formally categorised not as *nomoi* but as *psēphismata*. Nevertheless, there are contexts in which respect for *nomoi* and respect for interstate agreements are represented as being closely connected. In one of the *Letters* attributed to Philip II (and preserved in the Demosthenic corpus), the description of *paranomia* is applied to the behaviour of the Athenian general Callias, on the grounds that he has attacked cities although they are ὑμῖν μὲν ἐνόρκους, ἐμοὶ δὲ συμμαχίδας, 'tied by oath to you, but allied to me' ([Dem.] 12.5). For Isocrates in the *Panegyricus*, the murder of the Greek leaders of the Ten Thousand by the Persian Tissaphernes, in spite of the existence of a truce, is, again, a deliberate act of *paranomia* (4.147).[80] Rather

---

[79] Note that, according to Andocides, Alcibiades' 'lawlessness' extends (seamlessly) from his domestic life to his treatment of foreign states.

[80] Xenophon's description of the event (*An.* II.v.31–5) is fuller, and puts a different interpretation on the nature of the Persian's misdemeanour: it is discussed in more detail below: 119–20.

more generally, the behaviour of the Thebans in attacking Plataea is consistently characterised by Isocrates' Plataeans as being a breach of treaties (e.g., at 14.5, 10), and is equally consistently described as being an act of *paranomia* (e.g., at 14.4, 22). What these claims illustrate, I think, is a belief not so much that treaties themselves should be counted as *nomoi*, as that the creation, and observance, of interstate agreements are themselves instantiations of some more fundamental interstate *nomos* – one which might be described as the (familiar) obligation *pacta sunt servanda*, and which, although never explicitly formulated, is no less strongly felt or frequently invoked.[81]

The existence, and nature, of the connection between interstate agreements and *nomoi* is perhaps most clearly expressed in a section of Xenophon's *Memorabilia* (IV.iv.15–17). In the course of the argument for the identity of τὸ νόμιμον (the *nomimon*) and τὸ δίκαιον ('the just'), Socrates is made to consider the role of *homonoia* in producing respect for laws, and the importance of laws, in turn, in creating happiness and success, for both the individual and the *polis*:

ἰδίᾳ δὲ πῶς μὲν ἄν τις ἧττον ὑπὸ πόλεως ζημιοῖτο, πῶς δ᾽ ἂν μᾶλλον τιμῷτο, ἢ εἰ τοῖς νόμοις πείθοιτο; πῶς δ᾽ ἂν ἧττον ἐν τοῖς δικαστηρίοις ἡττῷτο ἢ πῶς ἂν μᾶλλον νικῴη; τίνι δ᾽ ἄν τις μᾶλλον πιστεύσειε παρακαταθέσθαι ἢ χρήματα ἢ υἱοὺς ἢ θυγατέρας; τίνα δ᾽ ἂν ἡ πόλις ὅλη ἀξιοπιστότερον ἡγήσαιτο τοῦ νομίμου; παρὰ τίνος δ᾽ ἂν μᾶλλον τῶν δικαίων τύχοιεν ἢ γονεῖς ἢ οἰκεῖοι ἢ οἰκέται ἢ φίλοι ἢ πολῖται ἢ ξένοι; τίνι δ᾽ ἂν μᾶλλον πολέμιοι πιστεύσειαν ἢ ἀνοχὰς ἢ σπονδὰς ἢ συνθήκας περὶ εἰρήνης; τίνι δ᾽ ἂν μᾶλλον ἢ τῷ νομίμῳ σύμμαχοι ἐθέλοιεν γίγνεσθαι; τῷ δ᾽ ἂν μᾶλλον οἱ σύμμα-χοι πιστεύσειαν ἢ ἡγεμονίαν ἢ φρουραρχίαν ἢ πόλεις . . . τῷ δ᾽ ἄν τις ἧττον πολεμήσειεν ἢ ᾧ μάλιστα μὲν φίλος εἶναι βούλοιτο, ἥκιστα δ᾽ ἐχθρός, καὶ ᾧ πλεῖστοι μὲν φίλοι καὶ σύμμαχοι βούλοιντο εἶναι, ἐλάχιστοι δ᾽ ἐχθροὶ καὶ πολέμιοι;

'And how is the individual citizen less likely to incur penalties from the *polis*, and more certain to gain honour than by obeying the laws? How less likely to be defeated in the courts or more certain to win? Whom would anyone rather trust as guardian of his money or sons or daughters? Whom would the whole city think more trustworthy than the man of lawful conduct? From whom would parents or kinsfolk or servants or friends or fellow-citizens or

---

[81] The point is made by Sheets 1994: 54, with reference to Thucydides' characterisations of interstate agreements.

strangers more surely get their just rights? Whom would enemies rather trust in the matter of a truce or treaty or terms of peace? Whom would men rather choose for an ally? And to whom would allies rather entrust leadership or command of a garrison, or cities? . . . Whom would anyone less willingly make war on than him whose friendship he covets and whose enmity he is keen to avoid, who attracts the most friends and allies, and the fewest opponents and enemies?' (IV.iv.17)

What the flow of Xenophon's argument in this passage suggests is that interstate agreements – whether with friends or enemies – are as open to regulation by *nomoi* as behaviour in the law-courts or as guardianship of money or of minors. It is possible to perceive a steady progression in the passage, from the most concrete examples – appearances in the law-court – to the more abstract – friendship, enmity. But it is not possible to define a fixed point where the boundary between 'law' and 'custom' is crossed. No rigid distinction is imposed between these different applications of *nomos*.[82]

This passage of Xenophon is also helpful in its illustration of another way in which the connection between positive and customary *nomos* should be considered – a way which involves returning more directly to the question of the sources of international law: the interstate agreements which were discussed in the earlier part of this section had an immediately identifiable source; what, then is the source of these other *nomoi*?

For Xenophon, the answer to that question would, again, point to a single answer, applying to all types of *nomos*, and based in the necessary connection between what is *nomimos* and what is just: the gods establish what is just, and what is lawful; *nomoi*

---

[82] This approach conflicts with Aristotle's creation (in the *Rhetoric*) of a stronger distinction between different types of *nomos* (written/unwritten, private/common), but seems to be more in keeping with the approaches to *nomos* which can be found in Athenian forensic oratory. Although written and unwritten *nomoi* may be distinguished, they are generally portrayed as being mutually confirming parts of the same system (see Carey 1996). It is also worth noting the absence from the Xenophontic passage of any marked division between activities within the *polis* and those connected to external relations. A contrast might usefully be drawn with Roman approaches to the *ius gentium*, which is closer to (and, in some of its manifestations, clearly influenced by) the Aristotelian model: there is a strong dividing line between *ius civile*, positive laws of the state, and *ius gentium*, laws perceived as being observed by and applicable to all, regardless of their citizen status (see Jolowicz & Nicholas 1972: 102–7).

come, ultimately, from the gods.[83] This connection applies to all laws, whether they are restricted in scope (as are the νόμοι πόλεως, '*nomoi* of the city', with which this section of discussion begins (IV.iv.13)) or ἀγράφοι νόμοι, 'unwritten *nomoi*', of universal validity (IV.iv.19).[84]

The possibility of a connection between what is *nomimos* and what is just shows, too, how the question of the sources of international law connects to a much bigger subject: the role and nature of justice in interstate relations. If law and justice are held to be identical, who, then, defines what is just? Can the creation of law be distinguished from the will of the stronger; or, to put it in more familiar terms, does might create right? That problem will be considered more fully at a later stage (see ch. 4, sec. 4), but it is relevant here to point to one alternative to the Xenophontic approach. For Demosthenes, in *For the Liberty of the Rhodians*, justice is determined not by the gods, but by the powerful:

τῶν μὲν γὰρ ἰδίων δικαίων τῶν ἐν ταῖς πολιτείαις οἱ νόμοι κοινὴν τὴν μετουσίαν ἔδοσαν καὶ ἴσην καὶ τοῖς ἀσθενέσιν καὶ τοῖς ἰσχυροῖς· τῶν δ' Ἑλληνικῶν δικαίων οἱ κρατοῦντες ὁρισταὶ τοῖς ἥττοσι γίγνονται.

Of private rights within a state, the laws of that state grant an equal and impartial share to all, weak and strong alike; but the international rights of Greek states are defined by the strong for the weak.[85] (15.29)

And there is a sense in which Demosthenes (who is, it should be noted, discussing a treaty at this point) can be seen to be supported in this claim by the examples which have been discussed above. The inspiration of a dominant power – notably Athens – is clearly visible in several of those interstate agreements. Even though the creator of the law may not, formally speaking, have been Athens, Athenian control, backed by Athenian power, is nevertheless present. And a similar process might also be seen to be at work in the creation of the 'customary' *nomoi*. In the absence of any fixed code of such *nomoi*, their existence depends, ultimately,

[83] X. *Mem.* IV.iv.19–25. (Compare the opening exchange of Plato's *Laws* (624a).) On religious sources of ancient international law, see Bederman 2001: ch. 3.

[84] A comparable equation of justice with *nomos* can be found in Aristotle *Politics* 1324b, where, again (at 1324b22–36) the example is extended to the sphere of interstate relations. Further discussion of this passage in ch. 4, sec. 3 below; see also Kraut 1997: 67–8.

[85] Contrast Xenophon *Mem.* I.ii.40–5, where law and force (βία) are characterised as absolute opposites.

on their invocation. If the proposer of a decree, or the writer of a speech, has the power to declare that a particular action upholds or breaks an international *nomos*, then – if only in that decree, or that speech – the *nomos* comes into existence.[86]

It remains true, however, that the *representation* of these international laws – whether in inscribed decrees or in literary texts – is much closer to the Xenophontic view than the Demosthenic: international laws are shared creations, whether of a group of states or of all the Greeks (or of all mankind). Zimmern claimed, when discussing the sources of modern international law, that

> we shall not find them embodied in the habits or the will, still less in the affections, of a society. The peoples of the world know little of them. International Law is remote both from their hearts and their minds.[87]

But his description of international law in the early twentieth century seems to find its exact opposite in classical Greece: the rules and obligations of international law can be found, precisely, in the habits and the will, the hearts and minds of society. And it is this interaction between power and consensus which will also be important in considering the question of the application and enforcement of international law.

3.4 Application, enforcement and the problem of sanctions

If one way in which the status of international agreements (are they law, custom, both, or neither?) has traditionally been approached is through a consideration of their origins, equal (and often greater) importance has also been attributed to the other side of the problem: how, and by whom, are these agreements enforced? Are there, in fact, any secure mechanisms for ensuring adherence to interstate agreements?[88] The problem of sanctions in particular is one which has long troubled theorists of international law, largely because

---

[86] See Kratochwil 1989: esp. 40 on the importance of rhetoric to the construction of international law.

[87] Zimmern 1936: 97.

[88] On the problem and approaches to it in modern International Relations, see the review article of Koh 1997 (who describes the question of why states obey international law as, 'among the most perplexing . . . in international relations': 2599).

the presence of sanctions has, traditionally, been regarded as one of the defining features of law: even if it were possible for laws to come into existence without the positive action of a sovereign power, there would be no way for them to remain in force without the possibility of sanction imposed by a sovereign power. Such a sovereign power exists in domestic societies; it does not (and cannot) exist in an international society; therefore there can be no proper law in international society.[89]

Again, however, this traditional position has faced increasingly frequent challenges in more recent work on international law. These challenges have, in general, two bases. First, the observation that the observance of laws (or lack of it) does not have a necessary effect on their status as 'law': many domestic laws, it is pointed out, are frequently broken, without anyone seriously questioning either their validity or the legitimacy of the power which created or (attempts to) enforce them.[90] Second, the suggestion that sanctions may not in any case be the crucial factor in determining adherence to laws. Studies of attitudes to modern domestic law and law-breaking suggest that laws are obeyed not only through the fear of getting caught (and of the consequent punishment), but also because of considerations of personal morality, and, just as importantly, fears of peer disapproval of law-breaking.[91] Adherence to law may, that is, be less dependent on the possibility of enforcement or the threat of sanctions, and more related to societal, and ethical, factors. Such arguments do not, of course, necessarily prove anything about the situation in classical Greece, but what they do suggest is that the issue of enforcement should not be used to create a rigid divide between what can and cannot properly be considered law.[92]

If, then, enforcement should not be considered an essential feature of a legal system, what is the point of studying it? One reason why the subject remains important is not only because it can help in providing some sense of order and system to a wide range of

---

[89] Again, this is a view made most famous by Austin (see, e.g., Austin 1885, vol. II: 575). For a recent exploration of (and attempt to confirm) the argument, see Rubin 1997.

[90] See, e.g., Brierly 1958: 53; Kratochwil 1984: 347.

[91] Tyler 1990: 56 (a conclusion drawn from Tyler's own study, which was based on a sample of residents of Chicago).

[92] Nardin 1983: 131.

interstate behaviour,[93] but also – and more specifically – because it can reveal some interesting things about questions of force, power and consensus. How does law differ from 'the enforceable will of the stronger'?[94] To what extent is the enforcement of law conditioned by existing power relationships, and to what extent can that enforcement, in turn, lead to the creation or restructuring of hierarchies or communities of states?

Some sanctions are laid down within the agreements to which they apply, but this is not always the case, and it is therefore worth starting by considering briefly the procedures by which sanctions can be determined – especially since these procedures can themselves illustrate some of the issues which have just been outlined.

Some of the examples which were discussed in section 3 showed how attempts to control interstate behaviour could take place in contexts, and according to laws, which are, strictly speaking, domestic. Many of the comments which were made about the overlap between domestic and international factors in the creation and scope of law apply equally to these procedures for its enforcement, and do not need to be repeated at length here. However, one example – the decree of Hegesippus (RO 69) – does illustrate neatly how a domestic legislative process might nevertheless have some implications for the wider interstate community. This decree represents, as was seen, an example of law-enforcement in action: an 'illegal' act has been carried out, and Hegesippus' concern is to institute measures to ensure punishment (and to discourage repetition). The process envisaged for the punishment of the offender is, as was noted, fixed in Athenian procedure (and is very similar in appearance to an *eisangelia*).[95] The initiative for the action comes from a private Athenian citizen, and the authority for the enforcement of the penalty will come, ultimately, from the Athenian *demos*. What is interesting, however, is the broad reference of Hegesippus' proposal. Most *eisangeliai* are brought because of an action which is alleged to have harmed Athens, whether through

---

[93] That is: the types of activity which are considered below are extremely well known, and have frequently been studied as individual phenomena. What I hope to do in this discussion is not, therefore, to provide a thorough investigation of each subject – in most cases this has already been done – but to suggest how they could fit into a broader picture.
[94] Sheets 1994: 60.   [95] See above, 90.

corruption or outright treason.[96] In this case, the victim of the offence is not directly, and certainly not solely, Athens, but her allies. The typically inwardly focused procedure of *eisangelia* is, therefore, being significantly extended.[97] What this example illustrates is a case of a legal procedure within a *polis* being used in an attempt to maintain the stability of a larger group of *poleis*. In the process, the position of the protector of that stability is confirmed and strengthened: Athens, as hegemon, is displaying a conspicuous concern to preserve the agreements by which the system is maintained, and in doing so increases not only her own security, but also her prestige, and, finally, the ties of reciprocal gratitude which bind the members of that community to her.[98]

Law enforcement could also, however, take place in a more distinctively 'international' environment, through the procedure of arbitration.[99] As was mentioned above,[100] this is the mechanism of control which has received most attention from modern scholars, and which has traditionally been regarded as the major Greek contribution to the theory and practice of interstate relations. Even writers who are less enthusiastic in their claims for a Greek 'legacy' to modern international politics nevertheless continue to regard the practice as one of the 'fundamental institutions' of Greek interstate society.[101] Arbitration could be used in a wide variety of cases,

---

[96] Hansen 1975: 65.

[97] A possible parallel might be the charge brought against the general Timotheus in 373, on the grounds that he had failed to provide assistance to Athens' ally Corcyra (Dem. 49.9–10; D.S. 15.47.3; Hansen 1975: no. 80), although in this case the harm done to the allies is due more to omission than commission.

[98] *IG* ii² 109 (mentioned above, 93) shows a similar Athenian concern to be identified as a defender of *nomoi*. Compare Hunter 1994: 149, on the importance of law enforcement within Athenian domestic society for creating and developing the ties of reciprocity within that society. See also Kratochwil 1984: 348: 'power and influence are derived from the role as a protector of certain rules and core values of the game . . . the alleged antinomy between "power", "balancing" and "rule following" is a mistaken one'.

[99] Although, again, the procedure is one which is familiar from domestic dispute settlement: for brief discussion, see Todd 1993: 123–5, 128–9; on the basic similarity of domestic and international arbitration, see Roebuck 2001: 159.

[100] 82.

[101] See especially Reus-Smit 1999: chs. 1–3 (defining fundamental institutions as elements which 'provide the basic framework for cooperative interaction between states and . . . transcend shifts in the balance of power and the configuration of interests' (4)). Reus-Smit's position contrasts with that adopted by Ager (1993, 1996) who, while less optimistic on the success of arbitration as an institution, is much more concerned to claim significant parallels with modern practice.

from financial complaints, through territorial disputes (probably the most common), to cases of outright aggression.[102] They could also come about through more than one process. One of these could, indeed, be coercion. Ps.Demosthenes' criticism of Philip for his claim that he would force the Cardians to submit to arbitration ([Dem.] 7.43–4) is based not on an objection to such threats, but on Philip's *hubris* in assuming that he could succeed where Athenian power had failed.[103] But arbitration also occurred – and for practical reasons was more likely to occur – when both sides had agreed to it, whether in the terms of a treaty, or through mutual agreement after a dispute had arisen. (An example of the latter type is the (failed) attempt at arbitration before the Corinthian War (*Hell.Oxy.* 21.4). A more questionable example of the former is the possible arbitration clause in the Common Peace of 362/1 (Tod 145).)[104]

It is, perhaps, possible to give too much emphasis to the impact of arbitration: it is, after all, an extremely imperfect method of international law enforcement, particularly in circumstances where there is no suitable third party to perform the arbitration.[105] The motives of states in choosing (or refusing) to submit to arbitration might also be questioned. It has been argued that arbitration would be resorted to only by those who were too weak to get their own way by other (usually military) means.[106] This is a position

[102] Tod 1913: ch. 2; Ager 1996: 4–7.   [103] On coerced arbitration, see Tod 1913: 74–5.

[104] Discussed as Piccirilli 1973: no. 48; see also Bengtson, *ad SV* ii.292 (RO 42 omits this part of the document). The text of the inscription at the relevant point (lines 18–21) is very uncertain, but there seems to be a reference to judges and to settlements; this would fit with a claim earlier in the same inscription: the Greeks διαλέλυνται τὰ <δ>[ιάφορα πρὸ]|[ς κ]οινὴν εἰρήνην, 'have put aside their differences towards a common peace' (lines 4–5; echoed in D.S. 15.89.1). For a balanced discussion of the possibilities (tending towards the conclusion that arbitration had taken place within the framework of the Common Peace) see Jehne 1994: 103–4.

[105] An obvious problem in the Peloponnesian War (Ager 1993: 11), and one which continues even in the less 'bi-polar' world of the fourth century: see, for example, Demosthenes' claim (reported by Aeschines) that there 'could be no impartial arbitrator' (οὐκ εἶναι κριτὴν ἴσον) between Athens and Philip II (3.83).

[106] Martin 1940: 573. Tod 1913: 187, takes a less cynical view. A related problem is the one of how far arbitral decisions were respected: in the absence of any good evidence on this subject, the view which is taken tends to depend on one's general opinion of the morality of the Greek city-states (Tod 1913: 187, is optimistic; Ager 1996: 32–3, less so).

which finds some support in classical sources, as, for example, in Ps.Demosthenes' *On Halonnesus*:

ὁπότε δ' ἡ μὲν δύναμις ἡ ὑμετέρα, ἡ ἐλευθερώσασα τοὺς Ἕλληνας, μὴ δύναται ὑμῖν τὰ ἐν τῇ θαλάττῃ χωρία σῴζειν, οἱ δὲ δικασταί, οἷς ἂν ἐπιτρέψητε, οἱ κύριοι τῆς ψήφου, οὗτοι ὑμῖν σώσουσιν, ἐὰν μὴ Φίλιππος αὐτοὺς πρίηται, πῶς ὑμεῖς οὐχ ὁμολογουμένως, ὅταν ταῦτα διαπράττησθε, τῶν ἐν τῇ ἠπείρῳ ἁπάντων ἀφεστήκατε, καὶ ἐπιδείκνυτε ἅπασιν ἀνθρώποις ὅτι οὐδὲ περὶ ἑνὸς αὐτῷ διαγωνιεῖσθε, εἴγε περὶ τῶν ἐν τῇ θαλάττῃ, οὗ φατὲ ἰσχύειν, μὴ διαγωνιεῖσθε, ἀλλὰ δικάσεσθε;

If you cannot preserve your maritime possessions by your power, that which once saved Greece, but rely on any jury to whom you refer it, and whose verdict is final, to save them for you, provided always that Philip does not buy their votes, how is that not an open confession, when you adopt this policy, that you have abandoned everything on the mainland, and are you not advertising to all men that there is not a single thing for which you will put up a fight, if indeed for your possessions on the sea, where you say your strength lies, you do not put up a fight but go to law?[107] ([Dem.] 7.7–8)

There is no way of knowing how widespread such opinions were – the 'true' motives of those who did undertake arbitration are not available to us. Nevertheless, the sincerity or insincerity of the parties involved does not alter the fact that both suggestions of arbitration and examples of arbitration having taken place are common enough in this period to make it an important factor in interstate law-enforcement.[108] This importance means, in turn, that arbitration could have a significant impact on the nature of Greek interstate society. Although force and coercion may have had a part to play in the road to arbitration, the act of arbitration itself provides one of the strongest counter-arguments to the claim that simple force is the only available mechanism for resolving interstate disputes. And the process of arbitration can, again, become an important contributor to the creation of ties of obligation between sets of states. This process is most visible in the Hellenistic and Roman periods,[109] but it occasionally surfaces in earlier cases. Perhaps

---

[107] Contrast [Dem.] 12.16–17, where arbitration is presented as a more positive option – and one which is κάλλιον ('better') than resorting to military force.
[108] Piccirilli 1973: nos. 32–61, and Ager 1996: nos. 1–7, list 37 arbitrations between 410 and 323 (and do not include cases where arbitration was suggested but did not take place).
[109] Ager 1996: 19–34.

the most striking example from the classical period is the fourth-century arbitration by Athens in an internal dispute at Paros, where (as was seen in Chapter 2) the act of arbitration is associated with the development of a strong Athenian claim to kinship with the Parians.[110] Once more, therefore, active involvement in maintaining the stability of the interstate system both has intrinsic general benefits, and brings specific advantages to individual states.

At this point, it seems appropriate to move on to consider the sanctions themselves. It might, however, be argued that this discussion of procedures has omitted the most obvious, and possibly most fundamental, method of enforcing interstate *nomoi* – namely, physical force, which, in interstate relations, most frequently equates to war. This omission was deliberate: military action represents the point at which the distinction between process and sanction, and indeed between the enforcement of *nomoi* and a whole range of other motives and practices in interstate behaviour, is hardest to maintain. War, it might be argued, is always likely to be the consequence of a broken interstate agreement – most obviously in the case of truces between two hostile parties. On a stronger version of the argument, truces and treaties are mere interruptions in a permanent condition of war between states, and the breaking of a treaty or truce will simply result in the reversion of interstate relations to their natural (warlike) condition.[111] The unquestioning bellicosity of the Greek states can, perhaps, be overemphasised, but the frequency of the recourse to war as a first resort might help to explain why the appearance of an explicit threat of military sanction as part of the terms of interstate agreement is a relatively late development. Its appearance is also closely associated with the major diplomatic

---

[110] See the discussion in ch. 2, sec. 3.

[111] The point is made most clearly by Plato in the *Laws*: πάσαις πρὸς πάσας τὰς πόλεις ἀεὶ πόλεμον ἀκήρυκτον κατὰ φύσιν εἶναι ('all *poleis* are, by nature, constantly engaged in an undeclared war with every other *polis*'; 626a4–5). It is accepted by, for example, Momigliano 1966c; de Romilly 1968: 207; rejected by Badian 1991: 44, n. 38; and questioned at greater length in Shipley 1993; Constantineau 1998: 9–12; Reus-Smit 1999: 41–4. Plato's assertion of a universal, and default, state of war should be distinguished from the more widely attested belief that treaties might only interrupt a specific pattern of hostility between two (or more) parties: the best example comes from the fifth century, in Sparta's alleged fear that hostilities with Argos would recommence as soon as the thirty-year peace between the two parties expired (Th. v.14.4; see Bederman 2001: 158); compare also Isocrates' complaint (4.172) that peace treaties are used only to postpone wars, not settle them.

phenomenon of the fourth century, namely the development of the Common Peaces. The history of these peaces has been frequently and thoroughly discussed,[112] and does not need to be repeated at length here. What is important in this context is the introduction, in the first (Spartan) Common Peace of 371, of a clause giving the option of enforcing the terms of the peace by military action. Xenophon provides the details:

δοξάντων δὲ τούτων καλῶς εἰπεῖν, ἐψηφίσαντο καὶ οἱ Λακεδαιμόνιοι δέχεσθαι τὴν εἰρήνην, ἐφ᾽ ᾧ τούς τε ἁρμοστὰς ἐκ τῶν πόλεων ἐξάγειν, τά τε στρατόπεδα διαλύειν καὶ τὰ ναυτικὰ καὶ τὰ πεζικά, τάς τε πόλεις αὐτονόμους ἐᾶν. εἰ δέ τις παρὰ ταῦτα ποιοίη, τὸν μὲν βουλόμενον βοηθεῖν ταῖς ἀδικουμέναις πόλεσι, τῷ δὲ μὴ βουλομένῳ μὴ εἶναι ἔνορκον συμμαχεῖν τοῖς ἀδικουμένοις.

Since these men were thought to have spoken well, the Lacedaemonians voted to accept the peace, with the provision that all should withdraw their governors from the cities, disband their forces both on sea and on land, and leave the cities independent. And if any state should act in violation of this agreement, any which so desired could aid the wronged cities, but that any which did not wish to do so was not under oath to be the ally of those who were wronged. (*HG* VI.iii.18)

This is the first evidence which we have for a clause of this sort, and it seems likely that it is the first time that such a clause appears in the Common Peaces.[113] The innovation here does not lie in the provision for military action itself, which is, of course, a standard element in bilateral treaties: in the case of attack on one party, the other will provide (military) assistance with all their strength.[114] Similar provisions also appear in multilateral treaties: the charter of the Second Athenian League (*IG* ii² 43, lines 46–51) is an obvious example from this period, and the second Common Peace of 371

---

[112] Especially by Jehne 1994; see also Ryder 1965 (and, more briefly, Momigliano 1966a; Moritani 1988).

[113] It has been argued (by Hampl 1938: 17; see also Cawkwell 1973: 53; Badian 1991: 46) that such a clause also appeared in earlier peaces. There is, however, no evidence that this was the case, and the suggestion is rejected by Ryder 1965: 68, 125 and Jehne 1994: 40–1, 60–1. For further discussion of this clause of the peace see ch. 5, sec. 2. More generally on sanctions clauses in the Common Peaces, see Jehne 1994: 68–70. The mss (followed by Lewis 1997b: n. 1) have εὔορκον in the final clause, but ἔνορκον seems to make more sense in this context.

[114] There are many examples. Typical ones include *IG* i³ 74 (= *SV* II.184), lines 12–14 (Athens and Halieis, 424/3); *IG* i³ 83 (= Th. v.47), lines 8–10, 12–15 (alliance of Athens, Argos, Mantineia and Elis, 418); RO 6, lines 4–11 (Athens and Boeotia, 395); *IG* ii² 15 (= Tod 102), lines 4–9 (Athens and Locris, 395); *IG* ii² 97 (= Tod 127), lines 2–11 (Athens and Corcyra, c.375). See Baltrusch 1994: 68–82.

also includes such a clause (X. *HG* VI.v.2).[115] The novelty in the first 371 peace is that the military action will be taken not against an aggressor coming from outside the community created by the treaty, but against someone inside that community who has transgressed the rules by which it is constituted. The community, and the rules, established by the peace could, in other words, continue to exist even after the agreement had been violated.[116]

Part of the reason why this might seem less problematic in this context is, of course, the multilateral nature of the Common Peaces: one party could defect from the agreement, but still leave more than one party with an interest in preserving it. Nevertheless, the sanctions clause of this treaty does highlight something which is true of all clauses of this type – that is, that they complicate the issue of determining when an agreement is broken, when it stops having any binding force, and whether the two need necessarily be the same. The more straightforward idea – that breaking an agreement destroys it completely – is often implicit in discussions of treaties and treaty breaking, and is occasionally formulated more explicitly. In the Demosthenic *On the Treaty with Alexander*, for example, the case is made that, once one party has stopped abiding by the terms of an agreement, it is mistaken to assume that the agreement should be considered valid ([Dem.] 17.5). Sanctions

---

[115] Xenophon's version of the clause is ἐὰν δέ τις στρατεύῃ ἐπί τινα πόλιν τῶν ὁμοσασῶν τόνδε τὸν ὅρκον, βοηθήσω παντὶ σθένει ('if anyone campaigns against any city of those which have sworn this oath, I shall aid them with all my strength'). This has been interpreted (e.g. by Ryder 1965: 132) as a stronger version of the sanctions clause in the first 371 peace; however, it seems to me that this clause applies not only (or even not at all?) to those inside the peace, but to any party which attacks one of those who have sworn the oath.

[116] A similar logic might be thought to lie behind Athens' actions against rogue members of the Delian League (for example, those described by Thucydides at 1.98–100), although Thucydides' representation of those actions seems to indicate a very different approach: the emphasis is not so much on a desire to maintain the stability of a wider community, as on Athens' concern to secure a specific, bilateral, relationship (see Meiggs 1972: 83–4 on the possible role of the allies (not mentioned by Thucydides) in the dispute with Thasos). If τὸ καθεστηκός ('that which was settled'), which was, according to Thucydides (1.98.4), breached by Athens in her attack on Naxos, is one of the founding principles of the Delian League then the contrast with the first 371 peace would be even stronger (this is the interpretation of Meiggs 1972: 70; Hornblower 1991 *ad loc.* takes it to be a more general reference to the principles of Greek interstate interaction; *HCT ad loc.* argues that either or both interpretations are possible). RO 31, lines 42–9, shows that it was possible to argue (in 369/8) that the Common Peace of 386 was also patrolled in this way (by the Athenians, at least).

clauses of the sort found in the first 371 peace show that this approach was not the only one which was available, and highlight again the difficulty of assuming the existence of a strict dichotomy between valid treaties (creating and containing international law) on one side and international anarchy on the other. Broken treaties do not just disappear, but continue to control explicitly or influence implicitly the behaviour of states who had participated in them.

The clause of the first Common Peace of 371 represents, therefore, a significant development in the use of military sanctions as a formal part of the maintenance of interstate agreements. Its appearance in this context is not, however, entirely without parallel. A very similar clause is found in another multilateral agreement – the oath of the Amphictions, as reported by Aeschines:[117]

ἔνορκον ἦν . . . μηδεμίαν πόλιν τῶν Ἀμφικτυονίδων ἀνάστατον ποιήσειν, μηδ’ ὑδάτων ναματιαίων εἴρξειν μήτ’ ἐν πολέμῳ μήτ’ ἐν εἰρήνῃ, ἐὰν δέ τις ταῦτα παραβῇ, στρατεύσειν ἐπὶ τοῦτον καὶ τὰς πόλεις ἀναστήσειν, καὶ ἐάν τις ἢ συλᾷ τὰ τοῦ θεοῦ, ἢ συνειδῇ τι, ἢ βουλεύσῃ τι κατὰ τῶν ἐν τῷ ἱερῷ, τιμωρή-σειν καὶ χειρὶ καὶ ποδὶ καὶ φωνῇ καὶ πάσῃ δυνάμει· καὶ προσῆν τῷ ὅρκῳ ἀρὰ ἰσχυρά.

They swore . . . that they would raze no city of the Amphictyonic states, and would not shut them off from flowing water either in war or in peace; that if

---

[117] It is not clear precisely where this document should be placed in the diachronic story of international law. The Amphictionic Oath is usually represented as an extremely early manifestation of Greek interstate regulation (see, as well as Aeschines, Egger 1866: 21; compare also its early position (II.104) in Bengtson's *Staatsverträge*), and on the traditional dating this clause would be the precursor of, and arguably model for, the sanctions clause of the 371 peace, rather than a (later) parallel to it. However, it has recently, and I think persuasively, been argued that this oath, and certainly Aeschines' version of it, owes much more to the historical circumstances of the mid-fourth century (and in particular those of the Third Sacred War) than to any archaic original: Sanchez 1997 points to the failure of any author earlier than Aeschines to mention this oath, even though there are occasions when it would seem to be extremely relevant (in Thucydides' account of the Theban attack on Plataea, for example, or in Isocrates' version of the Plataeans' accusations against the Thebans, who have razed their city for a second time). He also notes the suspiciously good fit between the oath, as represented by Aeschines, and the circumstances of the Third Sacred War, not to mention the specific requirements of Aeschines' argument at this point. Lefèvre (1998: 160–1), while not going quite so far as Sanchez, does provide some support for his argument in his suggestion that there was unlikely ever to have been a fixed 'Oath' – instead, the form of the oath would have changed over time, and have been affected by changing historical circumstances. If, finally, the oath is seen as a fourth-century creation, it would fit quite neatly into the series of similar documents, oaths and treaties, which are created (or re-created) in the fourth century and which, while ostensibly relating to earlier events, also fulfil an important contemporary purpose (see Habicht 1961; Robertson 1976; Davies 1996. The Oath of Plataea (RO 88) is a particularly relevant parallel).

anyone should violate this oath, they would march against him and raze his cities; and if any one should despoil the shrine of the god or be accessory to such an act, or make any plot against the holy places, they would punish him with hand and foot and voice, and all their power. To the oath was added a mighty curse. (2.115)

Comments on this passage have tended to concentrate on the attempt apparently preserved here to produce a more 'civilised' code for the conduct of war.[118] But the system envisaged for the enforcement of those regulations is also of some interest. The form of the agreement – an oath – and its combination with a 'mighty curse' (ἀρὰ ἰσχυρά) are clearly important,[119] but the parallel with the first 371 Common Peace is most prominent in the provision for a military sanction: in the case of violation of the oaths, punishment will take the form of a combined military expedition against the offender.[120]

What these two examples show is that what might seem to be the most basic form of sanction is, in this period at least, intimately connected with more complex developments of diplomatic practice, and, in particular, with different constructions of an interstate community. The enforcement of interstate rules through military action becomes, itself, a rule of interstate behaviour, adherence to which can have an effect both on a community of states as a whole and on the status of individual states within that community. Not only could military action on behalf of an injured party become the basis for the establishment of further and stronger connections between those involved, but the claim to leadership of that action was also, of course, a central factor in establishing a state's prestige.[121] Once more, it is possible to see how conspicuous concern to enforce interstate *nomoi* could become in itself a medium for increasing status and power.

---

[118] See, for example, Larsen 1944: 147; Kiechle 1969; Ilari 1980: 364–6; Lefèvre 1998: 149.

[119] See below: 122–5.

[120] Note the repetition of the verb ἀνίστημι ('raze'): a state which transgresses the terms of the oaths loses the right to protection under those terms.

[121] On the possibility of 'winning' a Common Peace, see ch. 2, n. 114. For the Delphic Amphictiony, a good example is Philip II's evident concern to be identified as the protector of the shrine, and of Apollo (illustrated in the story that the Macedonian forces at the Crocus Field wore the laurel wreaths appropriate for defenders of Apollo: Justin 8.2.3, possibly using Theopompus (Hammond 1991: 502–3)).

Questions of power are more immediately obvious in a second, apparently relatively unsophisticated, method of ensuring compliance with interstate agreements – the taking of hostages. In this case, however, the nature of the evidence presents a significant barrier to understanding fully how this sanction would have worked in practice. Although references to the taking (and sometimes releasing) of hostages are widely scattered through the literary and epigraphic records of the classical period, this broad range of evidence is correspondingly shallow in terms of detail. It does seem that hostage-taking could be used for a variety of purposes,[122] which are often associated less with the behaviour of states after interstate agreements had been made, and more with the preliminaries to those agreements. Hostages could be used as short-term guarantees, held while a formal agreement was under negotiation, or taken by force and used as a form of blackmail to encourage the co-operation (or capitulation) of the opposing party. The frequency of the forceful seizure of hostages can even make it difficult on some occasions to distinguish their status from that of prisoners of war.[123]

Nevertheless, there are some indications that hostage-taking also operated on a more long-term basis, and at a more formal level.[124] The most famous hostage of Greek history is probably Philip II of Macedon, who spent a number of his formative years in Thebes. It is generally agreed that his stay was of some length, which implies that the reason for his presence was to guarantee a long-term, if not

[122] Amit 1970 finds four: hostages can be used during peace negotiations between belligerents; used to guarantee implementation of long-term clauses in treaties; used to ensure the loyalty of allies; children of rulers can be taken hostage to ensure the loyalty of their father. See also Panagopoulos 1978: 188–92. Pritchett 1971–91, vol. V: 308–12, concentrating on the military aspect of hostage taking, lists as possible reasons or occasions: surrender of hostages by a city under siege; surrender of hostages by a defeated party to guarantee obedience to the victor; hostages held as sureties of the faithfulness of fighting contingents.

[123] The comparison is implicit in Panagopoulos 1978, and is occasionally made explicit (e.g., at 188); the usefulness of imposing any firm distinction at all is questioned by Cartledge 1980: 296.

[124] Compare the Suda's definition of the term: ὅμηρον, παρὰ θουκυδίδῃ, ἐνέχυρον τὸ εἰς εἰρήνην διδόμενον ἐπὶ συνθήκαις, 'hostage, in Thucydides: a surety given to ensure peace in the context of treaties' (and see also Phillipson 1911, vol. I: 398–406, who concentrates almost exclusively on this aspect of hostage-taking; Panagopoulos 1978: 187).

permanent, agreement. Even in such a famous case, however, little is known of the reason for, or the details of, his stay there,[125] and the evidence relating to less famous hostages is even less coherent. Two tombstones found in Athens (*IG* i³ 1373 and 1374)[126] record the names of two Thasian hostages who had, presumably, died and been buried in the city. However, not only are these two examples unique, but almost everything about them – from their date to their original location – is uncertain.[127] It is, though, interesting to note, first, that hostages are given a burial which, whether or not it had any 'official' input, nevertheless makes quite clear the reason why these Thasians were in Athens; second, that this burial is by no means as grand as that allowed to other foreigners who die in Athens while on some sort of official business.[128] The impression that hostages could often have a formal, official status is supported by the indications in the recorded discussions of treaty and truce-making that formal stipulations on hostages might form an important part of that process. Xenophon, for example, describes in the *Anabasis* how some Thracian tribesmen come to negotiate 'about a truce and hostages' (περὶ σπονδῶν καὶ ὁμήρων:

[125] For a comprehensive study of Philip's time in Thebes, see Hammond 1997. The evidence is both scattered and late: D.S. 15.67.4; Plu. *Pel.* 26.5–8; Justin 6.9.7, 7.5.2–3. On the uncertainty of any of this evidence, see Aymard 1954.

[126] = *IG* ii² 8827 & 8828..

[127] *IG* i³ dates both inscriptions to the end of the fifth century, a suggestion which is based on a presumed connection with Thrasybulus' expedition of 407 (X. *HG* I.iv.9). However, Athenian–Thasian relations in the fifth and fourth centuries are sufficiently turbulent to allow for a number of other possibilities. Boeckh (*ad CIG* 851) states that the stele of Cleodemus (*IG* i³ 1373) should be dated 'haud dubie non diu post Olymp. 100 [380], qua de re disputare longum est'. A date around 380 would, it is true, allow a connection with the disturbances suggested by *IG* ii² 33 (*c.* 385), or perhaps even with Thasos' entry into the Second Athenian League. On the other hand, Pouilloux (1954: 106, n. 3) suggests prosopographical reasons for placing Cleodemus in the middle of the fifth century. It is not even necessary that the usual assumption that the stones are contemporary is correct: the circumstances of their excavation are not entirely clear, but it is certain that they were not discovered as a pair. (*IG* i³ 1373 was found near the Syntagma cemetery (Kyparissis 1924/5: 71); *IG* i³ 1374 must have been discovered earlier, since it is reported by Boeckh to have been located 'in Lusierii museo'. It is now lost.)

[128] For example, the graves of the *proxenos* Pythagoras of Selymbria (*IG* i³ 1154); of the ambassador Silenos of Rhegion (*IG* ii² 5220); or of the two Corcyrean ambassadors, Thersander and Simylos (*IG* ii² 5224). All these are impressive monuments, in terms of both size and location. The 'intermediate' status of hostages – somewhere between prisoners and diplomats – is suggested (although supported by evidence from a later period) by Phillipson 1911, vol. I: 405–6. Some further suggestions on how, where, and for how long hostages were held in Lonis 1977: 225–30.

An. VII.iv.12). Earlier in that work, Thracian refusal to accept terms relating to hostages leads to the collapse of a proposed truce:

ἐπεὶ δὲ ἀπορία πολλὴ ἦν, διελέγοντο περὶ σπονδῶν· καὶ τὰ μὲν ἄλλα ὡμολόγητο αὐτοῖς, ὁμήρους δὲ οὐκ ἐδίδοσαν οἱ Θρᾷκες αἰτούντων τῶν Ἑλλήνων, ἀλλ᾽ ἐν τούτῳ ἴσχετο.

Since their situation had become serious, they started to negotiate about a truce; and on every other point an agreement had been reached, but the Thracians refused to give the hostages for which the Greeks asked, and this became a sticking point. (VI.iii.9)

What the sources seem to indicate is that the system of hostage-taking was, and was characterised as being, not so much one of a mutual exchange of pledges, as one of domination on one side and subservience on the other. Although, therefore, modern commentators sometimes talk in terms of 'exchange' of hostages,[129] the operation seems more often to have been a one-sided one. In the examples from the *Anabasis* mentioned above, for example, there is no suggestion that the *spondai* will be dependent on the provision of hostages from the Greek side. To be in a position to demand and hold hostages is equated with being in a position of power: this is clearly visible in Demosthenes' criticism of Charidemus for unnecessarily giving up hostages and so, according to Demosthenes, weakening the Athenian position to a point where the capture of Amphipolis was no longer possible (23.149–50). The converse is also true: giving hostages can be claimed to be one of the signs of having been defeated: it appears, for example, alongside the more familiar signs of lost power (dismantling of walls, surrender of the fleet) in Lysias' description of the terms which Theramenes promised (but failed) to obtain at the end of the Peloponnesian War:

ὑπέσχετο δὲ εἰρήνην ποιήσειν μήτε ὅμηρα δοὺς μήτε τὰ τείχη καθελὼν μήτε τὰς ναῦς παραδούς.

He promised to arrange a peace without giving any hostages or demolishing the walls or surrendering the ships. (12.68)

---

[129] For example Phillipson 1911, vol. 1: 398; the co-operative aspect of hostage-taking is also emphasised by Lonis 1977. There is some support for this view (see, for example, X. *HG* III.ii.18) but examples of exchange are much less common than cases of a one-way transfer.

The general picture which emerges, therefore, is that the use of hostages to control interstate behaviour both implies a threat of force (if regulations are broken) and is most likely to be based upon an existing position of power.

Other types of sanction, however, have a less immediate connection to physical force, or the threat of it. And although such types of sanction might be considered a humanising advance on the more direct methods of enforcement just described, they too have a long tradition in Greek interstate behaviour.

An early interstate treaty, between Elis and Heraea, contains a sanctions clause which has little to do with direct (mortal) force: the penalty set out for infractions of the treaty is a fine (of 1T of silver, to be paid to Olympian Zeus).[130] Fining remains a relatively commonly used sanction, although the examples from the classical period serve more to expand and perhaps complicate the picture rather than to provide strict parallels for that early example. In some cases the connection between the proposed fine and the possible (or actual) offence is quite straightforward. The Spartan decision before the Olynthian expedition of 382 to allow the allies' contribution of military personnel to be commuted to one of money is backed up by a provision to impose a fine (of one stater per man per day) on those who default (X. *HG* v.ii.21).[131] Although there is clearly a punitive element here, the financial context makes the imposition of a financial penalty seem appropriate, and perhaps less unexpected than it might appear in the Elean–Heraean alliance. Another obvious difference, which is nevertheless worth emphasising, is, again, the question of the power relationships implied by the Spartan regulation: whereas in the Elean–Heraean alliance, the fine will be payable to a third party, in this case it is Sparta (as *hegemon* of the Peloponnesian League) to whom the fine will be owed, and Sparta who will be responsible for imposing the sanction (ἐξεῖναι Λακεδαιμονίοις ἐπιζημιοῦν,

---

[130] ML 17 (= *SV* II.110), lines 5–6: αἰ δὲ μὰ συνέαν τάλαντον κ᾽] ἀργύρο ἀποτίνοιαν τοῖ Δὶ ᾽Ολυνπίοι 'if they do not stand by each other, those who do wrong shall pay a talent of silver to Olympian Zeus' (discussed by Baltrusch 1994: 9–11). The date is uncertain: the treaty was traditionally dated to the early or mid sixth century (see *SV* II *ad loc.*; accepted by Baltrusch 1994: 9, n. 35); Jeffery 1990: 219–20, no. 6 places it around 500 (accepted by ML; noted without comment in the addendum to *SV* II: 339).

[131] For the decision and its implications, see Cartledge 1987: 271.

'it will be permitted for the Lacedaemonians to exact the fine': v.ii.22).

In other examples, the power of an individual *polis* is less obviously important. There are some well-known cases of fines imposed (or demanded) by the Delphic Amphictiony in response to infringements of regulations. The extensive fines paid by the Phocians in the aftermath of the Third Sacred War are striking not only for their size, but also for the length of time over which they are paid.[132] As with the Spartan fine, however, the appropriateness of this type of penalty is easy to understand: the Phocians, who had plundered the treasures of Delphi, are both compensating and paying a penalty directly to the party which their actions had injured. In fact, in this case it is hard to make any firm distinction between reparation and punitive fine.

A more interesting example is the attempt made by the Amphictiony to fine Sparta for their attack on the Theban Cadmeia. The episode is reported by Diodorus: after Leuctra, the Thebans had brought a complaint before the Amphictions, who imposed a fine of 500 talents; when the Spartans failed to pay, the fine was increased to 1000 talents (D.S. 16.29). The offence which is being considered here has no direct connection to Delphi, although it could be argued that the religious aspect of Sparta's action (the attack took place during a religious festival: X. *HG* v.ii.29) made Delphi an appropriate place to lodge the complaint.[133] The crucial element must, however, be that both Thebes and Sparta were members of the Delphic Amphictiony, and thus in some way thought to be subject to the control of that body, even in actions which had no direct impact on it. It is worth noting too that, although the Spartans fail to pay the fine, their reasons for doing so – at least as represented by Diodorus – are based on the size of the fine and a belief in the injustice of the judgement (λέγοντες ἀδίκως . . . καταδεδικάσθαι, 'they said that they had been unjustly condemned'; 16.29.3), rather

---

[132] *F.Delphes* 3.5.14 (= RO 67), records payments from 343 onwards (totalling around 460T). The total amount owed is unknown – although the value of the treasures plundered is estimated (by Diodorus, 16.56.6) at more than 10,000T. For the details, concentrating on the financial implications of the fine, see Roux 1979: 164–72; Bousquet 1988.

[133] Lefèvre 1998: 242.

than any claim that the Amphictiony had no legitimate interest in the matter.

In this case, then, more than any of those considered so far, it is possible to see how one type of sanction could be employed in a variety of ways, and could have a variety of implications for the relationships between the states involved. It is also possible to see how the legitimacy of the enforcing body need not always depend on force alone. In the case of Sparta, the importance of military or hegemonic authority seems plain. But this is less true for the Delphic Amphictiony, whose status as a controlling authority over and between a broad community of Greek states rests on less immediately obvious foundations.

It is at this point that it seems appropriate to turn directly to the factor which has (quite artificially) been excluded from the discussion so far, but which is arguably the most important controlling mechanism of all: religion. This is a form of sanction which – perhaps because it is relatively alien to modern conceptions of law-enforcement – can be overlooked in favour of more tangible forms of control. Dependence on religion might even be claimed to compromise the status of international law as law.[134] Such an approach was, however, rejected many years ago by Phillipson:

> the religious sanction did not impair but added force to the legal and political sanction. Religion in antiquity was co-extensive with the whole of life . . . it was at the bottom of law because it was at the bottom of life.[135]

Phillipson's assertion that religion can be a fundamental basis for international law should, I think, be accepted. It has already been seen that gods might be claimed to be the ultimate source of *nomoi* – especially those of the more general, unwritten, variety.[136] But the religious aspect of law, and law enforcement in particular, is also visible much closer to the surface of law and of life, and not only

---

[134] On the challenge which the presence of religion might be thought to pose to the status of ancient international law, see Bederman 2001: 48–51 (and ch. 3 generally on religion and ancient international law). On religion and international law in the modern world, see Janis ed. 1991 (esp. the preface).

[135] Phillipson 1911, vol. 1: 51. Vinogradoff 1922: 20, and Bengtson 1965: 71, also emphasise the importance of religion. Martin 1940: 401–3, acknowledges the apparent presence of religion, but is less convinced of its actual importance.

[136] Above: 100–1.

in unwritten *nomoi* but also in formal, written, agreements. In the case of *spondai* (literally, 'libations') the original connection with religious practice is obvious,[137] but it is also present in the language associated with other types of interstate agreement: treaties are frequently described not just as συνθῆκαι ('agreements'), but as ὅρκοι καὶ συνθῆκαι, 'oaths and agreements'.[138]

It is even possible to see how, from some perspectives, oaths could be seen as the most important element of a treaty. The swearing of the oaths by the parties to the treaty represents the sign that the treaty has been accepted by both sides – it is, in other words, the closest equivalent to the ratification of modern treaties.[139] The existence of an oath can be an incentive to maintain a treaty: when the Athenians are attempting to decide whether to help Sparta in 370/69, for example, according to Xenophon πλεῖστος ἦν λόγος ὡς κατὰ τοὺς ὅρκους βοηθεῖν δέοι, 'the most powerful argument was that they should offer help in accordance with the oaths' (*HG* VI.v.36).[140] And, when a treaty is broken, it is often the breaking of the oaths which is highlighted. A good example of this can be seen in the various accounts of the truce made between the Ten Thousand and the Persian Tissaphernes. There are two conflicting accounts of which side broke their oaths, but both versions are informative. According to Isocrates, it was the Persian who was at fault: his act (as was mentioned above)[141] was one of *paranomia*:

ὁ βασιλεὺς . . . τοὺς ἄρχοντας τοὺς τῶν ἐπικούρων ὑποσπόνδους συλλαβεῖν ἐτόλμησεν, ὡς εἰ τοῦτο παρανομήσειε συνταράξων τὸ στρατόπεδον, καὶ μᾶλλον εἵλετο περὶ τοὺς θεοὺς ἐξαμαρτεῖν ἢ πρὸς ἐκείνους ἐκ τοῦ φανεροῦ διαγωνίσασθαι.

---

[137] See Phillipson 1911, vol. I: 392–3; Adcock & Mosley 1975: 229; Baltrusch 1994: 99–104.

[138] See, for example, Aeschin. 3.66, 70; Dem. 15.26; [Dem.] 17.1. The same combination is found in references to *summachiai*: see, for example, Aeschin. 2.138.

[139] Heuß 1934: 14–53; Mosley 1961; Lonis 1980: 268 (with the example of the Plataean claim (Thuc. II.5.6) that their truce with the Thebans was not valid because an oath had not been sworn); Badian 1991: 37–9 (accounting for reports that the Persian King would have sworn to the Common Peace by pointing out that the idea of oath-swearing was so ingrained in the Greek conception of treaty-making that it was likely to be assumed to have taken place even in implausible contexts). An oath was last used to confirm a treaty in the Franco-Swiss alliance of 1777 (Wheeler 1984: 253, n. 5).

[140] On the question of the treaty to which these oaths belong, see Lewis 1997b: 30–1.

[141] 98.

The King . . . dared to arrest the commanders of the auxiliaries in violation of the truce, hoping by this lawless act to throw the army into confusion, and he preferred to offend against the gods rather than to fight in plain view. (4.147)

In Xenophon's version of events, it is not the Persians but the Greeks – and specifically Clearchus – who are (or who are allegedly) to blame:

Κλέαρχος μέν, ὦ ἄνδρες Ἕλληνες, ἐπεὶ ἐπιορκῶν τε ἐφάνη καὶ τὰς σπονδὰς λύων, ἔχει τὴν δίκην καὶ τέθνηκε.

Clearchus, men of Greece, since he was shown to be perjuring himself and violating the truce, has received his deserts and is dead.[142] (*An.* II.v.38)

These two versions also suggest two different approaches to how the violation of an oath might be punished. The Tissaphernic approach returns the action, once again, to the human sphere: violation of oaths is an act which demands immediate justice, administered by the injured party. This is not an unparalleled claim. A comparable assertion appears in a *Letter* of Philip, complaining about the Peparethian seizure of Halonnesus:

τί οὖν ἐχρῆν με ποιεῖν; οὐ δίκην λάβειν παρὰ τῶν ὑπερβεβηκότων τοὺς ὅρκους; οὐ τιμωρήσασθαι τοὺς οὕτως ὑπερηφάνως ἀσελγαίνοντας;

'What, then, was I to do? Was I not to punish those who had violated their oaths? Was I not to take vengeance for such an egregious outrage?' ([Dem.] 12.15)

However, the idea that oath-breaking, as an offence against the gods, could be left to the gods to punish is also a common one.[143] Before meeting his unfortunate end, Xenophon's Clearchus had made a strong statement of the case:

πρῶτον μὲν γὰρ καὶ μέγιστον οἱ θεῶν ἡμᾶς ὅρκοι κωλύουσι πολεμίους εἶναι ἀλλήλοις· ὅστις δὲ τούτων σύνοιδεν αὐτῷ παρημεληκώς, τοῦτον ἐγὼ οὔποτ' ἂν εὐδαιμονίσαιμι. τὸν γὰρ θεῶν πόλεμον οὐκ οἶδα οὔτ' ἀπὸ ποίου ἂν τάχους οὔτε ὅποι ἄν τις φεύγων ἀποφύγοι οὔτ' εἰς ποῖον ἂν σκότος ἀποδραίη οὔθ' ὅπως ἂν εἰς ἐχυρὸν χωρίον ἀποσταίη.

---

[142] Compare the version of Ctesias (*FGH* 688 F27, lines 21–2): Tissaphernes 'conquered' the Greeks 'by oaths' (ὅρκοις ἐχειρώσατο: line 24). It is, of course, not improbable that the Greeks and Persians understood and expected quite different things from these oaths (on Greek/Persian misunderstandings in general, see Mitchell 1997a: ch. 6) – what is interesting, however, is the Greek assumption of a universal system of values.

[143] Note also the reference to gods as *proxenoi* of the alliance between Sybaris and the Serdaeans (*SV* II.120, lines 5–8 (= ML 10); see Lonis 1980: 271). On belief in gods as punishers of wrongdoing in domestic law, see Saunders 1991: 75.

For, first and most important, our oaths, sworn by the gods, stand in the way of our being enemies of one another; and the man who is conscious that he has disregarded such oaths, I for my part should never call happy. For in war with the gods I do not know either by what speed of foot or to what place a man could escape, or into what darkness he could sneak away, or how he could withdraw himself to a secure fortress. (*An.* II.v.7)

In other contexts, it is easier to see that these two approaches should be seen as representing different ends of a continuous spectrum rather than two exclusive alternatives: human and divine action will combine to punish those who break their oaths. Again, Xenophon provides the best examples of the phenomenon. The most infamous of these is his analysis of Spartan decline in terms of the divine retribution visited on the Spartans for their infractions of the Common Peace and disregard of their oaths:

πολλὰ μὲν οὖν ἄν τις ἔχοι καὶ ἄλλα λέγειν καὶ Ἑλληνικὰ καὶ βαρβαρικά, ὡς θεοὶ οὔτε τῶν ἀσεβούντων οὔτε τῶν ἀνόσια ποιούντων ἀμελοῦσι· νῦν γε μὴν λέξω τὰ προκείμενα. Λακεδαιμόνιοί τε γὰρ οἱ ὀμόσαντες αὐτονόμους ἐάσειν τὰς πόλεις τὴν ἐν Θήβαις ἀκρόπολιν κατασχόντες ὑπ' αὐτῶν μόνων τῶν ἀδικηθέντων ἐκολάσθησαν.

One could produce many other examples, both Greek and barbarian, to prove that the gods do not ignore the wicked or those who do impious things; now, however, I will discuss only the present case. The Lacedaemonians had sworn that they would leave the cities independent, and, after seizing possession of the Acropolis of Thebes, were punished by the very men, unaided, who had been wronged. (*HG* v.iv.1)

Divine influence is, for Xenophon, apparent; but the agents of retribution are those who have been harmed by the Spartans' impiety.

The positive expression of that view can be seen most clearly in Xenophon's account of Agesilaus' attitude to oaths and treaties. It is worth noting that Agesilaus' respect for these things is one of the first items cited by Xenophon as evidence of the Spartan's respect for the gods (which, in turn, is the first of the virtues in Xenophon's catalogue):

Ἀγησίλαος γὰρ τὰ μὲν θεῖα οὕτως ἐσέβετο ὡς καὶ οἱ πολέμιοι τοὺς ἐκείνου ὅρκους καὶ τὰς ἐκείνου σπονδὰς πιστοτέρας ἐνόμιζον ἢ τὴν ἑαυτῶν φιλίαν.

Agesilaus had such reverence for religion that even his enemies considered his oaths and his treaties to be more trustworthy than their own friendship with one another. (*Ages.* III.2)

Agesilaus' approach has already been seen in action in the narrative with which the *Agesilaus* opens. The villain is, again, Tissaphernes, who, having arranged a truce with Agesilaus, immediately breaks his oath (I.10–11). Agesilaus, although aware of Tissaphernes' duplicity, nevertheless chooses to stick to his side of the agreement, secure in the knowledge, according to Xenophon, that the gods will now be on his side:

Ἀγησίλαος δὲ μάλα φαιδρῷ τῷ προσώπῳ ἀπαγγεῖλαι τῷ Τισσαφέρνει τοὺς πρέσβεις ἐκέλευσεν ὡς πολλὴν χάριν αὐτῷ ἔχοι ὅτι ἐπιορκήσας αὐτὸς μὲν πολεμίους τοὺς θεοὺς ἐκτήσατο, τοῖς δ᾽ Ἕλλησι συμμάχους ἐποίησεν

Agesilaus, with a beaming face, instructed the envoys to inform Tissaphernes that he was profoundly grateful to him for his perjury, by which he had established the gods as his enemies, and made them allies of the Greeks.[144] (I.13)

Xenophon's attitude to the role of the gods in interstate politics has been subject to some stern criticism from modern commentators,[145] but there are grounds for thinking that his views on divine sanctions should not immediately be dismissed. Not only are interstate agreements usually ratified by oaths, but these oaths are, in turn, frequently accompanied by a reference to the possible consequences of transgression.[146] These references can be left quite vague, as, for example, in the treaty of 375 between Athens and Corcyra (*IG* ii² 97 (= Tod 127)):

[ε]ὐο-
[ρ]κõντι μέμ μοι εἴη πολ[λ]ὰ καὶ ἀγαθά, εἰ δὲ
[μή], τἀναντία.

---

[144] The account in *HG* III.iv.11 is identical. (On Xenophon's representation of Agesilaus' piety, see Luppino 1991: 103–7; respect for oaths is also represented as a positive characteristic of Cyrus the Younger: *An.* I.ix.7–8.) On the emphasis on respect for oaths as a consistent feature of Xenophon's approach to religion, see Pownall 1998: esp. 253–4. Compare also [Dem.] 11.2: Philip's treachery is such that the Athenians should expect that the gods will be μεγίστους . . . συμμάχους καὶ βοηθούς, 'the greatest allies and helpers'; Isoc. 14.28–9: the seizure of the Cadmeia represents divine punishment for Theban perfidy.

[145] Note especially Cawkwell 1979: 45: 'The hand of God is an explanation that dulls the quest for truth, but it is the explanation to which Xenophon, so unlike Thucydides, readily had recourse'. (For the possibility that it is Thucydides', not Xenophon's, approach to religion that requires special explanation, see Hornblower 1992a; oaths and curses do, of course, play a significant role in even Thucydides' narrative of the Peloponnesian War: see Schmidt 1990.) A more sympathetic approach to Xenophon's attitude to the gods and religion can be found in Dillery 1995: ch. 7.

[146] A common feature in all oaths: see Plescia 1970: 11–12.

If I keep my oath, may I have many good things; if not, the opposite.[147] (lines 24–6 (Athenian oath); repeated in the Corcyrean oath, lines 36–8).

This general threat of unpleasant consequences is the most common formulation of a possible religious sanction,[148] but it was possible, too, for the general threat to be expanded into a more specifically formulated curse. It has been seen that the Amphictionic Oath described by Aeschines included provisions for a military sanction in case of transgression, but it was also supplemented by a 'mighty curse' (ἀρὰ ἰσχυρά: Aeschin. 2.115). Aeschines does not here specify the form of that curse, but, in a discussion of another Amphictionic oath (allegedly sworn after the First Sacred War), he is more specific. While it need not, of course, follow that the curse was the same in both cases, his description is nevertheless worth quoting to give some idea of the likely form of such an imprecation:

'εἴ τις τάδε' φησὶ 'παραβαίνοι ἢ πόλις ἢ ἰδιώτης ἢ ἔθνος, ἐναγής' φησὶν 'ἔστω τοῦ Ἀπόλλωνος καὶ τῆς Ἀρτέμιδος καὶ [τῆς] Λητοῦς καὶ Ἀθήνας Προναίας.' καὶ ἐπεύχεται αὐτοῖς μήτε γῆν καρποὺς φέρειν μήτε γυναῖκας τέκνα τίκτειν γονεῦσιν εοικότα, ἀλλὰ τέρατα, μήτε βοσκήματα κατὰ φύσιν γονὰς ποιεῖσθαι, ἧτταν δὲ αὐτοῖς εἶναι πολέμου καὶ δικῶν καὶ ἀγορῶν καὶ ἐξώλεις εἶναι καὶ αὐτοὺς καὶ οἰκίας καὶ γένος τὸ ἐκείνων. 'καὶ μήποτέ' φησιν 'ὁσίως θύσειαν τῷ Ἀπόλλωνι μηδὲ τῇ Ἀρτέμιδι μηδὲ τῇ Λητοῖ μηδ' Ἀθηνᾷ Προναίᾳ, μηδὲ δέξαιντο αὐτῶν τὰ ἱερά'.

'If any one should violate this', it says, 'whether city or private man, or tribe, let them be under the curse,' it says, 'of Apollo and Artemis and Leto and Athena Pronaea'. The curse goes on: That their land bear no fruit; that their wives bear children not like those who begat them, but monsters; that their flocks yield not their natural increase; that defeat await them in war and court and market-place, and that they perish utterly, themselves, their houses, their whole race; 'And never,' it says, 'may they offer pure sacrifice to Apollo, nor to Artemis, nor to Leto, nor to Athena Pronaea, and may the gods refuse to accept their offerings'.[149] (3.110–11)

---

[147] The interest of the gods in controlling this agreement is emphasised, too, by the appearance of Athena, Hera and Zeus in the relief which accompanies the inscription (Lawton 1995: no.96). On the document (and its relation to *IG* ii² 96 (Tod 126)), see most recently Fauber 1998: esp. 111–15.

[148] Compare *SV* II.297, lines 87–90 (*synoikia* agreement between Orchomenos and Euaimon, 360s/50s); *SV* II.307, lines 14–15 (alliance of Grabos, king of Illyria, and Chalkis, 357); RO 50, lines 5–7 (alliance of Philip II and Chalcideans, 357/6). On the consequences of broken oaths, see Parker 1983: 186–8.

[149] The Oath of Plataea provides a parallel, with a similarly explicit curse (RO 88, lines 39–51, with Siewert 1972: 98–101). On similarities of content between the two oaths,

The available evidence does not allow us to infer with certainty how regularly curses of this sort might have been used in this period. It is worth noting that curses were a relatively common feature in the contemporary domestic sphere, in both private (particularly in legal disputes)[150] and public contexts. A good example of the latter kind from a fourth-century text, although again allegedly preserving a much earlier action, is the 'sympathetic' curse of the foundation oath of Cyrene.[151] The association of curses with interstate agreements is visible in both earlier and later periods,[152] and has also been perceived to be present in agreements from this period, even when explicit evidence is lacking. It has been noted, for example, that the rituals associated with the oath sworn between the Persian Ariaeus and the Ten Thousand (X. *An*. II.ii.8–9) include elements which imply that there was a curse involved.[153]

see Daux 1953. At 3.121 Aeschines refers to a further clause, imposing a curse on those who fail to punish transgressions of the oath: again, therefore, the expectation of divine action does not exclude human action.

[150] See in general, Parker 1983: ch. 6; Watson 1991: ch. 1; Gager 1992; Cole 1996; Faraone 1999: esp. 103–11.

[151] ML 5, lines 40–51. See Faraone 1993.

[152] Earlier: e.g. the oath and curse of the Achaean-Trojan agreement of *Iliad* III.298–301 (on which see Karavites 1992: 104–6). Later (in terms of composition, if not dramatic date): e.g. the Roman *foedus*-making procedure described at Livy I.24. The importance of curses to Greek international law is noted briefly by Glotz 1915: 94; Lonis 1980 is less sure of their value. It has been suggested (by Dušanić 1994: 98–9) that we should assume that the 'charter' of the Second Athenian League was reinforced by curses – a claim for which, however, there is no positive supporting (or contradictory) evidence.

[153] Faraone 1993: 65–6, 79. The throwing of iron lumps into the sea associated with the oath of the Delian League ([Arist.] *Ath.* 23.5; Plut. *Arist.* 25.1) has also been reinterpreted (by Jacobson 1975; accepted by Faraone 1993: 79) as a form of sympathetic cursing. (That is, as accompanying some curse such as 'may any party that violates this treaty sink/disappear, just as this metal sinks', rather than as implying permanence.) Lonis 1980: 275–8, argues that the idea of sympathetic cursing cannot be applied to Greek practice. Not strictly relevant to the argument here, but worth noting nevertheless, is the question of the identity of the potential victim of a curse: in some cases (as in the Plataean oath and curse) the scope is explicitly broad (individual, family, *polis*); elsewhere (in the Athenian/Corcyrean alliance, for example) it is much narrower: the oath and curse apply only to the individual swearing it. Descriptions of the effects of curses show similar variation: X. *HG* v.iv.1 suggests that Spartan perfidy caused general Spartan disaster; contrast [X.] *Ath.* II.17, which suggests a much greater degree of individual liability. For representations of the opposing points of view, see Lonis 1980: 278–9 (emphasising the individual); Cole 1996: 240–1 (emphasising the collective). The variety in the formulation of these oaths and curses seems to me to illustrate quite neatly the fluid approach to questions of agency in interstate relations which is visible elsewhere too (see further ch. 4).

It has been pointed out that the strengthening of agreements in this way (whether through general imprecations or specific curses) is most appropriate in contexts where offences against the agreement would be 'particularly hard to guard against on a human level',[154] or when the likelihood of violations seems especially strong.[155] Both of these factors are, of course, extremely relevant to the sphere of interstate agreements, and suggest why the religious aspect of their enforcement might have been considered so important by Xenophon, and why it would be a mistake to exclude that aspect from any model of international law-enforcement in classical Greece.

The practice of invoking divine sanction also raises important issues of power and authority. To be in a position to proclaim a curse in a public context implies that the curser possesses some authority. This authority need not, however, be equated with pure power:

> it is, however, to rights rather than raw power that they [curses] relate, and if they commonly consort with authority that is because the rights of communities and parents are in fact very extensive. Even the strong can perhaps not curse effectively unless wronged, while the weak acquire the power to do so in so far as their recognized rights are infringed.[156]

This argument can also, I think, be applied to an interstate environment. The Delphic Amphictiony is a good example of an interstate organisation which possesses considerable authority in the Greek world, but has comparatively limited access to the direct force with which that authority could be asserted.[157] It is, therefore, in precisely this context that references to curses and divine sanctions might be expected to appear most prominently. The appeal to divine sanctions is a way, therefore, in which the inevitable inequalities of 'raw power' in the international system could, if not be evened out,

---

[154] Parker 1983: 194.   [155] Faraone 1993: 79; Faraone 1999: 108.

[156] Parker 1983: 197. The issue of 'recognized rights' is a problematic one in a Greek context (see Schofield 1999), and even if infringement of rights is taken in a fairly limited sense – the contravention of the terms of a treaty or other agreement – it is clear that the question could still be the subject of contestation.

[157] The Delphic Amphictiony does, of course, have the possibility of recourse to military power (as was noted above: 111–12), but in practical terms this power would be weakened by the fact that it was exercised not by the Amphictiony itself, but by member states who would act (or fail to act) on its behalf (see Lefèvre 1998: 159–61).

at least become less relevant to the question of the enforcement of international *nomoi*.

The international *nomoi* of the Greek world are not, therefore, entirely empty pledges. Although it is impossible to deny that they were frequently broken, it is also true that there existed a whole range of procedures and practices by which adherence to them could be encouraged, and breaches punished. It is important to emphasise that, although the various types of sanctions have been considered separately, they should not be considered as methods which were available only for isolated, exclusive use, or as forming a part of some sort of evolution of strategies of law enforcement.[158] Certain types of sanction are, admittedly, more common in certain contexts: religious sanctions, for example, are particularly appropriate in the enforcement of the 'unwritten' *nomoi* associated with treatment of heralds, burial of war-dead and so on.[159] But the choice of the type of sanction employed, and of the way in which it is used, and by whom (and even whether it is used at all) may often depend not only on the nature of the offence but also on the status and motives of the parties involved. Law enforcement may not, that is, always be dependent on force, but it is frequently very closely tied to questions of power.

3.5 Conclusions

The Greek society of states was not a lawless one. The *nomoi* of interstate activity may not always have been adhered to, but they are nevertheless a prominent feature of interstate life. These *nomoi* do not necessarily provide a rigid system by which every aspect of relations between states can be controlled and regulated, but what they do provide is a broader framework within which interstate behaviour takes place, and by which it can be judged.[160]

The presence of laws does not entail the presence of legalism: we need not assume 'that legal orders represent closed systems

---

[158] Whether towards a more 'humane' system (as suggested by Walker 1899: 43), or away from more abstract modes of enforcement (primarily appeal to the gods) and towards more concrete methods (suggested by Plescia 1970: 71–2). Bengtson 1965: 71 warns against evolutionary views of Greek international law.

[159] See Parker 1983: 43–4, 188.   [160] See Kratochwil 1989: 10–11.

which are susceptible to complete mapping *and* logical formalisation'.[161] The international rules, customs and laws of the Greek
world are always subject to creation, recreation and reinterpretation. This is a process which cannot take place in isolation – it
requires a community, or a society, of states. Although the creation and enforcement of law cannot be separated from questions
of power, and sometimes also of force, the importance attributed to
consensus cannot be ignored.[162] Treaties, for example, should be
made between equal, and consenting, partners (they are συνθῆκαι,
'agreements', not προστάγματα, 'instructions').[163] The unwritten *nomoi* of interstate relations are shared by all (right-thinking)
members of the society of states. And their maintenance is also,
often, a matter of consensus rather than enforcement. If one party
to a bilateral agreement breaks his oath, then the others need feel
no obligation to maintain theirs.[164] The (alleged) Athenian plan
to mutilate their prisoners of war after Aegospotami, for example, is an act of *paranomia* which means that their own prisoners
can no longer expect *nomimos* treatment (X. *HG* ii.i.32). Actions
within the society of states are, to an extent, constrained by *nomoi*,
but those *nomoi* rely in turn on the willingness of members of the
interstate society to accept them.[165]

The answers which have emerged from this study of international law also reinforce some of the conclusions which were
reached when considering the question of international society,
and, in particular, those related to the issue of the nature of the
boundaries of, and within, that interstate society. Several of the

---

[161] Kratochwil 1989: 41 (emphasis in original).

[162] Emphasised by Martin 1940: 402; see also the conclusions reached by Bederman 2001:
279: the story of ancient international law is 'the story of the creation of a nascent
community'.

[163] Isoc. 4.176. See also Andoc. 3.11–12 on the difference between a peace (which is made
ἐξ ἴσου, 'on the basis of equality') and a truce (in which terms are dictated by the victor
to the defeated). The representation of equality may, however, be quite distant from the
reality (as suggested by Missiou 1987). On equality and inequality in the formulation
of treaties and oaths, see Pistorius 1985.

[164] See [Dem.] 17.12 for the claim that violated treaties need no longer be considered
valid. Xenophon's description (*Ages.* 1.10–12) of Agesilaus' decision not to go back on
his agreement when Tissaphernes broke his oath implies that such behaviour was both
praiseworthy and unusual.

[165] Compare Dem. 21.224–5 on the connection between the support of the people and the
existence of domestic law. See also Cohen 1993, 1995: ch. 3.

examples used above have involved relations between Greeks and those outside the 'Greek world' proper. Although some *nomoi* are specifically described as being 'of the Greeks', this is perhaps less common than might be expected. Barbarians may often be represented as being conspicuously perfidious, and liable to violate international *nomoi*, but it is notable nevertheless that this behaviour is depicted, and criticised, in terms of those *nomoi*. The implication is, usually, that it would have been reasonable to expect that the same systems of rules and customs would apply to all members of the international society, not just the Greek society of states. It has also been possible to detect the creation of smaller communities within that larger society – bound by the *nomoi* of, for example, the Delphic Amphictiony, or the Common Peaces, or – at the smallest level – the regulations of bilateral agreements.

A question of boundaries of a different sort has also been raised: it has been seen that the distinction between domestic and external law is at times hard to maintain. This seems to reflect a more widespread uncertainty. Where does the *polis*, and its interests, stop and the outside world begin? What, exactly, constitutes a single *polis*? And how far are the patterns of behaviour which are appropriate within a state distinct from those used in external relations? These problems will be considered in the next two chapters.

4

DOMESTIC MORALITY, INTERSTATE
MORALITY

4.1 Introduction: a domestic analogy?

In the discussion in the previous chapter of the processes and structures which characterise the construction of *nomoi* within and beyond the *polis*, it became clear that the boundary between 'inside' and 'outside', between domestic and external, is often somewhat indistinct. What I intend to do in this chapter is to concentrate on that problem – the presence or absence of that boundary – but to approach it from a different angle: that of the morals (or ethics)[1] of interstate behaviour.

One of the most firmly held tenets of International Relations, and particularly of Realist approaches to it, is the belief that a strict line

---

[1] There is a problem of terminology here. Many philosophers, thinking of the technical philosophical distinction between 'ethics' and 'morality', would object to the use of the latter term in ancient Greek contexts (or at least insist that its use implies definite assumptions about specific characteristics of Greek philosophy. On the dissimilarity of ancient and modern approaches to ethics, see Williams 1981: 241–53; Williams 1993: esp. ch. 1; see Annas 1992 for the suggestion that there may be more common ground between ancient and modern). In non-philosophical usage, however, it is 'ethics' which is the more loaded term, implying systematised, usually philosophical, thought, as opposed to 'popular' approaches (see Dover 1974: 1). It is this second, non-technical, approach which will be found in what follows: 'ethics' will generally be used of (systematic) philosophical writing, 'morality' of non-philosophical. However, the difficulty of maintaining a strict distinction between those two categories must also be emphasised. It is certainly true that 'if we imagined that either Plato's work or Aristotle's represented an intellectual system-atization of the principles which were manifested in the moral choices and judgements of the ordinary unphilosophical Greek, it is possible that we might go badly astray' (Dover 1974: 1–2; similar views in Pearson 1962: 212; Whitehead 1993: 38–9). However, there is also some danger in overestimating the degree of access which any (literary) material allows to the opinions of the 'ordinary' Greek (are Xenophon and Isocrates 'popular' or 'philosophical', for example?), as well as underestimating the degree to which the arguments of Plato and Aristotle, while reaching novel conclusions, may nevertheless be grounded in more widely held assumptions (Annas 1978: 450; Taylor 1990; on the difficulty of maintaining a distinction between 'lived' and 'preached' morality, see Den Boer 1979: 2–4; on the possibility that philosophical arguments could influence 'popular' thought, see Adkins 1978: 143–6). The most sensible approach seems likely to be one which makes use of as broad a range of evidence as possible, but does so with sensitivity to its genre and context.

can be drawn between domestic and international life. The reasons for this attitude are not purely theoretical,[2] but a clear theoretical justification for it can be found in Hobbes (or in International Theorists' readings of him). If the international arena is to be characterised as a Hobbesian state of nature, then in that arena, in the absence of any true law, there can be no true justice (or injustice). It is only in civil society that law, and justice, can be found.[3]

Two basic responses to the Hobbesian position can be identified, both of which can be given the description of the 'domestic analogy'. The first approach is to deny the validity of Hobbes' basic claim, and to argue that moral values can have a place in a state of nature, and, therefore, in international relations.[4] The second, much more influential, approach is to accept the legitimacy of the Hobbesian view, but to attempt to find ways to overcome it. This leads to a domestic analogy of a different sort: the attempt to create order in the international system by extending features of civil society into the sphere of relations between states; to create, in Hobbesian terms, a 'greater Leviathan'. It is this tradition, closely associated with liberal, Idealist attitudes to international relations, which lies behind, for example, the establishment of the League of Nations.[5] The importance of this approach lies, however, not so much in its own achievements as in the reaction which it provoked. The idea developed, in conscious opposition to these liberal domestic analogy proposals, that relations between states cannot be understood as being analogous to those between individuals, and that any proper understanding of interstate relations must be based on the acceptance of this point.[6] The rejection of

---

[2] Disciplinary and methodological factors are important too (see ch. 1, sec. 2).

[3] The key text is Hobbes 1996 (1651): ch. 13: 'To this warre of every man against every man, this also is consequent; that nothing can be unjust. The notions of Right and Wrong, Justice and Injustice have there no place. Where there is no common Power, there is no Law: where no Law, no Injustice.' For a brief discussion of these ideas, and their relationship to interstate relations, see Boucher 1998: ch. 7; on the importance of the historical context to Hobbes' theory, see Jahn 1999.

[4] Such a reaction could be based on the Lockean state of nature, in which moral laws do exist independently of civil society. On this approach, see Bull 1966b: 48; Graham 1997: 17–20; Hobson 2000: 90.

[5] On this tradition, its origins, and responses to it, see esp. Suganami 1989.

[6] For the classic statement of the case, see Bull 1966b: 'although we may employ such analogies, we must in the end abandon them . . . The working of international society must be understood in terms of its own, distinctive institutions' (48); further discussion in

the analogy extends to the question of morality: even if it were to be enforceable, the moral framework which is appropriate to relations between individuals should not be thought to be appropriate to relations between states.[7]

It is this version of the argument which is, I think, most familiar to historians of ancient Greece, although they – with de Ste. Croix – may prefer to see Thucydides rather than Hobbes as the originator of the idea:

it is precisely this 'moral bleakness' of Thucydides *in regard to international affairs* which is for me his unique virtue, shared with no other historian of antiquity and with few of any age. It is his wholesale application of the principle that 'moral' considerations of the kind that can and should be regarded inside the State are simply not transferable in their existing form to international affairs, *even to the actions of one's own State*, that gives him his unparalleled realism.[8]

And it is also this version of the argument which I want to explore in this chapter, dividing the enquiry into three broad areas: the nature of the morally evaluative language used of interstate activity (and the extent to which it overlaps with that used of domestic activity); the evidence for more general assumptions of, or arguments for, the comparability of the two spheres of activity; and, finally, the evidence for arguments against that view.

In the course of this exploration, some other issues will arise: the problem of the relationship between the individual, groups of individuals and the *polis* in the conduct of foreign relations;[9] the extent to which moral judgements reflect on the community which makes them as much as on the individual (or thing) which is judged; the relationship between τὸ συμφέρον ('self-interest') and τὸ δίκαιον ('justice'). But the focus remains not so much an attempt to define

---

Suganami 1989: 11–12. The rejection of the domestic analogy, although clearly suited to a Realist approach to IR, is not restricted to it: even those who argue for the possibility of the creation of a moral code for international relations tend to accept as a starting point the idea that such a code could not be the same as that which applies to domestic behaviour (see Kokaz 2001: 30–2). The impossibility of interaction between inside and outside was, until relatively recently, a belief which was rarely challenged: see Beitz 1979; Walker 1993.

[7] Graham 1997: 19.

[8] De Ste. Croix 1972: 23–4 (emphases original). De Ste. Croix did see some echoes of this Thucydidean world-view elsewhere in classical Greek writing (especially in Demosthenes and Aristotle: 16–17).

[9] A version of the level of analysis problem: see Hollis & Smith 1990: ch. 7.

a substantive ethical or moral code of Greek interstate activity,[10] as an enquiry at the next level of abstraction: how are the various claims to the morality (or immorality) of interstate behaviour represented, and how do those representations relate to claims about domestic morality? In other words, I am, here, not particularly concerned with attempting to attack (or defend) the view that

Greeks, and Mediterranean people generally, have what today strikes Nordics and Americans as an incredible callous attitude to violence and suffering, and the same was true *a fortiori* in Antiquity.[11]

Nor, to take a less contentious example, is the existence of a moral code of helping friends and harming, cheating or deceiving enemies of direct interest in its own right;[12] what is of interest is the extent to which the manifestations of that code in interstate life replicate, or distort, the versions which appear in domestic contexts.

4.2 Moral language: individuals and groups, selves and others

One obvious way to begin an investigation into the similarities and differences between the moral judgements made of domestic activities and those applied to interstate relations is through the language used to express those judgements: the question, simply put, would be (less importantly) whether,[13] and (more interestingly) in what ways, the morally evaluative language used in domestic life recurs in the sphere of interstate relations. But, of course, the very simplicity of this 'lexical'[14] approach carries its own problems.

---

[10] For an attempt to produce a checklist of 'moral principles' of (fifth-century) Greek interstate relations, see Karavites 1984a; see also de Romilly 1979: chs. 9 and 10, on kindness (and unkindness) in interstate relations.

[11] Green 1999: 101.

[12] This is, of course, an example which has already been extensively studied (and will not therefore be treated in enormous detail in what follows): see, generally, Blundell 1989; on friendship in interstate relations, especially Mitchell 1997a; on deceiving enemies, Hesk 2000: ch. 2.

[13] That there was overlap of some sort is widely accepted: see, for example, Dover 1974: 310–11; Raaflaub 1979b: 245; Bauslaugh 1991: 8. There is, however, less consensus on how it should be interpreted.

[14] The label is Dover's (1974: 46). For a criticism of Dover's method, see Adkins 1978: esp. 147–53; for a defence, Dover 1983.

There is always some danger of expecting too much logic or rationality in the language of morality, of missing the nuances of that vocabulary, and, above all, of underestimating the importance of context in shaping the meanings and implications of a particular word.[15]

If, however, it is accepted that the language of morality might be a useful starting point (even if not a suitable end point) for this enquiry, the problem which immediately follows is that of defining precisely what is being looked for: what is to be counted as 'moral' language? A point which needs to be emphasised at the outset is that, here as elsewhere, the boundary between the moral and the political is not absolute: 'certain words, which usually bear a moral meaning, were used by the Greeks in a political or social sense as well'.[16] And this characteristic has obvious implications for the nature of the question which is being asked: the relevant factor is not simply the extension of a purely moral set of language into a more public (political) sphere; but the use of that language in characterising political behaviour both within and beyond the boundaries of the *polis*.

One area in which this overlap has already been identified is the language of interpersonal relationships, such as *philia* and *sungeneia*.[17] (Here, too, it is worth noting the blurring of the categories of moral, interpersonal and political activity.) A similar transfer of meaning has been noted in the language of tyranny (an area which, in contrast to friendship, we might want to see as primarily political, but which is also characterised in moral terms).[18] What I want

---

[15] Dover 1974: 47–50.

[16] Neil 1901: 202, who argues that the ethical meaning should be thought of as prior to the political (arguing against Grote 1888, vol. II: 419–20, n. 4, who suggests that the ethical meaning 'gradually grew up in Athens, and became popularized by the Socratic school of philosophers as well as by the orators'). The question of origins is not vital for the argument here: what is important is that the two senses are, by the classical period, coexistent. Such a phenomenon is in keeping with the broader pattern of the basic inseparability of Greek moral and political philosophy (Rowe 2000: 5): the nature of the interaction between the individual and the community in its various forms (*oikos*, *polis* and so on) is a fundamental concern of Greek philosophical writing (a point emphasised by Gill 1995: esp. ch. 4; see also Cartledge 2000b).

[17] See ch. 2, sec. 3.

[18] See Raaflaub 1979b, 1984; Tuplin 1985. Generally on tyranny, McGlew 1993. Some examples are discussed below: 154, 158–9. There are many other possible themes of this sort: slavery (noted by de Ste. Croix 1972: 36); ἡσυχία ('quiet', 'neutrality'; see

to concentrate on here, however, is the more abstract language of moral blame and, especially, praise.

This area of moral vocabulary has received a considerable amount of scholarly attention, much of it focusing on or responding to the canonical Platonic 'cardinal virtues': σοφία ('wisdom'), ἀνδρεία ('bravery'), σωφροσύνη ('prudence') and δικαιοσύνη ('justice').[19] However, while this formulation may well have had considerable influence on later writers,[20] it is just as unsafe here as it would be elsewhere to assume that it represented the definitive statement on the issue (or even a response to a well-defined question). Other sources – literary and epigraphic – suggest that the range of morally evaluative language, of 'cardinal virtues' (and vices), was much broader. Whitehead, working from the language of Athenian honorific decrees, establishes a list of ten significant abstract nouns: ἀνδραγαθία ('manly virtue'), ἀρετή ('virtue', 'bravery'), δικαιοσύνη ('justice'), ἐπιμέλεια ('concern'), εὔνοια ('goodwill'), εὐσέβεια ('reverence'), εὐταξία ('good order'), φιλοτιμία ('love of honour'), προθυμία ('enthusiasm') and σωφροσύνη ('prudence').[21] Dover, whose interest is in the literary (and non-philosophical) sources, is even less prescriptive, considering a broader range of adjectival as well as nominal vocabulary. The terms already listed are not, therefore, entirely absent from his account, but attention is also given to the language of being καλός (good, noble) and αἰσχρός (bad, shameful), its derivatives and its synonyms.[22] It would be possible to spend some time creating and refining such vocabulary lists, and even longer attempting to discern the diachronic and synchronic variations in the uses and

---

Bauslaugh 1991); ἀπραγμοσύνη ('lack of action'), φιλοπραγμοσύνη ('love of action') and πολυπραγμοσύνη ('busyness'; see esp. Ehrenberg 1947; Bauslaugh 1991: 8, n. 10; and the discussion in ch. 5, sec. 4).

[19] *Republic* 427e6–11 (and subsequent discussion). On these Platonic virtues see Ferguson 1958: 28–44; on their connection to Platonic ethics more generally, Irwin 1995a: ch. 14; on their (alleged) antecedents, Kunsemüller 1935.

[20] Ferguson 1958: 35–52.

[21] Whitehead 1993: 65. Veligianni-Terzi 1997 operates with a similar list, although she also includes related adjectives, adverbs and verbs. See also the brief summary in Henry 1983: 42–4. A notable absence from all these lists is ἀνδρεία ('courage'), which is not found in (inscribed) honorific decrees (its epigraphic appearances in this period are almost entirely confined to Athenian naval lists: *IG* ii² 1628, line 440, 1629, line 961 (both triremes)).

[22] Dover 1974: 69–73.

meanings of each member of them,[23] but that would involve too great a digression from the principal concern here: namely, the extent to which the same items (and sets) of vocabulary are found in domestic and external contexts.

The area where this transfer (or overlap) is easiest to perceive and categorise is at the least 'literary' end of the spectrum of evidence, in the language of inscriptions.[24] It has already been suggested[25] that it is in the epigraphic evidence for the making of 'international law' that the blurring of the boundaries between inside and outside can most clearly be perceived, and this is, I would suggest, also true in this case. The category of honorific inscriptions, in particular, is one which extends over both spheres of activity, and in which some interesting parallels can be seen.

A good example of this phenomenon can be found in the inscription which records the honours voted by Arcesine on Amorgos to its Athenian governor Androtion.[26] The decree is passed:

ἐ[π]ειδὴ Ἀνδροτίων ἀνὴρ
ἀγαθὸς γέγονε περὶ τὸν δῆμον τὸν Ἀρ-
κεσινέων

Since Androtion has been a good man to the people of Arcesine. (lines 2–4)

And Androtion is crowned,

ἀρετῆς καὶ δικαιοσύνης καὶ εὐνοίας ἕνεκα τῆς εἰς τὸν δῆμον τὸν Ἀρκ-
εσινέων.

---

[23] Specific studies: see, for example, North 1966; Rademaker 2005 (on *sōphrosunē*); Bourriot 1995 (on *kalokagathia*); Hobbs 2000 (on (specifically Platonic) *andreia*); Roisman 2003 on *andreia* in the Attic orators (esp. 132–6 on its use in Demosthenes' diplomatic rhetoric).

[24] On the importance of epigraphic evidence for the study of moral values (a source ignored by Dover 1974; but see Dover 1981), see Whitehead 1993: 39–42; Whitehead 1998. Whitehead restricts his study to Athens, and concentrates (as I will here) on honorific decrees, although the evidence of other categories of inscription (treaties, proxeny decrees, epitaphs) reveals a broadly similar pattern.

[25] Ch. 3, esp. sec. 3.

[26] *IG* xii.7 5 (= RO 51), usually dated to 357/6 (a date extrapolated from what is known of Athenian–Arcesinian relations, and from other information on Androtion's career). On Androtion's career, see Harding 1976 (194–5 for this incident); Harding 1994: 13–25. On the inscription as evidence for the history and nature of the Second Athenian League, see Cargill 1981: ch. 9.

on account of his *aretē* and his *dikaiosunē* [justice] and his *eunoia* [goodwill] towards the people of Arcesine. (lines 19–21)

Two general points arise from this example. First: in what sense (or senses) is this an 'interstate' honour at all? Most obviously, perhaps, it is concerned with the behaviour of someone from outside the *polis*: in this sense, it is, fundamentally, dealing with Arcesine's external relations.[27] But it would be equally possible to see this as primarily a domestic document: the decree is passed by the *boulē* and the *dēmos* of Arcesine; it relates, in the most part, to actions which have taken place within the territory of the *polis*; and it makes quite clear that Androtion's praiseworthy behaviour is not to be considered as an absolute. He has become an ἀνὴρ ἀγαθός περί ('a good man *concerning*') the people of Arcesine; similarly, his *aretē*, justice and goodwill have been demonstrated not as generalised abstract qualities, but specifically εἰς ('to') the people of Arcesine.[28] This phrasing illustrates quite neatly, therefore, the general point (made above: n. 16) of the close connection between individual morality and the community within which it is displayed: the moral qualities themselves may be abstract, but they are manifested in a specified, and carefully delimited, environment.

Second, of course: the question of the moral language used here. Androtion has, first of all, become an ἀνὴρ ἀγαθός (*anēr agathos*; literally, 'good man'). This is the most familiar of all terms of approbation – a concept which appears from the Homeric poems onwards,[29] and one which frequently features in honorific inscriptions of this sort.[30] It can be found, for example, in what is probably

---

[27] The outward-looking nature of the decree might also be argued to be visible in its dialect (which has some Atticism: ἐ|λάττω (lines 12–13)) and its (stoichedon) style of inscription. Austin (1938: 90–1) suggests that these are intended as a specific compliment to the Athenian honorand; this would, however, be an exception to the usual practice in honorific decrees (Buck 1913: 145–50), and more general linguistic and epigraphic influence may be a better explanation.

[28] The importance of these qualifying prepositions is noted (in relation to *IG* i³ 17) by Whitehead 1993: 47.

[29] On the *anēr agathos* in Homer, see Adkins 1960: ch. 3 (and ch. 8 on the continuation of the idea in the classical period).

[30] Generally on its use in Attic inscriptions, see Whitehead 1993: 45–7; Veligianni-Terzi 1997: 192–5; in external contexts, Veligianni-Terzi 1997: 247–54, 265–7; in internal, Veligianni-Terzi 1997: 279–80. The phrase is also widely used in non-Athenian

the earliest extant example of the genre, which records honours
voted by Athens to the people of Sigeion:

[ός ὅσιν ἀνδράσι]-
[ν ἀγ]αθοῖς ἐς [τὸν δῆμον τὸν Ἀθ]-
[εναίον.

since they are good men to the people of Athens.[31] (*IG* i[3] 17, lines 7–9)

The 'virtue' of ἀνδραγαθία (*andragathia*) has, convincingly, been
argued to be closely connected to the condition of being an *anēr
agathos*,[32] and, again, this is frequently found in these interstate
honours. The Samian Poses, for example (who has already been
described as an *anēr agathos* (*IG* ii[2] 1, line 65)), is honoured by the
Athenians for, among other things, his *andragathia* (line 70).[33] But
although these terms of approbation are commonly found in external contexts, they are not restricted to them. The same terms appear
in domestic contexts: they are used, for example, to describe the
conduct of the Athenian Eucles, who (in 400/399) is appointed herald of the *boulē* and *dēmos*, praised for his *andragathia* (*IG* ii[2] 145,
line 4), and said to be an *anēr agathos* (line 5).[34] However, this
overlap is not absolutely straightforward: the appearance of this
language in the domestic sphere seems, in Attic inscriptions, to
be a significantly later phenomenon than its presence in interstate

inscriptions: examples (apart from the honours for Androtion) include Tod 149, line 4
(Cius honours Athenodorus); RO 56, line 3 (Erythrae honours Mausolus); *IG* xii.5 114,
line 10 (Paros and Thasos honour Cephisophon).
[31] The decree is usually dated *c.* 450 (although Mattingly (e.g., 1996a: 102, 1996c: 350–1)
argues for 418/7). The restoration, though extensive, is generally accepted and can be
widely paralleled (see Henry 1983: 1; more generally, Whitehead 1993: 44–7; Veligianni-
Terzi 1997: no. A1).
[32] On the noun, its development and its relationship to *aretē*, see Whitehead 1993: 55–62.
Survey of its use (in Attic inscriptions) in Veligianni-Terzi 1997: 270–2 (external), 293–4
(internal). Other non-Athenian examples include: *IG* xii.5 1001, line 11 (Ios honours the
Macedonian Lysippus); *I.Délos* 75 (Delians honour Kallias, as an *anēr agathos* (lines
5–6) and for his *andragathia* (lines 13–14)); *I.Délos* 79 (Delians honour ?? (name not
preserved), again as an *anēr agathos* (line 4 – restored) and for *andragathia* (line 7)).
[33] Whitehead 1993: 49. A similar combination appears (if the restoration is correct) in *IG* i[3]
125 (405/4: honours for Epicerdes of Cyrene, who had ransomed the Athenian prisoners
held in Sicily): he is praised ὡς ὄντι ἀνδρ||[ὶ ἀγαθῶι ('because he is a good man'; lines
7–8), and crowned because of his *andragathia* (line 28). On the inscription, see Meritt
1970; Bielman 1994: no. 1; Veligianni-Terzi 1997: no. A43. On the context, Kelly 1970.
[34] For other examples, at a deme as well as a *polis* level, see Whitehead 1993: 48–51;
Veligianni-Terzi 1997: 279–80, 293–4.

contexts.[35] It has been suggested that this development can be connected to the various ideological shifts which were necessary before such 'aristocratic' language could unproblematically be applied to (living) democratic insiders.[36] But, even if that explanation were not correct, what is worth noting here is that, while in the end the language of moral approbation is shared, it seems that the process is not, in this case, one of extension of vocabulary from inside to outside, but the reverse.

It is possible to demonstrate a similarly wide pattern of use for the other terms which are applied to Androtion's behaviour: *aretē, dikaiosunē,* and *eunoia.* Much of what was said about *anēr agathos / andragathia* is also true of *aretē.* This too is a widely used word, with potentially aristocratic overtones, used especially of the dead, but also of the living.[37] As with *anēr agathos* and *andragathia,* the word is used in both internal and external contexts, but – in this case too – there is (in Athens, at least), some unevenness in distribution: again, this has been explained by reference to the aristocratic connotations of the word, which created some difficulties in using it of the Athenian citizen, at least while he was still alive.[38] With *dikaiosunē* the pattern is reversed: this is a term of approbation found especially in the context of domestic conduct; examples of its application to external behaviour are much rarer.[39] The final quality displayed by Androtion – *eunoia* –

[35] Whitehead 1993: 47; Veligianni-Terzi 1997: 217–18.

[36] Whitehead 1993: 47. On the democratisation of aristocratic terminology, see Loraux 1978, 1986a: esp. ch. 4; Ober 1989: 248–61. The hypothesis is, though, hard to test, both because of the imbalances in the state of the Athenian evidence (extant 'external' honours greatly outnumber 'internal', for example), and because the non-Athenian (or non-democratic) evidence is also too patchy to function as a proper control: the majority is fourth-century and later, and very little relates to internal affairs.

[37] Whitehead 1993: 57–60; Veligianni-Terzi 1997: 219–22, 272–4 (external), 294–300 (internal). There are, again, a few more non-Athenian instances: see, for example, *IG* iv 748, line 9 (Troezen honours Echilaus of Plataea); *IG* xii.5 1004, line 7 (Ios honours Zeno). There are, of course, many examples from funerary contexts (see Dover 1974: 67–9): particularly relevant here, perhaps, is the fifth-century epitaph of Pythagoras, proxenos of Selymbria (*IG* i³ 1154), to whom the quality of *aretē* is attributed (though it is also worth noting that, in this context, the *aretē* is not displayed εἰς ('towards') or περί ('concerning') anyone, but is left as a more free-floating virtue).

[38] Whitehead 1993: 60. The same difficulties (above: n. 36) apply to the testing of this hypothesis.

[39] This is a term which overlaps with the Platonic 'cardinal virtues', although it is possible that this overlap conceals a difference in meaning: Whitehead 1993: 67–8, suggests that

requires the construction of yet another model of distribution between internal and external. In this case, the great majority of the epigraphic evidence, in Attica and beyond, relates to external political activities: the first extant example of the application of the term to domestic behaviour comes in 337/6 (Schwenk 1985: no. 9, line 10) – although even this example, which appears in a (disputed) restoration, is only arguably extant.[40] This dominance of external examples would, of course, fit neatly with the prominence of *eunoia* in contemporary literary analyses of interstate behaviour.[41] But, if this literary evidence is to be taken into account, so too should the literary material which suggests that *eunoia* was also considered an important civic, as well as personal, quality in domestic (Athenian) life.[42]

The four qualities attributed to Androtion usefully illustrate, therefore, not only the basic fact of overlap between internal and external 'virtues', but also the messiness of that overlap. Some qualities are, it seems, more closely associated with one sphere than another. But the boundaries are not rigidly maintained, and the most important factor in determining the use or non-use of a particular term seems often to be not so much whether the behaviour is related to domestic or external politics, but the more specific aspects of that behaviour, the status of the honorand, and – possibly – the political and ideological context in which the honour is created.

It would be possible to show that other members of this set of vocabulary conform to this pattern, and variations on it.[43] However,

'honesty' (especially in financial contexts) might be a better translation than 'righteousness' or similar; and an implication of financial propriety would fit with Androtion's behaviour, as represented in this decree (the provision of interest-free loans, for example). For a survey of Attic examples, see Veligianni-Terzi 1997: 222–3, 299–302 (she lists no examples of its use in external decrees). Parallels for this use in external contexts can be seen in *I.Délos* 75, line 13; *I.Délos* 79, line 8; but epigraphic evidence for its use is otherwise scarce, even outside Athens. Note also Dem. 18.215, on the reasons for Theban honours to Athens (Athenian *andreia*, *dikaiosunē* and *sōphrosunē*).

[40] Whitehead 1993: 53–4. The first secure example comes in the (posthumous) honours for Lycourgos (*IG* ii² 457+513). For the external Attic examples, see Veligianni-Terzi 1997: 218–19, 274–5. Non-Athenian examples include (apart from the honours for Androtion) *IG* iv 748, line 10 (Troezen honours Echilaus of Plataea), xii.5 1001, line 9 (Ios honours Lysippus), xii.9 198, line 3 (Eretria honours Adimantus of Lampsacus).

[41] See ch. 2, sec. 3. [42] Whitehead 1993: 53.

[43] The data with which this claim could be supported (in the case of Attic honorific inscriptions) is collected in Veligianni-Terzi 1997: pt 2, ch. 2.

rather than spend more time on this basic point, it is more useful to attempt to broaden the question in two directions: the relationship between the group and the individual; and the identity of the group represented as having benefited from the honorand's behaviour.

These terms of approbation can be applied not only to individuals, or even to small collections of individuals,[44] but also to much larger groups. *IG* i³ 101, for example, records honours voted to the Neapolitans, for their loyalty to Athens during the closing years of the Peloponnesian War:

> [ἐπ]αινέσαι τοῖς Νεοπ[ολίταις] <τοῖς>
> παρὰ Θάσον [πρõτον μ]ὲν ⟦ [ὅτι ἄποικοι ὄντες Θασίον] ⟧ [καὶ πολιο]-
> ρκόμενοι ⟦ [ὑπ' αὐτõν] ⟧ καὶ Πελο[πονν]ησίον οὐκ ἠθ[έλησαν ἀ]-
> [πο]στῆνα[ι ἀπ' Ἀθηναί]ον, ἄνδ[ρες δ'] ἀγαθοὶ ἐγένο[ντο ἔς τε τὴ]
> [ν στρα]τ[ιὰν καὶ τὸν δῆ]μον τ[ὸν Ἀθηναίον κα]ὶ το[ὺς χσυμμά]
> [χους

Let the Neapolitans near Thasos be praised, first because, although colonists of Thasos and under siege by them and the Peloponnesians, they were not willing to revolt from Athens, and they became good men to the army and the people of the Athenians and to the allies.[45] (lines 6–11)

Here, then, it is the Neapolitans, *en masse*, who are represented as displaying the qualities and behaviour of ἄνδρες ἀγαθοί, 'good men'. A more usual formulation, though, is to specify that it is the *dēmos* of the city in question which has displayed a particular virtue. So, in *IG* ii² 28 (387/6), it is the δῆμον τὸγ Κλαζομενί|ων ('the *dēmos* of the Clazomenians') which is praised for being πρόθυμος . . . ἐς τὴμ πόλιν τὴν Ἀθηναίων ('devoted to the city of the Athenians'; lines 4–5). Similarly, at the other end of the century, the decree honouring Tenedos (*IG* ii² 233 (= RO 72)) records that it was decided:

---

44 See, for example, the multiple honours to the Spartocids (*IG* ii² 212 (= RO 64), 346 BC): Spartocus and Paërisades are praised ἀρετῆς καὶ εὐνοίας ἕνεκα ('on account of their *aretē* and *eunoia*'; line 32). On the granting of honours to more than one person (often members of the same family) in proxeny decrees, see Walbank 1978: 7. Ambassadors are a subset who are praised relatively regularly in these terms: see, for example, *IG* ii² 96 (=RO 24), lines 7–10.

45 = Veligianni-Terzi no. A33, ML 89. Generally on the historical background, see Andrewes 1953.

[ἐπαινέσαι μὲν τὸν δ]-
[ῆ]μον τῶν Τενεδίων ἀρε[τῆς ἕνεκα καὶ εὐνοίας τ]-
[ῆ]ς εἰς τὸν δῆμον τὸν Ἀ[θηναίων καὶ τοὺς συμμάχ]-
[ο]υς.

Let the *dēmos* of Tenedos be praised on account of their *aretē* and their goodwill towards the *dēmos* of Athens and the allies.[46] (lines 6–9)

The – obvious but important – point which these examples illustrate is that the overlap, from domestic to interstate, of the language of praise does not apply simply to individual actions but also to those of states: it is, therefore, legitimate to claim that this overlap operates in interstate relations, and not just in interpersonal relations in an interstate context. What these examples also suggest, however, is that the creation of a strict divide between individuals and states is not, in fact, appropriate.[47] The reference to the *dēmos* keeps the focus of attention on the people who make up the unit, rather than the unit itself, and can serve as a useful reminder that, even when this language is used of a *polis*, it refers as much to the collection of individuals who make up that *polis* as to any abstract entity.[48]

---

[46] See also *IG* ii² 107 (= RO 31), lines 37–8 (praise for the δῆμον τὸμ Μυτ[ιλ]||[ηναίω]ν, 'the *dēmos* of the Mytileneans'); *IG* ii² 273, line 7 ([τὸ]ν δῆμον [τὸν Βυζαντίων, 'the *dēmos* of the Byzantians').

[47] The absence of any 'State' in the Greek world is a relevant issue here: see Hinsley 1986: 28–31; Berent 2000: 259–63; Cartledge 2000b: 17–20. The tendency for discussions of interstate behaviour to focus on the people (οἱ Ἀθηναῖοι, for example) rather than, or as well as, the place is discussed (with reference to the language of defensive alliances) by Schiller 1996: ch. 3. On the importance of this factor for the nature of Greek theorising about interstate relations, see Purnell 1978: 28.

[48] On the variation in meanings and implications of *polis*, see Hansen 1998: ch. 4. On the interpretation of references to the *dēmos* in Athenian texts (arguing that they should be taken as references to the assembly), Hansen 1983a. On the significance of references to the *dēmos* in Athenian interstate relations in the mid-fifth century, Welwei 1986; see also Fauber 1998: 112, n. 13. But although a reference to the *dēmos* might sometimes imply that deliberate emphasis is being given to the (political) ideological aspect of interstate interaction, there are also occasions when a reference (or failure to refer) to the *dēmos* seems less likely to have any particular significance: for example, *IG* ii² 232, line 6, praises the *polis* of Tenedos; the almost contemporary *IG* ii² 233, lines 6–7, praises the *dēmos*; whatever the reason for the variation, it seems extremely unlikely that it is prompted by a change in the political situation at Tenedos between the two decrees (on the relationship between the two decrees, see Tracy 1995: 91). It is also relevant to note in this context the variation in the ways in which the Athenians refer to themselves in these honorific decrees (the Athenians, the *dēmos*, the *polis*): on this variation see Veligianni-Terzi 1997: 234–44.

The second point is less directly relevant to the main subject of this chapter, but is nevertheless worth making. A further way in which the scope of honours can be broadened relates to the identity of the party (or parties) which is represented as having benefited from the actions of the honorand. As was noted above, the most common formulation is to specify that an individual or group has displayed their virtue or virtues 'with respect to' the body which is presenting the honour. But there are also cases when the scope of that clause is wider. Specifically, it can include not only the honouring party, but also their allies. This can be seen in the honours for Neapolis and Tenedos quoted above: both the Athenians and their *summachoi* have been the subject of the honorands' good behaviour. A similar example can be found in *IG* xii.5 114: the Athenian general Cephisophon is honoured, in a Parian decree, for his behaviour [πε|ρ]ì τὸν δῆμο[ν] τὸ[μ] Π[α]|[ρ]ίων καὶ Θασίων ('towards the *dēmos* of the Parians and the Thasians'; lines 10–12).[49] That honorific decrees reflect, and are intended to reflect, as much on the nature of the honouring party as on the honorand is widely accepted.[50] What it is possible to see here is that these decrees might be used not only in constructing the identity of the honouring party, but also in shaping the boundaries of the community which is interested, and implicated, in the praiseworthy behaviour of the honorand; moreover, these boundaries may be substantially wider than those of the single *polis*.[51] The connection which is being established, or asserted, in these decrees operates not only between the honouring body and the honorand, but also between the honouring body and those who are associated with it in these prepositional clauses: what is good for Athens is also good for her allies; what is good for Paros is good for Thasos.

It should, however, be noted that it is very difficult to find (in the epigraphic record) cases where the honouring *polis*, with or without a wider community, is represented as having no direct interest in the virtuous behaviour of an honorand: cases, that is,

---

[49] On relations between Thasos and Paros at this time (339), see Pouilloux 1954: 430–2.

[50] See esp. Dem. 20.64, with West 1995 (esp. 237–8); generally, Henry 1996; Hedrick 1999: 408–25.

[51] A similar process, that is, to the one which was noted in the discussion of the creation of 'international laws' (ch. 3, sec. 3). On the relationship between communities and moral judgements in interstate relations, see Kratochwil 1988: esp. 209.

where an individual is praised for behaviour which has benefited a third party. This could, of course, be a problem of evidence rather than of attitudes (or require explanation with reference to attitudes other than those specifically related to moral behaviour): there are very few extant decrees detailing the honours voted to a member of the home *polis* for his behaviour overseas.[52] But one example does illustrate the point quite well. In the closing lines of the 361/0 treaty between Athens and Thessaly the, otherwise unknown, [Th]e[ai]tetos of Erchiea is complimented on the way in which he has performed his duties:

εἶναι δὲ καὶ [Θ]ε[αί]τ-
ητον τὸν Ἐρχιέα ὡ[ς] λέγο[ν]τα [ἄρ]ιστα [κα]ὶ [πρ]άττοντα ὅ-
[τ]ι ἂν δύνηται ἀγα[θὸ]ν τῶ[ι δήμ]ω[ι] τῶι Ἀ[θην]α[ί]ω[ν κα]ὶ Θε-
τταλ[ο]ῖς ἐν τῶι τεταγμέ[ν]ωι.

Let Theaitetos of Erchiea, since he said and did the best that he could for the people of Athens and Thessaly, be deemed to have done his duty.[53] (RO 44, lines 45–8)

[Th]e[ai]tetos has behaved well not only to his native *polis* but also to outsiders – the Thessalians. But those outsiders are not, of course, entirely removed from the Athenian sphere of interest: they are allies of the Athenians; what benefits the Thessalians, it might be argued, necessarily benefits the Athenians too – and *vice versa*.[54]

The picture which emerges from the use of this sort of language in literary sources is broadly comparable to that found in the epigraphic material, although – particularly in this last area – some

---

[52] The literary evidence provides a different picture: see below n. 54 and pp. 147–8.

[53] *IG* ii² 116 (with a different text at these lines). On the meaning of ἐν τῶι τεταγμένωι, see Tod 147, commentary; ML: p. 180; and compare RO 64 (= *IG* ii² 212), lines 63–5.

[54] One possible example with a much broader circle of benefit is the decree of Ctesiphon honouring Demosthenes, which, according to Demosthenes, specified that he καὶ λέγει καὶ πράττει ὅ τι ἂν δύνηται ἀγαθὸν ὑπέρ τε αὐτῶν Ἀθηναίων καὶ τῶν ἄλλων Ἑλλήνων ('both spoke and did all the good he could on behalf of the Athenians and the other Greeks'; Dem. 18.84). The beneficiaries are still a distinct, circumscribed, group, but there is a clear difference between the nature of this group and the narrower, formally defined, sets of allies seen in the epigraphic examples. The uniqueness of this example, however (in the context of epigraphic evidence), and its similarity to the approach found in other literary material should, perhaps, encourage some distrust of the accuracy of this version of the wording of the decree (if, indeed, the text of this paragraph bears any relation at all to the Demosthenic original: for a sceptical view, see Yunis 2001: 29–31).

significant differences can be seen. The move to these sources must, however, be accompanied by a small disclaimer. In considering the literary material it is even harder to maintain the narrow focus on vocabulary; and the artificiality of such an approach is even more obvious. What follows is – it should be emphasised – an attempt to provide a general survey of some basic points, and to highlight those important similarities and differences, rather than an effort at comprehensiveness.

As with the epigraphic material, the reasons for praising (or blaming) an individual often focus on the effect of his actions on the domestic community. Often, indeed, the language of 'virtues' outlined above is entirely absent. Aeschines' summary, in *Against Ctesiphon*, of reasons why Athenian generals have been honoured illustrates the point well:

ἐπερώτησαν δὴ τοὺς δικαστὰς εἰ ἐγίγνωσκον Χαβρίαν καὶ Ἰφικράτην καὶ Τιμόθεον, καὶ πυθοῦ παρ' αὐτῶν διὰ τί τὰς δωρεὰς αὐτοῖς ἔδοσαν καὶ τὰς εἰκόνας ἔστησαν. ἅπαντες γάρ σοι ἅμα ἀποκρινοῦνται, ὅτι Χαβρίᾳ μὲν διὰ τὴν περὶ Νάξον ναυμαχίαν, Ἰφικράτει δὲ ὅτι μόραν Λακεδαιμονίων ἀπέκτεινε, Τιμοθέῳ δὲ διὰ τὸν περίπλουν τὸν εἰς Κέρκυραν, καὶ ἄλλοις, ὧν ἑκάστῳ πολλὰ καὶ καλὰ κατὰ πόλεμον ἔργα πέπρακται.

Ask the jury whether they knew Chabrias and Iphicrates and Timotheus, and enquire why they gave them those rewards and set up their statues. All will answer with one voice, that they honoured Chabrias for the sea-battle at Naxos, and Iphicrates because he destroyed a regiment of the Lacedaemonians, and Timotheus because of his voyage to Corcyra, and other men, each because of many glorious deeds in war. (3.243)

Given the nature of his case against Ctesiphon (and, indirectly, Demosthenes), Aeschines obviously has a specific motive here for making military success the sole motivating factor in the judgement of leaders. Nevertheless, the claims which he makes in this passage do seem to fit, to at least some extent, with what can be seen in other texts. One of the honorands mentioned by Aeschines – the general Timotheus – is also praised at some length by his mentor Isocrates (15.101–39), and, here too, his merits are conceived of primarily in terms of his military successes: Timotheus' achievement, summed up by Isocrates, is to have captured more cities κατὰ κράτος ('by force') than any other man (15.107), and it is this (together with his economic effectiveness) which forms the focus of Isocrates' encomium.[55] And although Isocrates does go on to discuss some of the other qualities which indicate that Timotheus was a καλὸς κάγαθὸς ἀνήρ ('a noble and good man'; 15.138) – above all, his restrained and fair treatment of other states – the specific evaluative language which has been described above does not appear in that discussion.[56]

This tendency is not, however, universal, and there are cases where the 'cardinal virtues', or versions of them, do appear. For example, in the same excursus in which Timotheus' activities are eulogised, Pericles is described by Isocrates as holding μεγίστην ἐπὶ σοφίᾳ καὶ δικαιοσύνῃ καὶ σωφροσύνῃ δόξαν ('the highest reputation for wisdom and justice and prudence'; 15.111).[57] The best, and most extensive, example can be found, however, in Xenophon's *Agesilaus*. It has been suggested that this whole work can be seen as a Xenophontic attempt to (re)define the list of 'cardinal virtues'.[58] Xenophon's list would, on this interpretation, be εὐσέβεια ('piety'; §3); δικαιοσύνη ('justice') – especially in relation to financial conduct (§4); ἐγκράτεια ('self-control'; §5); ἀνδρεία ('courage') and σοφία ('wisdom'; §6). To these is added a range of qualities which are expressed in adjectival rather than nominal form: the virtues of being φιλόπολις ('a lover of his city'), and also φιλέλλην ('a lover of Greece'; §7); the characteristics of being εὔχαρις ('engaging'), εὔελπις ('optimistic'), εὔθυμος ('cheerful'; §8). Agesilaus, of course, is the paradigmatic exponent of these virtues, but what is of more particular interest here

---

55 Military successes: victory over Spartans (15.109); conquest of Samos (15.111); capture of Sestos and Crithote (15.112); defeat of Chalcideans (15.113). Economic skill: 15.109, 111. On the excursus, see generally Alexiou 1995: 69–87. On Timotheus as general, see Tuplin 1984; Heskel 1997: pt 1; on the economic aspect, Millett 1993: 191–4.

56 *Eunoia* – an important theme in Isocratean thought on interstate relations (see de Romilly 1958; Mitchell 1997b: esp. 42–4) – is referred to during the excursus, but is attributed not to Timotheus but to those with whom he had dealings (15.122, 134–5). For Isocrates' use of the inside/outside model in other ways, see below: 155–60.

57 It could be that these qualities are intended to be applied by extension to Timotheus: the context is Isocrates' discussion of Pericles' capture of Samos, an action which, according to Isocrates, was surpassed by Timotheus. On the other hand, it might also, of course, be possible that Isocrates' silence on Timotheus' possession of these virtues is deliberate: he excelled Pericles precisely because he did not rely on *sophia*, etc. But this seems, to me, less likely (note, for example, Isocrates' characterisation of Timotheus' policy as a *philosophia* (15.121)).

58 Dover 1974: 66. More generally on the encomium, see Plezia 1982 (comparing its form and content with the Isocratean praise of Timotheus); Cartledge 1987: 56; Luppino 1991.

is the fact that he displays this set of characteristics in situations which span the range of activity from treatment of immediate family, through behaviour within the city, dealings with soldiers and with allies, to treatment of enemies. Here too, some qualities are more visible in one sphere than another: his *andreia* is, unsurprisingly, illustrated with reference only to military activities; *eusebeia* ('piety') too is a virtue which is exemplified with reference to Agesilaus' attitude to interstate relations (particularly, the making of oaths and treaties).⁵⁹ His *dikaiosunē*, on the other hand, can be seen not only in his financial uprightness in domestic contexts, but also in his refusal to allow his conduct of external relations to be affected by bribes. Similarly, his *sophia* ('wisdom') is manifested in his treatment of his friends and family, and in his dealings with his enemies – especially in military contexts.

As in the epigraphic material, this language can be applied not only to individuals but also to groups. Xenophon again provides a good example, in another encomium – that of the Phliasians (*HG* VII.ii).⁶⁰ A dominant theme of this passage is the Phliasians' bravery and general military prowess. But, in this example too, this is not the only quality which the Phliasians display. Their loyalty to their friends and allies – in particular their προθυμία ('enthusiasm') towards the Spartans (VII.ii.4) – is another recurring theme of the digression. This loyalty is maintained not only when the fortunes of their friends suffer (the Phliasians stay loyal to the Spartans even after Leuctra (VII.ii.2)), but also, in some cases, when these friends could even be considered to have become enemies:

καλὸν δὲ καὶ τοῦτο διεπράξαντο οἱ Φλειάσιοι· τὸν γὰρ Πελληνέα πρόξενον ζῶντα λαβόντες, καίπερ πάντων σπανιζόμενοι, ἀφῆκαν ἄνευ λύτρων. γενναίους μὲν δὴ καὶ ἀλκίμους πῶς οὐκ ἄν τις φαίη εἶναι τοὺς τοιαῦτα διαπραττομένους;

The Phliasians also carried out this good deed: when they had captured the Pellenean proxenos alive, even though they were in want of everything, they let him go without a ransom. How could anyone deny that men who performed such deeds were noble and bold?⁶¹ (VII.ii.16)

---

⁵⁹ See ch. 3, sec. 4.
⁶⁰ On this passage, see Cartledge 1987: 266; Tuplin 1993: 145–6; Dillery 1995: 130–8.
⁶¹ If Schneider's (1849 *ad loc.*) suggestion that Proxenos is a proper name, rather than a position, is accepted (as it is by Dindorf 1870; Brownson 1921; Warner 1979), then the action of the Phliasians would be still more remarkable: not merely maintaining

A consideration of the *epitaphioi* – which are, predictably, the most fruitful sources of this 'honorific language' among literary texts – makes it possible to develop this picture, and to show more clearly how fluid the boundary between individual and group can be. The object of praise in these speeches – as has been well established[62] – slips from the specific *aretē* of the commemorated dead to the qualities of the city as a whole. And, again, it is possible to see that this slippage is made easier by the terms in which the praise of the wider group is expressed: it is not so much a contrast, between individuals on the one hand and a defined entity (the *polis*) on the other, as a continuum of thought: the individuals, by themselves and as a group, have displayed qualities which have typified the behaviour of other (groups of) citizens over the course of Athenian history, and which, by extension, can come to characterise the *polis* itself. (And even this characterisation adds a somewhat artificial level of solidity to the distinction.) The Lysianic *epitaphios* provides perhaps the clearest illustration of the phenomenon. The speech starts from the *aretē* of those who have just died (2.1); but, in later passages, that *aretē* is represented also as a quality belonging to the *polis* itself: for example, the Amazons, in their defeat, τῆσδε μὲν τῆς πόλεως διὰ τὴν ἀρετὴν ἀθάνατον <τὴν> μνήμην ἐποίησαν, 'created an immortal memory for this city because of its *aretē*' (2.6).[63]

At this point it is worth, again, digressing slightly in order to point to an important difference between the epigraphic and literary

---

an existing relationship, but perhaps even acting out of spontaneous goodwill to the Pellenean.

[62] See, especially, Loraux 1986a.

[63] On the theme of *aretē* in the speech, see Prinz 1997: 237–44. A similar process can be seen in the Demosthenic *epitaphios*. It is established at the outset that the dead possessed a range of virtues beyond simple courage: εἰ μὲν οὖν τὴν ἀνδρείαν μόνον αὐτοῖς τῶν εἰς ἀρετὴν ἀνηκόντων ὑπάρχουσαν ἑώρων, ταύτην ἂν ἐπαίνεσας ἀπηλλαττόμην τῶν λοιπῶν· ἐπειδὴ δὲ καὶ γεγενῆσθαι καλῶς καὶ πεπαιδεῦσθαι σωφρόνως καὶ βεβιωκέναι φιλοτίμως συμβέβηκεν αὐτοῖς ('if it were my view that, of those qualities that constitute *aretē*, courage alone was their possession, I might praise this and leave it at that; but since they also happened to have been nobly born and strictly brought up and to have lived with lofty ideals'; Dem. 60.3); the speech goes on to demonstrate how these virtues were fostered not by the individuals themselves, but by the Athenian (and, especially, democratic) environment in which they lived: note esp. §27. (On this, see Prinz 1997: 257–64.) Compare also Isocrates 6.93, for the claim that the glory of the individual (τῆς ἰδίας δόξης) and that of the community (τῆς κοινῆς) can and should not be considered separable.

material. In the literary material, as in the epigraphic, it is possible to see that the praiseworthy behaviour of an individual or group may affect more than a single party, and here too it is, I think, possible to attribute some significance to the scope of that community of beneficiaries. What is notable in this set of material, however, is how much wider the boundaries of that group might be. Agesilaus' actions do benefit those to whom he has a formal, defined, bond – his family, his *polis*, his allies – but his virtues also affect the Greeks as a whole (in fact, his concern for the Greeks as a whole is, precisely, one of his virtues).[64]

The boundaries of that community of beneficiaries could also be not only widened but also made more flexible: Agesilaus' enemies, once defeated, do not remain enemies, but become the recipients of Agesilean φιλανθρωπία ('magnanimity'; *Ages.* 1.22). Lysias' *epitaphios* provides a variation on the theme: Athenian δικαιοσύνη ('justice') and εὐψυχία ('firmness of heart'; 2.14) are demonstrated not only to their existing friends and allies, but also, in their assistance to the sons of Heracles, to those with whom they have no pre-existing connection. Such actions are, of course, best understood in terms of the establishment of bonds of reciprocal obligation, rather than as purely other-benefiting behaviour.[65] The point which needs to be made here, however, is simply that, in these texts, it is possible to see moral language being used not just of relations between specific pairs or sets of states, but also of 'interstate relations' in a much wider, more general, sense.

Returning to the specific linguistic question, one final general point which should be made is that this linguistic crossover can – in the literary texts – be seen not only in positive but also in negative assessments of individual and group behaviour. And if the

---

[64] On the representation of Agesilaus' philhellenism in the *Agesilaus*, see Dillery 1995: 114–18.

[65] The practical benefits of Agesilaus' policy in the treatment of defeated enemies are emphasised by Xenophon (1.20–2). Lysias, on the other hand, makes the point that the Athenians had no guarantee that they would receive benefits in return (2.13); nevertheless, the story as a whole has to be seen in the context of the account of the creation and maintenance of Athenian hegemony. The extent to which any Greek approaches to morality or ethics can properly be characterised as primarily other-benefiting or altruistic is disputed: see Gill 1998; Konstan 2000; on the question of the 'egotistic' nature of Greek ethics, see Annas 1992: 130–2; Taylor 1998: 49–53. For more on the role of reciprocity in interstate relations, see ch. 2, sections 2 and 3; ch. 5.

epitaphioi are the best places in which to find positive moral language, then deliberative oratory is the best place to find the negative versions of such ideas. Accusations of *hubris*, for example, are regularly found in both formal and informal contexts in Athenian domestic life.[66] But the term can also be applied to interstate behaviour – especially to expansionist, 'imperialistic' behaviour. Philip's activities, for example, are repeatedly represented in this way by Demosthenes (for example, the catalogue of Philip's *hubris* in the *Third Philippic*, 9.32–5).[67] Again, the accusation can also be applied to groups and to cities. Xenophon, for example, uses the term to describe the Athenians' own perception (after the fact) of their behaviour in the latter part of the fifth century:

ἐνόμιζον δὲ οὐδεμίαν εἶναι σωτηρίαν – εἰ μὴ παθεῖν ἃ οὐ τιμωρούμενοι ἐποίησαν, ἀλλὰ διὰ τὴν ὕβριν ἠδίκουν ἀνθρώπους μικροπολίτας οὐδ᾽ἐπὶ μιᾷ αἰτίᾳ ἑτέρᾳ ἢ ὅτι ἐκείνοις συνεμάχουν.

And they thought that there was no salvation, except to suffer the same things as they had carried out, not in retaliation, but in *hubris* and unjustly upon the people of small states, for no other single reason than because they were in alliance with the Spartans.[68] (*HG* II.ii.10)

Isocrates, too, uses the term both of Athens' fifth-century imperialism (8.99), and of Sparta's fourth-century behaviour (8.108), as well as applying it to an assertion of a more general rule of the rise and fall of empires:

εὑρήσετε τὴν μὲν ἀκολασίαν καὶ τὴν ὕβριν τῶν κακῶν αἰτίαν γιγνομένην, τὴν δὲ σωφροσύνην τῶν ἀγαθῶν.

You will discover that arrogance and *hubris* have been the cause of our misfortunes while prudence has been the source of our blessings.[69] (8.119)

A similar pattern can be identified for the more general language of shame – αἰσχύνη (*aischunē*) and its related forms. A passage

---

[66] See, in general, MacDowell 1976; Fisher 1976, 1979; Murray 1990; and, most comprehensively, Fisher 1992. On the *graphē hubreos*, see also Fisher 1990; Todd 1993: 270–1.

[67] For discussion and other examples see Fisher 1992: 141–2.

[68] See Fisher 1992: 130–42 for a survey of the (fifth- and fourth-century) evidence. Note, in the fifth century, the use of the allegation in imperialist contexts, directed against those who rebel: see especially Cleon's characterisation of the behaviour of Mytilene (Th. III.39).

[69] Note the contrast between *hubris* and *sōphrosunē*: see Davidson 1990: 26–7.

from *On the Chersonese* is worth quoting at some length, since it demonstrates both the force which could be attached to such arguments, and the precise terms in which they might be expressed:

εἰ μὲν γάρ ἐστί τις ἐγγυητὴς θεῶν (οὐ γὰρ ἀνθρώπων γ᾽ οὐδεὶς ἂν γένοιτ᾽ ἀξιόχρεως τηλικούτου πράγματος) ὡς, ἐὰν ἄγηθ᾽ ἡσυχίαν καὶ ἅπαντα προῆσθε, οὐκ ἐπ᾽ αὐτοὺς ὑμᾶς τελευτῶν ἐκεῖνος ἥξει, αἰσχρὸν μὲν νὴ τὸν Δία καὶ πάντας θεοὺς καὶ ἀνάξιον ὑμῶν καὶ τῶν ὑπαρχόντων τῇ πόλει καὶ πεπραγμένων τοῖς προγόνοις, τῆς ἰδίας ἕνεκα ῥαθυμίας τοὺς ἄλλους πάντας Ἕλληνας εἰς δουλείαν προέσθαι, καὶ ἔγωγ᾽ αὐτὸς μὲν τεθνάναι μᾶλλον ἂν ἢ ταῦτ᾽ εἰρηκέναι βουλοίμην.

For if you have the guarantee of some god (since no mere mortal could be a satisfactory guarantor for such an event) that if you keep quiet and abandon everything, Philip will not in the end march against yourselves, by Zeus and all the gods, it would be a disgraceful thing, unworthy of you and of the resources of your city and the record of your ancestors to abandon all the other Greeks to enslavement for the sake of your own indolence, and I for one would rather die than be guilty of proposing such a policy.[70] (Dem. 8.49)

The interesting point here is that Demosthenes appeals not only to the idea of an absolute wrong (αἰσχρόν, 'a disgraceful thing'), but also to a shame which is characterised in a more relative sense: failure to act would be unworthy of the Athenians now (ὑμῶν, 'you'), and of the *polis*, and of their ancestors. Athenian policy should be considered, that is, not only in its own context but also in the broader scheme of the Athenian 'tradition' of behaviour in these situations. (The positive model of the *epitaphioi*, and the idealising pictures of Athens' past actions found in those speeches, can function as a background against which such claims can more clearly be understood.) A similar argument can be seen in Isocrates' *Archidamus*, where it is the imagined Spartan tradition of past behaviour in interstate behaviour which is represented as the paradigm, deviation from which should cause shame – shame which would attach to the *polis* itself:

εἰ δὲ φοβηθέντες τοὺς ἐπιόντας κινδύνους προησόμεθά τι τῶν ἡμετέρων αὐτῶν, βεβαιώσομεν τὰς Θηβαίων ἀλαζονείας καὶ πολὺ σεμνότερον τρόπαιον τοῦ περὶ Λεῦκτρα καὶ φανερώτερον στήσομεν καθ᾽ ἡμῶν αὐτῶν· τὸ μὲν γὰρ ἀτυχίας, τὸ δὲ τῆς ἡμετέρας διανοίας ἔσται γεγενημένον. μηδεὶς οὖν ὑμᾶς πείσῃ τοιαύταις αἰσχύναις τὴν πόλιν περιβαλεῖν.

---

[70] Compare the similar claims in, for example, Dem. 10.25; 18.66, 200.

If through fear of the dangers which now threaten us we relinquish anything that is ours, we shall justify the boasts of the Thebans, and erect against ourselves a trophy far more imposing and conspicuous than that which was raised at Leuctra; for that will stand as a memorial of our misfortune; but this, of our abject spirit. Therefore, let no-one persuade you to surround the city with such shame. (6.10)

These examples also, however, highlight once more the difficulty of attempting to treat these lexical items in isolation from their context. It is at this point, therefore, that it seems sensible to extend the terms of enquiry: how does this overlap (and it is, I think, best seen as overlap rather than absolute, mechanical, replication) fit into larger patterns of the representation of interstate morality and its connection to morality inside the *polis*?

4.3 Assumptions of and arguments for similarity

A factor which can be closely associated with this linguistic overlap is the tendency of discussions of various aspects of political, and moral, activity to slip between domestic and external behaviour, without any apparent attempt to signal any significant difference between the two spheres. This has already been noted briefly in the discussion of Xenophon's *Agesilaus*: the primary aim of the work is to demonstrate Agesilaus' various virtues, and the precise location of the actions which are described – whether they are within or beyond the *polis* – seems to be much less important than the general qualities which they exemplify.

The phenomenon can be seen elsewhere, in a variety of authors and a variety of genres. In *To Nicocles*, for example, Isocrates' advice to the king shifts constantly and seamlessly from the domestic sphere to the external: the king should keep an eye on the expenditure of the citizens (2.21); he should behave honourably in dealing with outsiders and in making interstate agreements (2.22); he should ensure that his subjects are secure and free from fear (2.23); and so on. The advice slips equally easily between that relating to the treatment of people (whether inside or outside the *polis*: the scope of the reference to πάντας, 'all' (below) is vague) and of *poleis*:

ἀρχικὸς εἶναι βούλου μὴ χαλεπότητι μηδὲ τῷ σφόδρα κολάζειν ἀλλὰ τῷ πάντας ἡττᾶσθαι τῆς σῆς διανοίας καὶ νομίζειν ὑπὲρ τῆς αὐτῶν σωτηρίας ἄμεινον αὐτῶν σὲ βουλεύεσθαι. πολεμικὸς μὲν ἴσθι ταῖς ἐπιστήμαις καὶ ταῖς παρασκευαῖς, εἰρηνικὸς δὲ τῷ μηδὲν παρὰ τὸ δίκαιον πλεονεκτεῖν. οὕτως ὁμίλει τῶν πόλεων πρὸς τὰς ἥττους, ὥσπερ ἂν τὰς κρείττους πρὸς ἑαυτὸν ἀξιώσειας.

Do not be willing to show your authority by harshness or by undue severity in punishment, but by bettering all in your judgement and believing that your plans for their safety are better than their own. Be warlike in your knowledge of and preparations for war, but peaceful in your avoidance of all unjust aggression. Deal with weaker states as you would expect stronger states to deal with you. (2.24)

This tendency to draw examples from both domestic and external activities in order to support a more general argument is also visible in Plato's writings. It is, in fact, in this sort of context that the references to interstate relations in Plato's work are most commonly found: not, that is, as a particular subject of interest in their own right, but as a small part of a much bigger picture. So, for example, at an early stage of the *Republic*, Socrates briefly uses the example of an imperialist *polis*, enslaving other cities unjustly, as an illustration in his attempt to demonstrate to Thrasymachus the superiority of the just over the unjust life (350e11–351b3). Callicles' attempt, in the *Gorgias*, to demonstrate the opposite is also represented as drawing on both interstate and interpersonal examples (the invasions of Xerxes and Darius: 483d6–8; the actions of Heracles: 484b1–c3).

The possibility of this straightforward, unmarked, movement between internal and external is not very striking to look at, although it is nevertheless important to note. But it is also possible to find cases where more use is made of perceptions of or claims to similarity between the two spheres.

One of the more common ways of suggesting the connection appears in the claim that morality (or lack of it) in one area can be used in an argument which relates to behaviour in the other. The examples are generally negative. In his speech against Timarchus, for example, Aeschines claims that Timarchus' record of dubious moral practices at home makes him entirely unsuited for service overseas:

καὶ τὸν αἰσχρῶς οἴκοι βεβιωκότα ἔξω τῆς πόλεως πρεσβευτὴν πέμψομεν καὶ τούτῳ περὶ τῶν μεγίστων διαπιστεύσομεν;

And shall we send abroad as ambassador, and entrust with the most important matters, a man who has lived shamefully at home? (1.188)

Demosthenes' arguments against Philip II play on a similar set of ideas: the depravity of Philip's domestic life (described at 2.18–20), not only parallels his duplicity in interstate conduct (described at 2.5–8), but also provides another reason why his success in foreign affairs will not last for long:

ἀλλ᾽, οἶμαι, νῦν μὲν ἐπισκοτεῖ τούτοις τὸ κατορθοῦν· αἱ γὰρ εὐπραξίαι δειναὶ συγκρύψαι τὰ τοιαῦτα ὀνείδη· εἰ δέ τι πταίσει, τότ᾽ ἀκριβῶς αὐτοῦ ταῦτα ἐξετασθήσεται.

At the moment, I think, his prosperity obscures all of this; for success is good at concealing faults of this sort. But if he slips up at all, then we shall know all about his vices.[71] (2.20)

The assumption, or claim, of the transferability of judgements from one area of activity to the other can, then, be used, as here, as a subsidiary part of some larger case, but it is also possible to make these ideas more central to the logic, and presentation, of an argument.

One place where the identity of domestic and external does seem to be crucial to the argument is in Aristotle's fullest account of the morality of interstate behaviour (in the seventh book of the *Politics*, especially at 1324a35–25b33, 1333b5–34b4). This passage has been interpreted as demonstrating precisely the opposite of the claim which I want to investigate here: that is, as showing that Greek states approached their external relations with significantly different attitudes from those which they used in their domestic affairs.[72] And it does seem that this is what Aristotle alleges to be the case:

ἀλλ᾽ ἐοίκασιν οἱ πολλοὶ τὴν δεσποτικὴν πολιτικὴν οἴεσθαι εἶναι, καὶ ὅπερ αὑτοῖς ἕκαστοι οὔ φασιν εἶναι δίκαιον οὐδὲ συμφέρον, τοῦτ᾽ οὐκ αἰσχύνονται πρὸς τοὺς ἄλλους ἀσκοῦντες· αὐτοὶ μὲν γὰρ παρ᾽ αὑτοῖς τὸ δικαίως ἄρχειν ζητοῦσι, πρὸς δὲ τοὺς ἄλλους οὐδὲν μέλει τῶν δικαίων.

---

[71] The point that success based in immorality is fragile has also been made in the earlier passage: some slight slip (πταῖσμα; 2.9) will, in the end, cause Philip's downfall. Such claims also, of course, rely on the belief that immorality (in any sphere) will not bring success: for one of the more literal manifestations of that idea, see Theopompus (*FGH* 115) F40, on the fate of the Ardiaeans, whose lack of self-control leads to a violent bout of food-poisoning, and so to military disaster; for the reverse process (excesses in foreign relations leading to decline at home), see Xenophon *Lac.* xiv. Generally on this subject, see de Romilly 1977: chs. 3 and 4.

[72] De Ste. Croix 1972: 17.

Yet the majority seem to think that despotic rule is statesmanship, and are not ashamed to practise towards others treatment which they would not claim to be just or beneficial for themselves; for in their own cases they seek just government, yet in their relations with others they pay no attention to justice.[73] (1324b32–6)

What is less often made clear, however (and what justifies the inclusion of this passage in this section of this chapter, rather than the next), is not only that Aristotle does not endorse this view – it is, for him, ἄγαν ἄτοπον ('excessively illogical'; 1324b23) – but that his opposition to it is not based on any moral objection to imperialism as such, but on a more fundamental attitude to the connection between domestic and interstate behaviour. The assumption of this connection is, I think, implicit in the extension of Aristotle's arguments about natural and unnatural slavery (and tyranny) to the case of interstate despotism:

ἄτοπον δὲ εἰ μὴ φύσει τὸ μὲν δεσποστόν ἐστι τὸ δὲ οὐ δεσποστόν, ὥστε εἴπερ ἔχει τὸν τρόπον τοῦτον, οὐ δεῖ πάντων πειρᾶσθαι δεσπόζειν, ἀλλὰ τῶν δεσποστῶν.

Yet it is strange if there is not a natural distinction between peoples suited to be despotically ruled and those not suited; so that if this is so, it is not proper to attempt to exercise despotic government over all people, but only over those suited for it.[74] (1324b36–9)

External policies (especially warfare) should not, Aristotle argues, be seen as a special case, but treated, like other activities, as a means to an end; and that end is – for the individual and for the state – the achievement of the good life and of *eudaimonia* (1325a5–11).[75] And it is the failure to recognise this, or to appreciate the fact that

[73] It is possible to read this accusation not as one of inconsistency between domestic and external behaviour, but of inconsistency over time: when people are under someone else's control, they believe in the just treatment of the ruled, but they forget it when they have the upper hand (for this interpretation, see Kraut 1997 *ad loc.*). However, the context of this statement (and especially the reference at 1324b24–5 to the statesman who ἄρχῃ καὶ δεσπόζῃ τῶν πλησίον, 'rules and controls his neighbours') makes it more likely that it is a contrast between domestic and interstate which is intended here.

[74] On Aristotle's use of this analogy, see Garnsey 1996: 115–19; Kraut 1997: 63–4. Compare 1333b38–1334a14: military training should have the aim not of 'enslaving those who do not deserve it' (καταδουλώσωνται τοὺς ἀναξίους), but of avoiding one's own enslavement, and of 'ruling over those who deserve to be slaves' (δεσπόζειν τῶν ἀξίων δουλεύειν).

[75] Similar reasoning lies behind Aristotle's objection to the Spartan constitution (1334a40–b3): the error of the Spartans is to privilege one aspect (warfare) of the means to the end (the acquisition of virtues) over the virtues themselves. For the claim that the same reasoning must be applied to states as to individuals, a point repeatedly made in book VII, see also, for example, 1324a33–5; 1334a11–13.

ethical schemes developed with reference to domestic life must also include interstate behaviour, which makes illogic, or oddity (ἄτοπον) the most appropriate charge against the attitude of 'the many'.

A second example, very different in many ways but relying on a very similar set of basic ideas, can be found in Isocrates' *On the Peace*. In this speech the analogy between domestic and foreign conduct – expressed in a variety of ways – becomes a central theme, which it is worth exploring in some detail.

Isocrates' speech was delivered – or purports to have been delivered – in the context of the Social War: it is an attempt to divert the Athenians from their journey down the road to ruin; to show them how best to restore their hegemony of the Greek world.[76] Isocrates' master-plan is, broadly speaking, based on the idea that Athenian success will best be achieved not through conquest, or through any sort of aggression, but through a more subtle blend of restraint, good deeds and general inspiration of *eunoia* among the Greek states. Isocrates is not, therefore, proposing that Athens should give up any ambitions to be the leading state among the Greeks – it is the means, not the desired end, which need to be changed. This is not, of course, an idea which is restricted to this speech;[77] what distinguishes this version of the argument is its presentation through the assertion of parallels and analogies between life inside the *polis* and the behaviour of the *polis* towards those on the outside.

The opening sections of the speech introduce Isocrates' topic in relatively familiar and conventional ways. The first theme is that of the difficulty of providing proper advice to the Athenians, or – more accurately – of getting them to pay any attention to the best advice (§1–15).[78] Isocrates then moves on to provide a reasonably focused

---

[76] On the 'seriousness' of this speech – a traditional problem for Isocratean scholarship (see Baynes 1955) – see (against) Harding 1973 and (for) Moysey 1982. The value of the speech as evidence for one (not necessarily *the*) way of thinking about Athenian imperialism (in its past and present manifestations) is convincingly argued for by Davidson 1990 (which is also the best recent analysis of the speech). On the structure of arguments in the speech, see also Gillis 1970; Michelini 1998; on its attitude to Athenian foreign policy, Mathieu 1925: ch. 10; Bringmann 1965: ch. 4; Grieser-Schmitz 1999: 172–94.

[77] Although Isocrates' writing is far from being entirely consistent on the subject of foreign relations, the works of the 350s (*On the Peace, Areopagiticus, Antidosis*) do present a relatively coherent line. See Wallace 1985: 158–60; more generally on the coherence of Isocrates, Too 1995: ch. 2.

[78] Compare, for example, the opening of Demosthenes' *Second Olynthiac*.

and straightforward account of his policy (§16–27): a peace should be made, and its terms should be modelled on those of the Common Peaces; this will lead to increased political and economic security – even prosperity; Athens' position as leader of the Greeks will not be compromised.

The point where the argument takes an unexpected turn is at §28, when Isocrates embarks on his justification of this policy. It is not the behaviour of cities, but that of men which forms the starting point of his explanation:

ἔχει γὰρ οὕτως. ἐμοὶ δοκοῦσιν ἅπαντες μὲν ἐπιθυμεῖν τοῦ συμφέροντος καὶ τοῦ πλέον ἔχειν τῶν ἄλλων, οὐκ εἰδέναι δὲ τὰς πράξεις τὰς ἐπὶ ταῦτα φερούσας, ἀλλὰ ταῖς δόξαις διαφέρειν ἀλλήλων· οἱ μὲν γὰρ ἔχειν ἐπιεικεῖς καὶ στοχάζεσθαι τοῦ δέοντος δυναμένας, οἱ δ' ὡς οἷόν τε πλεῖστον τοῦ συμφέροντος διαμαρτανούσας. ὅπερ καὶ τῇ πόλει συμβέβηκεν.

For this is how it is. It seems to me that, while all men crave their advantage and desire to be better off than the rest, they do not know what kind of conduct leads to this end but differ from each other in judgement; some behave reasonably and are capable of hitting the right course of action; others completely miss their true advantage. And this is the very thing which has happened to our city. (§28–9)

The analogy between the failures of individuals and that of cities (in this case, the *polis* as a whole, rather than the Athenians as a collection of individuals) is emphasised here, and Isocrates goes on to illustrate his point – that men and cities have a misguided impression of what is in their best interests – with the example of Athenian foreign policy: the Athenians persist in their belief that imposing their authority is the way to success, while the evidence suggests that a more gentle approach might bring better results (§29–30).[79] But in the sections which follow, as Isocrates turns to consider the question of what sort of behaviour will produce success, the expression of the argument slips almost imperceptibly back into terms which suggest that Isocrates is thinking now of the individual in his everyday life (τὸν βίον τὸν καθ'ἡμέραν; §31): how should the ἀγαθοῖς οἷς ἔχομεν ἐν τῇ ψυχῇ ('the good things which

---

[79] The point is reiterated, again with the explicit comparison of individual life and interstate politics, at §110. The argument (without the analogy) is used elsewhere of interstate relations: see, for example, Aeschines 2.70–3 (acquisitiveness of Athenian generals causes Athens to lose hegemony); Isocrates 14.39–41 (hegemony goes to those who behave justly, or oppose injustice).

we have in our soul'; §32) best be cultivated? This is, therefore, a reverse example of the phenomenon noted above in the discussions of Plato and Aristotle: the broad context, and the main focus, of the work are the morals of interstate politics, but the morality of the individual repeatedly intrudes.

This slippage can be seen again when Isocrates returns to this theme later in the speech. This time, the discussion seems to start at the level of the morality of individuals. A reference back to the earlier treatment of the subject reinforces that impression:

ἃ μὲν οὖν ὑπάρχειν δεῖ τοῖς μέλλουσιν εὐδαιμονήσειν, τήν τ᾽ εὐσεβείαν καὶ τὴν σωφροσύνην καὶ τὴν δικαιοσύνην καὶ τὴν ἄλλην ἀρετήν, ὀλίγῳ πρότερον εἰρήκαμεν.

Therefore, the qualities which we must possess if we are to be happy and prosperous, namely, piety and prudence and justice and *aretē* in all other respects, I mentioned a moment ago. (§63)

But, here as there (although the direction of the shift is reversed), the focus of attention subtly moves towards the behaviour of those individuals as a group, directing the affairs of the *polis*. Indeed, the inextricable connection between what is good for the individual and what is good for the *polis* is made explicit at this point:

ἐγὼ γὰρ ἡγοῦμαι καὶ τὴν πόλιν ἡμᾶς ἄμεινον οἰκήσειν καὶ βελτίους αὐτοὺς ἔσεσθαι καὶ πρὸς ἁπάσας τὰς πράξεις ἐπιδώσειν, ἢν παυσώμεθα τῆς ἀρχῆς τῆς κατὰ θάλατταν ἐπιθυμοῦντες.

For I believe that we shall manage our city to better advantage and be ourselves better men and go forward in all our undertakings, if we stop hankering after the empire of the sea. (§64)

What makes Isocrates' approach more interesting, however, is the fact that the boundary between domestic and external is not always allowed to be so fluid. Because, although Isocrates wants to insist on the permeability of that boundary – on the absolute applicability of the morality of individual life to the interstate relations of the *polis* (and *vice versa*) – his argument also requires him to acknowledge that the Athenians have not always realised this obvious fact. This – undesirable – gap is therefore emphasised when Isocrates returns to this theme for a third time towards the end of the speech:

ἦν [i.e. τὴν σωφροσύνην] ὑμεῖς ἐπὶ μὲν τῶν ἰδιωτῶν ἐπαινεῖτε, καὶ νομίζετε τοὺς
ταύτῃ χρωμένους ἀσφαλέστατα ζῆν καὶ βελτίστους εἶναι τῶν πολιτῶν, τὸ
δὲ κοινὸν ἡμῶν οὐκ οἴεσθε δεῖν τοιοῦτον παρασκευάζειν. καίτοι προσήκει τὰς
ἀρετὰς ἀσκεῖν καὶ τὰς κακίας φεύγειν πολὺ μᾶλλον ταῖς πόλεσιν ἢ τοῖς ἰδιώταις.
ἀνὴρ μὲν γὰρ ἀσεβὴς καὶ πονηρὸς τυχὸν ἂν φθάσειε τελευτήσας πρὶν δοῦναι
δίκην τῶν ἡμαρτημένων· αἱ δὲ πόλεις διὰ τὴν ἀθανασίαν ὑπομένουσι καὶ τὰς
παρὰ τῶν ἀνθρώπων καὶ τὰς παρὰ τῶν θεῶν τιμωρίας.

But, while you commend *sōphrosunē* in individual men and believe that those
who practice it enjoy the most secure existence and are the best of the citizens,
you do not think it fit to make the state practise it. And yet it is fitting for cities
much more than individuals to cultivate the virtues and to shun vices; for a man
who is godless and depraved may die before paying the penalty for his sins, but
cities, since they are immortal, must endure punishment at the hands both of men
and of the gods. (§119–20)

But while at one level Isocrates' line here seems to conflict with
his presentation earlier in the speech, it is, in fact, precisely that
early insistence on, or rather assumption of, the naturalness of
the analogy which allows him to represent the Athenians' current
attitude as so unnatural, and so misguided.

A rather different sort of analogy between domestic and
external – that between the tyrant and the tyrant empire – is also
prominent in this speech, and is presented in a similar way. There
is, first of all, some overlap in content: the idea of tyranny – as
it is portrayed by Isocrates – is also closely related to his more
general moral ideas on the importance of restraint, the necessity
of avoiding superficially easy routes to power, and so on.[80] And in
this case too, Isocrates seems initially to assert as an accepted fact,
rather than specifically argue for, the congruence of the two types
of behaviour (and their consequences). The idea of the misery of
the tyrant is first explicitly developed at §91, where it is inserted
into a discussion of the Athenians' fifth-century empire:

τῶν μὲν γὰρ ἀρχόντων ἔργον ἐστὶ τοὺς ἀρχομένους ταῖς αὐτῶν ἐπιμελείαις
ποιεῖν εὐδαιμονεστέρους, τοῖς δὲ τυράννοις ἔθος καθέστηκε τοῖς τῶν ἄλλων
πόνοις καὶ κακοῖς αὐτοῖς ἡδονὰς παρασκευάζειν. ἀνάγκη δὲ τοὺς τοιούτοις
ἔργοις ἐπιχειροῦντας τυραννικαῖς καὶ ταῖς συμφοραῖς περιπίπτειν, καὶ τοιαῦτα
πάσχειν οἷά περ ἂν καὶ τοὺς ἄλλους δράσωσιν. ἃ καὶ τῇ πόλει συνέπεσεν.

[80] See Davidson 1990: 31–2; more generally on Isocrates' use of the concept of tyranny in
this speech, Wehrli 1968.

For it is the duty of those who rule to direct their efforts towards making their subjects happier, whereas it is a habit of those who dominate to provide pleasures for themselves through the toils and hardships of others. But, by necessity, those who attempt the latter method must encounter the disasters which befall tyrannical power and be afflicted by the very things which they inflict upon others. And it is just this which has happened to our city.

Again, therefore, the shift of focus from interstate to internal politics is not very strongly marked, although the move back to the affairs of the *polis* is given rather greater emphasis. The legitimacy of the analogy is not, it would seem, a subject of great dispute.[81] And again, this allows Isocrates to represent the Athenians' behaviour as even more misguided when he returns to this theme towards the end of the speech. The account of the wretched condition of the tyrant is repeated, and expanded upon (not only will the tyrant meet an unpleasant end, he is also condemned to live in constant fear and uncertainty: §111–13). But on this occasion Isocrates does not argue for, or even assert, the relevance of the tyrant's life to the conduct of a hegemonic *polis*, but immediately reproaches the Athenians for their failure to appreciate this relevance:

οὐκ ἀγνοῶ δ' ὅτι τὸν μὲν περὶ τῶν τυράννων λόγον ἀποδέχεσθε, τὸν δὲ περὶ τῆς ἀρχῆς δυσκόλως ἀκούετε· πεπόνθατε γὰρ πάντων αἴσχιστον καὶ ῥᾳθυμότατον· ἃ γὰρ ἐπὶ τῶν ἄλλων ὁρᾶτε, ταῦτ' ἐφ' ὑμῶν αὐτῶν ἀγνοεῖτε. καίτοι τῶν φρονίμως διακειμένων οὐκ ἐλάχιστον τοῦτο σημεῖόν ἐστιν, ἢν τὰς αὐτὰς πράξεις ἐπὶ πάντων τῶν ὁμοίων φαίνωνται γνωρίζοντες.

But I do not fail to realize that while you accept readily what I say about tyrants, yet you hear with intolerance what I say about empire. For you have fallen into a most shameful and lazy way of thinking, since what you see clearly in the case of others, you ignore in yourselves. And yet it is not the least important sign of whether men are possessed of intelligence if they are seen to recognize the same course of conduct in all cases that are comparable.[82] (§114)

---

[81] A feature of Isocrates' argument noted as puzzling by Tuplin 1985: 361: 'despite the admission that Athenians were unwilling to perceive similarities between τυραννίς and ἀρχή Isocrates provides surprisingly little exposition of these similarities and largely treats them as a *datum*, an assumption at which nobody *ought* to cavil' (emphasis original).

[82] Compare also the analogy between Athens' internal democratic government, and her failure to apply these principles to her external relations: ὅτι μὲν οὖν οὐ δίκαιόν ἐστι τοὺς κρείττους τῶν ἡττόνων ἄρχειν, ἐν ἐκείνοις τε τοῖς χρόνοις τυγχάνομεν ἐγνωκότες, καὶ νῦν ἐπὶ τῆς πολιτείας τῆς παρ' ἡμῖν καθεστηκυίας ('in that period we recognised the fact that it is not just for the strong to rule over the weak, as now in the constitution which is established among us'; §69). Here too Isocrates does not argue for the legitimacy of the comparison, but moves immediately to criticise the Athenians' failure to appreciate it.

There are various reasons why this type of argument is particularly useful for Isocrates in this speech. In terms of rhetorical artistry, the representation of interstate politics as analogous to human conduct reinforces, and is reinforced by, the extensive use of the language of personal experience and emotion. The language of love and desire, for example, is an especially prominent theme in the speech,[83] and not only functions in its own right as a powerful source of imagery and metaphor (for example, the representation of empire as a destructive *hetaira*, killing those who are seduced by her: §103), but also reinforces Isocrates' moral argument of the dangers of unrestrained desire and ambition for the private individual, the tyrant and the *polis*. At a much more general level, the connection between domestic and external can also be linked to Isocrates' long-standing views on the intrinsic connection between Athenian domestic and external stability: foreign success increases domestic prosperity (see, for example, 8.20); but domestic failings are also responsible for external weakness – in the *Areopagiticus*, for example, it is argued that the reason for Athens' poor standing in the Greek world can be found in the debased condition of her internal politics (e.g., 7.11–15, 79–83).[84] But what needs to be emphasised here is the fact that, whatever Isocrates' motive in focusing on the identity of domestic (whether personal or public) and interstate morality, this identity is represented as the unquestioned starting point, not the object, of his argument: it is, for Isocrates in this speech, the proper and natural approach; and it is the Athenians' misguided deviation from that approach that Isocrates wants to demonstrate.

4.4 Arguments for difference? Power, self-interest and justice

It could, however, be objected that, even if this is a plausible interpretation of Isocrates' approach to the subject, any explanation of

---

[83] See Davidson 1990: 24–9.

[84] An argument which is linked, in turn, to another recurring Isocratean complaint: the failure of the Athenians to select or listen to the correct leaders: see, for example, 8.13. For a variation on the theme, note the culmination of the account of the career of Timotheus in the *Antidosis*: Timotheus put Isocrates' ideas into practice, and succeeded in external politics; but failed to use the same techniques in his conduct of domestic politics, and so met an unpleasant end (15.135).

Greek interstate' morality which is modelled on Isocrates is likely to be extremely incomplete, if not entirely misleading. And it is true that there might seem to be one striking lacuna in the account which has been presented so far: where is the dialogue between 'might' and 'right'; or that between the (weak) demands of justice and the (powerful) claim of self-interest?

Although distinct, and worth treating separately, these two types of argument are closely connected. Versions of both can be seen in the arguments given to Thrasymachus in the first book of the *Republic*.[85] Thrasymachus' first claim is that justice can be defined as, and identified with, what is in the interests of the stronger: τὸ δίκαιον οὐκ ἄλλο τι ἢ τὸ τοῦ κρείττονος συμφέρον ('justice is nothing other than that which benefits the stronger'; 338c1–2). Those in power define what justice is, and will do so in their own interests. It is this argument which is closest, although not identical, to a 'conventionalist' position: that justice is created by those in power; or to put it another way, that might makes right.[86]

Thrasymachus' second line of argument is rather different, per-haps even contradictory:[87] the problem with justice is not that it is purely conventional, but that it is irrelevant. Justice involves acting in another's interest (and against one's own interests); injustice is the way to happiness and success (343a–344c).[88]

A third variation on the theme is that offered by Callicles in the *Gorgias*, in an argument based on a distinction between two types of justice. His 'conventional' justice is a justice which allows the weaker to restrain the stronger, and relies on a *nomos* developed by

---

[85] Generally on Thrasymachus' arguments, see Annas 1981: 34–57.

[86] On 'conventionalism' and Thrasymachus' argument, see Annas 1981: 39–43, who emphasises (at 42) that in rejecting Cleitophon's amendment to his definition (340b6–8: that justice is what the stronger *think* good for them (not necessarily what really is good for them)), Thrasymachus also avoids committing himself to a fully conventionalist position.

[87] For an attempt to resolve the contradiction, see Nicholson 1974; for the suggestion that the contradiction is deliberate and important to the broader structure of the *Republic*, see Everson 1998.

[88] The 'immoralist' argument: see Annas 1981: 36–7. For a weaker version of this, made with reference to interstate relations, see Isocrates 12.117–18: faced with a choice between doing or suffering injustice, Athens was right to choose the former. Again, this choice is presented as being in accordance with a universal moral norm: ἅπερ ἅπαν-τες μὲν ἂν οἱ νοῦν ἔχοντες ἕλοιντο καὶ βουληθεῖεν ('which all sensible people would choose and plan for'; 12.118). (On Isocrates' ambivalent approach to the subject of the benefits of justice in this speech, see Dawson 1996: 81–2.)

οἱ ἀσθενεῖς . . . καὶ οἱ πολλοί ('the weak and the masses'; 483b5–6). By a different route, therefore, Callicles arrives at the same problem reached by Thrasymachus in his second argument: for the strong, adhering to this justice will involve acting in the interest of others. However, Callicles' solution to this problem is not to recommend unjust behaviour as the way to success, but to develop a new idea of justice – a 'natural' justice, which is equated to the wishes of the strong:

ἡ δέ γε οἶμαι φύσις αὐτὴ ἀποφαίνει αὐτὸ ὅτι δίκαιόν ἐστιν τὸν ἀμείνω τοῦ χείρονος πλέον ἔχειν καὶ τὸν δυνατώτερον τοῦ ἀδυνατωτέρου. δηλοῖ δὲ ταῦτα πολλαχοῦ ὅτι οὕτως ἔχει, καὶ ἐν τοῖς ἄλλοις ζῴοις καὶ τῶν ἀνθρώπων ἐν ὅλαις ταῖς πόλεσι καὶ τοῖς γένεσιν, ὅτι οὕτω τὸ δίκαιον κέκριται, τὸν κρείττω τοῦ ἥττονος ἄρχειν καὶ πλέον ἔχειν.

But nature, in my opinion, herself proclaims the fact that it is right for the better to have more than the worse, and the more powerful to have more than the less powerful. It is obvious in many cases that this is so, not only in the animal world, but in the states and races, collectively, of men, that right has been judged to consist in the rule and advantage of the stronger over the weaker.[89] (483c9–d6)

None of these arguments, as they appear in Plato's work, have any specific connection to interstate relations: in fact, as was noted above (152) they are supported (and opposed) by reference to examples from both domestic and interstate behaviour.[90] But it is in the context of interstate relations that these arguments, and versions of them, receive their most prominent 'practical' (or non-philosophical) application: most famously, and most influentially, in the speeches of Thucydides.[91] It is in the Melian dialogue that it seems possible to find an approach which comes closest to the 'immoralist' view – justice exists, but it is irrelevant:

δίκαια μὲν ἐν τῷ ἀνθρωπείῳ λόγῳ ἀπὸ τῆς ἴσης ἀνάγκης κρίνεται, δυνατὰ δὲ οἱ προύχοντες πράσσουσι καὶ οἱ ἀσθενεῖς ξυγχωροῦσιν.

[89] On Callicles' arguments, and their relation to those of Thrasymachus, see Annas 1981: 48–50.

[90] See Kokaz 2001: 33 for the observation that, although the *nomos/phusis* distinction does not map onto a division between inside and outside, there is a strong tendency among International Theorists to assume that it does.

[91] See, for example, Adkins 1960: 234: in order to see the extent of the acceptance of Thrasymachean/Calliclean ideas, 'it is only necessary to consider Athens' (fifth-century) foreign policy'. The same connection is made by Barker 1960: 83–6. For a recent example of this view, see Green 1999.

Justice, in human affairs, is only in question between equals in power, while the strong do what they can and the weak suffer what they must. (v.89)

It is also here that the practical consequences of such an argument are made explicit: if justice has no place in the hierarchised world of interstate relations, then decision-making in that sphere must be made purely on the basis of τὸ συμφέρον (*to sumpheron*; 'expediency'; a point conceded by the Melians: v.90).[92]

This model of the operation of interstate morality, and interstate decision-making, has (as was suggested earlier)[93] been enormously influential, not only for interpretations of modern international relations, but also for analyses of Greek interstate relations. And it is true that there does seem to be at least one other expression of this 'Thucydidean' approach: namely, Demosthenes' assertion in his speech *For the Liberty of the Rhodians*:

τῶν μὲν γὰρ ἰδίων δικαίων τῶν ἐν ταῖς πολιτείαις οἱ νόμοι κοινὴν τὴν μετουσίαν ἔδοσαν καὶ ἴσην καὶ τοῖς ἀσθενέσιν καὶ τοῖς ἰσχυροῖς· τῶν δὲ Ἑλληνικῶν δικαίων οἱ κρατοῦντες ὁρισταὶ τοῖς ἥττοσι γίγνονται.

Of private rights within a state, the laws of that state grant an equal and impartial share to all, weak and strong alike; but the rights of Greek states are defined by the strong for the weak. (15.29)

In fact, this claim is not so much an heir to the sentiments of the Melian Dialogue,[94] as a variation on Thrasymachus' first argument. Demosthenes is not suggesting here that power makes justice irrelevant to interstate relations: justice exists, but it is defined by the powerful. What is striking, however – because it marks an important difference from the Platonic version of the argument and because it makes explicit what is only implicit in the version found in the Melian Dialogue – is the insistence that this is not true of justice within the *polis*. Only interstate relations are affected.

---

[92] Note that, even here, the Athenians state this as a global truth: it may be more likely to apply in interstate politics, but is not explicitly confined to that sphere. Sharper distinctions between inside and outside do appear elsewhere in the dialogue: the allegation made by the Athenians (at v.105.4), that the Spartans have a habit of calling τὰ ξυμφέροντα δίκαια ('what is convenient, just'), is claimed to apply only to their conduct in interstate politics. (On this claim, see further n. 108 below, and ch. 6, sec. 3.)

[93] See ch. 1, sections 4 and 5.

[94] Which is how it is often presented: see, especially, de Ste. Croix 1972: 16–17; Radicke 1995 *ad loc*. There is, clearly, a shared interest in the relationship between power and justice, but this can perhaps obscure the fact that the way in which that relationship is expressed is significantly different.

The fact that such a forceful claim to the distinction between domestic and external could be made should not, of course, be ignored. But it is equally important not to give too much emphasis to this one passage: Demosthenes may present the statement as indisputable fact (much as Isocrates presents his, very different, approach to the question), but it is extremely hard to find any parallel examples.[95]

It is, however – or at least seems initially to be – much easier to find examples of the alternative formulation of the argument: justice is irrelevant to interstate relations; expediency, self-interest, *to sumpheron*, is what matters. The most systematic account of that view appears towards the start of Aristotle's *Rhetoric*. In introducing the three divisions of rhetoric (symbouleutic, forensic, epideictic), Aristotle sets out what should be the proper concerns of each type.[96] The goal of the deliberative orator seems clear enough:

τέλος δὲ ἑκάστοις τούτων ἕτερόν ἐστι, καὶ τρισὶν οὖσι τρία, τῷ μὲν συμ-βουλεύοντι τὸ συμφέρον καὶ βλαβερόν· ὁ μὲν γὰρ προτρέπων ὡς βέλτιον συμ-βουλεύει, ὁ δε ἀποτρέπων ὡς χείρονος ἀποτρέπει, τὰ δ' ἄλλα πρὸς τοῦτο συμπαραλαμβάνει, ἢ δίκαιον ἢ ἄδικον, ἢ καλὸν ἢ αἰσχρόν.

Each of the three kinds has a different goal, and as there are three kinds of Rhetoric, so there are three goals. The goal of the deliberative speaker is the expedient or harmful; for he who exhorts recommends a course of action as better, and he who dissuades advises against it as worse; all other considerations, such as justice and injustice, honour and disgrace, are included as accessory in reference to this. (1358b20–5)

When Aristotle returns to the point shortly afterwards his position has been slightly modified: just (*dikaion*) and unjust (*adikon*) are no longer simply less important parts of an argument than *to sumpheron*, they have no necessary part in the argument at all:

---

[95] Thucydidean endorsement of this approach is less whole-hearted than is sometimes suggested: the opinion that domestic and interstate morality is distinct is expressed (especially in the Melian Dialogue), but the work also includes claims (made by speakers, and in the authorial voice) pointing to a closer connection between the morality applicable between states and that which operates between individuals within states (e.g. 1.144.3: Pericles on the best route to honour for citizen and city; III.82.2: Thucydides on the corrosive effects of war on cities and individuals). For further discussion and examples, see Hornblower 1987: 178–82.

[96] On the tripartite division, see Rorty 1996.

οἱ συμβουλεύοντες τὰ μὲν ἄλλα πολλάκις προΐενται, ὡς δὲ ἀσύμφορα συμβουλεύουσιν ἢ ἀπ' ὠφελίμων ἀποτρέπουσιν οὐκ ἂν ὁμολογήσαιεν· ὡς δ' [οὐκ] ἄδικον τοὺς ἀστυγείτονας καταδουλοῦσθαι καὶ τοὺς μηδὲν ἀδικοῦντας, πολλάκις οὐδὲν φροντίζουσιν.

Similarly, the deliberative orator, although he often sacrifices everything else, will never admit that he is recommending what is inexpedient or is dissuading from what is useful; but often he is quite indifferent about showing that the enslavement of neighbouring peoples, even if they have done no wrong, is not an act of injustice. (1358b33–7)

However, although Aristotle's chosen example seems best interpreted as referring to interstate relations, it is important to note that the divide for which he is arguing is not, in fact, between domestic and interstate conduct, but between various types of behaviour, which could relate to actions either within or outside the *polis*. Symbouleutic rhetoric is not concerned only with the foreign relations of the *polis*, but with all deliberation in the assembly, as well as with advice offered in private (ἰδίᾳ; *Rhet.* 1358b9–10). In the *Rhetoric*, therefore, as in the *Politics*, the boundary between domestic and external is not emphasised.[97]

The consideration of the *Rhetoric* could, therefore, stop at this point: the argument for a distinction between *to dikaion* and *to sumpheron* may be visible in that work, but the claim that this distinction corresponds to one between behaviour inside and outside the *polis* is not. And since it is extremely hard to find such a claim being endorsed anywhere else either, the issue becomes, strictly speaking, irrelevant to the subject of this chapter.[98] In spite of this, however, it does seem worth pursuing this subject a little further, not only because the (alleged) dichotomy between justice and expediency seems so important to accounts of the (im)morality

[97] Noted by Yatromanolaki 1997: 1–2, 11–12.

[98] The one place where such a distinction might be seen is in the speech of Diodotus at the Mytilenean debate (III.41–8): *to dikaion* and *to sumpheron* are treated as discrete concepts, and the former is argued to be irrelevant to the decision facing the Athenians. Note, however, both that this approach is also applied by Diodotus (by implication) to domestic security (in the argument on deterrence: III.45), and that Diodotus' approach to interstate morality is juxtaposed with one (that of Cleon, at III.37–40) which, although more keen to insist on a distinction between conduct appropriate to domestic and interstate politics (see esp. III.37.1), relies heavily on the applicability of both *to dikaion* and *to sumpheron* to interstate affairs. (On the use of justice and other arguments in this debate, see esp. Macleod 1983a.)

of interstate relations,[99] but also because, although *dikaion* and *sumpheron* do appear extensively in both the theory and practice of 'interstate' rhetoric, the relationship between them is not always, I think, quite as antithetical as is sometimes assumed, nor are the concepts themselves quite as straightforward as they might sometimes seem.

The language of justice is widely used in classical rhetoric (both domestic and interstate), particularly, although not exclusively, in fourth-century texts.[100] Moreover it often appears alongside discussions of expediency. Indeed, even the 'buzzwords' *to sumpheron* and *to dikaion* regularly appear in combination: the two factors are represented as distinct, but rarely as independent. This last characteristic was noted, and regretted, by Dover:

unfortunately, 'just and advantageous' became a cliché which by no means implied that both the justice and the advantage of the action so commended could be demonstrated independently.[101]

It is certainly true that many of these words do seem to appear most frequently as a sort of catchphrase, as, for example, in the closing sentiment of [Dem.] *On Halonnesus*: the speaker states the intention:

[99] 'The most important point', according to Dover 1974: 311; see also Walbank's (1985a: 175) description of Carneades' speech against justice (delivered in Rome in 156/5 BC: Cic. *Rep.* 3.6–7; Lactantius *Inst.Div.* 5.14.3–5): 'to a Greek already preoccupied with the question of empire the idea of τὸ συμφέρον [*to sumpheron*] as a criterion of conduct was of course familiar, and Polybius will have regarded much of Carneades' thesis as consisting of truisms. But for the Romans it was different.' Even Phillipson concedes the primacy of self-interest in Greek interstate relations (especially 'under the stress of unexpected conditions': Phillipson 1911, vol. II: 90). The importance of the subject, and its controversial status, continues into modern International Relations: on Hobbes' line (and its relation to Thucydides), see Johnson 1993: ch. 2; for a more recent statement of a similar view (the 'national interest' is to be separated totally from ideas of right and wrong), Oppenheim 1987. See also Osgood 1953, both for the claim that 'the conflict between ideals and self-interest is as much a part of the international life of the United States as it was of Athens' (1), and for an account of the interaction of these two ideas in US foreign policy of the first half of the twentieth century. For more theoretical approaches to the question of interest in IR, see Kratochwil 1982; Brown 2001a; for investigations of the problem from a philosophical perspective, see Gauthier ed. 1970.

[100] See Heath 1990 for an analysis of the language of justice in both Thucydidean and non-Thucydidean rhetoric.

[101] Dover 1974: 309. Compare Dawson 1996: 82–4, who notes that the two are often used in combination in fourth-century rhetoric, but sees this as a marker of a lack of sophistication (in contrast to the Thucydidean approach). Kennedy 1959 also argues for diachronic development, from the polarised model of the fifth century, through the middle ground of Demosthenes, to the synthetic approach adopted by Isocrates.

γράψαι τὴν ἀπόκρισιν, ἣν ἡγοῦμαι δικαίαν τ' εἶναι καὶ συμφέρουσαν ὑμῖν.

of proposing the resolution which I conceive to be in accordance with justice and your interests. (7.46)

Isocrates, in the *Antidosis*, claims that, if the Athenians were to listen to his advice,

ὅλην τὴν Ἑλλάδα καλῶς ἂν διοικοῖτε καὶ δικαίως καὶ τῇ πόλει συμφερόντως.

you might direct the whole of Hellas with honour and justice and, at the same time, with advantage to Athens.[102] (15.79)

The impression that the two factors should be seen as mutually reinforcing (rather than mutually exclusive) incentives to action is strengthened by the analysis given in the *Rhetoric to Alexander*, in the course of a discussion of types of arguments which should be used when discussing peace and war:

προφάσεις μὲν οὖν εἰσι τοῦ πόλεμον ἐκφέρειν πρός τινας αἵδε· πρότερον ἀδικηθέν-
τας νῦν καιροῦ παραπεπτωκότως ἀμύνασθαι τοὺς ἀδικήσαντας, ἢ νῦν ἀδικουμένους ὑπὲρ αὑτῶν πολεμεῖν ἢ ὑπὲρ συγγενῶν ἢ ὑπὲρ εὐεργετῶν, ἢ συμμάχοις
ἀδικουμένοις βοηθεῖν, ἢ τοῦ τῇ πόλει συμφέροντος ἕνεκεν ἢ εἰς εὐδοξίαν ἢ εἰς
εὐπορίαν ἢ εἰς δύναμιν ἢ εἰς ἄλλο τι τῶν τοιούτων.

These are the reasons for waging war against someone: having been wronged previously and now, when the opportunity arises, taking action against the wrongdoers; or, being wronged now, fighting on one's own behalf, or on behalf of kin or benefactors; or providing help to allies who have been wronged; or because it benefits the city; or for the sake of good reputation or resources or power or other similar motive. (1425a10–16)

Similarly, when arguing against war, the same range of considerations (and their inapplicability to the situation) should be demonstrated (1425a28–35).[103] Here too, then, there is a clear attempt to

---

[102] See Dover 1974: 309–10, 311–12, for further examples from domestic and interstate politics respectively.

[103] Arguments for war and peace come under the general heading of protreptic rhetoric, for which the appropriate criteria of argument are listed as: δίκαια . . . καὶ νόμιμα καὶ συμφέροντα καὶ καλὰ καὶ ἡδέα καὶ ῥάδια πραχθῆναι ('things which are just . . . and lawful and beneficial and good and sweet and easy to effect'; 1421b24–6). It is worth noting that the emphasis on *sumpheronta* and *dikaia* is not found in all discussions of interstate activities: the making of treaties, according to the *Rh.Al.*, should be debated at a more immediately practical level (1424b28–25a9; here too, though – although it is expressed in a different way – there is a combination of tangible considerations (what is the power of the state in question?) and more abstract concerns (are they just?)). But the

distinguish between the two factors; but there is no clear sign that one should be used to the exclusion of the other.[104]

It might, however, be possible to say something more about at least some of the instances of this 'cliché'. While modern ethics tends to characterise moral and prudential reasoning as being distinct parts of rational argument, it has been argued that this separation is much harder to identify in ancient ethical writing: a moral argument need not, therefore, replace or exclude practical, possibly even self-interested, considerations.[105] And this is a position which can be defended with reference to Aristotle's *Rhetoric*, to which it now, therefore, seems helpful to return. Although the statements at *Rhetoric* 1385b20–37 might seem to leave little room for manoeuvre, not everything which is said on the subject is contained in those paragraphs. First of all, it can be noted that considerations of justice, while in theory either demoted or entirely excluded from deliberative oratory, sometimes seem to creep back into the picture, and even to assume a prominent position:

ἐν δὲ τοῖς δημηγορικοῖς ἢ ὡς οὐκ ἔσται ἀμφισβητήσειεν ἄν τις, ἢ ὡς ἔσται μὲν <ποιοῦσιν> ἃ κελεύει, ἀλλ' οὐ δίκαια ἢ οὐκ ὠφέλιμα ἢ οὐ τηλικαῦτα.

In deliberative oratory, it may be maintained either that certain consequences will not happen, or that what the adversary recommends will happen, but that it will be unjust, inexpedient, or not so important as supposed. (*Rhet.* 1417b34–6)

This might seem to be nothing more than a variant expression of the familiar catchphrase, and another piece of supporting evidence for the divisibility of its two constituent parts.[106] But it could also encourage a consideration of some other sections of the work, where Aristotle seems to argue for a more intricate connection between justice and expediency. In book one of the *Rhetoric*, Aristotle produces an extensive definition of *to sumpheron*. The

appeal to *sumpheron* and *dikaion* is not restricted to discussions of war and peace: the advice on debating religious policy (1423a30–b9) is also based around those criteria. Again, therefore, there is variation in the appropriate type of argument for a given situation, but this variation does not map neatly onto a boundary between domestic and external politics.

[104] Although it is worth noting that justice appears first in the list of arguments; according to Heath 1990: 395, 'this priority is not casual'.

[105] See generally Annas 1995; Irwin 1995b.

[106] Further Aristotelean examples which might be used to support this view in Halliwell 1994: 223.

first move in this definition is the claim that τὸ δὲ συμφέρον ἀγαθόν ('what is beneficial is good'; 1362a20). A consideration of the nature of ἀγαθόν ('the good') follows: it is defined first of all as ὃ ἂν αὐτὸ ἑαυτοῦ ἕνεκα ᾖ αἱρετόν, καὶ οὗ ἕνεκα ἄλλο αἱρούμεθα ('that which is desirable for its own sake, or for the sake of which we choose something else'; 1362a21–3). This definition is backed up by an extended list of examples, and the concluding item in this list is: τὸ δίκαιον· συμφέρον γὰρ τι κοινῇ ἐστιν ('justice; since this is beneficial in general'; 1362b28). In Aristotle's scheme of things, therefore, *to sumpheron* seems not to be something detachable from justice, or from ethical values in general, but something which 'falls unequivocally within the sphere of ethically pertinent values or 'goods' (*agatha*)'.[107]

This definition (or redefinition) of *to sumpheron* to include ethical *agatha* can, therefore, be seen as an important indication of how the potential tension in the relationship between morality and self-interest might be relaxed; it is important, too, to note that, in Aristotle's account, it is the scope and meaning of self-interest, not of justice, which is liable to redefinition.[108] What still needs to be considered, however, is the question of how far Aristotle's views, or versions of them, can be detected anywhere else.[109]

The *Rhetoric to Alexander* provides support for the possibility of a broader conception of *to sumpheron*, and for the view that self-interest need not equate to selfishness, but might include consideration of more abstract propositions:

συμφέρον δ' ἐστὶ τῶν ὑπαρχόντων ἀγαθῶν φυλακὴ ἢ τῶν μὴ προσόντων κτῆσις ἢ τῶν ὑπαρχόντων κακῶν ἀποβολὴ ἢ τῶν προσδοκωμένων γενήσεσθαι βλαβερῶν διακώλυσις. διαιρήσεις δὲ τοῦτο τοῖς μὲν ἰδιώταις εἰς σῶμα καὶ ψυχὴν καὶ τὰ ἐπίκτητα. σώματι μὲν οὖν ἐστι συμφέρον ῥώμη κάλλος ὑγίεια, ψυχῇ δὲ ἀνδρεία σοφία δικαιοσύνη· τὰ δ' ἐπίκτητα φίλοι χρήματα κτήματα· τὰ δ' ἐναντία τούτοις ἀσύμφορα. πόλει δὲ συμφέροντα τὰ τοιαῦτά ἐστιν· ὁμόνοια, δυνάμεις πρὸς πόλεμον, χρήματα καὶ προσόδων εὐπορία, συμμάχων ἀρετὴ καὶ πλῆθος.

---

[107] Halliwell 1994: 224; see also Yatromanolaki 1997: chs. 1 and 2, and esp. (on this passage) 48–53.

[108] Contrast the Athenian allegation at Th. v.105.4, that the Spartans are notorious for redefining justice to equate with their self-interest; on this claim, and its implications for Thucydides' analysis of normative argument, see ch. 6, sec. 3.

[109] On Aristotle's engagement (or attempt to engage) with 'popular morality', see Lloyd 1968: 264–5; Halliwell 1994: esp. 211–16.

What is beneficial is to protect existing good things, or to acquire those which are missing, or to throw off existing troubles, or prevent predicted harm from coming into being... For the body, robust good-health is beneficial; for the soul, courage; for wisdom, justice; the acquisition of friends and money and possessions; the opposite of these is not beneficial. For the city, these sorts of things are beneficial: harmony, power in war, money and well-resourced supplies, good and plentiful allies.[110] (1422a4–14)

Another example of a similar, if differently argued, version of the Aristotelean point of view can be seen in Isocrates' *On the Peace*. As was outlined above, one of the major themes of the speech is that, although some might hold the misguided opinion that injustice is 'profitable' (συμφέρουσαν) and justice is positively disadvantageous (8.31), Isocrates will demonstrate that this is not the case:

οὔτε πρὸς χρηματισμὸν δόξαν οὔτε πρὸς ἃ δεῖ πράττειν οὔθ' ὅλως πρὸς εὐδαι-μονίαν οὐδὲν ἂν συμβάλοιτο τηλικαύτην δύναμιν, ὅσην περ ἀρετὴ καὶ τὰ μέρη ταύτης.

Nothing in the world can contribute so powerfully to material gain, to good repute, to right action, in a word, to happiness, as virtue and the qualities of virtue.[111] (8.32)

Such explicit definitions are not, however, a feature of 'real' delib-erative oratory (and the rhetorical advantages of keeping such con-cepts usefully vague are obvious). Nevertheless, although the point may not be provable, it does seem that interpreting *sumpheron* and *dikaion* as different aspects of a single type of beneficial behaviour, rather than as absolute opposites juxtaposed for rhetorical effect, might often – although certainly not always[112] – allow for a more helpful approach to some texts. The Demosthenic *On the Treaty with Alexander*, for example, opens with a claim which, if *to dikaion* and *to sumpheron* are irreconcilable opposites, is some-what puzzling:

[110] A clear difference here from the Aristotelean position is the distinction between indi-vidual and *polis*: the *agatha* of the *polis* are much more practical than those of the individual, but abstract qualities (ὁμόνοια; 'harmony') are not entirely absent.

[111] The μέρη ('parts') of *aretē* are defined (at §63) as δικαιοσύνη ('justice'), εὐσέβεια ('piety'), σωφροσύνη ('prudence'). On *sumpheron* and *dikaion* in this speech, see Gillis 1970; Schmitz 1988: 266–75.

[112] The separation of the two is insisted on, for example, in Isocrates' *Archidamus*, 6.34–7: *to sumpheron* is too changeable to be relied on as a guide to action; *to dikaion* is what should be pursued.

προελόμενοι περὶ πλείστου ποιήσασθαι τὸ δίκαιον ἀνεγκλήτως πρὸς ἅπαντας χρῆσθε τῷ συμφέροντι μηκέτι μέλλοντες.

Having definitely resolved to put justice before all other claims, may you pursue your own interests, clear from all reproach, without further hesitation.[113] ([Dem.] 17.2)

A commitment to just behaviour is, it seems, the – necessary – gateway to a profitable future in pursuit of self-interest. A similar interaction between the two concepts can be seen to be operating much more widely in Demosthenes' speech *For the Megalopolitans*. Here, a constant awareness of and appeal to what is *sumpheron* for the city[114] is found alongside some of the strongest claims for the necessity of just behaviour:

καὶ τοῦτο λυμαινόμενον πάνθ' εὑρήσομεν, καὶ ταύτην ἀρχὴν οὖσαν πάντων τῶν κακῶν, τὸ μὴ 'θέλειν τὰ δίκαια πράττειν ἁπλῶς.

And we shall find that what ruins everything – and this is the start of all bad things – is unwillingness to act justly in all circumstances.[115] (16.24)

One thing which is rarely left unspecified, however, is the matter of whose benefit is in question. But here too there is some variation in the possible scope of the group of beneficiaries. There are cases where the interests of a particularly wide group are claimed to be at stake. Demosthenes' characterisation of Athens' (traditional) foreign policy represents it as having been directed ὑπὲρ φιλοτιμίας καὶ τῶν πᾶσι συμφερόντων ('for the sake of honour and of benefiting all [Greeks]'; 18.66): this selflessness was, according to Demosthenes, both the most admirable and the most unusual of Athens' qualities.

A more restricted conception of the scope of *to sumpheron* is, however, more common. It is possible for this scope to extend as far as an alliance: a striking example is a passage of the *Second Olynthiac*, where, in a discussion of Philip's power-base, a shared

---

[113] The comments made at §24 imply that justice is nevertheless an essential first step: simply pursuing self-interest will not bring success. On the emphasis given to questions of justice in this speech, see Culasso Gastaldi 1984: 32–3.

[114] Note especially 16.4–5, 9–10, 30–2.

[115] The appeals to self-interest have traditionally attracted more attention: note, especially, Jaeger's identification of this speech as containing the earliest expression of the (fundamentally Realist) doctrine of the Balance of Power (Jaeger 1938: 87–8). For a more balanced analysis of *sumpheron* and *dikaion* in the speech, see Yatromanolaki 2000.

conception of *to sumpheron* is depicted as being a central part of a stable alliance:

ὅταν μὲν γὰρ ὑπ' εὐνοίας τὰ πράγματα συστῇ καὶ πᾶσι ταὐτὰ συμφέρῃ τοῖς μετέχουσι τοῦ πολέμου, καὶ συμπονεῖν καὶ φέρειν τὰς συμφορὰς καὶ μένειν ἐθέλουσιν ἄνθρωποι.

For when a league is knit together by goodwill, when all the allies have the same interests, then men are willing to remain steadfast, sharing the toil and enduring the hardships.[116] (2.9)

It should, however, be noted that this situation is presented as a counterfactual: no such shared purpose exists among Philip's followers.

Where references to the scope of *to sumpheron* appear in more positive terms, and – especially – where they appear in combination with a reference to *to dikaion*, they typically have a still more restricted group of beneficiaries: τῇ πόλει ('the city'; at, for example, Isoc. 8.16; 15.79); ὑμῖν ('you'; [Dem.] 7.46; Dem. 14.3); ἡμῖν ('us'; Isoc. 8.66; the preceding verb makes it clear that 'we' are the Athenians). A more recent example of the use of similar ideas can provide a helpful contrast:

now our actions can be guided by a more subtle blend of mutual self-interest and moral purpose in defending the values we cherish. In the end values and interests merge. If we can establish and spread the values of liberty, the rule of law, human rights and an open society then that is in our national interests too.[117]

While the claim that 'moral purpose' contributes to, rather than contradicts, self-interest may seem authentically Isocratean, what is significantly different here is the – carefully vague, but always potentially broad – impression of whose 'self-interest' is under

---

[116] Compare the decree recording Athenian honours for the people of Tenedos (*IG* ii² 233 (= RO 72)). The Tenedians (as was noted above) are commended for their *aretē* and *eunoia*, which have been displayed εἰς τὸν δῆμον τὸν Ἀ[θηναίων καὶ τοὺς συμμάχ|ο]υς ('towards the Athenian *dēmos* and the allies'; fr.a, lines 8–9). This shared interest between the Athenians and their allies recurs later in the decree: the reason for this commendation is, among other things, that the Tenedians πρ[άττουσιν]| . . . τὰ συμφέροντα τῶι δή[μωι τῶι Ἀθηναίων καὶ]| τοῖς συμμάχοις ('do . . . what is beneficial for the Athenian *dēmos* and the allies'; fr.b, lines 21–3); on the formula, and variations on it, see Veligianni-Terzi 1997: 264–5, 282–3.

[117] Tony Blair, speech on the 'doctrine of the international community' (Chicago, 22 April 1999); quoted in Fairclough 2000: 149–50.

discussion: the 'we' of this speech is sometimes Britain; sometimes left-of-centre governments; sometimes NATO or the G7/8; sometimes an undefined grouping of nations (the 'international community').[118]

In Greek rhetoric, by contrast, an action which is *sumpheron* will, it seems, most usually benefit a much smaller group, and above all, if not exclusively, the *polis* which performs it. And it is, I think, here – in the focus of the action rather than its intrinsic quality – that the divide between *to sumpheron* and *to dikaion*, when they appear in this close pairing, can most usefully be seen. What the use of this 'cliché' points to is not necessarily a contrast between generally virtuous behaviour and hard-nosed self-interest, but between two complementary aspects of a single (commendable) type of behaviour: that which is directed beyond an immediate community of interest; and that which reflects *agatha* back onto the *polis*.

4.5 Conclusions

My main conclusion should, by now, be predictable. Classical Greek texts, of a variety of sorts, display an approach to describing and discussing interstate activity which relies on the absence of any firm distinction between the morals (and ethics) of domestic life and those which apply beyond the *polis*. But it is also apparent that this approach, while pervasive, was not unchallenged. It is hard to determine the precise extent or severity of these challenges, but it does seem legitimate to suspect that the more explicit, analytical, versions of the 'domestic analogy' which appear in fourth-century writing in particular might best be understood as responses to, or indirect reflections of, the existence of direct attacks on that analogy.[119]

If this main conclusion is correct, then it might be possible to find here an explanation for a gap in ancient Greek thought which has long been found troubling: that is, the absence of any properly developed theories of interstate relations. Rather than supposing

---

[118] For this analysis of the speech, see Fairclough 2000: 151–3.
[119] A view suggested (indirectly) by Radicke's (1995: 52) concern to analyse Dem. 15.29 in relation to Isocrates' approach to Athenian foreign relations in *On the Peace*.

that the Greeks were simply too busy to get round to producing such a theory (or too exhausted after producing all their other theories),[120] it might be better to ask whether such a theory was felt to be necessary. The fact that the actors in interstate relations could be either individuals, or groups of individuals, or the *polis*, and that these actors are not, apparently, seen as falling into radically different categories, removes one major motivation for the creation of specific theories of inter*state* behaviour.[121] More generally, if interstate and domestic activity are regarded as fundamentally comparable, then theories which attempt to explain or guide behaviour in one sphere can be applied, by default, to the other. There is no need for a theory of interstate politics.[122]

One final, important, point can also be made. It is possible to point to a connection between morality and the boundary between inside and outside, but both the nature of connection and the location of the boundary are very different from the ones with which this chapter began. Descriptions of morality in interstate relations do not float freely: they are closely tied both to the individual or group which performs the action, and to those who are thought to benefit from (or be harmed by) it. The various applications of the language of morality and of interest provide a crucial insight into the shaping and reshaping of the boundaries of the many, often intersecting, 'communities' which participate in the Greek interstate system.

---

[120] The (not, I think, entirely serious) suggestion of Purnell 1978: 20: 'mental energy is limited among peoples as in individuals. When we survey what the Greeks did accomplish in the intensely exacting field of conceptualization we may feel like murmuring, "Lo, it is enough".'

[121] Purnell 1978: 28.

[122] A rather different answer, that is, to the question, 'why is there no international theory?' from that proposed by Wight 1966b (see ch. 1, sec. 4).

NORMS AND POLITICS: THE PROBLEM
OF INTERVENTION

5.1 Introduction: the importance of intervention

The last three chapters have approached aspects of interstate relations as more or less discrete entities, categorised under relatively broad and abstract headings. The artificiality of those distinctions will, however, have become obvious: international systems inevitably influence the functioning of international law; approaches to law and to morality are closely connected; claims to morality cannot be separated from constructions of international systems; and so on. The aim of this chapter, therefore, is to explore more closely how these various aspects of interstate behaviour might interact in practice, and to do so by focusing on one particular category of interstate behaviour: namely, intervention.

The use of this – modern – concept in an ancient context requires some explanation. Intervention (in the sense in which it will be used here) implies the interference by one state (or *polis*, or *ethnos*) in the quarrels of one or more other states (whether in an internal *stasis*, or in a bi- or multilateral conflict); such interference should mark a distinctive development in the pattern of relations between the two groups involved (that is, it should not, for example, be conditioned by some specific pre-existing treaty obligation).[1] On this

---

[1] This is only one of many possible definitions. Indeed, part of the reason for the perceived pervasiveness of intervention lies in the fact that it is quite possible to construct a plausible definition of the practice which would make almost every act of interstate relations an act of intervention: any behaviour in the international arena will inevitably impinge on other members of that arena. It can even be claimed that failure to take action in a given situation also amounts to an act of intervention (the claim is usually attributed to Talleyrand; see also Hoffman 1984: 8; Little 1993: 15. Compare the Corinthians' accusations against Sparta at Th. I.69: Sparta's failure to prevent the enslavement of Greece itself amounts to an act of enslavement). The closest approximation to a 'standard' modern definition is provided by Rosenau 1968: intervention should (i) involve a sharp break with the established pattern of behaviour between the intervening and the target states; (ii) have the conscious aim of changing or preserving the structure of political authority in the

definition, it is clear that intervention is not only endemic in modern international politics,[2] but also a pervasive activity in classical Greek interstate relations. In the fifth century, Thucydides' account of the background to Athenian intervention in Corcyra (1.31–44) provides a fine example of the possible range of arguments which could be used in such situations: the conflicting demands of justice and expediency, obligations to treaties, kinship, past favours, are clearly shown, and their complexity sharply illustrated.[3] Intervention is even more prominent in accounts of the post-Peloponnesian War world: examples could include Athens' decision to become involved in the Corinthian War (as described by Xenophon, *HG* III.v); or, to take a case of intervention in internal conflicts, Spartan policy towards Thebes or Phlius in the late 380s; or, again, just about any action of Philip II in Greece, whether intervening in *stasis* in the cities of Northern Greece, or becoming involved in the Third Sacred War.[4]

The goal of this chapter is not, however, simply to demonstrate and exemplify the existence of interventionist behaviour in Greek interstate relations. Rather, it is to investigate the debates which surround that behaviour. The importance of intervention lies not just in its prominence as an activity, but also (and more interestingly) in the arguments which that activity is liable to provoke. This chapter will, therefore, consider three aspects of the arguments which

target state. For a critique of this definition, see Little 1993: 15–21. To a great extent, however, the instability of the concept is inevitable and intrinsic: the question of precisely what should be counted as an intervention is often the end point, not the starting point, of discussion (see, generally, Hoffman 1993; Weber 1995; Ramsbotham 1997). On the fluidity of the concept, Chesterman 2001: 1–6, and ch. 1 (who points out that this is not a purely postmodern complaint, but can be found in descriptions of the subject from the nineteenth century on).

[2] Especially and increasingly, of course, in recent years: see, for example, Mayall ed. 1996 (on UN interventions in Cambodia, Somalia and Yugoslavia); Burg 1999 for an account of the Bosnian war in terms of intervention; Wheeler 2000 on changing norms of intervention from the 1970s to the 1990s; Welsh ed. 2003: esp. pt 2, on the connection between intervention and international politics. On the history of the doctrine of humanitarian intervention, see Abiew 1999.

[3] For a study of the historical situation and Thucydides' presentation of it, see J. B. Wilson 1987.

[4] The question of why intervention should be a prominent feature of the interstate relations of any period is also an interesting one (see Hoffman 1984: 11–14; Regan 1998). It will not be dealt with directly in what follows, although the nature of the Greek states-system (see ch. 2) is clearly a relevant factor.

surround intervention in classical Greece: first, the basic question of the existence of a norm of (or against) intervention; second, a potential theoretical problem associated with intervention: that is, the problem of state autonomy; third, the potential practical implications of interventionism: above all, its use as a vehicle for imperialism.

The decision to concentrate on these three aspects is, as will become clear, prompted by debates which are prominent in contemporary interstate relations. My aim in choosing to investigate the subject in this way is not, however, to reveal continuities between ancient and modern interstate relations, but rather to make more apparent the important discontinuities. Ancient and modern interventionism may look like very similar practices, but these apparent similarities can often obscure significant (and fundamental) differences.

5.2 Helping the wronged: intervention as an ideal

In 1970, the United Nations passed a resolution on intervention which remains, in theory, the official and legal statement on the subject:

> no state, or group of states, has the right to intervene, directly or indirectly, for any reason whatever, in the internal or external affairs of any other state. Consequently, armed intervention and all other forms of interference . . . are in violation of international law.[5]

Modern international law, that is, operates with a norm of non-intervention. This does not, of course, mean that interventions never occur, or even that all interventions are necessarily

---

5 'Declaration on principles of international law concerning friendly relations and co-operation among states' (= UN Resolution 2625); published in *Official Records of the UN General Assembly, 25th Session (1970), Supplements 23–8*: 121–4. The declaration modifies the statement of the UN's charter (Article 2.7), which is a blanket prohibition of intervention 'in matters which are essentially within the jurisdiction of any state'. (On the declaration and its antecedents, see Abiew 1999: 68–71.) Proposals have been formulated which establish new guidelines for intervention (Evans & Sahnoun edd. 2001), but the formal legal position remains unchanged at the time of writing. It should be noted that, although most contemporary concern focuses on intervention within states, Resolution 2625 applies equally to internal and external intervention.

considered to be a breach of international law. What it does mean is that the burden of proof, or rather of justification, lies with the intervening party.[6] What I want to demonstrate in this section is that almost the exact opposite was the case in the Greek world: there is a strong tradition of positive representation of intervention in classical sources; intervention can be represented as a norm, sometimes even as an obligation; and it is failure to intervene which is a cause of unease, or even shame.

Intervention, like imperialism, is something for which the Greeks did not have a word. Nevertheless, it is also an activity for which – in its positive manifestation[7] – there is a recurring, and widespread, mode of description. The typical characterisation of such action is that of helping, protecting, or saving the wronged: the most frequently appearing variant, perhaps common enough to be categorised as a slogan, is βοηθεῖν τοῖς ἀδικουμένοις, 'to help the wronged'.[8]

This characteristic is appealed to both as a traditional element of interstate behaviour, and as a continuing, and desirable, part of contemporary policy-making. Both of these tendencies can be seen very clearly in the Lysianic *Epitaphios*, a speech produced, allegedly, to commemorate the dead of the Corinthian War.[9] Lysias'

---

[6] Discussions of the question have often, therefore, been based around attempts to formulate 'rules of disregard' for the norm of non-intervention: the most influential early attempt to do so is that of Mill 1984 (1859); for a discussion of Mill's views on (non-)intervention see Varouxakis 1997; see also McMahan 1986; Walzer 2000: ch. 6. For an extensive study of the principle of non-intervention, in its historical and contemporary forms, see Vincent 1974.

[7] For the question of how a positive version of intervention might be distinguished from a negative, see sec. 4 below. It should, nevertheless, be emphasised that many, if not all, of the examples referred to in this section are also open to less idealistic interpretation.

[8] The phrase is also used in relation to internal political and inter-personal relationships: for example, by Demosthenes (e.g. 21.225 (of self-help); 30.25 (of a jury helping the wronged party)). Βοήθεια, 'help', (and related forms) is, of course, a standard piece of military/diplomatic vocabulary (frequently appearing in clauses of mutual aid in defensive alliances; for examples, see Tod, Index 3, *s.v.* βο(ι)ηθέω). Signs that this concept alone could be seen as an ideal as well as a description of practice might be argued to be visible in the popularity of the word as a name for Athenian triremes: there are four (or perhaps five, depending on one's faith in the reconstruction) examples between the mid-350s and 320; only *Demokratia* ('Democracy'), *Nikē* ('Victory') and *Salaminia* (the name given to one of Athens' official, 'state', ships) are as popular (*IG* ii² 1611, line 76 (cf. lines 128, 140, 170); 1615, line 67; 1631, line 445; 1632, lines 122–3; possibly 1618, line 139 (βο[?ή]θεια]); see Miltner 1931; Casson 1995: 352, n. 45).

[9] Generally on the speech, see Walz 1936; Prinz 1997: 231–52. The exact date of the work is unclear: Walz (1936: 51–3) suggests 392/1; but – especially if the view is taken that the

survey of the high points of Athenian history produces a list of cases when Athenians have rushed to right a wrong committed against some third party. The Athenians insist on the proper burial of Adrastus and Polynices, and are prepared to use armed force to impose it, even though – according to Lysias – there was no history of conflict (οὐδεμιᾶς διαφορᾶς; 2.8) between Athens and Thebes, nor any specific Athenian desire to earn the goodwill of the Argives. The motive is, quite simply, a desire to see justice done and wrongs righted. Similar reasoning, according to Lysias, can account for Athens' decision to provide asylum to the sons of Heracles. Again, there is no pre-existing tie or obligation between Heracles and Athens, and again – and the point is made more explicitly here – there is no expectation that Athens will receive any direct benefit as a result of her action: they cannot know what sort of people the sons of Heracles will grow up to be (2.13). The Athenians fought:

τοὺς μὲν ἀδικουμένους ἐλεοῦντες, τοὺς δ' ὑβρίζοντας μισοῦντες . . . ἡγούμενοι ἐλευθερίας μὲν σημεῖον εἶναι μηδὲν ποιεῖν ἄκοντας, δικαιοσύνης δὲ τοῖς ἀδικουμένοις βοηθεῖν.

pitying the wronged and hating the aggressor . . . believing it a sign of freedom to do nothing unwillingly, and of justice to help the wronged. (2.14)

The events of the Persian Wars can be fitted into the same explanatory framework. The Persian rationale for making Athens the first Greek city attacked was that:

αὐτοῖς ἐκ τῶν προτέρων ἔργων περὶ τῆς πόλεως τοιαύτη δόξα παρειστήκει, ὡς εἰ μὲν πρότερον ἐπ' ἄλλην πόλιν ἴασιν, ἐκείνοις καὶ Ἀθηναίοις πολεμήσουσι (προθύμως γὰρ τοῖς ἀδικουμένοις ἥξουσι βοηθήσοντες)· εἰ δ' ἐνθάδε πρῶτον ἀφίξονται, οὐδένας ἄλλους τῶν Ἑλλήνων τολμήσειν ἑτέρους σῴζοντας φανερὰν ἔχθραν πρὸς ἐκείνους ὑπὲρ αὐτῶν καταθέσθαι.

from the former actions of our city, this impression had arisen: they thought that if they attacked another city first, they would be at war both with them and with Athens (for the Athenians would eagerly come to help the wronged); but if they came here first, none of the other Greeks would dare to save the others and for their sake incur the open hostility of the Persians. (2.22)

speech is not a genuine *epitaphios* – Snell's (1887: 17–19) argument for a date after the Peace of Antalcidas is not implausible (he sees an implicit reference to the abandonment of the Greeks of Asia Minor in Lysias' praise (2.57) of Athens for saving Greek cities from enslavement by the barbarian).

Even in the years before the Persian Wars, according to Lysias, the norm was so firmly established as a basis of Athenian policy that others have to take it into account when making their own plans.

Lysias' story, and his appeal to this norm, do not, however, end here.[10] The motif of 'helping the wronged' recurs in the most recent of Athenian external activities – the fighting in which the commemorated dead had lost their lives:

οἱ δὲ νῦν θαπτόμενοι, βοηθήσαντες Κορινθίοις ὑπὸ παλαιῶν φίλων ἀδικουμένοις καινοὶ σύμμαχοι γενόμενοι, οὐ τὴν αὐτὴν γνώμην Λακεδαιμονίοις ἔχοντες (οἱ μὲν γὰρ τῶν ἀγαθῶν αὐτοῖς ἐφθόνουν, οἱ δὲ ἀδικουμένους αὐτοὺς ἠλέουν, οὐ τῆς προτέρας ἔχθρας μεμνημένοι, ἀλλὰ τὴν παροῦσαν φιλίαν περὶ πολλοῦ ποιού-μενοι) πᾶσιν ἀνθρώποις φανερὰν τὴν αὐτῶν ἀρετὴν ἐπεδείξαντο. ἐτόλμησαν γὰρ μεγάλην ποιοῦντες τὴν Ἑλλάδα οὐ μόνον ὑπὲρ τῆς αὐτῶν σωτηρίας κιν-δυνεύειν, ἀλλὰ καὶ ὑπὲρ τῆς τῶν πολεμίων ἐλευθερίας ἀποθνήσκειν· τοῖς γὰρ Λακεδαιμονίων συμμάχοις περὶ τῆς ἐκείνων ἐλευθερίας ἐμάχοντο.

Those who are being buried now went as new allies to help the Corinthians, who were wronged by ancient friends; they did not act in the same spirit as the Lacedaemonians (who envied the Corinthians their good fortune, whereas our men pitied them for the wrongs they suffered, and forgot their former enmity, but made much of their present friendship), but made a clear display of their *aretē* to all men. They dared, in making Greece great, not only to risk danger for their own safety, but also to die for their enemies' freedom; for they fought the allies of the Lacedaemonians for the sake of the freedom of those allies. (2.67–8)

In this example, the theme is not only repeated but also expanded upon. As before, the Athenians' decision to help the Corinthians is not determined by any pre-existing friendship or obligation. In this case, however, it even runs against those existing ties: the Corinthians, although current allies, are former enemies of Athens; in a still more paradoxical move, it can be claimed that, by attempting to preserve their *eleutheria*, Athens has been helping even those against whom she has been fighting.

The message from this speech is, therefore, clear enough: the mission of the Athenians has always been, and continues to be,

---

[10] Cf. Adcock 1963 who accepts that stories of 'generosity, the protection of the weak' have a place in accounts of Athens' mythical past, but denies their role in 'real' politics (52). Piccirilli 2001: 20–1, is similarly sceptical, noting the existence of claims to 'help the wronged', but preferring to see self-interest as the central determining factor in foreign policy making.

active intervention in the cause of safeguarding the rights of others, whether or not they are old friends of Athens (and perhaps even, as in this last claim, if they are old enemies), and, according to Lysias, whether or not they are likely to reciprocate the benefit which is done to them.

It must be admitted that this speech is unusual in the degree of emphasis which it gives to the theme of helping the wronged. The theme itself, however, is a common one, and is not restricted to a single genre. The picture of an Athenian approach to foreign relations which is dominated by interventionism in support of the 'rights' (δίκαια) of others is one which recurs in the *epitaphioi*.[11] This is, perhaps, precisely what would be expected in these idealistic, idealising, versions of the Athenian past,[12] but it is possible to find similarly positive assessments of interventionism in less abstract contexts.

One such context is deliberative oratory, or pseudo-deliberative oratory. The speech attributed by Xenophon to the Phliasian Procles does include some practical reasons why Athens should help Sparta against Thebes (after the Theban invasion of the Peloponnese in 370/69).[13] But he concludes his speech by turning to the same examples which appear in the *epitaphioi* (the burial of Adrastus and Polynices, the asylum given to the sons of Heracles: *HG* vi.v.46–7). The lesson which these examples are intended to illustrate is also the same:

ἐγὼ δέ, ὦ ἄνδρες Ἀθηναῖοι, πρόσθεν μὲν ἀκούων ἐζήλουν τήνδε τὴν πόλιν ὅτι πάντας καὶ τοὺς ἀδικουμένους καὶ τοὺς φοβουμένους ἐνθάδε καταφεύγοντας ἐπικουρίας ἤκουον τυγχάνειν.

[11] On the *topos* in the *epitaphioi*, see Ziolkowski 1981: 102–8 (esp. 104–5). Isocrates 4.54–70 should be seen as drawing on the same tradition.

[12] See, generally, Walters 1980; Loraux 1986a: esp. ch. 3. See also Brock 1998: esp. 234–6 for the suggestion that the *epitaphioi* are markedly less interested than other sources (particularly tragedy) in the complexities of the (mythical) interventions which they describe. (Brock, however, sees this difference as being connected more to period (fifth *vs* fourth century) than to genre.)

[13] That this speech is attributed to Procles (the only character of the *Hellenica* to be given more than one speech) is not without significance, particularly in view of his nationality: the Phliasians (as the excursus of vii.ii demonstrates) are in many ways Xenophon's model state in their conduct of foreign relations (on Phlius as Xenophontic paradigm, see Dillery 1995: 130–8; see also ch. 4, sec. 2). For an analysis of this debate, and of Procles' speech in particular, see Tuplin 1993: 110–13.

In former days, men of Athens, I used to hear things which made me admire this city, for I heard that all who were wronged and all who were afraid fled here for refuge, and found assistance. (VI.v.45)

Demosthenes' speeches work with a similar model of Athenian behaviour. In some cases, admittedly, it is depicted as being the behaviour of earlier times, but those earlier times were also better times. This is an ideal which it is, according to Demosthenes, shameful for Athens to have abandoned. So, for example, in the *Second Olynthiac*:

ἀλλ' ἐκεῖνο θαυμάζω, εἰ Λακεδαιμονίοις μέν ποτε, ὦ ἄνδρες Ἀθηναῖοι, ὑπὲρ τῶν Ἑλληνικῶν δικαίων ἀντήρατε, καὶ πόλλ' ἰδίᾳ πλεονεκτῆσαι πολλάκις ὑμῖν ἐξὸν οὐκ ἠθελήσατε, ἀλλ' ἵν' οἱ ἄλλοι τύχωσι τῶν δικαίων, τὰ ὑμέτερα αὐτῶν ἀνηλίσ-κετ' εἰσφέροντες καὶ προυκινδυνεύετε στρατευόμενοι, νυνὶ δ' ὀκνεῖτε ἐξιέναι καὶ μέλλετ' εἰσφέρειν ὑπὲρ τῶν ὑμετέρων αὐτῶν κτημάτων.

But I am surprised at this: that you, men of Athens, who once withstood the Lacedaemonians in defence of the rights of Greece; who, although the opportunity was often available, were not willing to enrich yourselves privately; who spent your own possessions and ran risks on campaign so that others might enjoy their rights, now shrink from an expedition and are slow to pay your contributions for the sake of your own possessions. (2.24)

It is also an ideal which – albeit balanced with considerations of prudence – can be put forward as a suitable guide to Athens' future policies:

τῶν πάντων οὐδέν' ἂν ἀντειπεῖν οἴομαι ὡς οὐ καὶ Λακεδαιμονίους καὶ πρότερον Θηβαίους καὶ τὸ τελευταῖον Εὐβοέας ἔσωσεν ἡ πόλις, καὶ μετὰ ταῦτα συμμά-χους ἐποιήσατο, ἕν τι καὶ ταῦτ' ἀεὶ βουλομένη πράττειν. ἔστι δὲ τοῦτο τί; τοὺς ἀδικουμένους σῴζειν.

I do not think any one man would deny that Athens has saved the Lacedaemonians, and the Thebans before them, and lastly the Euboeans, and has afterwards made alliance with them, having always one and the same object in view. And what is this? To save the wronged.[14] (16.14–15)

---

[14] Note the sequence of events: the alliance follows the intervention (Aeschines (3.93) repeats this version of events, but represents Demosthenes' actions as being entirely reprehensible: on Aeschines' ambivalent attitude to intervention, see n. 64 below). It is also worth noting that in both Demosthenic passages the positive ideal (helping/saving the wronged) is represented as distinct from, and opposite to, the negative pursuit of πλεονεξία ('greed', 'over-ambition').

There is, then, scope for seeing the norm of intervention as a strong theme in discussions and representations of Athenian interstate relations. There are also grounds – in spite of occasional Athenian claims to a monopoly on such actions[15] – for regarding it as a more widespread phenomenon. Athenian writers can certainly be found projecting this ideal onto non-Athenian states and individuals. Plato's account, in the *Laws*, of an archaic agreement made between Argos, Messene and Sparta claims that it included an undertaking:

βοηθήσειν δὲ βασιλῆς τε βασιλεῦσιν ἀδικουμένοις καὶ δήμοις καὶ δῆμοι δήμοις καὶ βασιλεῦσιν ἀδικουμένοις.

that the kings should aid both kings and peoples when wronged, and the peoples aid both peoples and kings when wronged.[16] (684b1–3)

Isocrates' *Archidamus*, apparently referring to the same tradition, describes Spartan intervention in an attempted coup at Messene (6.22–5), and, again, characterises this action as an attempt βοηθεῖν τοῖς ἀδικουμένοις ('to help the wronged'; 6.31). In the *Hellenica*, the claim is attributed to Agesilaus as his motivation for military intervention in Phlius: he is invading, he says, 'not in order to do wrong but to help the wronged' (οὐχ ἵνα ἀδικοίη στρατεύοιτο, ἀλλ' ὅπως τοῖς ἀδικουμένοις βοηθήσειεν: v.iii.14). Xenophon also makes a Spartan ambassador (attempting to win Athenian support for Sparta in the aftermath of Leuctra) place great emphasis on the Spartan tradition of helping those in need – and in particular on their assistance in ridding Athens of tyrants (vi.v.33–4).[17]

---

[15] Especially visible in the *epitaphioi*: see, for example, Lysias 2.22 (quoted above: 179). For an argument in favour of seeing the norm as a uniquely Athenian characteristic, see Missiou 1992: 113–14.

[16] See also *Laws* 737d3–5: the ideal *polis* should be of sufficient size not only to be able to defend itself, but also γείτοσιν ἑαυτῶν ἀδικουμένοις βοηθῆσαι ('to help its neighbours when they are wronged').

[17] It is, presumably, not a coincidence that the Spartan ambassador should make such explicit use of typically Athenian modes of argumentation in this Athenian context. That the Spartans are moving into an Athenian role is hinted at too, perhaps, in Xenophon's comment that the Spartan ambassadors 'happened to be present' (ἔτυχον δὲ παρόντες) – this is reminiscent of the similarly fortuitous presence of the Athenian ambassadors at Sparta (in the debate there before the Peloponnesian War (Th. 1.72.1)), whose speech makes particularly explicit, and self-conscious, use of the Athenian claim to be defender of the Greeks against aggression.

The ideal could even be imagined to exist among societies still more remote than that of Sparta. Xenophon's *Cyropaedia* includes an episode in which an embassy from India arrives at the court of Cyrus, with instructions to find out which of the warring sides – Medes or Assyrians – has been wronged, and to offer support to that side (ὁ Ἰνδῶν βασιλεύς, τὸ δικαίον σκεψάμενος, φαίη μετὰ τοῦ ἠδικημένου ἔσεσθαι; 'the King of the Indians, looking out for the just thing, said that he would take the side of the wronged party'; II.iv.7).[18] But it is, again, Demosthenes who provides the strongest assertion of the universality of the norm – expressed here, it should be noted, as an obligation:

ἀλλ' ὅμως οὔθ' ὑμῖν οὔτε Θηβαίοις οὔτε Λακεδαιμονίοις οὐδεπώποτε, ὦ ἄνδρες Ἀθηναῖοι, συνεχωρήθη τοῦθ' ὑπὸ τῶν Ἑλλήνων, ποιεῖν ὅ τι βούλοισθε, οὐδὲ πολλοῦ δεῖ· ἀλλὰ τοῦτο μὲν ὑμῖν, μᾶλλον δὲ τοῖς τότ' οὖσιν Ἀθηναίοις, ἐπειδή τισιν οὐ μετρίως ἐδόκουν προσφέρεσθαι, πάντες ᾤοντο δεῖν, καὶ οἱ μηδὲν ἐγκαλεῖν ἔχοντες αὐτοῖς, μετὰ τῶν ἠδικημένων πολεμεῖν.

But neither to you nor to the Thebans nor to the Lacedaemonians did the Greeks ever, men of Athens, allow the right of unrestricted action, or anything like it. On the contrary, when you, or rather the Athenians of that day, were thought to be behaving unreasonably towards someone, all felt it their duty, even those who had no grievance against them, to go to war in support of those who had been wronged.[19] (9.23–4)

It is, of course, true that although these examples may claim to relate to states other than Athens, they remain fundamentally

---

[18] For other examples of – deliberate – anachronism in the *Cyropaedia*, see Due 1989: 38–42.

[19] Compare Andocides 3.13: οἶμαι γὰρ ἂν πάντας ἀνθρώπους ὁμολογῆσαι διὰ τάδε δεῖν πολεμεῖν, ἢ ἀδικουμένους ἢ βοηθοῦντας ἠδικημένοις ('I think that all men would agree that it is necessary to fight for these reasons: either being wronged, or going to help the wronged'); similar argument in *Rh.Al.* 1425a11–15; and – with more sceptical undertones – in Ar. *Ach.* 535–56: Spartan intervention on behalf of Megara is in keeping with Athenian custom (and the Athenians would intervene to defend the rights of a wounded puppy). Contrast this with Demosthenes' – apparently provocative – claim in *On the Peace* (5.16) that states will not usually get involved in another's conflicts unless they have a particular interest in the outcome of the struggle: the claim is, though, introduced as one with which he expects his audience to disagree; Demosthenes also admits that most states will eagerly seek a πρόφασις ('excuse') for intervention (5.17). The speech as a whole (not surprisingly, in view of its overall aim) is generally opposed to the idea of intervention (mostly on practical grounds): Demosthenes claims, for example, that he was opposed to Athenian involvement in Euboea, because he knew it would be unsuccessful (5.5). For other Demosthenic representations of intervention as a positive ideal, see 8.46; [Dem.] 10.46; compare also the negative characterisation of isolationist policies at [Dem.] 10.52.

Athenian creations. Nevertheless, the fact that the ideal could be projected onto other states – even non-Greek ones – is an important indication of its embeddedness in (at least) Athenian conceptions of interstate behaviour.

More convincing evidence that the norm of helping the wronged should be seen as a general rather than purely Athenian ideal can be found in the language of interstate agreements. A striking example comes in a clause of the Common Peace of 371, as reported by Xenophon. Peace is made on terms of withdrawal of governors, disbanding of military forces, and granting of *autonomia* to cities; the final clause is that:

εἰ δέ τις παρὰ ταῦτα ποιοίη, τὸν μὲν βουλόμενον βοηθεῖν ταῖς ἀδικουμέναις πόλεσι, τῷ δὲ μὴ βουλομένῳ μὴ εἶναι ἔνορκον συμμαχεῖν τοῖς ἀδικουμένοις.

If any state should act in violation of this agreement, it was provided that any which so desired might aid the injured cities, but that any which did not so desire was not under oath to be the ally of those who were injured.[20] (*HG* VI.iii.18)

What seems to be happening here – if Xenophon's account of the terms of the treaty is accurate – is a combination of the language of intervention, of 'helping the wronged', with the phraseology which is more familiar from the specific mutual aid clauses of bilateral treaties.[21] The novelty here lies not in the use of the concept of βοηθεία ('help'), but in the potentially broad scope of the wrongs which might need redressing, and of the number of states which might feel obliged or entitled to redress those injustices. Here, then, intervention is given a kind of official sanction.[22]

---

[20] On the question of the novelty of this clause (in the context of the Common Peaces), see ch. 3, n. 113.

[21] On βοηθεία, 'help', in bilateral treaties, see n. 8 above. For the combination of βοηθεία ('help') and ἀδικία ('wrongs'), see also *IG* ii² 112 (= RO 41; alliance of Athens, Arcadia, Achaea, Elis and Phlius; 362/1), lines 32–4: βοηθεῖν Ἀθηναίους τ]|ούτοις παντὶ σθ[ένει καθότι ἂν ἐπαγγέλλωσιν οἱ ἀ]|δικούμενοι κατ[ὰ τὸ δυνατόν ('the Athenians will help them with all their strength, as called on by those who are being wronged, as far as they are able'); perhaps also *IG* ii² 111 (= RO 39; agreement between Athens and Iulis; 362 BC), lines 75–9: ἐὰ|[ν δέ τις τολμᾶι ἀδικεῖν Κείων . . .]βοηθή|[σω δὲ παντὶ σθένει κατὰ τὸ δυνατόν ('if anyone dares to wrong those of the Ceans . . . I will offer help with all my strength as far as I am able').

[22] In the Athenian peace of 371/0 (X. *HG* VI.v.1–2) the option of not helping is removed, but the scope of the potential obligation is made narrower (restricted to wars between parties who have participated in the peace). Compare also Tod's text for the foundation treaty of the Corinthian League, *IG* ii² 236, lines 17–19 (= Tod 177; accepted, with caution, by

Appeal to the principle of 'helping the wronged' seems, therefore, to be a widespread phenomenon in Greek interstate relations: the concept not only functions as an ideal, but can even sometimes be argued to involve some obligation. It can, then, be claimed that there existed a norm of intervention in classical Greece. But if such a claim is made, it must also be emphasised that the intervention entailed by the description βοηθεῖν τοῖς ἀδικουμένοις, 'helping the wronged', does not equate exactly to the type of intervention which is found so problematic in contemporary interstate relations. The key to the difference lies in the notion of the ἀδικούμενοι, 'wronged parties', a term which has two significant implications. The first is that the passive voice implies an agent: some other party has already carried out the offensive action. Acceptable intervention, under this description, is therefore necessarily counter-intervention.[23] The second, connected, factor is that explicit identification of the implied agent is, in this general formulation, unnecessary: the same injunction can be, and (as the examples cited above demonstrate) is, as much applied to those wronged in internal conflict as to those under attack from another state. This apparent failure to mark a strict division between actions outside and inside the *polis* represents another sharp difference from modern practice; it also, however, contrasts with some ancient approaches to interventionist activity. It is this aspect of the problem – the relationship between intervention and the *polis* – which will be considered in the next section.

Schmitt, *SV* III.403, and repeated in RO 76): ἂν δέ τις ποῆι τι] παράσπονδον πε‖[ρὶ τὰς συνθήκας, βοηθήσω] καθότι ἂν παραγ‖[γέλλωσιν οἱ ἀδικούμενοι ('if anyone commits any breach of the treaty concerning these agreements, I shall go in support as called on by those who are wronged'). On Philip's use of the pre-existing language of Greek diplomacy, see Perlman 1985.

[23] The one possible counter-example to this is Demosthenes' argument in *For the Liberty of the Rhodians* (15.14) that intervention in Rhodes would be justified even if no third party were already involved. At this point, however, Demosthenes' argument in favour of intervention is based not on the general principle of helping the oppressed, but on the more specific – ideological and practical – criterion of helping democrats. It is also worth noting that the statement is phrased as counter-factual: a third party *is* involved, as Demosthenes' earlier arguments have shown. The comment could in fact be read as a piece of implicit *praeteritio* of the purely moral argument: Persian involvement at Rhodes guarantees the ethical right to help the wronged; even if that were not the case, the practicalities of the situation recommend the same course.

5.3 Intervention, autonomy and *autonomia*

The major impediment to the development of an unproblematic norm of intervention in the modern states-system is the perceived incompatibility between acts of intervention and a commitment to the inviolable sovereignty of the autonomous nation-state. This incompatibility can be seen, in fact, in the UN resolution (cited above: 177) in which the norm of non-intervention is declared. That resolution goes on to insist on the right to self-determination of 'peoples' within sovereign states, and of the rights of these peoples to the support of the international community.[24] The resolution illustrates on a small scale, therefore, a tension which underlies much of the moral anxiety associated with acts of intervention in contemporary international relations: how can the preservation of the sovereignty of the nation-state be made consistent with the responsibility of the international community to defend human rights within those nation-states?[25]

These concerns must, of course, be located in specific chronological and geographical contexts: the modern world of the sovereign nation-state;[26] and the post-1945 world of explicit commitment by the international community to the ideal, and defence, of universal human rights. However, it might also seem that similar concerns existed in classical Greece: it has already been argued that alleged infringement of *dikaia* was often at the heart of positive

---

[24] UN Resolution 6265: 124. The question of how 'peoples' are to be defined is not addressed. On the inherent inconsistency of the declaration as a statement of the legality of intervention, see Roberts & Kingsbury 1993: 26–7.

[25] The bibliography on the question is huge, and rapidly expanding: but see, for recent overviews, Lyons & Mastanduno edd. 1995; Parekh 1997; Chesterman 2001; Walzer 2000: xi–xxiii; Wheeler 2000, 2001; Evans & Sahnoun edd. 2001; Lepard 2002; Chatterjee & Scheid edd. 2003; Jokic ed. 2003. See Moore ed. 1998 for a more practical approach.

[26] The point at which this world begins is disputed: traditionally, the turning-point is set at the Treaty of Westphalia (1648), but it has been argued that the location of the 'birth' of the nation-state at this date is primarily a nineteenth-century idea, based on anti-Hapsburg propaganda (Osiander 2001). Sovereignty is a highly disputed concept in contemporary politics (see, for investigations of the problem from an IR perspective, Hinsley 1986; Biersteker & Weber 1996; Murphy 1996; Jackson ed. 1999; Navari 1993 and Weber 1995 investigate the specific problem of the relationship between sovereignty and intervention); its possible application to the ancient city-state is also controversial: see, generally, Hinsley 1986: ch. 2; Davies 1994; Hansen 1998: 73–83.

187

representations of intervention, and, while *dikaia* are by no means equivalent to 'human rights', reference to them does, at least, suggest the existence of some sort of common interest in the question of justice and injustice.[27] It has also been argued that the Greek states-system, like the modern, operated with a strong belief in an autonomous, sovereign state. In this section I want to explore that second point more thoroughly: what is the nature of the connection between *autonomia* and the Greek *polis*; and how does the rhetoric of *autonomia* intersect with depictions of intervention, and with the norm of helping the wronged?

For many years, autonomy, or *autonomia*, was widely held to be one of the defining characteristics of the Greek city-state.[28] This approach affected discussions not only of domestic politics, but also of interstate relations. Although leagues, alliances and treaties clearly were formed, these were depicted as undermining the absolute autonomy of the *polis*, and, correspondingly, were understood as temporary aberrations from that ideal. For a *polis* to be in any state of permanent union with, or – worse – subjection to another would have been a contradiction in terms. The city-state was, or at least should have been, self-sufficient (the concept of *autarkeia* can also be invoked here)[29] and self-determining, and, as such, should neither require nor accept the assistance of another state.

More recent work on the nature of the city-state, and on the meaning of *autonomia*, has resulted in the creation of a rather different picture. This work, spearheaded by Mogens Hansen, has repeatedly, and convincingly, attacked the idea that being *autonomos* and being a *polis* are, from the time of the city-state's origins,

---

[27] On the (absence of) a concept of human rights in classical Greece, see Schofield 1999. For a different view, see Bauman 2000: ch. 2, who attempts to argue that the concept can be seen in the Greek world in the language of *philanthrōpia*.

[28] From works on interstate relations, see, for example, Ténékidès 1993: 253: autonomy is 'l'attribut essentiel de la Cité grecque'; similar assertions in Phillipson 1911, vol. 1: 32, Martin 1940: 84–7. (Autonomy is taken to be an uncomplicated translation of *autonomia* in these discussions.) Generally on *autonomia*, see Bickerman 1958 (similar arguments can be found in Lévy 1983). On the origins of the Greek word and concept see Ostwald 1982. On its definition and usage, especially in the fourth century, Hansen 1995, 1996, 1998: 78–83; or – with more concern for its use as a political slogan – Bosworth 1992; Keen 1996.

[29] On the term and its implications, see Morpeth 1993.

necessarily co-extensive conditions.[30] Nevertheless, although
Hansen would not make *autonomia* an intrinsic characteristic of
the city-state, he does accept that the concept becomes increasingly
important over the course of the fourth century, to the extent that,
by the death of Alexander, the desire of all cities to be autonomous
(most clearly indicated, he suggests, in the stipulations of the Common Peaces) has mutated into an assumption that all *poleis* should
be autonomous, and from there into a belief that anything not
autonomous could not be counted a *polis*.[31]

This model of development seems to be perfectly plausible, and
does at least remove an apparent tautology of the Common Peaces:
it has been pointed out that to declare that all *poleis* were to be
autonomous, would, on the old model, have been as pointless as
expressing a desire that the sky be blue.[32] But the formulation of
these peaces also makes clear the fact that guarantees of *autonomia*
were not always straightforward or universal. In the peace of 386,
for example, the 'rescript' of Artaxerxes declares that:

Ἀρταξέρξης βασιλεὺς νομίζει δίκαιον τὰς μὲν ἐν τῇ Ἀσίᾳ πόλεις ἑαυτοῦ εἶναι καὶ
τῶν νήσων Κλαζομενὰς καὶ Κύπρον, τὰς δὲ ἄλλας Ἑλληνίδας πόλεις καὶ μικρὰς
καὶ μεγάλας αὐτονόμους ἀφεῖναι πλὴν Λήμνου καὶ Ἴμβρου καὶ Σκύρου· ταύτας
δὲ ὥσπερ τὸ ἀρχαῖον εἶναι Ἀθηναίων.

King Artaxerxes thinks it just that the cities in Asia should belong to him, as well
as Clazomenae and Cyprus among the islands, and that the other Greek cities, both
small and big, should be left *autonomos*, except Lemnos, Imbros, and Scyros; and
these should belong, as of old, to the Athenians. (Xen. *HG* v.i.31)

The question of who might be entitled to *autonomia* was not, that is,
one to which there was a settled answer; in fact, it could become,
as Jehne has argued, a central *Machtfrage*.[33] *Autonomia* is not,
therefore, something which can be asserted as an absolute but is
always, and necessarily, a relative condition asserted by a weaker
power in the face of a stronger (or conceded by that stronger
power to weaker states).[34] *Autonomia* is an assertion of partial

[30] According to Hansen (1995: 37; see also Hansen 1998: 78), around 500 city-states, which
are called *poleis* in contemporary sources, would not qualify for the title if this criterion
were strictly applied.
[31] Hansen 1995: 38–43.   [32] Keen 1996: 121.   [33] Jehne 1994: 45.
[34] See especially Bickerman 1958: 336–7. This view of the meaning of *autonomia* fits well
with the apparent circumstances of its mid-fifth century coinage: although the earliest

independence rather than a statement of absolute freedom, and a claim to, or assertion of, *autonomia* necessarily implies the involvement of another state.

The problem of definition, however, remains: what sort of (partial) independence is at issue? This is a question to which there is no single answer: the types and extent of independence entailed by a guarantee of *autonomia* were not securely fixed, although they do fit within certain broad parameters. The -*nomos* of the suffix is sometimes best understood in the strong sense of 'law', but more often seems to imply 'norms' or 'customs'.[35] Thus, the term need not necessarily mean 'using their own laws' (although there are occasions when it could mean this). Ostwald's suggestion of the range of conditions which might come under a heading of *autonomia* is:

[a state] can make its own decisions, free from violent interference by a stronger state, about what is and what is not in the interests of its own survival, and . . . it can dispose of the military means necessary to implement measures necessary to ensure its survival.[36]

Others have suggested that such an elusive concept is easier to perceive through its absence, and therefore best defined in negative terms.[37] These negative conditions have been listed as follows: a state is not *autonomos* if it is ruled by a tyrant, ruled by the

securely dated example of the word (in Sophocles' *Antigone*, lines 821–2) applies to an individual, rather than to a *polis*, the more common usage in this period is of relations between *poleis*, and, in particular, of the unequal relations of the Delian League: on this, see Figueira 1993. (It would also fit with another possibly early instance of the word, in an agreement between Gortyn and Rhittenia (*I.Cret* IV.80, line 1): it has been suggested (by Van Effenterre & Ruzé 1994–5, vol. I: no. 7) that this agreement should be placed in the early fifth century.) An implication of this argument is that *autonomia* cannot be seen as a synonym of *eleutheria* – or at least not of *eleutheria* in its strong sense of freedom from all external coercion. For this view of the relationship between *autonomia* and *eleutheria*, see Karavites 1982a; note also Raaflaub 2004: 147–60, arguing that the fundamental difference between the terms is in their focus: *eleutheria* is outward looking, *autonomia* focuses on domestic self-determination. This argument works well as a description of the semantic ranges of the two words at their origin and in their early history. In the fourth century, however, it seems that the distinction between the two is not always so rigidly maintained: the process seems often to be not so much a strengthening of the force of *autonomia*, but a dilution of the power of *eleutheria* (see Karavites 1984b: esp. 191). For the suggestion that Sparta (in the fifth century) treated *autonomia* as a synonym of *eleutheria*, see Figueira 1993: 257–60; Figueira 1998: 249.

35 Ostwald 1982: 10–11.   36 Ostwald 1982: 29.

37 For *autonomia* as a 'trouser' word ('a word largely defined by its negative') see Bosworth 1992: 123; his approach is followed by Hansen 1995: 34.

fifth-century Athenian empire, ruled by Persia, ruled by a Spartan harmost (except on the Spartan definition of the word), a member of the Peloponnesian League (again, except for Sparta), a cleruchy or a perioikic community.[38] But even this extensive list does not seem to capture the whole range of meanings which could be associated with the concept; more importantly, even Hansen is prepared to concede that there might be an element of subjectivity involved in defining what could be claimed as a breach of *autonomia*. The absence of a fixed definition is, in fact, the most consistent feature of the word, and allows it, in Ostwald's description, to become 'merely useful as a political football'.[39] This seems to be entirely fair – although it is possible to question the adverb 'merely'. Rather than being an unfortunate diminution of the integrity of the term, it is precisely its value as a political football which gives the idea of *autonomia* its usefulness.[40]

The slipperiness of the idea applies, moreover, not only to the question of what particular freedoms might constitute *autonomia*, but also the issue of to whom that *autonomia* is to be granted. Or, to put it another way: must the boundaries of the autonomous unit necessarily coincide with those of the state? Although the general consensus holds that *autonomia* is a term properly used only in an interstate context, of relations between smaller states and larger powers, there are – in the fifth and fourth centuries – a number of possible counter-examples to this claim. One of these is the first (securely dated) occurrence of the word, in the *Antigone* (lines 821–2), where it is used by Cleon as a (negative) characterisation of Antigone's behaviour. The standard explanation of this personal use of a piece of interstate vocabulary is to categorise it as 'metaphorical'.[41] There are, however, other examples where the term is used in non-interstate contexts, where a metaphorical explanation seems implausible. In the Hippocratic *Airs, Waters,*

---

[38] Hansen 1995: 34–5. For an attempt to challenge this definition, with special reference to the contestable *autonomia* of the members of the fourth-century Boeotian League, see Keen 1996, and, for a counter-attack, Hansen 1996.

[39] Ostwald 1982: 42.

[40] For a good discussion of this, see Bosworth 1992; see also Rhodes 1999: esp. 40 on the fluidity of the concept, and Raaflaub 2004: 155–7 (suggesting, however, that this instability of meaning was less apparent to the Greeks than it is to modern scholars).

[41] Ostwald 1982: 11.

Places, the term is used to describe the condition of Greek states, in contrast to those which are under despotic rule (16.70.22, 71.4; 23.76.20); again, in Herodotus (1.96.1), the word is used with reference to the internal politics of a community – its negation would be tyranny. This tyranny might, it is true, be imposed from outside, but it could also come from within. In its only appearance in Aristotle (at *Politics* 1315a4–8), it is used to describe the opposite of monarchic rule.[42] There is, then, some evidence to suggest that the idea of *autonomia* did not always have to be used of relations between states and nothing else, and some of the (ab)uses of the term in interstate discourse – in particular when used in descriptions of acts of intervention – show how that potential ambiguity could be exploited.

One of the best demonstrations of how this manipulation of the meanings and boundaries of *autonomia* could operate in practice comes in the fifth book of the *Hellenica*, where Xenophon focuses his narrative on Spartan activities in the aftermath of the 386 King's Peace.[43] Xenophon describes a series of Spartan actions, in Mantineia, Phlius, Olynthus and Thebes (*HG* v.ii–iii): of these, the last three can be categorised as interventions.[44] The section is, therefore, worth considering in some detail not only as a case study of the use of the rhetoric of *autonomia*, but also because it is possible to see here one way in which that language might combine with that of helping the wronged.

The claim that the question of *autonomia* should be counted as an ordering principle of the section does, however, require rather more justification. Abstract criteria of any sort are, in fact, notably absent from Xenophon's account of the Spartan decision-making process, which is conspicuously driven by motivations of self-interest and security. Mantineia is attacked because the Spartans believe it to be disloyal, and a potential threat (v.ii.1–2); the intervention at Phlius is, Xenophon claims, unpopular at Sparta because the risk seems to

---

[42] Bosworth 1992: 123–4.

[43] For discussions of the section, see Tuplin 1993: ch. 4; Dillery 1995: 207–21.

[44] The attack on Mantineia is accompanied by constitutional change (Xen. *HG* v.ii.7; see also Gehrke 1985: 103–5), but this change – in Xenophon's account at least – follows the Spartan attack rather than (as in the cases of Phlius and Thebes) acting as a justification for it.

outweigh the potential benefit (v.iii.16);[45] Olynthus is supported because to do so would be ἄριστον τῇ Πελοποννήσῳ τε καὶ τοῖς συμμάχοις ('best for the Peloponnese and for the allies'; v.ii.20); Phoebidas avoids punishment for his unauthorised attack on the Theban Cadmeia on the grounds that his action was not harmful to the city:

ὁ μέντοι Ἀγησίλαος ἔλεγεν ὅτι εἰ μὲν βλαβερὰ τῇ Λακεδαίμονι πεπραχὼς εἴη, δίκαιος εἴη ζημιοῦσθαι, εἰ δὲ ἀγαθά, ἀρχαῖον εἶναι νόμιμον ἐξεῖναι τὰ τοιαῦτα αὐτοσχεδιάζειν. αὐτὸ οὖν τοῦτ', ἔφη, προσήκει σκοπεῖν, πότερον ἀγαθὰ ἢ κακά ἐστι τὰ πεπραγμένα.

Agesilaus, however, said that if what he had done was harmful to Sparta, he deserved to be punished, but if advantageous, it was an ancient custom that it was permitted to act, in such cases, on one's own initiative. 'This, then, is the thing', he said, 'which should be considered, whether what has been done is good or bad'. (v.ii.32)

If moral justifications are, in general, notably absent, the failure of one particular word to appear is even more striking: *autonomia* (and its related forms) – which occur six times in the first chapter of book five,[46] are not used again until the first paragraph of chapter four of the book, where – in his reflection on the divine punishment which arises from breaking treaties – Xenophon characterises the seizure of the Cadmeia as a breach of the commitment to uphold *autonomia* which was made by Sparta in the peace of 386:

Λακεδαιμόνιοί τε γὰρ οἱ ὁμόσαντες αὐτονόμους ἐάσειν τὰς πόλεις τὴν ἐν Θήβαις ἀκρόπολιν κατασχόντες ὑπ' αὐτῶν μόνων τῶν ἀδικηθέντων ἐκολάσθησαν πρῶ-τον, οὐδ' ὑφ' ἑνὸς τῶν πώποτε ἀνθρώπων κρατηθέντες.

The Lacedaemonians had sworn that they would leave the states independent, but after seizing possession of the Acropolis of Thebes they were punished by the very men, unaided, who had been thus wronged, although before that time they had not been conquered by any single one of all the peoples that ever existed. (v.iv.1)

This striking omission has been explained as indicating that it was only this last action which breached the terms of the 386 peace. This, in turn, has been explained by the suggestion that this peace

---

[45] See also v.ii.8, where the Phliasians encourage intervention on the grounds that their loyalty enhances Sparta's military strength.
[46] v.i.31, 32, 33 (twice), 36 (twice).

should not be classed as a 'Common Peace': only those who swore to it were protected by its terms, and *autonomia* is not, therefore, invoked in the first three cases because it is simply not an issue.[47]

This does not, however, seem to be the most plausible interpretation of the Peace of Antalcidas. Moreover, it is possible to explain why, even though the Peace applied to all *poleis*, Xenophon chose to emphasise the breach of the principle of *autonomia* only in relation to the attack on Thebes. To some extent, the neat *peripateia* of this case – Sparta's greatest act of impiety is the first cause of her downfall – must encourage Xenophon's emphasis in v.iv.I.[48] But it is also possible to see how this last action might be presented as being qualitatively different from the three which precede it. *Autonomia* is, I think, an issue in all four cases, but what is being demonstrated is how far the concept can be pushed, how far its boundaries can be stretched before they are unquestionably broken. This manipulation applies, however, not so much to the meaning which is given to the word, as to the nature and boundaries of the unit to which it is claimed to be applicable.

The *dioikismos* of Mantineia provides one of the most concrete examples this process.[49] Mantineia was originally made up of four (or five) separate villages.[50] This synoecism could be interpreted as compromising the *autonomia* of those villages, and Sparta's imposition of the *dioikismos* could therefore conceivably be regarded not as 'a clear violation of the autonomy clause of the Peace of Antalcidas',[51] but as being designed to uphold the principles to which she had subscribed in that peace.[52] This was, of course, just one of many possible ways in which the proper extent of the state could be constructed, a point which emerges in a neat reversal later

---

[47] For this argument, see Badian 1991: esp. 40–4. (Convincingly criticised by Jehne 1994: 41–2.) Diodorus (15.5.1) suggests that *autonomia* was thought to extend more widely.

[48] This is the line taken by Tuplin 1993: 100.

[49] Account of the *dioikismos* and of the issues involved in Cartledge 1987: 258–61.

[50] Xenophon (*HG* v.ii.7) has four; Ephorus (*FGH* 70, F79), Diodorus (15.5.4) and Strabo (viii.3.2) have five. On the topography and archaeology of Mantineia, see Hodkinson & Hodkinson 1981: esp. 261–3 on this problem.

[51] Cartledge 1987: 261.

[52] The fact that the Athenians, according to Diodorus (15.5.5), could choose not to see this action as a breach of the peace might support this view; the fact that the Thebans (according to Plutarch, *Pel.* 4) did take this as a reason for involvement indicates that the Athenian (and Spartan) interpretation need not be seen as definitive.

in the *Hellenica*: the first demonstration made by the Mantineians of the *autonomia* which they believe is granted to them by the peace of 370 is their vote μίαν πόλιν τὴν Μαντίνειαν ποιεῖν καὶ τειχίζειν τὴν πόλιν ('to make Mantineia one *polis* and to fortify the *polis*'; VI.v.3). But the Spartan preference in this case (for obvious reasons), was for a minimalist view of *autonomia*, a preference which can be seen again – albeit in a less physically destructive form – in their intervention in Olynthus. Here, the immediate aim is one of preservation rather then reversal of the *status quo* – the prevention of the incorporation of Acanthus and Apollonia into the Chalcidean Confederacy.[53] The ultimate goal, though, is the same as that seen at Mantineia, as is the means of achieving that goal through the manipulation of the boundaries of the (*autonomos*) political unit.[54]

There are indications elsewhere that it was the individual *polis* – no matter how artificially constructed – which was felt by Xenophon to be properly associated with *autonomia*. This approach appears, for example, in the speech given by Xenophon to the Athenian Autocles: in his attack on the Spartan claim to promote *autonomia* (VI.iii.7–9), he picks out as the Spartan action which is τὸ πάντων ἐναντιώτατον αὐτονομία ('the most opposed to *autonomia* of all'; VI.iii.8) their meddling in the constitutions of states. On this view, therefore, interfering in the internal affairs of *poleis* – particularly in their constitutions, and particularly if it

---

53 On the league, and these events, see Zahrnt 1971: 91–7; Cartledge 1987: 266–73; Beck 1997: ch. 9 (esp. 156–7). Xenophon's version here is strikingly different from that preserved in Diodorus (15.19), who makes the appeal for help come from the Macedonian king Amyntas. Such a version would make any appeal to the Peace of Antalcidas irrelevant, and it could be argued that Xenophon's preference for the alternative version here indicates, again, his desire to connect all these events to that Peace (Tuplin 1993: 94).

54 The Spartan insistence on the breakup of the Boeotian League and on the division of the recently united Corinth and Argos (X. *HG* v.i.32–4), are equally relevant examples of the flexibility of the boundaries of the basic political unit, and of the possible manipulation of that flexibility (see Rhodes 1993: 171–2, 174–5). Another possible example, although the evidence is less certain, of a similar attempt to break up a confederation in the context of an affirmation of the principle of *autonomia*, appears in the Athenian treatment of the cities of Ceos. Although the cities of the island do appear to have formed a confederation (see, for example, *IG* xii.5 594 (= Tod 141)), they appear as separate units on the stele of the Second Athenian League (*IG* ii² 43 (= RO 22), col. b, lines 23–6), and are shown elsewhere as being dealt with individually by Athens (e.g., *IG* ii² 1128 (= RO 40)). For discussions of the relevant evidence and of the historical context, see Brun 1989; on the Cean federation, Lewis 1997d.

is done by force rather than consent – is an infringement of their *autonomia*.[55] Such a view of *autonomia* would, of course, neatly explain why the attack on Thebes is depicted by Xenophon as a breach of that principle, while the attack on Mantineia and the intervention at Olynthus are not. But the intervention at Phlius,[56] which is in many ways very similar to that at Thebes – in both cases the intervention is made in support of a particular (oligarchic) faction, and both are followed by the overthrow of the existing constitution – seems to require further explanation. Why is the intervention at Thebes noted as a breach of the Peace of Antalcidas, while that at Phlius is not?

Two factors might, perhaps, distinguish the Phliasian intervention. The first difference lies in the outcome of the intervention, in the element of consent which is used in the establishment of the new regime: Agesilaus sets up a commission made up not only of the restored exiles but of the Phliasians who had remained in the city, and it is these who are entrusted with administering justice and with drawing up a new constitution.[57] The second, and, I would suggest, more significant difference lies in the origins of the (second, military) intervention. As was noted above (183), Agesilaus is able to claim that his objective is τοῖς ἀδικουμένοις βοηθήσειεν ('to help the wronged'; v.iii.14); Xenophon's narrative does, in fact, add some background to this claim:

ἔρχονται εἰς Λακεδαίμονα οἱ κατελθόντες κατηγορήσοντες τῆς πόλεως, καὶ ἄλλοι δὲ τῶν οἴκοθεν συνηκολούθουν, λέγοντες ὅτι πολλοῖς καὶ τῶν πολιτῶν οὐ δοκοῖεν δίκαια πάσχειν.

---

[55] A similar, explicit, association of *autonomia* with the maintenance of the *politeia* of a state can be seen in *IG* ii² 43 (= RO 22), lines 20–1 (where *autonomia* is also connected with freedom from garrison, *archon* and tribute). Note also in this context the evidence for the idea that priority should be given to the preservation of the existing (legitimate) constitution (whatever its type), visible in *IG* ii² 112 (= RO 41; alliance of Athens, Arcadians, Achaeans, Eleans and Phliasians, 362/1): the participants are obliged to take action if anyone attempts to overthrow the *dēmos* of Athens (line 25) or Phlius (line 30), or the *politeia* of the Acheans, Arcadians or Eleans (lines 30–1); similar provision in *IG* ii² 116 (= RO 44; alliance of Athens and Thessaly, 361/0), lines 18–19, 28–9.

[56] Strictly two interventions: a 'diplomatic' (*HG* v.ii.8–10) and a 'military' (v.iii.10–25).

[57] For the idea that consent could be argued to be a (or one of the) defining feature(s) of an *autonomos* relationship between a smaller and larger state, see Ostwald 1982: 29; Hansen 1995: 28.

the exiles arrived at Sparta and accused the city, and other people came with them
from home, saying that many of the citizens thought that the exiles were suffering
unjustly. (v.iii.11)

There is, then, some way in which it is possible to argue that a
wrong has already been committed, that the Phliasian exiles do
have a right to be supported, and that the Spartans' action here
is not so much an intervention as a counter-intervention. This is
notably different from Xenophon's, minimal, introduction to the
background to the Theban intervention, where the internal conflict
is described simply as *stasis* (v.ii.25), and where the question of
who might claim to be the injured party is not explored.[58]

Such claims – to be righting injustices, or to be operating with
the consent of the target state – might well be largely spurious (and
it is equally possible that we are intended to draw this conclusion
from Xenophon's account).[59] Nevertheless, these claims do seem
to explain how, in this case, the Spartan intervention could avoid
both a breach of the King's Peace and divine retribution. These
two types of behaviour – helping the wronged and maintaining
autonomia – seem, then, to be operating in this account not as
absolute opposites, nor as absolute equivalents, but as two different
ways in which intervention could be justified.

It is, however, possible to find some traces of a different construction of the scope of *autonomia*, and a correspondingly different attitude to its relationship to intervention. Where it is the
individual, not the *polis*, which is seen to have the greater claim
to *autonomia*, internal interference can be argued to be not only
compatible with, but also necessary for, the preservation of the liberty of the members of a state or community. In the *Panegyricus*,
Isocrates argues that it is not intervention but tyranny which should
be seen as a violation of *eleutheria* and *autonomia*:

τοσοῦτον δ' ἀπέχουσι τῆς ἐλευθερίας καὶ τῆς αὐτονομίας, ὥσθ' αἱ μὲν ὑπὸ τυράννοις εἰσί, τὰς δ' ἁρμοσταὶ κατέχουσιν, ἔνιαι δ' ἀνάστατοι γεγόνασι, τῶν δ' οἱ
βάρβαροι δεσπόται καθεστήκασιν.

---

[58] On Phliasian politics in the period, see Legon 1967 (with de Ste. Croix 1981: 608, n.
49); on Thebes, Hack 1978, who suggests the existence of a much more complicated
background (in the internal politics of Thebes in the 380s) than is revealed in Xenophon's
account.
[59] Tuplin 1993: 90–3.

So far are they removed from freedom and *autonomia* that some of them are ruled by tyrants, some are controlled by harmosts, some have been sacked, and some have become subject to barbarian masters. (4.117)

While in some ways these comments (describing the situation under the Spartan empire) seem quite similar to the complaints made by Xenophon's Autocles against Sparta (above: 195), there is, I think, a fundamental difference: for Autocles it is primarily the process of imposition which is the violation of *autonomia*; for Isocrates, the condition resulting from having such things imposed. And this difference in the interpretation of *autonomia* fits neatly with Isocrates' (positive) attitude to the Athenian empire in this speech.[60] The fifth-century Athenians interfered in the constitutions of other *poleis*; such a policy, however, which brought about stability, freedom and fairness, deserves not criticism but praise:

οὐ γὰρ ἐφθονοῦμεν ταῖς αὐξανομέναις αὐτων, οὐδε ταραχὰς ἐνεποιοῦμεν πολιτείας ἐναντίας παρακαθιστάντες, ἵν' ἀλλήλοις μὲν στασιάζοιεν, ἡμᾶς δ' ἀμφότεροι θεραπεύοιεν, ἀλλὰ τὴν τῶν συμμάχων ὁμόνοιαν κοινὴν ὠφέλειαν νομίζοντες τοῖς αὐτοῖς νόμοις ἁπάσας τὰς πόλεις διῳκοῦμεν, συμμαχικῶς ἀλλ' οὐ δεσποτικῶς βουλευόμενοι περὶ αὐτῶν, ὅλων μὲν τῶν πραγμάτων ἐπιστα-τοῦντες, ἰδίᾳ δ' ἑκάστους ἐλευθέρους ἐῶντες εἶναι, καὶ τῷ μὲν πλήθει βοηθοῦντες, ταῖς δὲ δυναστείαις πολεμοῦντες.

For we were not jealous of the growing states, nor did we stir up unrest among them by setting up conflicting constitutions side by side, so that there would be civil war among them, and that both sides would cultivate our support. On the contrary, we regarded harmony among our allies as a common benefit for all, and therefore we governed all the cities under the same laws, deliberating about them in the spirit of allies, not of masters; guarding the interests of the whole, but leaving each unit free; supporting the people but making war on despotic powers.[61] (4.104–5)

The suspicion with which this section began – that the concept of *autonomia* and the practice of intervention might be connected – turns out, therefore, to have some foundation. But this connection is not, it seems, as fundamental to the practice of intervention as is

---

[60] On the policies of the *Panegyricus*, see Bringmann 1965: ch. 2; Harding 1981; Porciani 1996; Grieser-Schmitz 1999: 100–46. On the historical context of the speech, Cloché 1963: 33–41.

[61] Compare the approach found in the *Archidamus* (6.64–5), where, again, *autonomia* is depicted as a quality enjoyed within *poleis* (but, in this case, one which revolt from Spartan control and establishment of democracy has destroyed).

the relationship between sovereignty and intervention in contemporary international relations. Nor is the relationship between the two concepts necessarily so strained as it is in the modern world:[62] the tension is eased, above all, by the fluidity of the meaning and scope of the two ideas. It is possible, perhaps, to see how abstract theoretical problems might arise; but the abstract concepts remain, precisely, sufficiently abstract to allow a direct confrontation of those problems to be avoided. But what the examples discussed here also demonstrate is that interventions do not present only theoretical problems: they are closely connected to practical outcomes, and it is those outcomes – and their difficulties – to which I now want to turn.

5.4 Intervention, imperialism and ideology

It will probably have been noticed that all of the positive depictions of the norm of intervention considered so far have come from the point of view of the active, intervening party, not that of the injured group. This bias is a fair reflection of the balance of the sources themselves. There are, however, a few, partial, exceptions to this rule, in which the practice of intervention is represented as being equally desirable from the point of view of the target state as it is for the intervening party. One interesting example comes in Lysias' *Epitaphios*: Lysias – unusually – refers to the role of the non-Athenians who had helped in the overthrow of the Thirty in 403:

ἄξιον δὲ καὶ τοὺς ξένους τοὺς ἐνθάδε κειμένους ἐπαινέσαι, οἳ τῷ πλήθει βοηθήσαντες καὶ περὶ τῆς ἡμετέρας σωτηρίας μαχόμενοι, πατρίδα τὴν ἀρετὴν ἡγησάμενοι,
τοιαύτην τοῦ βίου τελευτὴν ἐποιήσαντο.

It is right that we should also praise the foreigners who lie here: they came to help the masses, and fought for our salvation; they considered courage to be their homeland, and made this the goal of their lives.[63] (2.66)

---

[62] Cf. Karavites 1982b: 114, who sees the ideal of 'helping the weak' as a significant constraint on the sovereignty of the Greek city-state.

[63] On the more usual exclusion of non-Athenians from the *epitaphioi* (and on the exceptional nature of Lysias' comments here), see Loraux 1986a: 35. Lysias' reference to outsiders here seems especially striking in view of the general tendency (noted by Todd 1985: 166–8) among Athenian sources to underplay the role of non-Athenians in the events of 404/3. The fact that Lysias himself was an outsider may, of course, be significant.

A second example is more extensive, but probably less useful: the imaginary speech (imagined by Isocrates) of Plataean ambassadors at Athens after the sack of their city by Thebes, seeking Athenian help in righting that wrong. Although the speech does, superficially, play on the familiar themes from the opposite perspective, and suggests that the Plataeans too perceived intervention as an unquestionable good, it would, surely, be a mistake to treat it as anything other than another, if more imaginative, expression of an Athenian point of view. And apart from these examples, the emphasis of the extant evidence – when describing intervention as a positive ideal – is on the desirability of helping rather than being helped.

The reasons for this must lie partially, of course, in the fact that being the wronged party would, in practice, be a fairly unpleasant experience and not one which it would be easy to present as a welcome condition. But it must also have something do to with the fact that intervening to help those in need could bring advantages more tangible than simply a warm glow of moral superiority.

Evidence of an awareness of the potential practical advantages of intervention is not hard to find, although the perceived benefits do take a variety of forms. In some cases, the focus is less on the active expansion of power, and more on self-defence. For Demosthenes in the *Olynthiacs*, for example, the assertion that Athenian failure to help Olynthus would be dishonourable is combined with a strong practical argument: if Olynthus falls to Philip II, Athens will be next:

χωρὶς γὰρ τῆς περιστάσης ἂν ἡμᾶς αἰσχύνης, εἰ καθυφείμεθά τι τῶν πραγμάτων, οὐδὲ τὸν φόβον, ὦ ἄνδρες Ἀθηναῖοι, μικρὸν ὁρῶ τὸν τῶν μετὰ ταῦτα, ἐχόντων μὲν ὡς ἔχουσι Θηβαίων ἡμῖν, ἀπειρηκότων δὲ χρήμασι Φωκέων, μηδενὸς δε ἐμποδὼν ὄντος Φιλίππῳ τὰ παρόντα καταστρεψαμένῳ πρὸς ταῦτ' ἐπικλῖναι τὰ πράγματα.

For, quite apart from the disgrace that we should incur if we shirk our responsibilities, I see not a little danger, men of Athens, for the future, if the Thebans maintain their present attitude towards us, and the Phocians have run out of money, and there is nothing to hinder Philip, when he has overcome his current problem, from turning his attention against us.[64] (3.8–9)

[64] Note the combination of more abstract argument (the shame of failing to help) with the practical case here. For the practical argument alone, see Dem. 1.12. The argument that

Potential benefits could also be more positive. Some gains might be relatively small in scale. The apparently disinterested Indian ambassadors of the *Cyropaedia*, for example (above: 184), are described in a later chapter as having come to Cyrus' court in order to spy (III.ii.27). Other benefits might have more long-lasting implications. The idea that intervention need not, indeed ideally should not, be reliant on any pre-existing friendship between the two states involved is one which recurs (particularly, though not exclusively, in the *epitaphioi*): Lysias' comments (above: 180) on Athens' willingness to help even her traditional enemies are an excellent example of that approach.[65] This does not, however, mean that such acts could not be, and were not, used as the starting point to build up such networks of obligation. Intervention, that is, has to be seen in the context of the reciprocal patterns of Greek interstate behaviour: by doing someone a favour, it is legitimate to expect, or demand, something in return.[66] That something might, it is true, be no more than the promise of assistance in the case of attack: this is the sort of benefit which, according to Xenophon, the Phliasian Procles suggests will result if Athens helps Sparta against Theban aggression (*HG* VI.v.43–8). But more often, it amounts to rather more than that: namely, 'empire'.[67]

an intervention was too dangerous to undertake can also be found: see, for example, the arguments of Aeschines (2.76), who, while accepting (or claiming to accept) the moral value of the Athenian tradition of intervention, argues strongly that prudential considerations should take precedence (and gives the disastrous Athenian intervention in support of Leontini as evidence of the consequences when this is not the case); later in the same speech (2.173–6), he returns to the theme, presenting much of Athens' fifth-century history as a series of (misguided) excursions into the affairs of others. Similar, practical, concerns are mentioned, but dismissed, in pro-interventionist texts, for example Dem. 15.11–13; Isocrates 14.2.

[65] Outside the *epitaphioi* see, for example, Dem. 18.95–101.

[66] On reciprocity, see ch. 2, esp. sections 2 and 3.

[67] 'Empire' can, here, encompass both *hegemonia* and *archē*. There is a tendency among historians to characterise the two as representing distinct forms of activity (with *archē* as 'hegemony's evil twin': Van Wees 2004: 8): for an example of this approach, see Cargill 1982; or (to a lesser extent) Griffith 1978. References to *hegemonia* do generally seem entirely positive (note especially its use as a trireme name, a context in which the word's connotations of specifically military leadership are likely to be important: *IG* ii² 1618, line 110; perhaps also *IG* ii² 1609, line 90; *Hegemonē* appears in *IG* ii² 1612, lines 111, 122; 1629, lines 771, 845; 1631, lines 133, 202). And it is also possible to find undeniably negative references to *archē* (especially to the ἀρχή τῆς θαλάττης, '*archē* of the sea': see Ober 1978: 125–8): Isocrates' *On the Peace* is a good source for such views. But this distinction is not always rigidly maintained, and *archē* can be presented

The link between intervention and imperialism is one which is firmly established in modern international theory. (Studies tend, not surprisingly perhaps, to focus on twentieth-century US foreign policy.[68]) And, in this case, there does appear to be a substantial similarity between ancient and modern. That being in a position to intervene in the affairs of others can be seen as a marker of stability and power should not be surprising: just as being in the position of requiring help was, presumably, undesirable, so the opposite condition should be seen as an indication that things are going well. Again, this is a theme that recurs in Athenian writing – often, in the fourth century, with a tinge of nostalgia: one of the ways that the past greatness of the city was manifested was in the fact that she was, in the good old days, always the first port of call for those in distress.[69]

But what should also be considered are the ways in which acts of intervention could become not only a sign of a leading position among the Greek states, but also a method by which that position could be achieved. The classic statement of the connection comes in Xenophon's *Hellenica*, in the mouths of Theban ambassadors sent to Athens in 395 in an attempt to persuade the city to abandon her post-Peloponnesian War quietism and to help defend Thebes against a threatened Spartan invasion. After a few opening remarks, the Thebans get to the point:

καὶ μὴν ὅτι μέν, ὦ ἄνδρες Ἀθηναῖοι, βούλοισθ' ἂν τὴν ἀρχὴν ἣν πρότερον ἐκέκτησθε ἀναλαβεῖν πάντες ἐπιστάμεθα· τοῦτο δὲ πῶς μᾶλλον εἰκὸς γενέσθαι ἢ εἰ αὐτοὶ τοῖς ὑπ' ἐκείνων ἀδικουμένοις βοηθοῖτε;

Furthermore, men of Athens, we all understand that you would like to recover the *archē* which you formerly possessed; and how is this more likely to come about than if you help those who have been wronged by the Lacedaemonians?[70] (III.v.10)

<hr>

as favourably as *hegemonia*: this elision of the gap between the two is especially visible in the *Hellenica* (see Wickersham 1994: 81–4; and below n. 70).
[68] On the general link between intervention and imperialism, see Dunn 1994: 249; for a case study of how the connection can work in practice (with reference to American foreign policy after the Second World War), see Robinson 1996.
[69] See, for example, And. 1.107; Aeschin. 3.134; Isoc. 4.34–40, 8.174; X. *Mem.* III.v.12, *Vect.* v.5–10. See also Chambers 1973: esp. chs. 3 and 4.
[70] Note that intervention will, according to the Thebans, bring *archē*, not *hegemonia*.

Some details of the evils of the Spartan empire follow, before the ambassadors return to their theme:

πῶς οὖν οὐκ εἰκός, ἐὰν ὑμεῖς αὖ προστῆτε τῶν οὕτω φανερῶς ἀδικουμένων, νῦν ὑμᾶς πολὺ ἤδη μεγίστους τῶν πώποτε γενέσθαι;

How, then, is it unlikely that if you in your turn offer yourselves as leaders of those who are so manifestly wronged, you will now become by far the greatest of all the states that have ever been? (III.v.14)

The idea that intervention could be a painless way to empire is not, either, simply an invention of the Thebans (or of Xenophon). Thucydides' Alcibiades, urging the Athenians to go through with their intervention in Sicily, claims that such behaviour – παραγιγνόμενοι προθύμως τοῖς αἰεὶ ἢ βαρβάροις ἢ Ἕλλησιν ἐπικαλουμένοις ('readily coming to the side of whoever called, whether Greek or barbarian'; vi.18.2) – is the safest and quickest route to empire. In *On the Peace* (8.30), Isocrates claims that it was by behaving justly and helping the oppressed that Athens was 'willingly' (παρ' ἑκόντων) entrusted with the hegemony of the Greeks. In the section of the *Archidamus* mentioned above (183), Sparta's willingness to help the wronged is directly connected to her conquest of Messene. A negative expression of the connection can be seen in Plato's *Menexenus* (244c4–5): in the aftermath of the Peloponnesian War, Athens' acceptance of defeat and of the loss of empire was made manifest by her decision to abandon her role as international policeman of the Greek world.

It is, however, when the connection between intervention and imperialism is most closely made that it is possible to find the strongest objections to that activity – although the activity is also, in these circumstances, differently categorised: the behaviour involved may seem objectively extremely similar to that which came under the heading of 'helping the wronged', but the response to it is violently different. Thucydides' Hermocrates, addressing the Sicilians as the prospect of Athenian intervention looms, presents as uncontroversial the fact that this act of kindness to injured kinsmen (cf. Th. III.86) is nothing but a prelude to full-scale invasion and conquest (IV.60). The phenomenon can be observed even more clearly in Demosthenes' depictions of the behaviour of one of the fourth century's prime exponents of interventionism, Philip II. It is not, I think, impossible to imagine how Philip might have been able to present his activities in, for example, Oreus: the city was terribly riven with factional strife, grave injustices were being done, and he stepped in only to protect the innocent from being harmed. The practical consequences of his action were merely an unforeseen, if fortunate, side-effect. In the *Third Philippic*, however, Demosthenes interprets these actions rather differently:

καὶ μὴν εἰ μέχρι τούτου περιμενοῦμεν, ἕως ἂν ἡμῖν ὁμολογήσῃ πολεμεῖν, πάντων ἐσμὲν εὐηθέστατοι· οὐδὲ γὰρ ἂν ἐπὶ τὴν Ἀττικὴν αὐτὴν βαδίζῃ καὶ τὸν Πειραιᾶ, τοῦτ᾽ ἐρεῖ, εἴπερ οἷς πρὸς τοὺς ἄλλους πεποίηκε δεῖ τεκμαίρεσθαι . . . τοῖς ταλαιπώροις Ὠρείταις τουτοισὶ ἐπισκεψομένους ἔφη τοὺς στρατιώτας πεπομφέναι κατ᾽ εὔνοιαν· πυνθάνεσθαι γὰρ αὐτοὺς ὡς νοσοῦσι καὶ στασιάζουσιν, συμμάχων δ᾽ εἶναι καὶ φίλων ἀληθινῶν ἐν τοῖς τοιούτοις καιροῖς παρεῖναι.

If we are going to wait until Philip acknowledges that he is at war with us, we are indeed the simplest of all men; for even if he marches straight against Attica and the Piraeus, he will not admit it, if we may judge from his treatment of the other states . . . he informed those wretched people in Oreus that he had sent his soldiers to pay them a visit of sympathy in all goodwill, for he understood that they were sick and stricken with civil war, and it was the duty of true friends and allies to be at their side on such occasions. (9.10, 12)

Philip's behaviour, in other words, is not only aggressive, it is also deceitful: under a pretence of friendship, he is able to take over cities without even fighting a battle.[71]

In terms of the actions involved, it might seem difficult to distinguish Philip's behaviour in Euboea from, for example, the proposed expedition to support the democrats of Rhodes during the *stasis* there – an expedition which Demosthenes had enthusiastically

---

[71] The actual evidence for Philip's actions in Oreus (and elsewhere in Euboea) is uncertain: it is quite possible that Demosthenes is exaggerating the extent of Philip's involvement (see Tritle 1993). The use of intervention as an underhand method of extending empire is one of Demosthenes' favourite allegations against Philip: cf. 6.20–5; 9.33; 18.43. Compare Isoc. 5.20: it is the combination of benefaction and of force which is the basis of Philip's success. On the manipulability of arguments for and against Philip's interventions, see Squillace 2000.

promoted a few years earlier. It might, therefore, seem legitimate to suspect that the difference lies solely in the perspective from which such actions are seen: intervention carried out by the right side is good; by the wrong side, terrible. Certainly, the importance of such subjective criteria in the assessment of interventions should not be ignored. But in many cases it is possible to find some indications that something else might be at stake too: the issues – not, of course, unconnected to imperialism – of domestic political structures, political ideology and constitutional change.[72] Although, as was argued above (in section 3), interference in the domestic politics of another state need not, necessarily, conflict with a positive representation of interventionism, there are also occasions when such behaviour is closely connected with negative portrayals of that activity.

Isocrates' *On the Peace* provides an interesting, if inconclusive, approach to the problem. Intervention is a prominent theme in the speech, but is presented in more than one way. Isocrates wants to distinguish between two types of intervention. There is a negative variety – *polypragmosunē* (πολυπραγμοσύνη, 'meddlesomeness'; 8.26, 30, 58, 108) – exemplified above all by the behaviour of fifth-century Athens, although Sparta and Thebes are also culprits.[73] This is to be contrasted, however, with the positive version of that behaviour – helping the wronged:

καὶ γὰρ τὸ πρότερον ἐκ μὲν τῆς τοιαύτης πολυπραγμοσύνης εἰς τοὺς ἐσχάτους κινδύνους κατέστημεν, ἐκ δὲ τοῦ δίκαιαν τὴν πόλιν παρέχειν καὶ βοηθεῖν τοῖς ἀδικουμένοις καὶ μὴ τῶν ἀλλοτρίων ἐπιθυμεῖν παρ' ἑκόντων τῶν Ἑλλήνων τὴν ἡγεμονίαν ἐλάβομεν.

---

[72] The question of the link between *stasis* and external intervention has provoked great controversy. For *stasis* as class struggle, see de Ste. Croix 1981: 78–9 (and 298); for the 'elite strife' thesis, see Ruschenbusch 1978. Overviews in Lintott 1982; Gehrke 1985.

[73] For an overview of the word's use (with particular reference to the fifth century) and its association with imperialism, see Ehrenberg 1947; Kleve 1964; Whelan 1983. Isocrates presents *polypragmosunē* as being opposed to *sōphrosunē* (on the contrast between the two, see North 1947), and to ἡσυχία ('quiet', 'neutrality'); a similar pattern appears in Xenophon's *Poroi*, where ἀπραγμοσύνη ('lack of action') is equated with ἡσυχία (Dillery 1993: 6–9). On *polypragmosunē* in Isocrates, see Bringmann 1965: 62–4 (noting the relationship to Thucydides' approach); Too 1995: 92–8 (but Too's suggestion (96) that the opposite of *polypragmosunē* should be seen as 'pacifism' is, I think, misleading (on Isocrates' attitude to war, see Bettalli 1992)).

For previously, as the result of such *polypragmosunē*, we were placed in the utmost danger, while as the result of keeping our city in the path of justice and of helping the wronged and not coveting the possessions of others we were given the hegemony by the willing consent of the Greeks. (8.30)

But although this is one of the clearest assertions of the distinctiveness, and opposition, of the two concepts, the basis for their distinction is not immediately obvious.[74]

A comment later in the speech suggests that the potential 'wrongdoers' against whom Athens should be prepared to act are other *poleis*:

ἢν οὖν ἐμμείνητε τοῖς εἰρημένοις . . . οὐ μόνον εὐδαίμονα ποιήσετε ταύτην τὴν πόλιν ἀλλὰ καὶ τοὺς Ἕλληνας ἅπαντας. οὐδὲ γὰρ ἄλλη τῶν πόλεων οὐδεμία τολμήσει περὶ αὐτοὺς ἐξαμαρτάνειν, ἀλλ᾽ ὀκνήσουσι καὶ πολλὴν ἡσυχίαν ἄξουσιν, ὅταν εἰδῶσιν ἐφεδρεύουσαν τὴν δύναμιν τὴν ἡμετέραν καὶ παρεσκευασμένην τοῖς ἀδικουμένοις βοηθεῖν.

If, then, you will abide by the advice which I have given you . . . you will make not only this city but all the Greeks happy. For no other city will dare to wrong them; on the contrary, they will hold back and studiously avoid aggression when they see our power prepared and ready to go to help the wronged. (8.136–7)

This might suggest that 'helping the wronged' is, for Isocrates, an activity which takes place not within but between states. Is *polypragmosunē*, then, a label properly applied to intervention in disputes within states? Again, it might seem possible to support this argument. According to Isocrates, Athens' insistence on establishing democratic government in the subject states of her fifth-century empire caused (justified) hostility (8.79); the Spartan empire of the early fourth century was similarly doomed by its policy of subverting the constitutions of the states under its control, and, in this case, dismantling πολιτείας ('legitimate constitutions') and setting up τυράννους ('tyrannies'; 8.99–100). It might, then, be possible to

---

[74] Adkins 1976: 311–16, raises the problem of the categorisation as *polypragmosunē* of behaviour which might in some circumstances be considered virtuous, and suggests that the basis for distinction might lie not in the nature of the action, but in the identity of the agent which carries it out: the actions of the *dēmos* during the Athenian empire are classed as *polypragmosunē* not because they are intrinsically bad, but because they trespass on the traditional *aretē* of the elite. But while an ideological element to Isocrates' objections is extremely likely, this need not, I think, be restricted to the question of agency, but might also be connected to outcome.

construct an argument in which *polypragmosunē* – 'bad' intervention – can be defined as intervention within states; and 'helping the wronged'– 'good' intervention – implies a restriction to involvement in disputes between states. But such a rationale is never made so explicit by Isocrates (and a distinction of this sort might in any case seem implausible in a speech which, generally, blurs the boundaries between domestic and interstate behaviour).[75] It should also be noted that Isocrates' representation of Athenian-imposed democracy is so negative as to make it seem almost identical to tyranny. It may, then, be better to see the basis for the distinction as one which, insofar as it relies on logic at all, is based more on Isocrates' attitude to the result of an action than his belief in the inviolable integrity of *politeiai*, whatever their political ideology.

In the *Panegyricus*, as was noted above (197), Isocrates' position, and the reasoning behind it, are much clearer: the line taken is that intervention in domestic affairs with the aim of setting up nontyrannical government is an unimpeachable activity. This applies not only, as was seen, to Athens, but also to the Spartans, who:

καὶ πρότερον μὲν τοὺς τυράννους ἐξέβαλλον, τῷ δὲ πλήθει τὰς βοηθείας ἐποιοῦντο

Previously, it is true, they used to expel tyrants and help the people (4.125)

Intervening in order to remove legitimate governments is, correspondingly, necessarily bad:

νῦν δὲ τοσοῦτον μεταβεβλήκασιν, ὥστε ταῖς μὲν πολιτείαις πολεμοῦσι, τὰς δὲ μοναρχίας συγκαθιστᾶσιν.

but now they have so far reversed their policy that they make war on legitimate constitutions and aid in establishing monarchies. (4.125)

It is this version of the argument which is closest to that which appears elsewhere. For Demosthenes too, the crucial factor seems to be the form of government which results from an intervention, although it is more obvious that, for Demosthenes, that form of government should be democracy: Athenian interventions help democracies, and this is a good thing. The speech *For the Liberty of the Rhodians* – a speech intended precisely to encourage the

---

[75] Ch. 4, sec. 3.

Athenians to intervene in order to restore democracy – provides, unsurprisingly, a clear statement of the case:

τοὺς μὲν οὖν ἄλλους τοὺς ἀδικοῦντάς τινας αὐτῶν τῶν κακῶς πεπονθότων ἐχθροὺς ἡγεῖσθαι χρή· τοὺς δὲ τὰς πολιτείας καταλύοντας καὶ μεθιστάντας εἰς ὀλιγαρχίαν κοινοὺς ἐχθροὺς παραινῶ νομίζειν ἁπάντων τῶν ἐλευθερίας ἐπιθυμούντων.

Now, all other wrongdoers must be considered the enemies of those only whom they have wronged, but when men overthrow legitimate constitutions and change them to oligarchies, I urge you to regard them as the common enemies of all who love freedom. (15.20)

By contrast, according to Demosthenes, the oligarchic regime currently in power at Rhodes should not be supported by Athens even if it had gained control without the help of others (15.14); Athens' general rule – as a point of security as well as ideology – should be to encourage and defend democracies (15.17–18).[76] Such an approach to the legitimacy of intervention – that it is support for democracy which makes it justifiable – makes Demosthenes' opposition to Philip's activities entirely consistent. Philip's interventions bring not democracy but tyranny, and so should be resisted by all right-thinking people. The point is made strikingly in the *Second Philippic* (6.20–5): the immediate effect of Philip's incursion into Olynthus and Thessaly is their subjection to Macedonian control; the general lesson which can be extrapolated from this is that free states should never trust tyrants – kings and tyrants are necessarily the enemies of freedom and law (ἐλευθερίᾳ καὶ νόμοις; 6.25).

It is also possible to find some traces of a third point of view: that the problem with intervention is that it strengthens democracies.[77]

---

[76] On Demosthenes' views of tyranny, see Leopold 1981; a similar view of intervention in internal politics – that it is justified if it brings about democracy or removes tyrannies – can be found in Lysias 2.56.

[77] Contrast the dominant modes of argument against pro-democratic intervention in modern interstate relations: either that it is an illegitimate infringement of state sovereignty; or that it is a disguised form of western imperialism. (For a recent analysis of this problem, see Byers & Chesterman 2000.) A third variant of the argument – that imposed liberty is not true liberty – can also be found: see, for example, Mill 1984 (1859): 122 (followed by Walzer 2000: 88): 'if they have not sufficient love of liberty to be able to wrest it from merely domestic oppressors, the liberty which is bestowed on them by hands other than their own, will have nothing real, nothing permanent.' The argument that democracy itself is a bad thing is, unsurprisingly, rare.

This view is – for obvious reasons – both less frequently and less clearly expressed. Nevertheless, it seems to be what lies behind, for example, Andocides' criticisms of Athens' foreign policy in *On the Peace* (a speech aimed at persuading Athens to withdraw from her involvement in the conflict between Corinth and Argos):

ἐγὼ μὲν οὖν ἐκεῖνο δέδοικα μάλιστα, ὦ <ἄνδρες> Ἀθηναῖοι, τὸ εἰθισμένον κακόν, ὅτι τοὺς κρείττους φίλους ἀφιέντες ἀεὶ τοὺς ἥττους αἱρούμεθα, καὶ πόλεμον ποιούμεθα δι' ἑτέρους, ἐξὸν δι' ἡμᾶς αὐτοὺς εἰρήνην ἄγειν.

What alarms me above all else, men of Athens, is our familiar fault of invariably abandoning powerful friends in preference for weak, and of going to war for the sake of others when it is possible for us to remain at peace.[78] (3.28)

The same criticism appears, in very similar terms, in Plato's *Menexenus*. Aspasia's funeral oration portrays Athens' tendency to rush to the help of the oppressed as her greatest single failing: the only accusation which can justly be made against the city is that she ἀεὶ λίαν φιλοικτίρμων ἐστὶ καὶ τοῦ ἥττονος θεραπίς ('always too liable to pity and a helper of the weak'; 244e3). Both these writers (Plato and Andocides) are associated with a generally unsupportive, if not actively hostile, attitude to Athenian democracy, and in both cases, the key to their objection to Athenian (democratic) behaviour seems to lie in the fact that Athens' help is always directed at the ἥττους ('the weak'). The ambiguity of this phrase – does it refer to weaker states or the democratic mob? – is suspiciously convenient.[79] What it is perhaps possible to see here is another way in which the traditional antithesis between oligarchy and Athenian imperialism might manifest itself:[80] if intervention, in Athenian policy in particular, is associated with support for democracies, as well as with the expansion of empire, then it is not all that surprising to find those with anti-democratic leanings

---

[78] Note that this criticism comes in the same speech as Andocides' assertion of a universal norm of helping the wronged (3.13, and n. 19 above). 'Helping the weak' (identified by Karavites 1982b as a dominant norm of Greek interstate relations) and 'helping the wronged' are not, therefore, to be seen as absolute equivalents.

[79] On this phrase, see Missiou 1992: 113 n. 11 and 138.

[80] For a fourth-century assertion of the connection, see *Hell.Oxy.* 9.2–3; the classic statement of the case in modern scholarship is that of de Ste. Croix 1954/5; see also Jaeger 1945: 77. For an argument against the existence of any significant link, see Harding 1981.

providing some of the most explicit challenges to Athenian policies of intervention.

5.5 Conclusions

Intervention in classical Greece is, therefore, governed by not one but several, often intersecting, norms. There is a strong positive norm of helping the wronged, to which it is very hard to find any direct challenges: even those who oppose, for practical or ideological reasons, a particular intervention are not found denying the validity of the general rule; they can even, in fact, be found asserting it. The ideal itself – that helping the wronged is, when all other things are equal, an acceptable and even admirable principle of interstate relations – is never openly challenged. When, as is more usually the case, things are not equal, the greater burden of proof, or of justification, lies not with those wanting to intervene, but with those attempting to argue against such behaviour.

But that norm of helping the wronged co-exists with the (fluid) ideal of *autonomia*. And the ideal of *autonomia*, in turn, runs alongside, and sometimes contrary to, a widely asserted belief that political ideology is the crucial factor in determining the legitimacy of any act of intervention. And to all this must be added, finally, the question of political expediency, and of practical benefit: interventions both represent and sustain positions of power.

Intervention is, rightly, seen as one of the most complex aspects of modern interstate relations:

intervention . . . is an inherently tricky business, subject to no clear-cut guidelines and liable to numerous difficulties and embarrassments . . . There appears to exist a continuum of moral action of an Aristotelian sort, ranging from busybodiness to just intervention to callous indifference. The boundaries separating these categories are not easy to draw on either the level of personal morality or on the level of international relations. For this reason, the decision to intervene must always be an agonizingly imprecise one.[81]

Many aspects of classical Greek intervention may be specific to classical Greece, but this fluidity is, I think, a characteristic which,

---

[81] Elfstrom 1983: 725.

although identified by a scholar of modern interventions, can also be perceived in the Greek world. But here too there is a difference: there is, it seems to me, little sign that there was much agonising over the imprecision of intervention. Rather, it is its indistinctness, its openness to perpetual redefinition and recharacterisation, which gives it much of its usefulness as a tool of practical interstate politics.

6

STABILITY AND CHANGE

6.1 Introduction: an evaded dimension

Back in Chapter 1, the modern discipline of International Relations was criticised for its unwillingness, or inability, to confront the question of change. That accusation will, however, perhaps have come to seem increasingly hypocritical, since this study too has generally paid little attention to the possibility of diachronic progression, or regression, in the conduct of interstate relations. Such an approach might seem perverse: the period owes its traditional popularity (or at least some of it) to the fact that it is characterised by important, even exciting, historical developments (the rise and fall of several empires; various political revolutions; the transformation of warfare – to name just three possible subjects); and it is also regularly argued to include – at 404/3 – at least one major historical rupture. Moreover, a theme which has recurred in this study is the importance of an awareness of temporal progression to the conduct of Greek interstate politics: actions are regularly motivated and justified by reference to past events, and in the hope of shaping future patterns of behaviour. In that sense, therefore, diachronic progression is entrenched in Greek interstate politics.

What is less immediately clear, however, is how far changes of this sort influence the larger framework of interstate interaction – the approaches to society, norms and morals which have been described in preceding chapters. That is the question which this chapter seeks to address, first by setting out a case for the basic stability of interstate norms throughout the classical period; and second by providing some suggestions about the sorts of changes of which even a basically synchronic study needs to take account. This second question is the more difficult both to frame and to answer, and will involve turning to two elements of Greek interstate history which have been conspicuously marginal to this study so far: namely Thucydides, and the Athenian Empire.

6.2 A stable system

First, however, it is worth providing a very brief reassertion of the argument for the basic stability of the structure, methods and ideals of the Greek interstate system throughout this period. The assumption of stability has, of course, underpinned much of the argumentation of the preceding chapters: the small-scale nature of those developments which have been mentioned (shifts in honorific vocabulary, the changing implication of the label *autonomia*, and so on) should serve to illustrate rather than undermine that point.[1] Nevertheless, it is worth taking the time to make a more explicit statement of the case for continuity.

I am going to reject (after brief consideration) one possible solution to the question of change (or, to put it more honestly, one way of sidestepping the problem entirely). It could be argued, not without justification, that the model of historical change briefly sketched above is one which is relevant only to a small proportion of the Greek world. It is, after all, in Athenian history (and, in no small part, in Athenian domestic history) that the strongest evidence of dramatic change is visible – a change focused on and driven by the loss of the Peloponnesian War, and consequently of the Athenian Empire, in 404. This revolution in Athenian power would clearly have had an effect on many other states in the Greek world, from the powerful (Sparta, for example) to the more puny (notably, the subject states of the Empire).[2] But it is worth wondering how

---

[1] Ch. 4, sec. 2 and ch. 5, sec. 3 respectively.

[2] Generally on the consequences of the Peloponnesian War, see Cartledge 2001a; Hornblower 2002: ch. 14. The precise connection between the outcome of the Peloponnesian War and Sparta's subsequent history is, of course, disputed: for an authoritative study of the problem, see Hodkinson 2000: esp. 423–32. For a particularly clear example of the effects of Athens' downfall (and Sparta's rise) on smaller states, see RO 4: Spartan activities on Delos, around 403. Broader assessments of change between the fifth and fourth centuries have often tended to be pessimistic in tone: see especially Mossé 1973; compare Dobbs 1907: 203 ('There is something infinitely tragic in this page of history'); Murray 1946: 166 ('all the fourth century is touched by the feeling of disillusion that goes with a lost cause'). Other works, particularly more recent ones, have been more optimistic: see Rhodes 1994: 589–91; Carlier 1996; and, for an early example, Bury 1900: 537 (arguing

world-shaking an event this might have been for other Greek cities. In spite of modern historical obsessions, and in spite of Thucydides' assertion of the all-encompassing nature of the events he describes in his history (Th. I.I.I), it seems likely that some parts of Greek interstate activity did manage to remain relatively unaffected by the evolution of the Athenian Empire, or by the struggles of the Peloponnesian War.

Admittedly (and not surprisingly) we can catch only glimpses of this, but the glimpses are suggestive. For example: ML 42, the fragmentary record of an agreement between the cities of Tylissos, Knossos and Argos, regulates diplomatic, military and economic relations between the two Cretan cities (the Argives apparently act as guarantor or arbitrator to the settlement).[3] Although the agreement is conventionally (if inexactly) dated to the period before the start of the Peloponnesian War – around 450 – there is no good reason to think that it could not still have been in operation twenty or thirty years later, or that this sort of regular, routine, relatively unspectacular interaction between Greek states did not continue into the second part of the fifth century: it seems likely that Knossos and Tylissos continued to quibble over the precise location of their borders, the allocation of booty from shared campaigns and the content of their shared sacrifices, no matter what the Spartans and Athenians were getting up to further north; it also seems unlikely that the ultimate outcome of that larger conflict would have had much impact on the day-to-day pattern of interstate relations between the two Cretan cities.[4]

---

for 'the general fact that the Greeks of the fourth century were more humane than the Greeks of the fifth'). Davies 1995 rejects the idea of a crisis in Athenian domestic politics, but suggests that one might be found in 'the city state system of which she was . . . a part' (36).

[3] The precise nature of the relationship implied by this agreement is unclear: the suggestion (associated especially with Kahrstedt 1942 and Gschnitzer 1958: 44–7) that the main agreement is between Knossos and Argos, and that Tylissos is only a dependency of the latter, seems less plausible than the interpretation (supported by ML *ad loc*, Van Effentere & Ruzé 1994–5, vol. I: no. 54) which points to some sort of tripartite agreement. For full discussion, and further bibliography, see Van Effentere & Ruzé.

[4] Compare the experience of Acarnania amd Ambracia in the mid-420s. Both states do become embroiled in the Peloponnesian War, but the agreement reported by Thucydides (III.114.3) indicates that it was still possible to plan (arguably, over-optimistically) for disengagement from the conflict: neither Athens nor Sparta plays any direct part in the creation of the treaty described by Thucydides, the main object of which seems to be

It is, therefore, important to be clear about the fundamental Athenocentricity of the models of change – particularly of revolutionary change – which are typically applied to the diachronic history of the classical period. Nevertheless, such an observation does not justify the avoidance of the issue altogether. In part, this is simply a quantitative issue: a history of Greek interstate relations which did not include Athens, or states affected by Athens, would be exiguous in the extreme. More important, however, is the centrality of Athenian accounts of foreign relations to any analysis of the subject: since we are, almost exclusively, restricted to studying Athenian perceptions of Greek interstate relations, then it is reasonable to assume that even events which affect only Athens might have some impact on those perceptions.

Even from an Athenian perspective, however, a case for stability can be made. In support of that case, I offer here just two examples, which, although relatively trivial, seem to provide sufficient demonstration of the crucial points.

The first example is a simple case of academic misattribution. It does, however, offer a good insight into the considerable uncertainty which often lurks behind academic convictions about the tone of foreign politics in the fifth and fourth centuries. The text in question is an Athenian decree, honouring the *koinon* of the Eteocarpathians for services which they have provided to Athens:

[ἔδοξεν τῆι βο]λῆι καὶ τῶι δή-
[μωι· . . . ηὶς ἐπ]ρυτάνευε, Τει-
[σίας ἐγραμμά]τευε, Ἀθηνόδω-
[ρος ἐπεστάτ]ε, Κτησίας εἶπε·
[. . . . 8. . . . τὸ]γ Καρπάθιον κα-
[ὶ τὸς παῖδας] καὶ τὸ Ἐτεοκαρ-
[παθίων κοιν]ὸν γράψαι εὐερ-
[γέτας Ἀθην]α[ί]ων, ὅτι ἔδοσα[ν]
[τὴν κυπάριτ]τον ἐπὶ τὸν νε[ὼ]-
[ν τῆς Ἀθηναί]ας τῆς Ἀθηνῶμ μ-
[εδεόσης, καὶ] ἐὰν τὸ Ἐτεοκαρ-
[παθίων κοινὸ]ν [α]ὐτονόμος κ-

to minimise the extent to which the two smaller states are engulfed by the war which is going on around them. A clearer picture of the breadth and the (general) stability of political life in the Greek world beyond Athens and Sparta now emerges from Hansen & Nielsen edd. 2004.

[αἱ . . .

(Lines 13 to 17 omitted)

[. . . ὅσοι δὲ] νῦγ καθελήφασ[ι]
[τῶν στρατι]ωτῶν ἐξιέναι ἐ[κ]
[τῆς ἀκροπόλ]εως. ἐὰν δέ τις [.]
[. . . 11 . . .] Ἐτεοκαρπαθ[ί]-
[. . . 10 . . .] ἢ ἀφαιρῆται ἢ λ-
[. . . 10 . . .]Λ.Ν [. . . 6 . . .]ων, ὀ-
[φέλεν πεντ]ήκοντα τάλαντα
[Ἀθηναίοις κ]αὶ τὸπιδέκα[το]-
[ν τῆς θεõ εἶνα]ι· δίκην δὲ ἔνα-
[ι πρὸς τὸς θεσμο]θέτας ΕΝΑ[.]
[. . . 11 . . .] ἐὰ]γ δὲ Ἐτεοκα-
[ρπάθιοι ἄλλο τ]ι δέωνται, Κω-
[ίος καὶ Κνι]δίος καὶ Ῥοδίος
[καὶ ξυμμάχ]ων οἵτινες ἂν δ[υ]-
[νατοὶ ὦσιν] περὶ ταῦτα τὰ χ[ω]-
[ρία ὠδελε͂]ν ὅ τι ἂν δύνωνται.
[γράψαι δὲ τ]αῦτα ἐν στήληι [λ]-
[ιθίνηι ἐμ] πόληι καὶ ἐγ Καρ[π]-
[άθωι ἐν τῶι] ἱερῶι τõ Ἀπόλλ[ω]-
[νος ὅθεν] ἐτμήθη ἡ κυπάρι[ττ]-
[ος· . . . 5 . . .]ρχον δὲ τὸν Λίνδ[ιο]-
[ν . . . 7 . . .]τησ[. .] Ἀθηναίο[. .]
[. . . 7 . . .]ναι τὴγ κυπάριτ[το]-
[ν.]

The Council and the People decided, in the prytany of [----], Tei[sias] was Secretary and Athenodoros was President, on the proposal of Ctesias: to record [----] the Carpathian and his sons and the state of the Eteocarpathians as benefactors of the Athenians because they gave the cypress wood for the temple of Athena who rules at Athens; and to allow the *koinon* of the Eteocarpathians to be *autonomos*... The soldiers who now occupy it are to depart from the acropolis. If anyone . . . wrongs either the Eteocarpathian state or takes away [or razes the stele?] he is to owe . . . fifty talents to the Athenians and a tenth of it is to belong to the goddess. The case is to be tried before the Thesmothetai in Athens. The Coans and the Cnidians and the Rhodians and all the allies who are capable around the region are to provide all the good they can to the Eteocarpathians if they ask for anything. This is to be written on a stone stele on the Acropolis, and at Carpathos, in the sanctuary of Apollo, from which the cypress was cut. Hagesarchos the Lindian, as he requested, is to deliver the cypress to the Athenians.

From the moment of its discovery, in the 1880s, until the middle of the 1980s, this text was usually dated, on the grounds of script, language, formulae and historical context, to the early years of the fourth century.[5] But in the 1980s, examination of some rediscovered squeezes revealed letter-forms that were clearly those of the fifth century;[6] the text was re-dated to the third quarter of that century, and it is as a document of the Athenian Empire that it now appears in *IG* (as *IG* i[3] 1454) and in other studies and anthologies of this period of history.[7]

I will return later in this chapter to explore this text in more detail. Here, I want only to make a very simple point: the argument for redating this text to the fifth century is, above all, a technical one, based on the physical appearance of the document. What the dating does not – and cannot – rely on is any safely observable difference in the 'tone' of the decree or the structures of the relationships which it describes: it is possible, as will be seen later, to fit the document quite neatly into a fifth-century historical context, but, at the same time, the historical arguments for placing the decree in the 390s remain (in their own terms) entirely plausible.[8] Although the Carpathians were members of the Athenian Empire, there is nothing obviously, or necessarily, 'imperial' about the relationship described in this document.

A second case-study might help to show how the confusion over the dating of the Carpathian decree could have arisen. This example consists of two texts: the first is the treaty made in the summer of 420 between Athens and a group of Peloponnesian states (Argos, Mantineia and Elis), which is recorded in Thucydides v.47 (and, in part, in *IG* i[3] 83);[9] the second is another treaty between Athens and the Peloponnesians (Elis again, but also Achaea, Phlius and the Arcadians), made in 362 and preserved as RO 41 (*IG* ii[2] 112). The dating of these texts is not disputed: the Thucydidean context

---

[5] The first publication of the inscription is Foucart 1888: 153–61 (reporting a discovery made a few years earlier by Mondry Beaudouin). His argument for the dating (of *c.* 393) was based (157) on 'les formules, l'écriture, l'orthographe . . . et les circonstances historiques'. This initial assessment was persuasive: Foucart's reasoning is followed almost exactly by Tod (110) in his summary of the historical context of the document.

[6] Lewis 1997a: 123.

[7] Notably in Osborne 2000a: no. 220. For other discussions of the text in an Athenian imperial context, see Smarczyk 1990: 67–70; Anderson & Dix 1997; Alfieri Tonini 1999.

[8] The most clear and convenient argument for a 390s date (arguing that the circumstances of the decree neatly fit the historical situation after the battle of Cnidus) appears in the commentary to Tod 110.

[9] On the relationship between the Thucydidean and the inscribed texts, see Cohen 1956.

provides a precise setting for the fifth-century document, and the archon's name is preserved in the heading of the fourth-century decree. There are also specific aspects in both documents which allow them to be tied down to particular moments in Greek history. The fifth-century treaty includes, in its reference to 'the allies whom the Athenians rule', something which might be thought to be an allusion to the existence of empire.[10] The treaty of the 360s, meanwhile, undeniably contains a reference to the Second Athenian League: the *synedrion* of the League has been involved in the preliminary negotiations of the terms of the agreement (lines 12–17).

However, other aspects of the treaties divide less neatly between imperial and post-imperial, or fifth and fourth-century, templates of behaviour: not only is there extensive continuity between the treaties, there are also present, in each case, features which do not neatly fit the conventional picture of the relevant period of history.

At the most basic level, and least surprisingly, the mechanics of treaty-creation are essentially the same in both cases: the processes of ratification by oath-swearing, and of multiple inscription and display of the agreement, are unchanged. What is perhaps less expected, however, is the continuity in the relative role of Athens' allies in these formalities. The failure of the members of the Delian League to take any active part in the formalisation of the treaty might not be hard to predict. It is, however, more surprising that, although the *synedrion* of the Second Athenian League seems to have had some role in the origination of the second treaty, this body is entirely absent from its formal frame: the agreement is presented straightforwardly as a decree of the Athenian council and people.[11] The Athenocentricity of the treaty's origins emerges, too, from the

---

[10] It must be noted that the expression is (as far as I have been able to find) unparalleled in Thucydides and in epigraphic texts: the juxtaposition of ruling with the idea of alliance is awkward. Using the language of 'ruling' in other contexts is a familiar part of imperial rhetoric, both in Athens (see Mattingly 1996b) and elsewhere (e.g., *IG* i³ 89, line 40, *c.* 417–413, of Perdiccas of Macedon's sphere of influence; RO 34, line 19, 368, of Dionysius I).

[11] Contrast this with a full-bodied decree of the *synedrion* (RO 29.ii); although note that even here the earlier decree recorded on the stone appears to be a purely Athenian affair. Similar inconsistency is visible in RO 33 (honours for Dionysius I, with reference to a *dogma* of the allies) and RO 34 (similar honours, but no visible allied involvement), and might even be thought to be built into the structure of the alliance: in Tod 127 (alliance between Athens and Corcyra), a division is made between matters of peace and war (to be

phrasing of the vow which is to be made by the herald: a sacrifice and procession will be offered if things turn out well; but the group which has to benefit for the gods to get their reward is a very specific one – only the Athenians:

> εὔξασθαι μὲν τὸγ κήρυκα αὐτίκα μ-
> άλα τῶι Διὶ τῶι Ὀλυμπίωι καὶ τῆι Ἀθηνᾶι τῆι Πολια-
> δι καὶ τῆι Δήμητρι καὶ τῆι Κόρηι καὶ τοῖς Δώδεκα [Θ]-
> εοῖς καὶ τας Σεμναῖς Θεαῖς, ἐὰν συνενείγκηι Ἀ[θη]-
> ναίων τῶι δήμωι τὰ δόξαντα περὶ τῆς συμμαχία[ς].

The herald shall vow forthwith to Zeus Olympios and Athena Polias and to Demeter and to Kore and the Twelve Gods and the August Goddesses, that, if what is resolved about the alliance is to the advantage of the people of Athens.[12] (RO 41, lines 6–10)

In both treaties, similarly, the Athenians take sole responsibility for swearing the oaths, on behalf of the members of their alliance.[13] There is, then, more continuity in the presentation of the relationship between Athens and her allies – whether of the Delian League or of the Second Athenian League – than might initially have been expected: in both cases, the role attributed to the allies is never more than subsidiary, and the focus of attention remains fixed on Athens.

But it could be argued that procedures are always less likely to change than substantive content, and it could also be pointed out that one feature of the fourth-century treaty does look distinctly specific to that period of history – namely, the detailed regulations governing the maintenance of existing political constitutions in each party to the agreement:

> [ἐὰν δέ τις ἴηι ἐπὶ τὴν Ἀττι]-
> [κὴ]ν ἢ τὸν δῆμον [καταλύηι τὸν Ἀθηναίων ἢ τύραννον]
> [κα]θιστῆι ἢ ὀλι[γαρχίαν, βοηθεῖν Ἀρκάδας καὶ Ἀχαι]-

decided by Athens and the allies) and τἄλλα, 'the rest' (to be decided by *dogmata* of the allies). Generally on the problem, see Cawkwell 1981: 48–51, and for allied involvement in the creation of Athenian decrees, see the further examples discussed in ch. 3, sec. 3.

[12] Contrast, for example, *SIG*³ 581 (= *SV* III.551): treaty of Rhodians and Hierapytnians, c. 201/200, which includes (at lines 2–8) a clause which is identical in all respects save for the scope of *to sumpheron*: here, this applies to both parties to the treaty. See also ch. 4, sec. 4, on the connection between interest and the shaping of the interstate community.

[13] This is explicit in the fifth-century treaty (at lines 26–8: the Athenians are to swear on behalf of their allies), but visible only in the absence of the allies from the oath-clause of the fourth-century text (lines 37–40; it should be noted, however, that the oath-clause is not completely preserved).

[ὸς] καὶ Ἠλείους κ[αὶ Φλειασίους Ἀθηναίοις παντὶ σ]-
[θέ]νει καθότι ἂν [ἐπαγγέλλωσιν Ἀθηναῖοι κατὰ τὸ δ]-
[υν]ατόν· καὶ ἐάν [τις ἴηι ἐπὶ ταύτας τὰς πόλεις ἢ τὸν]
δῆμον καταλύε[ι τὸν Φλειασίων ἢ ἐὰν τὴν πολιτεία]-
ν τὴν Ἀχαιῶν ἢ τ[ὴν Ἀρκάδων ἢ τὴν Ἠλείων καταλύηι ἢ]
μεθιστῆι, ἢ φυγα[δεύηι τινάς, βοηθεῖν Ἀθηναίους τ]-
ούτοις παντὶ σθ[ένει καθότι ἂν ἐπαγγέλλωσιν οἱ ἀ]-
δικούμενοι κατ[ὰ τὸ δυνατόν]

If anyone goes against Attica or overthrows the people of Athens or sets up a tyrant or an oligarchy, the Arcadians and Achaeans and Eleans and Phliasians shall go in support of the Athenians with all their strength as called on by the Athenians as far as they are able; and if anyone goes against these cities or overthrows the people of Phlius or overthrows or changes the constitution of Achaea or Arcadia or Elis, or exiles anyone, the Athenians shall help them with all their strength as called on by those who have been wronged, as far as they are able. (RO 41, lines 24–35)

Certainly this appears to contrast sharply with the stereotypical fifth-century Athenian approach to the preservation of constitutions (which is generally thought to be focused much more directly on the expansion of democracy)[14] and to coincide quite neatly with a wider fourth-century concern to respect the domestic *autonomia* of the Greek *poleis*.[15] But even here it is worth noting that the apparent transition might not be as smooth or absolute as it can sometimes appear: the fifth-century Athenians did not, it seems, always insist on the imposition of democracy;[16] and it is even more clear that it was still possible, even in the fourth century, to argue for policies which required, and celebrated, interference in a city's domestic politics.[17]

In other respects, however, less seems to have changed. The core purpose of each agreement is fundamentally similar: each

[14] This picture emerges particularly strongly from Thucydides (see, for a clear example, III.82.i), but is echoed in other sources too: e.g. [X.] *AP* 3.10–11.

[15] The argument for the novelty of this commitment to preserving the variety of domestic regimes has a long pedigree: see Foucart 1898. Dušanić 1979 (followed by Jehne 1994: 110 n. 84) argues for an alternative reconstruction of these lines, which would make Arcadia the democracy and the other three states the *politeiai*: his suggestion does not, however, affect the basic point about Athenian ideological tolerance.

[16] Argued for strongly by Ostwald 1993, 2002.

[17] Notably in Demosthenes 15; for further discussion of attitudes to political interference, see ch. 5. The particular historical context of RO 41 might be relevant to its interest in constitutional matters: Koehler 1876 suggests a connection between the protections set out in lines 24–35 and the policy of democratisation which, according to Xenophon (*HG* VII.i.42–3) the Thebans were pursuing in the Peloponnese in this period.

side makes a primarily military commitment to provide mutual assistance to the other. In both treaties the arrangements for leadership of military forces are based on careful and equal division of responsibilities.[18] And, perhaps most surprisingly, Athens' other allies (the members of the Delian or Second Athenian Leagues), seem to be equally marginal to the protections and responsibilities established by each agreement: the commitment to mutual territorial defence does not apply to the land of the allies, and the allies have no obligation (or no stated obligation) to participate in any military expeditions which arise from either of these agreements.[19] Just as both sets of allies were sidelined in the framing of the treaty, so too they are equally marginal to the substantive content of each agreement. The different historical context seems to make little difference to the representation, at least, of the relationship between Athens and her allies, or to the sorts of ties which the Athenians are interested in building up with the wider Greek world.

Or – to put it more exactly – changes in historical context seem to have little impact in these two particular cases. But how representative are these cases? It could be objected that the fifth-century document, in particular, is far from typical of that period of history, and, more precisely, that it does not give proper emphasis to those things which are seen to be most characteristic of the period: the Athenian Empire, the Peloponnesian War and – something inextricably linked with those two historical phenomena – Thucydides' *History*. Although the existence of the Athenian Empire is relevant to the understanding of the text, it is also marginal to the treaty's main focus. Moreover, the document comes from the part of the fifth century – the pause for breath in the middle of the Peloponnesian War – which, in many ways, is most unlike the history of the surrounding period (and most like that of the years after 404). And, perhaps most crucially, the document, although Thucydidean, comes from the section of Thucydides' narrative which is usually regarded as least representative of the overall tone of his work – a section so atypical that it could even be alleged to have been

---

[18] *IG* i[3] 83, lines 20–6; RO 41, lines 34–5.

[19] It need not follow that the actual obligations of the allies were also constant (nor is it clear whether the failure to specify the allies' rights or duties should be seen as a positive or negative feature). But the continuity in representation is significant in itself.

composed by Xenophon.[20] If the case for stability is to stand, then, it needs to confront these (alleged) fifth-century idiosyncrasies more directly, in order to attempt to establish just what is different about them, and how much attention they really deserve to be paid.

6.3 The problem of Thucydides

The problem of Thucydides is hard to avoid, but it is also hard to formulate – or at least to formulate in any manageable way. The core issue appears relatively straightforward, and was neatly summed up many years ago by Paul Shorey: the task is 'to apportion responsibility for the cynicism of the history between the historian and his time'.[21] But that apparently simple task conceals a range of further, much less straightforward, problems. The hardest of these to resolve is the challenge of circularity. If we want to establish the extent to which Thucydides is representative of his age, then the thing we need is precisely what we lack: a clear sense of what a history of the fifth century would look like without Thucydides' contribution to it. Without that control, a proper assessment of Thucydides' relationship with the history of the period will always be more speculative than definitive.[22] Some speculation is, however, essential, and will appear towards the end of this section (and in the one which follows). Most of what follows, however, will tackle a still more important question, and attempt to establish precisely what form of 'cynicism' should be attributed to Thucydides.

Before starting on that exercise, however, it is worth establishing that the problem cannot simply be sidestepped entirely: is it possible to construct a case for ignoring Thucydides altogether? Such a case would have to rest largely on the appearance of detachment which the historian himself creates: in self-consciously marketing

---

[20] The allegation is made by, among others, Canfora (1970: esp. ch. 6); for a discussion of its implausibility, see *HCT*, vol. v: 431–37. For a more positive analysis of this section of the *History* (arguing that its unusual form and tone is a deliberate authorial ploy, rather than a sign of interpolation or incompleteness), see Rood 1998: ch. 4.

[21] Shorey 1893: 85.

[22] For the methodology, and the density of evidence, required to assess the relationship between individual theorists and popular ideologies, see Freeden 1996: chs. 2 and (esp.) 3.

his work as a κτῆμα . . . ἐς αἰεί ('an eternal possession'; 1.22.4), Thucydides neatly provides at least the beginnings of a justification for those readers who would like to make him either entirely ahistorical or, more usually, a contemporary of their own time.

The problems with and objections to that contemporising approach were discussed in the first chapter of this book, and do not have to be repeated here. What does perhaps need a little more comment, however, is the extent to which Thucydides should be seen to be embedded in the intellectual and political culture of his own period. Thucydides' engagement with contemporary intellectual trends has been clearly demonstrated in recent work,[23] and, although it remains hard to pin down the precise nature and extent of his contemporary audience, it must be safe to assume that one of some size and importance did exist.[24] Thucydides' role in political life has received rather less attention, but is also relevant here. His (relatively) obvious disenchantment with many aspects of Athenian political life, particularly the excesses of the post-Periclean democracy,[25] can perhaps too readily distract attention from the fact that he was an active participant in that political system. He may have held the post of general only once, and with less than satisfactory military consequences, but the generalship was not purely, or necessarily even primarily, a military role: those who were elected to this post tended to be active in both domestic and external politics, and to have an input in the shaping of policy as well as its execution.[26]

[23] Generally on Thucydides' intellectual affinities, see Hornblower 1987: ch. 5. On his relationship with philosophical, sophistic and scientific thought, see Parry 1969; Guthrie 1971: 223–4; Kerferd 1981: 123–5; Hussey 1985; Farrar 1988; with Herodotus, Hornblower 1987: ch. 1, 1992b, 1996: 19–38; with Pindar, Hornblower 2004; with tragedy, Finley 1967: ch. 1; Macleod 1983b. In general, the intellectual context identified and described for Herodotus by Thomas 2000 must overlap significantly with Thucydides' intellectual context.

[24] Some speculations – emphasising that Thucydides' anti-populist jibe at I.22.4 should not be taken too literally – in Hornblower 1991 *ad loc.*; Hornblower 2004: 33. Thomas' (2000: ch. 8) observations on the context of performance for Herodotus' work must also be, at least partly, relevant to Thucydides; on the possible relationship between oral performance and written text, see Thomas 1992: 123–7.

[25] See, most clearly, Th. II.65.10–13, VIII.97.2–3. On the dangers of assuming too readily that Thucydides can be labelled an 'oligarch', see Hornblower 1987: ch. 7; generally on Thucydides' portrayal of various forms of government (emphasising that he sees problems in both democracy and oligarchy), see Leppin 1999.

[26] Hamel 1995; Hamel 1998: 5–14.

Thucydides, then, was a practitioner as well as an observer of fifth-century interstate politics, and it therefore seems to be both unwise and unjustifiable to exclude him from consideration on the grounds that his characterisation of the subject must necessarily be too far divorced from the reality of events to be worth studying. And that conclusion, arrived at largely on the grounds of external probabilities, is reinforced by the content of much of Thucydides' work. His writings demonstrate a clear knowledge of the practicalities of interstate interaction, and it is a straightforward task to extract from them a large amount of material illustrating all sorts of interstate activities – procedures for dealing with embassies; the formalities associated with the declaration of war; the duties of *proxenoi*, and so on – none of which look dramatically different from the activities of later periods.[27] It is also, more significantly, possible to see evidence of a range of concerns and expectations which are directly comparable to those which are visible in fourth-century writing: appreciation of the potential power of appeals to *xenia*, *philia* and kinship, between people and between states; reference to the shame associated with the breaking of treaties; and an awareness of the whole range of *nomoi* which surround interstate activity.[28]

One episode in the work illustrates that point quite well: after the disastrous (for Athens) battle of Delion in 424, the Boeotians and Athenians become involved in a protracted dispute over the

---

[27] See, for example: Th. v (embassies and treaty negotiations); II.1, v.113 (use of heralds in wartime); II.85.5, IV.78.1, v.45 (*proxenia* – the last example being the formally atypical, but practically still representative, case of Alcibiades). Generally on Thucydides' knowledge and depiction of diplomatic activity, see Westlake 1989.

[28] Reciprocity: the Spartan peace negotiations with Athens (Th. IV.19.3), including the claim that generosity will encourage the other party ἀνταποδοῦναι ἀρετήν, 'to return benefit for benefit'; kinship: appeal of Leontini to Athens (III.86); *xenia*: Alcibiades and Endius the Spartan (VIII.6.3); *philia* is typically used in a semi-technical sense, to characterise a tie which is less formal than actual alliance (as of the Argive relationship with Sparta and Athens at the start of the war, II.9.2, or the Melians' preferred relationship with Athens, v.94–5), but also appears in more persuasive contexts (v.44.1: Argives hope to make a deal with Athens φιλίαν ἀπὸ παλαιοῦ, 'on the grounds of an old friendship'). Treaties: Athenian behaviour after alleged Spartan infractions of the Peace of Nicias is instructive (v.56); compare also Thucydides' assessment of perception of war-guilt (VII.2). For a general discussion of all this, see Karavites 1984a; for an assessment of the role of international law in Thucydides, see Sheets 1994; and for an analysis (from a philosophical perspective) of Thucydides' representation of interstate norms, see White 2002: 139–43.

treatment of the dead of that battle (Th. IV.97–9). The episode is, in many ways, extremely unedifying, especially in the petty squabbling in which both sides are happy to indulge while the bodies of the dead rot on the battlefield.[29] But the terms in which this squabbling is conducted are illuminating. Neither side justifies their actions simply by appeal to the strength of their position, or their overall power. Instead, both sides attempt to prove that they have the force of interstate *nomoi* on their side – not just the widely observed conventions on the treatment of the war-dead, but also customs which protect (or are alleged to protect) the status of sacred territory:

ἐκ δὲ τῶν Ἀθηναίων κῆρυξ πορευόμενος ἐπὶ τοὺς νεκροὺς ἀπαντᾷ κήρυκι Βοιωτῷ, ὃς αὐτὸν ἀποστρέψας καὶ εἰπὼν ὅτι οὐδὲν πράξει πρὶν ἂν αὐτὸς ἀναχωρήσῃ πάλιν, καταστὰς ἐπὶ τοὺς Ἀθηναίους ἔλεγε τὰ παρὰ τῶν Βοι-ωτῶν, ὅτι οὐ δικαίως δράσειαν παραβαίνοντες τὰ νόμιμα τῶν Ἑλλήνων· πᾶσι γὰρ εἶναι καθεστηκὸς ἰόντας ἐπὶ τὴν ἀλλήλων ἱερῶν τῶν ἐνόντων ἀπέχεσθαι, Ἀθηναίους δὲ Δήλιον τειχίσαντας ἐνοικεῖν, καὶ ὅσα ἄνθρωποι ἐν βεβήλῳ δρῶσι πάντα γίγνεσθαι αὐτόθι, ὕδωρ τε ὃ ἦν ἄψαυστον σφίσι πλὴν πρὸς τὰ ἱερὰ χέρνιβι χρῆσθαι, ἀνασπάσαντας ὑδρεύεσθαι.

Meanwhile a herald came from the Athenians to ask for the dead, but was met and turned back by a Boeotian herald, who told him that he would do nothing until he himself had returned, and who then went on to the Athenians, and told them on behalf of the Boeotians that they had acted unjustly in transgressing the law of the Greeks. It was an established and universal custom that those who invaded a country should keep away from local temples, but the Athenians had fortified Delion and were living there, acting exactly as if they were on unconsecrated ground, and drawing and using for their purposes the water which the Boeotians never touched except for sacred uses. (Th. IV.97.2–3)

The fact that such assertions of shared Greek conventions might be contentious is demonstrated in the next chapter: the Athenians respond to the Boeotian complaint by claiming that their occupation of the sanctuary, although forced on them by circumstances, is itself legitimated by the existence of a νόμον τοῖς Ἕλλησιν ('a Greek law'; IV.98.2). But the truth-value of the various claims is, in this context, irrelevant. What I want to emphasise here is simply the fact that the manner in which this dispute is conducted would

---

[29] For some speculations on the likely condition of the bodies by the time they are finally handed over (seventeen days after the battle, Th. IV.101.1), see Vaughn 1991: esp. 52.

not look dramatically out of place in a non-Thucydidean context: it would sit quite comfortably alongside, for example, the Thebans' use of Spartan corpses as a bargaining tool after the Battle of Haliartus (X. *HG* III.v.23–4),[30] or the dispute between Sparta and Argos over the existence of divine support for their respective policies (on the Argive side, the extension of sacred months to postpone the threat of Spartan invasion; on the Spartan side, the invocation of direct divine permission to ignore that plea: *HG* IV.vii.2–7).

But Thucydides' account of the events after the Battle of Delion, and the majority of scholarly reactions to it, also indicate quite clearly the potential problem with that de- (or re-) contextualising approach to the text. This is not a section of Thucydides' work which is typically thought to be in any way uncharacteristic of his writing, or of his ideas about foreign politics (there has never been any suspicion, as far as I know, that Xenophon might have dabbled with this bit of the text), and the majority of commentators on this passage have found no difficulty in seeing here yet another instance of a characteristically Thucydidean demonstration of the cynicism inherent in interstate negotiations: while it might be acknowledged that these arguments are 'traditional', it is also regularly emphasised that the Athenian (and/or Boeotian) use of them is 'specious'.[31] The incident sits neatly, for the reader of Thucydides, between earlier debates over aspects of interstate morality (the dialogue between Archidamus and the Plataeans at II.71–4; the debate over Mytilene at III.36–49)[32] and the even more shocking discussions which are to come (above all, the Melian Dialogue).[33] To remove it from that context and treat it simply as one of a number of comparable episodes, found throughout the classical period and across the Greek world, runs the risk of distorting, or destroying, the whole point of Thucydides' argument. And

---

[30] Compare also the Theban insistence after Leuctra (as reported by Paus. IX.13.11–12, but not by Xenophon) that the Spartans collect their dead only after the allied bodies had been removed from the battlefield.

[31] Eatough 1971: 245. For a similarly anti-Athenian reading, see Jordan 1986: 129–30; Orwin 1994: 90–6. *HCT ad loc.* is more critical of the Boeotians.

[32] The first parallel is suggested by Westlake 1989: 20.

[33] A formal similarity between the two debates is suggested by Hornblower 1991: 308; a similarity in content and tone is perceived by Eatough 1971: 245 and n. 24; Orwin 1994: 96.

the same could be argued to be true of any of the individual examples of apparently conventional behaviour: excerpted and treated as discrete episodes, they tell us nothing; it is only when they are read as parts of a whole that their full significance emerges.[34]

This is not the place to attempt to provide a proper account of what the overall message or intention of Thucydides' work might be. What is needed here, however, is a more direct consideration of the way in which episodes like the one just discussed fit into the work as a whole, and of the functions which they are intended to perform. Even this, however, is not a straightforward task. A great range of moral perspectives appear in the work, from the relatively conventional to the virtually amoral – the latter, most notoriously, in the Melian Dialogue:

ἡμεῖς τοίνυν οὔτε αὐτοὶ μετ' ὀνομάτων καλῶν . . . λόγων μῆκος ἄπιστον παρέξ-
ομεν . . . δίκαια μὲν ἐν τῷ ἀνθρωπείῳ λόγῳ ἀπὸ τῆς ἴσης ἀνάγκης κρίνεται,
δυνατὰ δὲ οἱ προύχοντες πράσσουσι καὶ οἱ ἀσθενεῖς ξυγχωροῦσιν.

For ourselves, we shall not trouble you with specious pretences . . . Justice, in human affairs, is only in question between equals in power, while the strong do what they can and the weak suffer what they must.[35] (v.89)

One way of explaining that variety would be to view it as a genuine reflection of the variety of the tone of interstate discourse in this period: some states, at some times, used fairly conventional modes of argument; others, particularly the Athenians, were prepared to be more frank about their motivations. The explanation is superficially attractive – not least because it removes the problem of having to excavate any Thucydidean interpretation of these opinions – but it is also, surely, wrong. There is no evidence to prove that nobody ever addressed the Athenian assembly in the style of Diodotus, or bullied smaller states in the style of the Athenian ambassadors at Melos, or attempted to justify Athenian hegemony in the brutal terms employed by Euphemus at Camarina. Nor, however – and this is a point which can too readily be obscured – is there any

---

34 Expressed as a principle by, for example, Pelling 2000: esp. chs. 5 and 6; for the policy in action, see, as well as Pelling, Hornblower 1994; Rood 1998.

35 This is not, of course, a statement of absolute amoralism, but a more limited claim that justice is irrelevant in a context where power relationships are unequal: might excludes right rather than might is right. See ch. 4, sec. 4 for further discussion.

evidence to indicate that they did. Contemporary rhetorical evidence is, of course, hard both to locate and to interpret,[36] but the best contemporary evidence for the tone of 'real' interstate diplomacy – that is, the language of, primarily Athenian, inscriptions – fails to provide any good support for the Thucydidean characterisation of the amorality of interstate discourse.[37] The language of Thucydidean speeches stands out as something unique, isolated from all contemporary and near-contemporary evidence for the tone of interstate diplomacy, and this must be the strongest argument against believing in their authenticity – or, more precisely, their authenticity as records of the actual tone of interstate exchange in the fifth century.[38]

Taking that line on the authenticity of Thucydides' speeches makes, incidentally but importantly, a significant contribution to the overall theme of this section (and this chapter): the views expressed in some of Thucydides' speeches have been taken – precisely because they are unparalleled in other periods – as evidence for the uniqueness of this period of classical history. By seeing them as products of a single author rather than the culture as a whole, one important element of the argument for the specificity of the second half of the fifth century disappears. But the removal of that problem, of course, creates space for another, equally troubling, one: it may no longer be necessary to account for the idiosyncrasy of a whole period, but some explanation for the way it is represented by this well-informed observer is still required, as (still) is an explanation for the range of opinions about

[36] But see Heath 1990 for a good attempt to do so and, in particular, to explore the relationship between Thucydides and the rhetorical handbooks. The absence of any comparative evidence from other periods is striking, and has been noted by Strasburger 1958 (concentrating on fourth-century Athenian discourse), by Andrewes 1960: 9 (making a more general comparative point: 'no people could endure to think of themselves as actuated only by the motives which Thucydides ascribes to the Athenians in the [Melian] Dialogue'), and by Pelling 2000: 114: 'if this is verisimilitude, the truth it mimics points to a strange world indeed'. Since the point at issue here is, precisely, the strangeness of Thucydides' world, non-contemporary evidence, although suggestive, cannot be allowed too great a place in the argument.

[37] I have argued this point at greater length in Low 2005.

[38] As Heath 1990 notes, such a conclusion does require that Thucydides' characterisation at 1.22.1 of the speeches in his work be either ignored or creatively re-interpreted. Rejecting the reliability of this elusive, internally inconsistent and argumentative assertion seems, however, to be preferable to ignoring the weight of evidence against it.

the nature and value of the norms of foreign politics which appear in the work.

That variety of opinions provides the best argument against seeing these viewpoints – whether conventional or not – as straightforward reflections of the historian's own views. However, it is possible to detect a recurring theme, if not in the nature of the normative arguments themselves, then in the role they play in the bigger analytical structure of the work.

First of all, to reiterate and amplify a point already made, it is clear that conventional concerns about goodness, justice, morality and so on, are not absent from Thucydides' world; nor are claims about their existence found only in the speeches.[39] A famous instance of direct authorial interest in such themes appears, for example, in Thucydides' obituary for the Athenian general Nicias:

καὶ ὁ μὲν τοιαύτῃ ἢ ὅτι ἐγγύτατα τούτων αἰτίᾳ ἐτεθνήκει, ἥκιστα δὴ ἄξιος ὢν τῶν γε ἐπ' ἐμοῦ Ἑλλήνων ἐς τοῦτο δυστυχίας ἀφικέσθαι διὰ τὴν πᾶσαν ἐς ἀρετὴν νενομισμένην ἐπιτήδευσιν.

This, or something like it, was the cause of the death of a man who, of all the Greeks in my time, least deserved such a fate, seeing that the whole course of his life had been conditioned with strict attention to *aretē*. (VII.86.5)

Conventional *aretē* can, then, be identified in fifth-century foreign politics; and, as this passage shows, Thucydides is not entirely out of sympathy with those actors in his history who display such qualities.[40]

But if being good is still something to be admired in Thucydides' world, it is far less clear that it brings any tangible advantages. Nicias failed to win either domestic respect or international success as a result of his upright approach to politics (a stark contrast with the hero of Xenophon's *Agesilaus*),[41] and his fate is not unparalleled. The unfortunate Plataeans, for example, provide a

---

[39] A point emphasised by (among others) Gomme 1937; Finley 1977; Hornblower 1987: 189–90; Orwin 1994.

[40] Thucydides' post-mortem assessment is, of course, 'more generous than much of the preceding narrative' (Pelling 2000: 33). On Nicias' *aretē*, see Adkins 1975.

[41] On Agesilaus' morality, and its excellent results (for Agesilaus and for Sparta) see ch. 3, sec. 4. For Nicias' international failures, Th. VI and VII, *passim*; for his domestic unpopularity, note especially the allegation in Pausanias 1.29.12 that his name was omitted from the public memorial for the Sicilian Expedition, as a marker of his disgrace.

story of suffering which seems similar in many ways: loyalty to
an old ally drags the city into a war in which it wants to play
no part (Th. II.71–2); it is then abandoned by that same ally (Th.
III.68.5) and utterly destroyed in order to pander to the wishes of a
long-term enemy (Th. III.68.4).[42] At one – fairly simplistic – level,
therefore, a limitation of conventional moral behaviour, for participants in and interpreters of this period of history, is that it does not
necessarily align with power or success. It is not the case that
the good guys never win (Pericles provides a counter-example; as
does Brasidas); but moral uprightness – adherence to the norms of
domestic or interstate society – is in itself neither a necessary nor
a sufficient condition for success.

But that argument elides too many important complexities, of
which the most pressing is this: it is rarely a simple matter to decide
who the good guys are, or who has legitimate occupation of the
moral high ground. Returning, briefly, to the case of the Plataeans
will illustrate the point. The Plataeans are not absolutely, or at least
not uncomplicatedly, innocent. It is not necessary to accept some
of the Thebans' more extreme allegations about Plataean duplicity
(at Th. III.63–7) to believe that their behaviour after the initial
attack on their city is, at best, morally questionable: their decision
to put to death the Theban prisoners taken in the initial attack (Th.
II.5.7) puts them in an awkward position, which their conspicuously
flustered speech at III.53–9 does little to ameliorate.[43] Even the
Plataeans, then, are not morally spotless, and there is a less stark
divide between their position, and their attempts to justify it, and
that of the Athenians and Boeotians at Delion than might initially
be assumed. And, as observed earlier in this section, there is not an
unbridgeable gap, either, between the 'sophistry' of that exchange
and some of the ideas raised in the Melian Dialogue. An allegation
made against the Spartans there seems particularly relevant:

Λακεδαιμόνιοι γὰρ πρὸς σφᾶς μὲν αὐτοὺς καὶ τὰ ἐπιχώρια νόμιμα πλεῖστα
ἀρετῇ χρῶνται· πρὸς δὲ τοὺς ἄλλους πολλὰ ἄν τις ἔχων εἰπεῖν ὡς προσφέρονται,
ξυνελὼν μάλιστ' ἂν δηλώσειεν ὅτι ἐπιφανέστατα ὧν ἴσμεν τὰ μὲν ἡδέα καλὰ
νομίζουσι, τὰ δὲ ξυμφέροντα δίκαια.

---

[42] For the Plataeans as victims of the machinations of great powers, see Crane 2001.
[43] On this speech, see Macleod 1983c: 103–13; Hornblower 1991: 445–6.

The Lacedaemonians, when their own interests or their domestic laws are in question, are the worthiest men alive; of their conduct towards others much might be said, but no clearer idea of it could be given than by saying, in summary, that of all the men we know they are most conspicuous in considering what is agreeable honourable, and what is expedient just. (v.105.4)

The hypocrisy of this allegation is not revealing only of Athenian self-delusion; it also usefully picks out one of the crucial problems with the application of moral criteria to the judgement of the conduct of interstate relations. The problem with moral arguments – made explicit here, but implicit too in the examples which have already been discussed – is not that they are irrelevant to the conduct of foreign affairs, but that they can be made to be relevant to anything, and, more crucially, be made part of an argument justifying just about any course of action.[44] And an argument which explains everything is not all that different from an argument which explains nothing at all.

It is this feature of moral argumentation which provides the best explanation for Thucydides' apparent unease with attributing much, if any, explanatory power to it: the contingency of moral perspectives is something which is fundamentally opposed to an analytical programme which seeks to identify and explain the recurrent, and therefore predictable, features of interstate politics.[45] This unease manifests itself in different ways in the course of the history: sometimes, as at Delion, the challenge to the validity of normative argument is never more than implicit; elsewhere, it emerges from the strained relationship between debate and action;[46] and at times – as in the Melian dialogue – it is explicitly expressed by participants in debate.

Having established a clearer picture of the actual role of conventional and moralising behaviour in Thucydides, it also becomes much easier to explain why different approaches to the work can come up with such different interpretations of the picture of

---

[44] See Macleod 1983c: 120: 'moral arguments . . . both tend to entangle themselves and can easily be reversed'.

[45] On this, see Pelling 2000: 99–103.

[46] Notably in the aftermath of the 'trial' of the Plataeans: after two extended speeches, the Spartans simply repeat the same question they had asked before the debate took place (II.68.1), '*as if the speeches had never been delivered at all*' (Hornblower 1991: 446; emphasis original).

foreign policy it presents. In Thucydides' world, unlike – to take an obviously different example – Xenophon's, conventional arguments, although available to the actors of foreign politics, fail to provide an adequate explanation for the actions of states.[47] The Spartans kill the survivors of the siege of Plataea because this is the action which suits their predetermined policy, not because they are swayed by any of the arguments of duty, honour or betrayal which are presented to them by either Thebans or Plataeans (III.68.1); the Athenians intervene in Leontini because they want to expand westwards, not because they feel a tie of kinship with the Sicilian city (III.86.4). And this tactic of marginalising normative explanations, employed by Thucydides in his analysis of events, can also be attributed by him to the political actors themselves, particularly when those actors occupy a position of power: the Melians should not expect that their previous links with Sparta will do them any good (V.105.3); the little states of Greece should submit to Athens because they recognise Athenian power, not (or at least, not only) because they feel any gratitude for Athens' services in the Persian Wars (IV.83–7). In Thucydides' world, the behaviour of states – particularly powerful and successful states – can be explained purely by reference to motivations of power and self-interest. Any claims that might be made to work in the service of more abstract ideals of honour, or even virtue, although not absent, and certainly not uninteresting,[48] are ultimately epiphenomena of interstate politics, and irrelevant to a true understanding of its nature.

The most important gap which exists between Thucydides and other sources is, then, a gap in the interpretation of the behaviour they describe, not in the behaviour itself. However, this is still a gap and, arguably, something which still demands explanation. Is it easier to arrive at this sort of interpretation of interstate politics in the fifth century than it would be at other periods of history? Here it is probably worth repeating the disclaimer made at the start of this section: only speculation is possible; there is simply not the density of evidence available to allow for a definitive answer to that question. But, once more, some speculation does seem worthwhile.

---

[47] The distinction is analysed by J. E. Lendon, in a forthcoming paper on 'Xenophon's theory of foreign relations'.

[48] Emphasised by Hornblower 1987: 189–90.

The key question is this: how specific is Thucydides' analysis of the nature of interstate politics to the period of history which he describes? That is not a question which can be answered by looking only at Thucydides' text.[49] At this point, therefore, a broadening of focus, and a rephrased question, is needed: not what is special about Thucydides, but what is special about the period he describes?

6.4 The Athenian Empire: structures, institutions and ethics

The title of this section needs some justification. It might be argued that the Athenian empire is not the only phenomenon of early classical foreign politics with a claim to uniqueness. The other, of course, is the Peloponnesian War: κίνησις . . . μεγίστη δὴ τοῖς Ἕλλησιν ('the greatest war in Greek history') according to Thucydides (I.I.2). But assessments of the specificity of that conflict are, of course, complicated precisely by Thucydides' close involvement with it: it is impossible to place any serious sort of control on the claim that he makes for its greatness. We can, it is true, compare Thucydides' narrative of the war with other narratives of other wars, and attempt to create some sort of chart of qualitative or quantitative magnitude,[50] but any impression of objectivity produced by such a comparison would be entirely spurious: we cannot use Thucydides' account as a check on his own claim for the war's distinctive character; and there is no other source of evidence which is both sufficiently detailed and sufficiently independent of Thucydides to which we can turn instead.[51]

For the Athenian Empire, however, that richness of evidence is available, and allows for two vital sorts of contextualisation: it is possible to take a view which is both longer (setting the Athenian

---

[49] It is worth noting the apparent ambivalence of the text itself about the universality of its message: on this, see Ober 2001. Later classical and hellenistic views on the question appear to have been equally mixed: see Hornblower 1995.

[50] For example, relative length: if the Peloponnesian War is counted as a single conflict of twenty-seven years then it could have a claim to be the longest continuous war of the classical period. But counting the war as a single conflict is, of course, a fundamentally Thucydidean idea (Th. v.26; Loraux 1986b; Strauss 1997). Other attempts at objective testing (for example: attempts to quantify relative numbers of atrocities in different periods) would be equally compromised by the same circularity.

[51] For a pessimistic assessment of the value of almost all non-Thucydidean literary sources for the Peloponnesian War, see HCT, vol. I: 29–30, 39–84.

Empire in the context of other, similar, classical Greek institutions) and broader (seeing the Athenian empire through eyes other than those of Thucydides). As a result, it is possible to get a much clearer perspective on the key question: what is different about the Athenian Empire?

It is important not to be distracted by a feature which is, for the purposes of this study, incidental to the Empire: namely, the fact that it is Athenian. While it is true that the retention of such extensive power by this single state for three-quarters of a century is unparalleled in classical interstate relations, Athens' powerful position itself is less interesting than the means by which it was maintained: specifically, the structure, the institutions and the ethics of empire. It is these three themes which will, in turn, form the focus of the argument of this section.

The structural question is the most straightforward, and can be answered most directly by looking at the Empire at the moment of its (ultimate) creation, in 478.[52] There is a tendency in some modern scholarship to see in the Delian League the start of a self-consciously new era of interstate politics, 'for the allies and for Athens, a fresh start':[53]

A Greek nation was being formed, permanent, as nations naturally believe themselves to be; its immediate business was a war of liberation, and in the long future peace would undoubtedly have its victories no less renowned.[54]

Such a characterisation, however, elides a substantial level of uncertainty in the ancient sources not only over the precise nature and aims of the agreement reached in 479, but also over the revolutionary nature of that agreement.

It is certainly true that some sources – the Aristoteleian *Athenaion Politeia* (23–4) above all – do provide a description of events which emphasises the break with what had gone before: the Delian League, in this version, is a new alliance, with a new set of aims (not just continuing the fight against Persia, but much

---

[52] Such a statement obviously begs numerous questions about the development from League to Empire; but whatever form and however long that process took, it did not have any effect on the core structure of the alliance and can be ignored here. The historical and historiographical problems of the events of 478 are much discussed: for a useful overview of the range of approaches, see the review article of Chambers 1968/9: 247–9.

[53] *ATL* III: 225.   [54] *ATL* III: 227.

broader pledges of lasting friendship and enmity), whose creation is marked by oaths and by ceremony. But it is also true that other sources, notably Thucydides, present a version of events which highlights continuity, and suggest that the transition from anti-Persian alliance to Delian League, and from League to Empire, was a much less dramatic, more organic, process:

παραλαβόντες δὲ οἱ Ἀθηναῖοι τὴν ἡγεμονίαν τούτῳ τῷ τρόπῳ ἑκόντων τῶν ξυμμάχων διὰ τὸ Παυσανίου μῖσος, ἔταξαν ἅς τε ἔδει παρέχειν τῶν πόλεων χρήματα πρὸς τὸν βάρβαρον καὶ ἃς ναῦς· πρόσχημα γὰρ ἦν ἀμύνεσθαι ὧν ἔπαθον δῃοῦντας τὴν βασιλέως χώραν. καὶ Ἑλληνοταμίαι τότε πρῶτον Ἀθηναίοις κατέστη ἀρχή, οἳ ἐδέχοντο τὸν φόρον· οὕτω γὰρ ὠνομάσθη τῶν χρημάτων ἡ φορά. ἦν δ᾽ ὁ πρῶτος φόρος ταχθεὶς τετρακόσια τάλαντα καὶ ἑξήκοντα. ταμιεῖόν τε Δῆλος ἦν αὐτοῖς, καὶ αἱ ξύνοδοι ἐς τὸ ἱερὸν ἐγίγνοντο.

The Athenians having thus succeeded to leadership by the voluntary act of the allies through their hatred of Pausanias, fixed which cities were to contribute money against the barbarian, which ships; their professed object being to retaliate for their sufferings by ravaging the king's country. Now was the time that the office of 'Hellenotamiai' was first instituted by the Athenians. These men received the tribute, as the money contributed was called. The tribute was first fixed at four hundred and sixty talents. The common treasury was at Delos, and the congresses were held in the temple. (Th. 1.96)

Thucydides' evolutionary version of the League's formation has struck some readers as, if not wholly insufficient, then at least insufficiently forthcoming about the novelty of the transition:

it is clear that Th. thought of [this] as a wholly new phase of alliance even if he does not describe its formation in so many words.[55]

In fact, however, Thucydides' model is not at all unreasonable. The Delian League is in origin, and to some extent always remains, a multilateral alliance: this is, of course, a (arguably *the*) standard feature of the structure of Greek interstate politics in the fourth century, but it was also nothing particularly new in 478.[56] The

---

[55] Hornblower 1991, *ad* 1.96. The HCT characterises the account as 'defective' (*ad* 1.97.1). See also the more detailed arguments in the *HCT*, vol. I: 25, 370–85, suggesting that Thucydides' lack of emphasis on the innovative features of the League is a result of the unfinished nature of this section of the text.

[56] The Hellenic League against Persia is the obvious precedent, and can function as such even if it is not believed that the Delian League was a direct continuation of the earlier alliance. Another precedent might be identifiable in the Peloponnesian League, already in existence in some form by 479, even if there is little evidence for the details of

scope of the League's aims and objectives – at least as reported by [Aristotle] – might be more expansive than those of some other alliances, but these too are not unprecedented.[57]

But even if the logic of the Aristoteleian presentation might be questioned, the fact of its existence cannot be denied. Rather than treating the disparity between the two sources' perceptions of the events of 478 as a narrowly historiographical or historical problem, however, it is worth considering the possibility that the lack of clarity in the ancient sources reflects a genuine divergence in ancient perceptions of the novelty of the Athenian Empire.[58] Comparison with the inscribed 'charter' of the Second Athenian League (*IG* ii² 43 (= RO 22)) is instructive here: the League of which this document is the prospectus is clearly, and self-consciously, a new institution;[59] but at the same time it is inextricably, and explicitly, linked to the interstate interactions which have gone before: this alliance is to proceed ἐπὶ | δὲ τ[οῖς] αὐτοις ἐφ᾽ οἷσπερ Χῖοι καὶ Θηβαῖ|οι κα[ὶ] οἱ ἄλλοι σύμμαχοι ('on the same terms as the Chians and the Thebans and the other allies'; lines 23–5). There is no neat break with what has gone before. The, less complete and less reliable, sources for the foundation of the Delian League point, I suspect, in a similar direction: there was scope (with the *Ath. Pol.*) for seeing the events of 478 as the beginning of a new era of Greek, or at least Athenian, history; but there was also scope (with Thucydides) for emphasising the element of continuity. At the moment of its foundation, at least, the Delian League did not necessarily mark a revolution in interstate relations.

Structurally, then, the Athenians may have been within their rights to claim (as they are made to at Th. 1.76.1) that they were

its organisation until later in the century (for a summary of what is known, see de Ste. Croix 1972: 101–24 and App. XVIII, and for the structural similarities between the Peloponnesian League and the Delian League, de Ste. Croix 1972: 298–302). See Baltrusch 1994, part I, for a detailed discussion of the formal structure of the Delian League, and its relationship to late archaic and early classical practice.

[57] See ML 10 (treaty of Sybaris and the Serdaioi, *c.* 525–500) for an early instance of a permanent alliance (and, possibly, ML 17, if the reference to 100 years in that treaty is taken as a synonym for eternity).

[58] Raaflaub (1979a: 5) notes that the origins of the Empire were likely to already have been a matter of dispute when Herodotus and Thucydides were writing; the same must also apply, even more strongly, to the *Athenaion Politeia*.

[59] The rhetoric of novelty is, of course, central to this document, which is keen to emphasise the difference between the institution and preceding varieties of hegemony.

doing nothing new or unusual in setting up the Delian League. But what about institutionally? It is true that some institutions which are seen as characteristically 'imperial' are only patchily attested before 479: there are cleruchies before the Persian Wars, but there is little evidence for either garrisons or governors. On the other hand, all three of these are relatively commonplace in the fourth century.[60] One institution, however, stands out as both novel and distinctive: namely, tribute.

This is an institution which has a good claim to be the unique identifying feature of the Athenian Empire, and therefore, by extension, to provide the best support for seeing this period of history as unique. This is not just, or even particularly, a modern perception. The creation of the system of tribute forms a part of each of the four main ancient accounts of the early years of the Delian League,[61] including, as has been seen, that of Thucydides. In that case, it is worth noting the emphasis – explicit and implicit – which is given to the novelty of the tribute: it is an institution which requires a new set of magistrates; and whose name needs glossing. This is something new, in Greek interstate politics at least.[62]

Tribute is also central to modern conceptions of the nature of the Athenian Empire: modern historians of the period make extensive use of the tribute quota lists – partly, it is clear, for purely practical reasons, but often also for more abstract ones. Not everyone agrees with Thucydides that the start of Athenian imperialism should be made almost simultaneous with the start of the Delian League; but even those who disagree tend to follow Thucydides' assessment (made explicit in 1.99) that there is a close connection between the development of the tribute system and the extension of Athenian imperial control.[63]

---

[60] For early Athenian cleruchies, see, for example, Hdt. v.77.2 (Chalcis) and (possibly) ML 14 (Salamis), with Brunt 1993. On imperial garrisons, see Nease 1949; on officials, Balcer 1976. For the fourth-century manifestations of these institutions, see Cargill 1995 (cleruchies); RO 51, with Cargill 1981: ch. 9 (governors, garrisons).

[61] Th. 1.96–9; [Ar.] AP 23.5; Plu. Arist. 24; D.S. 11.46.4–47.1.

[62] There is a Persian precedent: see Murray 1966: esp. 149–50, and (for this and other non-Greek systems), Kallet-Marx 1993: 47–8. Both scholars note that the Athenians appear deliberately to emphasise the difference between their tribute and the Persian version; but see Aristophanes Birds 1021 for the suggestion that at least some observers saw Persian elements in Athenian imperial control.

[63] This is most visible, among those who want to make the 450s the crucial stage in the development of the empire, in the invocation of the transfer of the treasury of the

The practical and abstract aspects of the tribute are not, of course, entirely distinct, and the way in which they combine is significant. The Athenian Empire is, notoriously, an extremely shifty thing, hard to pin down either through abstract conceptualisation (the 'no word for empire' problem) or through concrete demarcation. There are no pink-shaded maps in the fifth-century Aegean, and if a selection of Athenians were asked to do the colouring-in then the results would probably be widely divergent: Aristophanes, for example (or a character in his *Wasps*, at least), would produce a version covering around 1,000 cities;[64] Thoudippos, proposer of the tribute reassessment decree of 425/4 (ML 69), seems likely to have come up with a figure around 400;[65] neither version is very close to the 'right' answer arrived at by modern historians of the empire.[66] The place where Athenian imperial control becomes most clearly visible is in practical activity, and payment of the tribute is the most important of the various imperial activities undertaken by Athens and the allies: it is, crucially, one of the few actions in which all – or nearly all – member states participate, and not paying the tribute – whether through arrangement or by rebellion – is, or can be argued to be, a marker of disengagement from the 'real' Athenian empire.[67]

Payment of the tribute dominated the experience of imperialism in other ways too. It required the creation of an extensive, and almost certainly unprecedented, network of human interaction:

league from Athens to Delos in the late 450s as evidence for a mid-century escalation of Athenian imperialism: see, for example, Rhodes 1993: 23 (the transfer is 'a useful symbol of growing Athenian imperialism to us, even if it did not seem sinister at the time').

[64] *Wasps* 707.

[65] The text in *ATL* (A9) has space for about 380 cities; Dow 1941 suggests that the list could have included over 400.

[66] There is no year in which we have evidence for more than 190 cities paying tribute (see ML: page 199). This vagueness is in keeping with the general lack of precision in Athenian terminology for their imperial subjects: if literary texts tend to talk in abstract terms (*archē*, or *hegemonia*), then documentary evidence is no more concrete: the records of imperial control talk, at most, of the 'cities which the Athenians rule'– in many ways a self-fulfilling assertion of the scope of empire – or, more usually and less helpfully (as, for example, in the Standards Decree, *IG* i^3 1453 (= ML 45)), simply of 'the cities'.

[67] Absence by arrangement: see, for example, the Mytilenean attempt to distinguish themselves from Athens' subject allies at Th. III.9–14 (esp. 13.6 for the economic aspect of their independence). Absence by revolt: non-appearance in the tribute lists is regularly used in modern studies as evidence for rebellion in the relevant city (or cities).

Athenian officials travelling to allied states, and allied representatives travelling to Athens.[68] It also, in the tribute assessment and quota lists, resulted in the creation of physical, permanent and visually impressive monuments to the relationship between leader and followers. These lists could be contrasted with, for example, the arguably no less burdensome, but, in the long term, far less prominently commemorated obligations to provide cow, panoply or phallus to the major Athenian festivals;[69] or with the infinitely more amateurish Spartan version of collecting and recording tangible contributions to its war-effort – the only document which comes anywhere close to providing a parallel to the Tribute Lists, but which ends up providing the clearest demonstration of their exceptionalism.[70]

Tribute, then, appears when Athenian imperialism appears (although the Empire, of course, outlives it at the other end of the century); it is the only imperial institution in which almost every member state of the empire is involved; and it results in the creation of some of the most distinctive physical markers of imperial obligation and exploitation. To all that can be added a fourth suggestive strand: the status accorded to tribute in ancient accounts of the Athenian empire. It has already been seen that tribute has a starring role in narratives of the origins of the empire; what is also important to note is the relatively prominent part it plays in other characterisations of this period of history, and particularly in attempts to demonstrate its distinctive nature. Most notorious of these is the Second Athenian League's ostentatious avoidance of any repetition of the fifth-century system (*IG* ii² 43 (= RO 22), line 22), together with Theopompus' equally notorious debunking of that pious declaration:

ἔλεγον δὲ καὶ τοὺς φόρους συντάξεις, ἐπειδὴ χαλεπῶς ἔφερον οἱ Ἕλληνες τὸ τῶν φόρων ὄνομα, Καλλιστράτου οὕτω καλέσαντος, ὡς φησι Θεόπομπος ἐν ī Φιλιππικῶν.

They used to call also the payments of phoroi 'syntaxeis', since the Greeks were upset by the name of 'phoroi'. It was Callistratus who gave them this name,

---

[68] On the mechanics of tribute payment, see Meiggs 1972: 236–8.

[69] The panoplies, as dedications to Athena, should have been deposited in the treasury, but do not appear in the inventories.

[70] Loomis 1992. Compare Th. 1.19 on Sparta's non-collection of tribute.

as Theopompus says in the tenth book of the *Philippica*. (Theopompus F98 = Harpocration *s.v.* Syntaxis)

More extensive, and more informative, is Isocrates' sustained attack on the tribute, and all it represented:

οὕτω γὰρ ἀκριβῶς εὕρισκον ἐξ ὧν ἄνθρωποι μάλιστ' ἂν μισηθεῖεν, ὥστ' ἐψηφίσαντο τὸ περιγιγνόμενον τῶν πόρων ἀργύριον διελόντες κατὰ τάλαντον εἰς τὴν ὀρχήστραν τοῖς Διονυσίοις εἰσφέρειν ἐπειδὰν πλῆρες ᾖ τὸ θέατρον· καὶ ταῦτ' ἐποίουν καὶ παρεισῆγον τοὺς παῖδας τῶν ἐν τῷ πολέμῳ τετελευτηκότων, ἀμφοτέροις ἐπιδεικνύντες, τοῖς μὲν συμμάχοις τὰς τιμὰς τῆς οὐσίας αὐτῶν ὑπὸ μισθωτῶν εἰσφερομένας, τοῖς δ' ἄλλοις Ἕλλησι τὸ πλῆθος τῶν ὀρφανῶν καὶ τὰς συμφορὰς τὰς διὰ τὴν πλεονεξίαν ταύτην γιγνομένας.

For so exactly did the Athenians gauge the actions by which human beings incur the worst odium that they passed a decree to divide the surplus of the funds derived from the tributes of the allies into talents and to bring it on the stage, when the theatre was full, at the festival of Dionysus; and not only was this done but at the same time they led in upon the stage the sons of those who had lost their lives in the war, seeking thus to display to our allies, on the one hand, the value of their own property which was brought in by hirelings, and to the rest of the Greeks, on the other, the crowd of orphans and the misfortunes which result from this policy of expansion. (8.82)

Tribute is, therefore, a key imperial institution, and also one which is regularly regarded, in ancient as well as modern accounts, as being unique to the fifth-century empire. But should it also be thought to have transformed the nature of fifth-century foreign politics? Tribute might have been important in its own right, but how much effect did it have on interstate life more generally?

This is where the third aspect of Athenian imperial distinctiveness – the ethics of interstate interaction – becomes relevant to the argument. That relevance might not be immediately apparent: attempts to assess the broader significance of the existence of tribute have traditionally focused on the basic economics of the institution: how much of a financial burden was it, on whom did the burden fall, and how much did it prevent the allies from investing in other, less Athenocentric, projects?[71] But more recent work has suggested that the tribute might have had a much wider effect on, or

---

[71] On the first two questions, see Finley 1978; Nixon & Price 1990. On the second, Osborne 1999.

been part of a bigger transformation in, the norms of interstate interaction in this period. Tribute, it is argued, is intimately connected
with a radical distortion of the patterns of reciprocal exchange
which, as was argued in Chapter 2, underpin large amounts of
interstate interaction in the Greek world.

This claim originates from work on the Thucydidean version
of the Athenian empire. Two recent studies have claimed to find
in Thucydides' narrative of Athenian imperial history a potent (if
sometimes implicit) argument for a radically new model of understanding models of power and prestige in Greek interstate politics –
a model which is inextricably linked with the introduction of
phoros.[72] From the Archaeology onwards, it is argued, Thucydides
is attempting to show that conventional methods of evaluating the
power and status of a city or leader – methods based on the acquisition of honour or prestige – are misguided. Power is something
which is

material and tangible, not abstract. Success and failure are measured by the presence or absence, respectively, of *periousiai chrematon*.[73]

This, then, explains why Thucydides makes the introduction of
tribute so central to his account of the origins of the empire: it
is tribute, more than anything, which enables the Athenians to
indulge their preference for real, tangible capital over the looser,
symbolic sort, and for the power which derives from the acquisition
of wealth over that which accrues to the participant in the reciprocal
exchange of gifts, honours or other services.

These arguments are based almost exclusively on a reading of
the Thucydidean account of the origins and nature of the Athenian empire, but it has been claimed that their conclusions reveal
something about the nature of all (not just Thucydidean) foreign
politics in the imperial period.[74] My question, predictably, is: is
that extrapolation legitimate? Or could this too be an idiosyn-
cratically skewed picture of the nature of interstate interaction in
this period? Does the creation of the Athenian empire, and the

[72] Kallet-Marx 1993: esp. chs. 1 and 2; Crane 1998: ch. 6.
[73] Kallet-Marx 1993: 33–4.
[74] Particularly clear in Crane (1998: 164): the Athenian Empire represents 'a fundamental
change and the emergence of possibilities that had not previously existed'.

introduction of tribute, really distort the whole structure, and ethics, of interstate politics in this way?

It has already been seen that there exists in the fourth century very good evidence, both epigraphic and literary, for precisely the sort of pattern of honorific exchange which is (allegedly) missing from Athenian imperial politics. One example, already alluded to (in ch. 2, n. 52) can usefully be repeated here: in (or around) 375, Athens makes an alliance with the small Thracian city-state of Elaious (*IG* ii^2 43 (= RO 22), line 123); in 357/6, the Athenians appear to have awarded honours to ambassadors from that city (*Agora* 16.53); and in 346/5, the citizens of Elaious award a golden crown to the *dēmos* of Athens (*IG* ii^2 1443, lines 93–5; cf. Dem. 18.92). The accounts of the Hecatompedon suggest that the Elaiousians were not alone in their actions: records of dedications stored in this treasury reveal that, from the 360s to the end of the century, thirty-three crowns were given to Athens by various Greek states, many of them (like Elaious) members of the Second Athenian League.[75]

In the fifth century, however, that pattern seems not to apply. The flow of honorific decrees between Athens and the members of the Delian League is remarkably unidirectional: while there are (to take an easily quantifiable example) over ninety extant inscribed proxeny decrees which originate in Athens and extend honours to other states, the Athenians seem to receive next to nothing in return.[76] Two further examples will help to illustrate the nature of the contrast. In the early years of the Delian League the Athenians

[75] For the details, see D. Harris 1995, App.II, with 238: the first attested dedication is 368/7, but there is also evidence that the records are seriously incomplete. For one version of the perception of the significance of these dedications, see Dem. 22.72: they are καλὰ καὶ ζηλῶτ᾽ ἐπιγράμματα ('fine and admirable inscriptions').

[76] I can find only one example of inscribed honours for an Athenian which might date to the period of the empire: this is *I.v.O.* 30: a proxeny decree for Diphilos of Athens, voted by the city of Alea (in Arcadia), which has been dated to the 420s and which, if the dating is correct, forms a neat pairing with an Athenian proxeny decree for an Alean citizen (*IG* i^3 80, 421/0). However, there is, of course, a strong element of circularity in that argument, and the 390s has also been proposed as a plausible date for the Alean decree. Other Athenian citizens did perform the role of *proxenos* for Greek states in this period: Monceaux's (1886, App. II) list of known examples includes (for the fifth century): Militiades and Cimon (Sparta), Alcibiades (Sparta), Callias (Sparta), Xenophon (Sparta), Nicias (Syracuse), Andocides (unknown). All examples involve powerful states (not members of the empire), and all are attested only in literary sources. On the potential importance of creating an inscribed record of such awards, see 248 below.

had intervened at Erythrae to (it might be argued) save them from falling into Persian, or tyrannical control.[77] We are relatively well informed about the Athenian response to that event – the installation of a democracy, and the imposition of certain obligations on the people of Erythrae – but we have no information on how, if at all, the people of Erythrae marked this act of 'liberation'. This silence can, however, be contrasted with the Erythraean response to a second Athenian intervention, over half a century later: Conon's liberation of the city, along with others in this region, from Spartan control after the battle of Cnidus.[78] Then, the Erythraeans resolve to vote Conon the status of *proxenos* and *euergetēs*, to allow him a range of practical and ceremonial honours (including citizenship), and to erect for him a gilded statue (RO 8). Later in the century, probably in the early 350s, the city of Arcesine on Amorgos, confers similar honours (including proxeny) on their Athenian governor Androtion, and awards him a 500 drachma crown (RO 51).[79] The things for which Androtion is being praised – for being a tolerant governor, for avoiding financial exploitation, for looking after the garrison – could easily be interpreted as evidence for Athenian backsliding into her bad old imperial ways.[80] If that is the case, however, it surely also needs to be noted that the people of Arcesine respond to that behaviour in a way which is not paralleled in the fifth-century empire.

How is the change in behaviour to be explained? The two examples briefly discussed above should discourage recourse to one superficially attractive explanation: that the change in allied response should be attributed to a fundamental change in Athenian treatment of the allies. In both these cases, it is not the basic

---

[77] ML 40 (*IG* i³ 14). On the date, see Meiggs 1943: 33–4. For a (rare) positive interpretation of Athens' fifth-century intervention (38: 'Athenian interference at this time in Erythraean affairs was dictated only by the purpose of helping the democracy to establish itself there'), see Highby 1936.

[78] For an account of this episode, see D.S. 14.84.3–4 (and X. *HG* IV.viii.1–2, who tells a similar story of liberation, but does not mention Erythrae by name).

[79] For Androtion's virtues, see ch. 4, sec. 2. A third example reveals that the practice is not restricted to celebrities: in or around the 330s, the people of Olbia award proxeny (and citizenship, and *ateleia*) to two otherwise unknown Athenians, probably grain merchants (Dubois 1996: no. 21).

[80] For a more positive explanation for Androtion's presence on Amorgos, see Cargill 1981: 155–6, 157–8.

behaviour of the Athenians which has changed (or not in any radical way, certainly); rather, it is in the responses of the targets of
that behaviour that a transformation can be identified. In the fourth
century, it is possible, or appropriate, for Athens' allies to honour
the Athenians; in the fifth century, as far as we can see, it is not.[81]

It is certainly possible that this change in allied response is
entirely independent of the shift in the nature of Athenian power:
there is, demonstrably, a general growth in honorific activity in
the Greek world in the fourth century (and even more in the
Hellenistic period), and the habit of inscribing those honorific
exchanges also becomes increasingly widespread.[82] If the change
were to be definitively and exclusively attributed to the existence of the Athenian empire, then it might be hoped that there
would be a vigorous set of honorific exchanges between Athens
and states outside the empire, or at least between states who had
nothing to do with Athens. Neither of those phenomena is easily
visible.[83]

---

[81] Compare the changes in honorific practice inside the Athenian *polis*: honours are awarded
to Athenian citizens (and those awards inscribed) with increasing frequency over the
course of the fourth century (see Lambert 2004): no one, I think, would want to argue
that this can be explained by reference to an improvement in standards of domestic
political behaviour.

[82] On the spread of honorific (and epigraphic) practice outside Athens, see Rhodes with
Lewis 1997: esp. ch. 6; Lewis 1997c.

[83] It is hard to produce a definitive list of examples, or a firm chronology, since dating
of non-Athenian inscriptions is so problematic. It is clear that the award of proxeny,
and other honours, is relatively well-attested in the archaic period outside Athens: for
details, see Wallace 1970, and add Van Effentere & Ruzé 1994–5 (Argive proxeny decree,
c. 475–470); SEG 36.982 (three proxeny decrees from Iasos, *c.* 500–450). See Hansen &
Nielsen edd. 2004, App.14, for a checklist of all cities at which *proxenia* is attested. For
other forms of honorific decree in the archaic and early classical period, see, for example,
I.v.O 11 (Chaladroi honours Deukalion, nationality not known, 6th cent.?); Van Effentere
& Ruzé 1994–5, vol. I: no. 32 (reinscribed decree from Cyzicus, originally 6th cent.),
no. 33 (Thessalian honours for Sotairos of Corinth). The reappearance of the practice as
the Athenian empire declines and falls is often easier to identify. Note especially ML 82,
Eretrian honours for Hegelochus of Tarentum, specifically awarded in thanks for his help
in liberating the city from Athens in 411. *I.Lindos* 15, 16 and 16a might also date from
shortly after Rhodian liberation from Athens, although the dating here is less secure (see
n. 85 below). The honorific habits of Olbia are also suggestive: Dubois 1996: nos. 1 and
5 seem likely to date from a period before the absorption of the region into the Athenian
Empire (particularly since no. 5 awards honours to a tyrant ousted by Athens from a
neighbouring city); there is then a gap in the evidence until the fourth century, when the
habit returns in force (Dubois 1996: nos. 15–21). Overall, however, no explanation for
the pattern of evidence can ever be more than tentative: as Osborne 1999: 331, notes, 'it
is hard enough to explain why people do things, harder still to explain why they fail to
do things'.

Nevertheless, explanations which relate these changes, even if only in part, to Athens' shifting imperial fortunes are both available and attractive. Again, more than one variant on the political theme is available. First – and perhaps most obvious – is the argument that the absence of honorific – and especially proxeny – decrees is a natural consequence of the absence of political liberty: if a city has no independent foreign policy, than it can have no need for, and perhaps no power to create, such decrees.[84] It seems to me, however, that in this case the obvious answer might not be the right one; or, at least, that it relies on various less straightforward, more controversial, assumptions, which are worth making explicit. First of all, it is necessary to believe that only a fully autonomous *polis* would be able to award this sort of status to an outsider. This seems, however, not necessarily to be the case: evidence from the fifth century is scanty and problematic,[85] but fourth-century material is more instructive, and reveals first, that proxeny decrees produced by federal states are as likely to emanate from the constituent parts of that state as from the federation as a whole;[86] and, second, that the practice of awarding these honours appears to flourish under other imperial powers.[87]

There is, then, or appears to be no necessary incompatibility between imperial subjection and the award of honours. If that is the case, then some more specific explanation needs to be identified for the curiously imbalanced pattern of honorific activity in the

---

[84] Suggested by Monceaux 1886: 141, as an explanation for the slow spread of the institution in fifth-century Greece; the same argument is employed by Knoepfler 2001: 425, to account for the pattern of Eretrian proxeny decrees in the fifth and fourth centuries.

[85] The key material is the set of inscriptions from Lindos: *I.Lindos* 16 (decree appointing a *proxenos* of the Rhodians) and *I.Lindos* 16a (decree, usually dated slightly earlier, appointing a *proxenos* of the Lindians). Conventionally, the difference between the two is attributed to the effects of the Rhodian sympolity: after this political union, Lindos would no longer be able to appoint its own *proxenoi*. There is, however, no good external reason to date *I.Lindos* 16a before *I.Lindos* 16 (on this, see Gabrielsen 2000: 185–6).

[86] On issuing bodies of proxeny decrees, see Hansen & Nielsen edd. 2004: 99: the practice of the Boeotian federation provides a good example (compare, for example, *IG* vii 2708, issued by Acraephia, with *IG* vii 393, issued by the *koinon*; for further examples, see Rhodes with Lewis 1997: 113–22).

[87] Notably the Macedonians: see, for a usefully clear example, the evidence for Eretrian response to Macedonian control, collected in Knoepfler 2001. For a full discussion of the more general phenomenon of honorific practice and imperial control in the Hellenistic period, see Ma 2000.

fifth-century Athenian empire. And it is in locating that explanation that the question of tribute – and its allegedly distorting effect on Athenian imperial politics – might become relevant once again. It is not quite the case that the epigraphic record for the fifth-century honorific habit exactly confirms the view that symbolic capital has absolutely no place in the Athenian empire: one party to the imperial relationship – namely, Athens – still seems to have a healthy interest in awarding honours to states and to individuals, inside and outside the empire. To that extent, then, a picture of interstate interaction which allows no space for, and attributes no importance to, such activities, should not be taken as an accurate reflection of reality.

But other parts of the imperial relationship do fit the model more neatly. Athens hands out honours, but in return she receives not reciprocal honorific gestures but tangible, regulated, and usually financial, contributions. So while it is not true that there is absolutely no space at all for symbolic capital in fifth-century interstate politics, it does seem to be absent from one important area of interstate relations – that is, from the typical allied experience of the Athenian Empire. In that context, tribute supplants honours; actual capital supplants symbolic capital.

It might be tempting to represent that pattern of behaviour as one which is beneficial to all sides: this is Athenian altruism of the sort apparently celebrated by Pericles in the Thucydidean funeral oration:

καὶ τὰ ἐς ἀρετὴν ἐνηντιώμεθα τοῖς πολλοῖς· οὐ γὰρ πάσχοντες εὖ, ἀλλὰ δρῶντες κτώμεθα τοὺς φίλους. βεβαιότερος δὲ ὁ δράσας τὴν χάριν ὥστε ὀφειλομένην δι' εὐνοίας ᾧ δέδωκε σῴζειν· ὁ δὲ ἀντοφείλων ἀμβλύτερος, εἰδὼς οὐκ ἐς χάριν, ἀλλ' ἐς ὀφείλημα τὴν ἀρετὴν ἀποδώσων.

In the matter of generosity too we are the opposite of most people: for we acquire our friends by conferring not by receiving favours. The one who confers a favour is the firmer friend of the two, in order by continued kindness to keep the recipient in his debt; while the feelings of the recipient are weaker, because he knows that the return he makes will be a payment, not a free gift. (Th. II.40.4)

This claim has often been thought to be tendentious at best: while it might provide an accurate account of Athenian imperial interventionism, its denial of Athenian imperial acquisitiveness is less obviously easy to accept.[88] In fact, however, the assertion that the Athenians were not particularly keen on being the recipients of (intangible) favours seems, on the basis of the pattern of evidence which has emerged here, to be not all that far removed from the truth. But the more menacing note of this passage should not be ignored: the Athenian preference for giving, rather than receiving, favours cannot be disentangled from their desire to maintain their superior position, and – the inevitable but centrally important corollary of that – their rigorous enforcement of the inferior position of their allies.

This model of behaviour is, therefore, in many ways, more disturbing than one in which honorific exchange is entirely irrelevant, since it represents a drastic distortion not only of the pattern but also of the etiquette of reciprocal exchange which, as was seen in Chapter 2, underpins so much interstate activity in so much else of the classical period. In one respect, the behaviour of states is constant: throughout, there is a concern to accumulate favours and use them to their own political advantage. What appears to be different, however, in the second half of the fifth century, is the extent to which the pattern of giving and receiving is kept in some sort of balance. The Athenians have not, it is true, established an absolute monopoly of benevolence: tribute is not the only thing which the Athenians receive from their allies, and other contributions – like, for example, the cypress wood sent by the Eteocarpathians – could be explicitly recognised as acts of euergetism (*IG* i^3 1454, lines 7–8).[89] But the balance of such behaviour is heavily weighted towards the Athenians. And, perhaps most importantly, the

---

[88] Rusten 1989 *ad loc.* advises that this statement 'must not be misinterpreted as a claim about the Athenian policy to the allies'. *HCT* and Hornblower 1991 *ad loc.*, are less explicitly sceptical, but both point out the fine line between the positive characterisation of interventionism here, and the more negative images of meddlesomeness which emerge from other depictions of the empire. For a more optimistic reading of the ethics of interstate interaction implied by the passage, see Missiou 1992: 114–21.

[89] The Thucydidean picture of an absolute refusal to accept favours (whether characterised as altruism, as by Pericles at II.40.4, or as threat, as by Euphemus at VI.83) is therefore an exaggeration. Similarly, the language of *philia* does not entirely disappear from Athenian imperial discourse, even if it might be strongly suspected that this friendship is extorted rather than freely offered (for example, in the oath of friendship sworn by the Colophonians to Athens after their forced reincorporation into the Empire: ML 47, with Mitchell 1997b); for further examples of *philia* language in fifth-century Athenian treaties, see Panessa 1999.

public recognition of such behaviour seems to be a solely Athenian preserve.

In other words, Demosthenes' fourth-century picture of the pattern of benefaction, and of the benefits which derive from the recognition of benefaction, could be applied with no difficulty to the imperial Athens of the fifth century:

προσήκει τοίνυν τὰς στήλας ταύτας κυρίας ἐᾶν τὸν πάντα χρόνον, ἵν᾽, ἕως μὲν ἄν τινες ζῶσι, μηδὲν ὑφ᾽ ὑμῶν ἀδικῶνται, ἐπειδὰν δὲ τελευτήσωσιν, ἐκεῖναι τοῦ τῆς πόλεως ἤθους μνημεῖον ὦσι, καὶ παραδείγμαθ᾽ ἑστῶσι τοῖς βουλομένοις τι ποιεῖν ὑμᾶς ἀγαθόν, ὅσους εὖ ποιήσαντας ἡ πόλις ἀντ᾽ εὖ πεποίηκεν.

It is fitting, therefore, to allow these *stelae* to be valid for all time, so that as long as any of these men are alive, they may suffer no wrong at your hands, and when they die, those inscriptions may be a memorial of our national character, and may stand as proofs to all who wish to do us service, declaring how many benefactors our city has benefited in return. (Dem. 20.64)

But – and this is where the crucial difference emerges – it could not be applied to the members of Athens' fifth-century empire. There is no sign that Athens' imperial subjects were, or felt, able to recognise Athenian benefactions in their (the allies') own terms. As a result, this method of acquiring and displaying status, which seems to be so enthusiastically exploited by the Athenians, is closed off to her allies.

The connection between the appearance of tribute and the disappearance of honours need not, therefore, be one of cause and effect. Rather, the two phenomena both result from and go on to contribute to a single and fundamental feature of this period of politics: the disparity in the distribution of power between the *poleis* of the Greek world. The imperial Athenians established a monopoly, it seems, not only, as has long been recognised, over the acquisition of physical strength, *dunamis*, but also over the less tangible sources of power and prestige to which the award of honours provided access.

6.5 Conclusion

By way of conclusion, I want to make good on my earlier promise to return to the island of Carpathos, and its errant inscription. It was suggested at the start of this chapter that it is very hard to pin down any objective historical (rather than technical) criteria for dating this document. It now seems possible both to amplify and refine that assertion. Although the precise status of this community on Carpathos is obscure, more confidence is possible when describing the nature of their relationship with Athens in the fifth century.[90] From 433, the Eteocarpathians appear in the tribute lists, paying a small amount of money (1000 drachmas) to Athens. But this was not the only contribution which the Eteocarpathians made to their Athenian masters: they also – in the act which prompts the creation of the decree – made this contribution of cypress wood, to be used to assist in constructing a temple for Athens' patron deity.[91] The Eteocarpathians are acting as euergetists; and, as was noted above, that is how they are labelled in the decree which honours them. The benefactions described in this decree, and the Athenian response to them, would not look out of place at any moment in Greek history, from the sixth century to the third (or beyond).

What is out of place, though, is the inscription itself. We never get to hear from the Eteocarpathians themselves about all the things they have done for Athens. The last word – and the last act of generosity – resides with the Athenians: this is an Athenian decree, demonstrating Athenian graciousness, and, on the Demosthenic model, enhancing Athenian prestige. The physical circumstances of the document's creation ram the point home just a bit more firmly: this decree was found on the island of Carpathos; but, if

---

[90] On the identity and status of the Eteocarpathians see Hansen & Nielsen edd. 2004: no. 489. On their appearance in the tribute lists, and the puzzling heading under which they appear (πόλες αὐταὶ φόρον ταχσάμεναι, 'cities arranging [?] their own tribute'), see Meiggs 1972: 250–2.

[91] It is usually assumed that the temple concerned is at Athens: when this decree was dated to the fourth century the building was identified as the 'old temple' of Athena (reported by X. *HG* I.vi.1 to have burned down in 406/5); with the redating, either the Parthenon (Meiggs 1982: 201) or Erechtheion (Lewis in *IG*) have become plausible candidates. Alfieri Tonini 1999 suggests that the reference to a temple of Ἀθηναίᾱς τῆς Ἀθηνῶμ μ|[εδεόσης ('Athena who watches over Athens') suggests a temple outside Attica (and on Carpathos). On the imperial connotations of this cult, see Parker 1996: 144–5. It is not entirely clear how much wood the Carpathians have donated: the reference to the tree is in the singular (lines 9, 38), and Meiggs 1982: 201 suggests that a single beam (from 'an exceptional tree') is all that has been provided, but it is possible that this does not accurately reflect the extent of the gift. For cypress wood as a standard import for religious building, see Hermipp. F63, line 14; for its use in other temple construction programmes, see Hodge 1960: 124.

David Lewis' identification of the letter-cutter is correct, it was not created by a Carpathian – the Athenians exported either stone or stonemason out to the southern Aegean, as if to make absolutely sure that their side of the story was properly conveyed.[92]

What emerges from all this, then, is an entirely one-sided conversation. It is possible to hear the voices of the allies, and to hear about the services and benefactions performed by the allies, but they are audible only as reported by the Athenians. This is not, in itself, an original observation – it is one of the conventional laments of anyone who studies fifth-century Greek history. What I would argue, though, is that this gap in our evidence is not simply an accident of preservation, or of historical chance, or of epigraphic practice. Rather, this distorted pattern is itself a key piece of evidence for the nature of this period of history, and a piece of evidence which, I think, is centrally important in pinning down just what it is which makes these years different from the rest of Greek foreign politics.

The difference is – to reiterate the argument of the early part of the chapter – not absolute, nor is it revolutionary: the picture of stability which emerged from the two treaties which were considered in the first section was not, I think, misleading. The basic shape of interstate relations does stay the same throughout the classical period. But this shape is flexible, and there are times – notably in the second half of the fifth century – when it is stretched so much that, viewed from certain angles, it is hard to recognise. The force which creates that distortion is the distribution of power among the *poleis* of the Greek world, and it is the massive disparity in power in the early classical period which can help to explain at least some of its oddities. Above all, the gap in power between the biggest states (especially Athens) and the smallest must have made it increasingly difficult for many Greek states to participate in the fiction that they formed part of a single community, bound by an agreed set of normative constraints. For some – Thucydides, for

---

[92] On the letter-cutter, see Lewis 1997a: 123. There may be a perfectly good practical reason for the export of Athenian epigraphic technology: the Carpathian epigraphic habit does not appear to have been well established, and it is quite plausible that there was no local stone-cutting expertise available (compare RO 14 for another example of a small state needing to use the stone-cutter of its larger neighbour).

example – this realisation might, perhaps, have either enabled or encouraged the adoption of a distinctive analytical approach to the subject of interstate relations. The strange disjunction in reciprocal activity suggests, moreover, that the consequences of the distorted power relations of this period were not only theoretical. What they do seem to have been, however, is short-lived: some of the norms of interstate interaction might be pushed to the margins in this period, but they return to the centre with remarkable speed. It is the conservatism, rather than the dynamism, of classical Greek inter-state activity which should be considered one of its distinguishing features.

CONCLUSION

At the start of this book, two conventional complaints about Greek interstate relations were given an airing: the undeveloped nature of Greek diplomatic interaction, with the corresponding preference for violence as the solution to most, if not all, external problems; and the absence of any clearly thought-out or expressed theories of interstate behaviour. What I hope has been demonstrated since then is that neither of these complaints is as easily justifiable as has often been assumed. A wide range of customs, beliefs and expectations shaped the practice, and the representation, of interstate politics in the classical Greek world. These norms are visible in all areas of interstate activity, from the broadest questions of the structures of interstate interaction, to specific approaches to particular problems. They do not make up a single, straightforward code of interstate behaviour, still less do they absolutely control the ways in which states or individuals behave. But they do provide an overall framework within which that behaviour operates and can be judged, and within which arguments about the proper conduct of interstate relations can be situated.

The most distinctive feature of this framework – particularly when it is compared with more recent approaches to interstate politics – is the extent to which it facilitates, encourages and sometimes even compels, participation in the world outside the city-state. The overwhelming pressure in Greek interstate relations is towards involvement rather than isolationism: the latter is not absolutely impossible, and is certainly not inconceivable, but rarely seems to be successful in the long term. (Sparta's short-lived attempt to withdraw from Greek politics in the immediate aftermath of the Persian Wars gives a useful, if partial, illustration of all three characteristics.[1]) Viewed from a distance, this extreme interconnectedness

---

[1] On this, see Thucydides 1.95.7, with Hornblower 1991 *ad loc.* (noting both the difficulties with Thucydides' account of Spartan objectives at this point, and, just as importantly, the

can look like chaos – and it is perhaps this appearance of unrestrained, self-indulgent interventionism which has contributed
most strongly to the undistinguished reputation of Greek diplomatic activity in the past. But closer inspection reveals that there
is a coherent, even logical, origin for these superficially confus-
ing entanglements: namely, the pervasive influence of an ethics of
reciprocity. Reciprocity not only provides – through friendship and
kinship – one of the most important methods of tying individuals,
groups and states to one another, it also offers specific motivation,
or justification, for further acts of intervention, whether hostile or
friendly, in the interstate arena. Even failures to act in ways determined by a strict pattern of reciprocity – as, most notably, in the
case of some Athenian interventions – derive much of their claimed
significance from their alleged subversion of this widespread norm.
These acts of intervention themselves serve to create and sustain
further links between the different members and sets of members
of the Greek society of states. And they also allow for a significant
degree of fluidity in the scope of that society: connections – particularly those at and beyond the margins of the Greek world – can
be created, allowed to lapse and revived as circumstances require.

Reciprocity, then, forms a basis for the type and extent of interstate interaction in this period; and a version of reciprocal morality
is also influential in shaping the quality of conduct in this sphere.
That is, the norms which shape the behaviour of states and individuals – conventions surrounding such issues as respect for treaties;
treatment for ambassadors; disposal of the war-dead; and so on –
depend largely on the existence of a consensus that all parties will
behave in, more or less, equivalent ways. In other words, adherence to certain modes of behaviour creates an obligation on others
to behave in a similar fashion; conversely, failure to follow any
given norm also removes that constraint from the other parties to
a relationship. And it should be noted, once more, that this reciprocal pattern of normative obligation does not necessarily stop at
the edges of the Greek world, but can, when necessary, be argued
to apply to any state or person with whom the Greeks come into

fact that, whether or not Thucydides' interpretation here is correct, Sparta soon became
involved again in affairs outside her borders, and outside the Peloponnese).

contact. Coercive measures do exist, but their importance is relatively restricted: socially determined motivations – shame, pity and so on – are regularly as prominent in accounts of Greek interstate behaviour as threats of force or financial impositions. Moreover, the authority by which coercive measures are enforced is itself, typically, socially constructed. In order to be in a position to insist on the maintenance of any norm, or to punish a failure to maintain it, a state (or group of states) must be recognised as a legitimate authority, and although it is clear this recognition can depend on the availability of force (as in the case of the Delian League, for example), it is equally apparent that this need not always be so (something for which the role of the Delphic Amphictiony provides the clearest evidence).

The society of states which these various forms of reciprocal action and justification combine to create is, therefore, of central importance in shaping the overall pattern of Greek interstate politics. It is essential to appreciate, however, that this society is not necessarily unhierarchical, and that it is certainly not always peaceful. And for this reason it would be a serious mistake to assume that this socially determined approach to interstate politics makes the acquisition and deployment of power irrelevant. At this point, it is perhaps worth quoting again E. H. Carr's observation on the relationship between norms and power:

If, however, it is utopian to ignore the element of power, it is an unreal kind of realism which ignores the element of morality in any world order.[2]

We now have a clearer picture of the 'elements of morality' in the Greek world order, and of the importance of these elements, but we have also, I think, confirmed rather than resolved the problem, identified by Carr, of separating the moral aspects of interstate activity from questions of power. Instead, the mutual and inextricable connection between these two themes has become clear. The connection is not the stark and simple version sometimes alleged – that of the powerful simply defining morality to suit their own purposes – but something rather more subtle. The appeal to moral criteria frequently relies upon, and more often is used to create or

[2] Carr 1946: 235–6. (see also ch. 1, sec. 4).

sustain, a position of power in the interstate system. This phenomenon is most clearly and consistently visible in the case of Athens, whose claims to primacy throughout this period are often intimately connected with assertions to be the arbiter and guarantor of appropriate behaviour in interstate affairs. It is not, however, restricted to that city: Xenophon's portrayal of Agesilaus' methodology of conquest in Asia Minor, for example, forms a persuasive argument for the potential practical benefits of ostentatious adherence to the norms of interstate conduct. Claims for the justice or morality of a particular course of an action are, as was seen in Chapter 4, regularly closely connected to assessments of its benefits for specific, carefully defined, groups. While, therefore, the existence of the normative framework discussed here may sometimes seem to even out inequalities of pure force in the Greek society of states, it does not lessen the importance of power, or of self-interest.

I do not want to suggest that this society is a utopia. Acquisition of high moral standing is not, obviously, the only way to acquire or maintain power in classical Greece: both Athens and Agesilaus were helped in their efforts by their access to extensive military and financial reserves. And the relationship between power and morality is not always so reassuringly symbiotic. There are undeniably occasions when power, however obtained, accumulates in the hands of a single state to such an extent that the normative constraints imposed by membership of the interstate society become almost invisible – something which is the case, most obviously, in the second part of the fifth century. Even here, however, the result of the distortion in the balance of power is not so much an absolute abandonment of all elements of morality, in favour of unrestrained force, but rather an amplification of the tendency, just described, to associate control of the norms of interstate society with control of the society itself: what emerges is an attempt to establish a monopoly over certain types of morally validated behaviour, and, most importantly, over the social status – the status within the society of states – which such behaviour could create.

It is, therefore, possible to find in classical Greek approaches to interstate politics something more complex and interesting than the internecine squabbling on which critics have concentrated. What it is not possible to find, however, is any contemporary description of those approaches to which the label of 'theory' could straightforwardly be applied. But it does not follow from this that the second conventional complaint against Greek interstate relations is any more justifiable than the first. The need for international theory is not inevitable, and the demand for such theory itself depends on the existence of a particular set of beliefs, not just about the nature of interstate politics, but also about the nature of the state and its role in external political life. Modern international theory has traditionally taken as its basic unit the autonomous nation state: it is the state which has been considered to be the principal actor in international politics, and it is the actions of the state which have been thought to require explanation by international theorists. Such a situation does not apply in classical Greece: interstate politics is not just the preserve of the state, and in fact the term 'interstate' – used in much of this work in an effort to avoid the more obviously anachronistic 'international' – fails, in the end, to provide an entirely adequate description of the nature of Greek practice. The actors of external politics are conceived of sometimes as *poleis*, sometimes as groups of individuals, sometimes as individuals; and while some of these sub-groups may fit quite neatly within the boundaries of the *polis*, others form units which cut across those divisions.

This fluidity in practice is significant in its own right, but also has important wider implications, of which the most relevant here is that it contributes to the difficulty of establishing a rigid dividing line, either practically or conceptually, between interstate behaviour and other sorts of political activity. The strict division between 'inside' and 'outside' which has formed the core of many modern approaches to international relations cannot straightforwardly be applied to the Greek example: on a practical level, it is often difficult to determine where the concerns of the domestic world stop and those of external relations begin; on a more abstract one, many of the norms of external activity replicate those of domestic life (and *vice versa*). There are signs, certainly, that some commentators on interstate politics – Thucydides and Demosthenes in particular – may have been attempting to develop arguments which relied on a stronger distinction between domestic and external conduct, but there are also even stronger indications that such arguments were not widely accepted. These indications can be found in popular practice, particularly in the form and content of the epigraphic record, and in theoretical or philosophical approaches to interstate ethics. It is this last point, above all, which should make the lack of a distinct theory of interstate politics unsurprising: the writers by whom we might have expected such a theory to be produced – namely, Plato, Aristotle, or one of their school – are precisely those who, as a consequence of their own theoretical approach to ethical and political philosophy, would see no need for a theory which explained only the behaviour of states and did not also concern itself with the ethics of the individual.

In spite of the claim to inclusiveness with which this book began, certain things have, inevitably, been excluded. This book has (deliberately) attempted to avoid many practical aspects of interstate relations – the technicalities of specific alliances and treaties; the realities of battles, campaigns and wars. It would be wrong to claim that such things do not matter: no matter how abstract the theories used to explain the nature of interstate interaction, the consequences of that activity are always – and often unpleasantly – tangible. But a complete picture of interstate relations cannot be achieved by focusing only on these details of 'what really happened'. An investigation of the norms of interstate relations must take as its starting-point the possibility – even the probability – that, in appealing to those norms, everyone could be lying; but it should also insist that the truth-value of such claims does not have any necessary bearing on their potential impact on the practical conduct of interstate relations. It is only through a proper awareness of the nature and role of interstate norms that the day-to-day realities of interstate politics can fully be understood.

BIBLIOGRAPHY

Abiew, F. K. (1999) *The Evolution of the Doctrine and Practice of Humanitarian Intervention*. The Hague, London, Boston

Accame, S. (1941) *La Lega Ateniese del Sec IV a.C.* Rome

(1951) *Ricerche Intorno alla Guerra Corinzia*. Naples

Adcock, F. E. (1924) 'Some aspects of ancient Greek diplomacy', *PCA* 21: 92–116

(1948) 'The development of ancient Greek diplomacy', *AC* 17: 1–12

(1963) *Thucydides and his History*. Cambridge

Adcock, F. E. & D. J. Mosley (1975) *Diplomacy in Ancient Greece*. London

Adkins, A. W. H. (1960) *Merit and Responsibility. A study in Greek values*. Oxford

(1975) 'The *arete* of Nicias: Thucydides 7.86', *GRBS* 16: 379–92

(1976) '*Polypragmosune* and "Minding one's own business": a study in Greek social and political values', *CPh* 71: 301–27

(1978) 'Problems in Greek Popular Morality', *CPh* 73: 143–58

Ager, S. (1993) 'Why war? Some views on international arbitration in Ancient Greece', *EMC/CV* ns 12: 1–13

(1996) *Interstate Arbitrations in the Greek World, 337–90 BC*. Berkeley and London

Alderson, K. & A. Hurrell (edd.) (2000) *Hedley Bull on International Society*. Basingstoke, London, New York

Alexiou, E. (1995) *Ruhm und Ehre. Studien zu Begriffen, Werten und Motivierungen bei Isokrates*. Heidelberg

Alfieri Tonini, T. (1999) 'Il decreto Ateniese per Carpato (*IG* i³ 1454 A). Una proposta di interpretazione', in *XI Congresso Internazionale di Epigrafia Greca e Latina, Atti*, vol. I. Rome: 157–65

Alker, H. (1996) *Rediscoveries and Reformulations. Humanistic methodologies for International Studies*. Cambridge

Alker, H. & T. Biersteker (1984) 'The dialectics of world order: notes for a future archeologist of international *savoir faire*', *International Studies Quarterly* 28: 121–42 (repr. in J. Der Derian (ed.) *International Theory. Critical Investigations*. Basingstoke and London 1995: 242–76; and in A. Linklater (ed.) *International Relations. Critical concepts in political science*. London and New York 2000, vol. I: 99–125)

Almeida, J. M. de (2003) 'Challenging Realism by returning to history: the British Committee's contribution to IR forty years on', *International Relations* 17: 273–302

Alonso Troncoso, V. (1995) 'Ultimatum et déclaration de guerre dans la Grèce classique', in E. Frézouls & A. Jacquemin (edd.) *Les Relations Internationales. Actes du colloque de Strasbourg, 15–17 juin 1993*. Paris: 211–95

(1999) '395–390/89 a.c., Atenas contra Esparta: ¿de qué guerra hablamos?', *Athenaeum* 87: 57–77

Alty, J. (1982) 'Dorians and Ionians', *JHS* 102: 1–14

Amit, M. (1970) 'Hostages in Ancient Greece', *RFIC* 98: 129–47

(1973) *Great and Small Poleis. A study in the relations between the great powers and the small cities in Ancient Greece*. Brussels

Anderson, C. A. & T. K. Dix (1997) 'Politics and state religion in the Delian League: Athena and Apollo in the Eteokarpathian decree', *ZPE* 117: 129–32

Andrewes, A. (1953) 'The generals in the Hellespont, 410–407 BC', *JHS* 73: 2–9

(1960) 'The Melian Dialogue and Perikles' last speech', *PCPhS* ns 6: 1–9

Annas, J. (1978) 'Plato and common morality', *CQ* ns 28: 437–51

(1981) *An Introduction to Plato's Republic*. Oxford

(1992) 'Ancient ethics and modern morality', *Philosophical Perspectives* 6: 119–36

(1995) 'Prudence and morality in ancient and modern ethics', *Ethics* 105: 241–57

Archibald, Z. H. (1998) *The Odrysian Kingdom of Thrace. Orpheus unmasked*. Oxford

(2000) 'Space, hierarchy, and community in archaic and classical Macedonia, Thessaly, and Thrace', in R. Brock & S. Hodkinson (edd.) *Alternatives to Athens. Varieties of political organization and community in ancient Greece*. Oxford and New York: 212–33

Arend, A. C. (1999) *Legal Rules and International Society*. New York and Oxford

Ashley, J. R. (1998) *The Macedonian Empire. The era of warfare under Philip II and Alexander the Great, 359–323 BC*. Jefferson and London

Ashley, R. K. (1984) 'The poverty of neorealism', *International Organization* 38: 225–86 (repr. in A. Linklater (ed.) *International Relations. Critical concepts in political science*. London and New York 2000, vol. IV: 1572–632)

Ashworth, L. M. (1999) *Creating International Studies. Angell, Mitrany and the Liberal Tradition*. Aldershot

Austin, J. L. (1885) *Lectures on Jurisprudence. Or, the philosophy of positive law*, 5th edn, 2 vols., ed. and rev. R. Campbell. London (1st edn 1863)

(1995 (1832)) *The Province of Jurisprudence Determined*, ed. W. E Rumble. Cambridge (repr. of 5th edn, London 1885; 1st edn London 1832)

Austin, R. P. (1938) *The Stoichedon Style in Greek Inscriptions*. Oxford and London

Axelrod, R. (1984) *The Evolution of Cooperation*. New York

Aymard, A. (1954) 'Philippe de Macédoine otage à Thèbes', *REA* 56: 15–36 (repr. in *Études d'Histoire Ancienne*. Paris 1967: 418–35)

Badian, E. (1958) 'Alexander the Great and the unity of mankind', *Historia* 7: 425–44

(1982) 'Greeks and Macedonians', in B. Bar-Sharrar & E. N. Borza (edd.) *Macedonia and Greece in Late Classical and Early Hellenistic Times*, Studies in the History of Art 10. Washington: 33–51

(1991) 'The King's Peace', in M. Toher & M. Flower (edd.) *Georgica. Greek Studies in Honour of George Cawkwell, BICS* Supplement 58. London: 25–48

(1995) 'The Ghost of Empire. Reflections on Athenian foreign policy in the fourth century BC', in W. Eder (ed.) *Die Athenische Demokratie im 4. Jahrhundert v. Chr. Vollendung oder Verfall einer Verfassungsform?* Stuttgart: 79–106

Bagby, L. M. J. (1994) 'The use and abuse of Thucydides in International Relations', *International Organization* 48: 131–53

(2000) 'Fathers of International Relations? Thucydides as a model for the twenty-first century', in L. S. Gustafson (ed.) *Thucydides' Theory of International Relations. A lasting possession.* Baton Rouge: 17–41

Balcer, J. M. (1976) 'Imperial magistrates in the Athenian empire', *Historia* 25: 257–87

Baldry, H. C. (1962) 'The idea of the unity of mankind', in O. Reverdin (ed.) *Grecs et Barbares*, Entretiens de la Fondation Hardt VIII. Geneva: 169–204

(1965) *The Unity of Mankind in Greek Thought.* Cambridge

Baltrusch, E. (1994) *Symmachie und Spondai. Untersuchungen zum griechischen Völkerrecht der archaischen und klassischen Zeit (8.–5. Jahrhundert v. Chr.).* Berlin and New York

Banks, M. (1984) 'The evolution of international relations theory', in *id.* (ed.) *Conflict in World Society. A new perspective on International Relations.* Brighton: 3–21

(1985) 'The inter-paradigm debate', in M. Light & A. J. R. Groom (edd.) *International Relations. A handbook of current theory.* London: 7–26

Barker, E. (1960) *Greek Political Theory. Plato and his predecessors*, 5th edn. London (1st edn 1918)

Barron, J. P. (1964) 'Religious propaganda of the Delian League', *JHS* 84: 35–48

Barry, J. A. (1998) *The Sword of Justice. Ethics and coercion in international politics.* Westport and London

Barry Jones, R. J. (1998) 'The English School and the political construction of international society', in B. A. Roberson (ed.) *International Society and the Development of International Relations Theory.* London and Washington: 231–45

Bauman, R. A. (2000) *Human Rights in Ancient Rome.* London and New York

Bauslaugh, R. A. (1991) *The Concept of Neutrality in Classical Greece.* Berkeley and Los Angeles

Baynes, N. H. (1955) 'Isocrates', in *Byzantine Studies and Other Essays.* London: 144–67

Bearzot, C. (1998) 'Criteri alternativi di applicazione dell'amnistia in Lisia', in M. Sordi (ed.) *Responsabilità, perdono e vendetta nel mondo antico*. Milan: 111–44

Beck, H. (1997) *Polis und Koinon. Untersuchungen zur Geschichte und Struktur der griechischen Bundesstaaten im 4. Jahrhundert v. Chr., Historia* Einzelschriften 114. Stuttgart

Bederman, D. J. (2001) *International Law in Antiquity*. Cambridge

Bedford, D. & T. Workman (2001) 'The tragic reading of the Thucydidean tragedy', *Review of International Studies* 27: 51–67

Beer, F. A. & R. Hariman (1996) 'Realism and rhetoric in International Relations', in *id.* (ed.) *Post-Realism. The rhetorical turn in International Relations*. East Lansing: 1–30

Beitz, C. R. (1979) *Political Theory and International Relations*. Princeton

Bellamy, A. J. (ed.) (2004) *International Society and its Critics*. Oxford

Bengtson, H. (1965) 'Zwischenstaatliche Beziehungen der griechischen Städte im klassischen Zeitalter', in *Rapports du XIIe Congrès International des Sciences Historiques*, vol. IV. Vienna: 69–76

Bentham, J. (1996 (1780)) *Introduction to the Principles of Morals and Legislation*, ed. J. H. Burns & H. L. A. Hart. Oxford (orig. pub. London 1780; 1st edn in this version London 1970)

Berent, M. (2000) 'Anthropology and the classics: war, violence, and the stateless *polis*', *CQ* ns 50: 257–89

Bethke Elshtain, J. (1995) 'International politics and political theory', in K. Booth & S. Smith (edd.) *International Relations Theory Today*. Cambridge and Oxford: 263–78

Bettalli, M. (1992) 'Isocrate e la Guerra', *Opus* 11: 37–56

Bickerman, E. J. (1950) 'Remarques sur le droit des gens dans la Grèce classique', *RIDA* 4: 99–127 (repr. in German tr. in F. Gschnitzer (ed.) *Zur Griechischen Staatskunde*. Darmstadt 1969: 474–502)

(1958) '*Autonomia*. Sur un passage de Thucydide (1.144.2)', *RIDA* 5: 313–43

Bielman, A. (1994) *Retour à la liberté: libération et sauvetage des prisonniers en Grèce ancienne. Recueil d'inscriptions honorant des sauveteurs et analyse critique*, Études Epigraphiques 1. Lausanne

Biersteker, T. J. & C. Weber (1996) 'The social construction of state sovereignty', in *eid.* (edd.) *State Sovereignty as Social Construct*. Cambridge: 1–21

Blake Reed, J. S. (1912) Review of Phillipson 1911, *CR* 26: 94–6

Blanco, W. & J. T. Roberts (edd. and tr.) (1998) *Thucydides* The Peloponnesian War. *A new translation, backgrounds and contexts, interpretations*. New York and London

Blundell, M. W. (1989) *Helping Friends and Harming Enemies. A study in Sophocles and Greek ethics*. Cambridge

Boak, A. E. R. (1921) 'Greek interstate associations and the League of Nations', *American Journal of International Law* 15: 375–83

Borza, E. N. (1990) *In the Shadow of Olympus. The emergence of Macedon.* Princeton and Oxford

(1999) *Before Alexander: Constructing early Macedonia,* Publications of the Association of Ancient Historians 6. Claremont

Bosworth, A. B. (1980) *A Historical Commentary on Arrian's* History of Alexander, vol. IV: *Commentary on Books I–III.* Oxford

(1992) 'Autonomia: the use and abuse of political terminology', *SIFC* 3rd ser. 10: 122–52

Boucher, D. (1998) *Political Theories of International Relations from Thucydides to the Present.* Oxford and New York

Bourriot, F. (1995) *Kalos Kagathos – Kalokagathia. D'un terme de propagande de sophistes à une notion sociale et philosophique,* 2 vols. Hildesheim, Zürich, New York

Bousquet, J. (1988) 'Etat des travaux sur les comptes du IVe siècle: l'amende des Phocidiens', in D. Knoepfler (ed.) *Comptes et Inventaires dans la Cité Grecque.* Neuchâtel and Geneva: 83–9

Bowen, J. (1989) 'Education, ideology and the ruling class: Hellenism and English public schools in the nineteenth century', in G. W. Clarke (ed.) *Rediscovering Hellenism. The Hellenic inheritance and the English imagination.* Cambridge: 161–86

Bozeman, A. B. (1960) *Politics and Culture in International History.* Princeton

Brierly, J. L. (1958) 'The basis of obligation in international law', in *The Basis of Obligation in International Law and Other Papers,* ed. H. Lauterpacht & C. H. M. Waldock. Oxford: 1–67

(1963) *The Law of Nations. An introduction to the international law of peace,* 6th edn, ed. C. H. M. Waldock. Oxford (1st edn 1928)

Bringmann, K. (1965) *Studien zu den politischen Ideen des Isokrates,* Hypomnemata 14. Göttingen

Brock, R. (1998) 'Mythical polypragmosyne in Athenian drama and rhetoric', in M. Austin, J. Harries & C. Smith (edd.) *Modus Operandi. Essays in honour of Geoffrey Rickman, BICS* Supplement 71. London: 227–38

Brown, C. (1992) *International Relations Theory. New normative approaches.* New York and London

(2001a) 'Ethics, interests and foreign policy', in K. E. Smith & M. Light (edd.) *Ethics and Foreign Policy.* Cambridge: 15–32

(2001b) *Understanding International Relations,* 2nd edn. Basingstoke, London and New York (1st edn 1997)

Brownson, C. L. (ed. and tr.) (1921) *Xenophon* Hellenica, *Books 6 & 7;* Anabasis, *Books 1–3.* London and Cambridge, Ma.

Bruce, I. A. F. (1960) 'Internal politics and the outbreak of the Corinthian War', *Emerita* 28: 75–86

Bruit Zaidman, L. & P. Schmitt Pantel (1992) *Religion in the Ancient Greek City,* tr. P. A. Cartledge. Cambridge (orig. pub. as *La religion grecque.* Paris 1989)

Brun, P. (1989) 'L'île de Kéos et ses cités au IVe siècle av. JC', *ZPE* 76: 121–38

Brunt, P. A. (1969) 'Euboea in the time of Philip II', *CQ* ns 19: 245–65

    (1993) 'Athenian settlements abroad in the fifth century BC' in his *Studies in Greek History and Thought*. Oxford: 112–36. (Orig. pub. in E. Badian ed. (1966) *Ancient Society and Institutions. Studies presented to Victor Ehrenberg*. Oxford: 71–92.)

Buck, C. D. (1913) 'The interstate use of the Greek dialects', *CPh* 8: 133–59

Buckler, J. (1980) *The Theban Hegemony, 371–362 BC*. Cambridge, Ma. and London

    (1989) *Philip II and the Sacred War, Mnemosyne* Supplement 109. Leiden

Bull, H. (1966a) 'International theory: the case for a classical approach', *World Politics* 18: 361–77 (repr. in K. Knorr & J. Rosenau (edd.) *Contending Approaches to International Politics*. Princeton 1969: 20–38; and in A. Linklater (ed.) *International Relations. Critical concepts in political science*. London and New York 2000, vol. II: 363–76)

    (1966b) 'Society and anarchy in International Relations', in H. Butterfield & M. Wight (edd.) *Diplomatic Investigations. Essays in the theory of International Politics*. London: 35–50 (repr. in J. Der Derian (ed.) *International Theory. Critical Investigations*. Basingstoke and London 1995: 75–93; in K. Alderson & A. Hurrell (edd.) *Hedley Bull on International Society*. Basingstoke, London, New York 2000: 77–94; and in A. Linklater (ed.) *International Relations. Critical concepts in political science*. London and New York 2000, vol. II: 601–14)

    (1972a) 'International Relations as an academic pursuit', *Australian Outlook* 26: 251–65 (repr. in K. Alderson & A. Hurrell (edd.) *Hedley Bull on International Society*. Basingstoke, London, New York 2000: 246–64)

    (1972b) 'The theory of international politics, 1919–1969', in B. Porter (ed.) *The Aberystwyth Papers. International Relations 1919–1969*. London: 30–55 (repr. in A. Linklater (ed.) *International Relations. Critical concepts in political science*. London and New York 2000, vol. I: 55–76)

    (1984) *Justice in International Relations*. Waterloo, Ontario (Hagey Lectures 1983) (repr. in K. Alderson & A. Hurrell (edd.) *Hedley Bull on International Society*. Basingstoke, London, New York 2000: 206–45)

    (1991) 'Martin Wight and the theory of International Relations', in G. Wight & B. Porter (edd.) *International Theory. The three traditions*. Leicester: ix–xxiii

    (1995) *The Anarchical Society. A study of order in world politics*, 2nd edn. Basingstoke, London, New York (1st edn London and New York 1977)

Bull, H. & C. Holbraad (1979) 'Introduction', in *eid.* (edd.) *Power Politics*. Harmondsworth: 9–22

Burg, S. L. (1999) *The War in Bosnia-Herzegovina. Ethnic conflict and international intervention*. Armonk and London

Bury, J. B. (1900) *A History of Greece to the Death of Alexander the Great*. London

Busolt, G. & H. Swoboda (1926) *Griechische Staatskunde*, vol. II, pt 2: *Darstellung einzelner Staaten und der zwischenstaatlichen Beziehungen*. Munich

Buzan, B. (2000) 'The theory and practice of power in International Relations: past and future', in J. V. Ciprut (ed.) *The Art of the Feud. Reconceptualizing International Relations*. Westport and London: 47–66

    (2001) 'The English School: a bibliography', [Online] Available: http://www.leeds.ac.uk/polis/englishschool/bibliography.htm (Accessed 21 January 2006)

Buzan, B. & R. J. Barry Jones (edd.) (1981) *Change and the Study of International Relations: the Evaded Dimension*. London and New York

Buzan, B. & R. Little (1994) 'The idea of 'International System': theory meets history', *International Political Science Review* 15: 231–55 (repr. in A. Linklater (ed.) *International Relations. Critical concepts in political science*. London and New York 2000, vol. IV: 1274–303)

    (2000) *International Systems in World History. Remaking the study of International Relations*. Oxford

    (2001) 'Why International Relations has failed as an intellectual project and what to do about it', *Millennium* 30: 19–39

Byers, M. & S. Chesterman (2000) '"You, the people": pro-democratic intervention in international law', in G. H. Fox & B. R. Roth (edd.) *Democratic Governance and International Law*. Cambridge: 259–92

Calder III, W. M. (1989) 'Ulrich von Wilamowitz-Moellendorff to Sir Alfred Zimmern on the reality of classical Athens', *Philologus* 133: 303–9

Canfora, L. (1970) *Tucidide Continuato*. Padua

Carey, C. (1996) '*Nomos* in Attic rhetoric and oratory', *JHS* 116: 33–46

Cargill, J. (1981) *The Second Athenian League. Empire or free alliance?* Berkeley, Los Angeles, London

    (1982) 'Hegemony, not empire: the Second Athenian League', *AncW* 5: 91–102

    (1995) *Athenian Settlements of the Fourth Century BC*. Leiden

Carlier, P. (1996) 'A propos du Chéronée', in *id*. (ed.) *Le IVe siècle av. J.-C. Approches historiographiques*. Nancy and Paris: 111–20

Carr, E. H. (1946) *The Twenty Years' Crisis, 1919–1939. An introduction to the study of International Relations*, 2nd edn. London (1st edn 1939)

Cartledge, P. A. (1980) Review of Panagopoulos 1978, *CR* ns 30: 296–7

    (1987) *Agesilaos and the Crisis of Sparta*. London and Baltimore

    (1995) '"We are all Greeks?" Ancient (especially Herodotean) and modern contestations of Hellenism', *BICS* ns 2: 75–82

    (1997) *The Greeks. A Portrait of self and others*, rev. edn. Oxford (1st edn 1993)

    (2000a) 'Boiotian swine f(or)ever? The Boiotian superstate, 395 BC', in P. Flensted-Jensen, T. Heine Nielsen & L. Rubinstein (edd.) *Polis and Politics. Studies in Ancient Greek History presented to Mogens Herman Hansen on his sixtieth birthday, August 20, 2000*. Copenhagen: 397–418

(2000b) 'Greek political thought: the historical context', in C. Rowe & M. Schofield (edd.) *The Cambridge History of Greek and Roman Political Thought*. Cambridge: 11–22

(2001a) 'The effects of the Peloponnesian (Athenian) war on Athenian and Spartan societies', in D. R. McCann & B. S. Strauss (edd.) *War and Democracy. A comparative study of the Korean War and the Peloponnesian War*. Armonk and London: 104–23

(2001b) 'Rebels and *Sambos* in classical Greece: a comparative view', in *Spartan Reflections*. London: 127–52 (orig. pub. in P. A. Cartledge & F. D. Harvey (edd.) *Crux. Essays in Greek History presented to G. E. M. de Ste. Croix on his 75th birthday*. London and Exeter 1985: 16–46)

Cartledge, P. A., P. C. Millett & S. C. Todd (edd.) (1990) *Nomos. Essays in Athenian law, politics and society*. Cambridge

Cartledge, P. A., P. C. Millett & S. von Reden (edd.) (1998) *Kosmos. Essays in order, conflict and community in Classical Athens*. Cambridge

Casson, L. (1995) *Ships and Seamanship in the Ancient World*, 3rd edn. Baltimore and London (1st edn Princeton 1971)

Cataldi, S. (1983) *Symbolai e Relazione tra le Città Greche nel V. Secolo a.C.* Pisa

Cawkwell, G. L. (1973) 'The foundation of the Second Athenian Confederacy', *CQ* ns 23: 47–60

(ed.) (1979) *Xenophon. A History of My Times*. Harmondsworth

(1981) 'Notes on the failure of the Second Athenian Confederacy', *JHS* 101: 40–55

Cecil, Lord (1936) 'The League of Nations Union and Gilbert Murray', in J. A. K. Thomson & A. J. Toynbee (edd.) *Essays in Honour of Gilbert Murray*. London: 79–94

Chambers, J. T. (1973) 'Studies on the fourth-century Athenians' view of their past', PhD Illinois

Chambers, M. (1968/9) 'Studies on Thucydides, 1963–1967', *CW* 62: 245–54

Chatterjee, D. K. & D. E. Scheid (edd.) (2003) *Ethics and Foreign Intervention*. Cambridge

Chesterman, S. (2001) *Just War or Just Peace. Humanitarian intervention and international law*. Oxford

Chittick, W. O. & A. Freyberg-Inan (2001) '"Chiefly for fear, next for honour, and lastly for profit": an analysis of foreign policy motivation in the Peloponnesian War', *Review of International Studies* 27: 69–90

Cloché, P. (1934) *La Politique Étrangère d'Athènes, de 404 à 338 avant Jésus-Christ*. Paris

(1963) *Isocrate et son Temps*. Paris

Cochran, M. (1995) 'Postmodernism, ethics and International Political Theory', *Review of International Studies* 21: 237–50

Cohen, D. (1956) '*IG* I² 86 and Thucydides v. 47', *Mnemosyne* 9, 289–95.

Cohen, D. (1993) 'Law, autonomy and political community in Plato's *Laws*', *CPh* 88: 301–17

(1995) *Law, Violence and Community in Classical Athens*. Cambridge and New York

Cohen, E. E. (2000) *The Athenian Nation*. Princeton

Cohen, M. (1984) 'Moral skepticism and International Relations', *Philosophy & Public Affairs* 13: 299–346 (repr. in C. R. Beitz, M. Cohen, T. Scanlon & A. J. Simmons (edd.) *International Ethics*. Princeton 1985: 3–50)

Cole, S. G. (1996) 'Oath ritual and the male community at Athens', in J. Ober & C. Hedrick (edd.) *Demokratia. A conversation on democracies, ancient and modern*. Princeton: 227–48

Constantineau, P. (1998) *La Doctrine Classique de la Politique Étrangère. (Thucydide, Xenophon, Isocrate, Platon et Aristote)*. Paris and Montréal

Cramb, J. A. (1915) *The Origins and Destiny of Imperial Britain*. London (rev. edn of *Reflections on the Origins and Destiny of Imperial Britain*. London and New York 1900)

Crane, G. (1996) *The Blinded Eye. Thucydides and the new written word*. Lanham

(1998) *Thucydides and the Ancient Simplicity. The limits of political realism*. Berkeley

(2001) 'The case of Plataea: small states and the (re-)invention of political realism', in D. R. McCann & B. S. Strauss (edd.) *War and Democracy. A comparative study of the Korean War and the Peloponnesian War*. Armonk and London: 127–60

Crawford, R. M. A. (2000) *Idealism and Realism in International Relations. Beyond the discipline*. London and New York

Cromer, Earl of (1910) *Ancient and Modern Imperialism*. London

Culasso Gastaldi, E. (ed. and tr.) (1984) *Sul Trattato con Alessandro. Polis, monarchia macedone e memoria demostenica*. Padua

Curty, O. (1994) 'La notion de la parenté entre les cités chez Thucydide', *MH* 51: 193–7

(1995) *Les Parentés Légendaires entre Cités Grecques. Catalogue raisonné des inscriptions contenant le terme syngeneia et analyse critique*. Geneva

Daskalakes, A. V. (1965) *The Hellenism of the Ancient Macedonians*. Thessaloniki

Daux, G. (1953) 'Serments amphictioniques et serment de Platées', in G. E. Mylonas & D. Raymond (edd.) *Studies Presented to David Moore Robinson on his Seventieth Birthday*, vol. II. St Louis: 775–82

Davidson, J. (1990) 'Isocrates against imperialism. An analysis of *de Pace*', *Historia* 39: 20–36

Davies, J. K. (1994) 'On the non-usability of the concept of "sovereignty" in an ancient Greek context', in L. A. Foresti, A. Barzanò, C. Bearzot, L. Prandi & G. Zecchini (edd.) *Federazioni e Federalismo nell'Europa antica*. Milan: 51–65

(1995) 'The fourth century crisis: what crisis?', in W. Eder (ed.) *Die athen-ische Demokratie im 4. Jahrhundert v. Chr. Vollendung oder Verfall einer Verfassungsform?* Stuttgart: 29–36

(1996) 'Documents and "documents" in fourth-century historiography', in P. Carlier (ed.) *Le IVe siècle av. J.-C. Approches historiographiques.* Nancy and Paris: 29–39

(2000) 'A wholly non-Aristotelian universe: the Molossians as ethnos, state, and monarchy', in R. Brock & S. Hodkinson (edd.) *Alternatives to Athens. Varieties of political organization and community in ancient Greece.* Oxford and New York: 234–58

Dawson, D. (1996) *The Origins of Western Warfare. Militarism and morality in the ancient world.* Boulder and Oxford

Den Boer, W. (1979) *Private Morality in Greece and Rome. Some historical aspects, Mnemosyne* Supplement 57. Leiden

Denemark, R. A. (1999) 'World system history: from traditional international politics to the study of global relations', *International Studies Review* 1: 43–75

Denyer, N. C. (1983) 'The origins of justice', in *Syzetesis: studi sull' epicureismo greco e romano offerti a M. Gigante*, vol. I. Naples: 133–52

Der Derian, J. (1989) 'The boundaries of knowledge and power in International Relations', in J. Der Derian & M. Shapiro (edd.) *International/Intertextual Relations. Postmodern readings of world politics.* Lexington and Toronto: 3–10

(1995a) 'Introduction: critical investigations', in *id.* (ed.) *International Theory. Critical Investigations.* Basingstoke and London: 1–11

(1995b) 'A reinterpretation of realism: genealogy, semiology, dromology', in *id.* (ed.) *International Theory. Critical Investigations.* Basingstoke and London: 363–96 (repr. in F. A. Beer & R. Hariman (edd.) *Post-Realism. The rhetorical turn in International Relations.* East Lansing 1996: 277–304)

(1997) 'Post-Theory: the eternal return of ethics in International Relations', in M. W. Doyle & G. J. Ikenberry (edd.) *New Thinking in International Relations Theory.* Boulder and Oxford: 54–76

Diller, A. (1937) *Race Mixture among the Greeks before Alexander.* Urbana

Dillery, J. (1993) 'Xenophon's *Poroi* and Athenian imperialism', *Historia* 42: 1–11

(1995) *Xenophon and the History of his Times.* London and New York

Dindorf, L. (ed.) (1870), *Xenophontis* Historia Graeca, 3rd edn. Leipzig (1st edn Oxford 1831)

Dobbs Jr, A. E. (1907) *Philosophy and Popular Morals in Ancient Greece. An examination of popular morality and philosophical ethics, in their interre-lations and reciprocal influence in ancient Greece, down to the close of the third century BC.* Dublin

Dobesch, G. (1968) *Der Panhellenische Gedanke im 4. Jh. v. Chr. und der 'Philip-pos' des Isokrates.* Vienna

Donnelly, J. (2000) *Realism and International Relations*. Cambridge

Dover, K. J. (1974) *Greek Popular Morality in the time of Plato and Aristotle*. Oxford

(1981) 'The language of classical Attic documentary inscriptions', *TPhS*: 1–14

(1983) 'The portrayal of moral evaluation in Greek poetry', *JHS* 103: 35–48

Dow, S. (1941) 'Studies in the Athenian Tribute Lists, III', *TAPhA* 72: 70–84

Doyle, M. (1990) 'Thucydidean Realism', *Review of International Studies* 16: 223–37

(1991) 'Thucydides: a Realist?', in B. S. Strauss & R. N. Lebow (edd.) *Hegemonic Rivalry: from Thucydides to the Nuclear Age*. Boulder and Oxford: 169–88 (repr. in W. Blanco & J. T. Roberts (edd. and tr.) *Thucydides* The Peloponnesian War. *A new translation, backgrounds and contexts, interpretations*. New York and London 1998: 489–501)

(1997) *Ways of War and Peace. Realism, liberalism, and socialism*. London and New York

Doyle, M. W. & G. J. Ikenberry (edd.) (1997) *New Thinking in International Relations Theory*. Boulder and Oxford

Dubois, L. (1996) *Inscriptions Grecques Dialectales d'Olbia du Pont*. Geneva

Dreher, M. (1995) *Hegemon und Symmachoi. Untersuchungen zum Zweiten Athenischen Seebund*. Berlin and New York

Ducrey, P. (1968) *Le Traitement des Prisonniers de Guerre dans la Grèce Antique. Des origines à la conquête romaine*. Paris

Due, B. (1989) *The Cyropaedia. Xenophon's aims and methods*. Århus

Dunn, J. (1994) 'The dilemma of humanitarian intervention: the executive power of the law of nature, after God', *Government and Opposition* 29: 248–61

Dunne, T. (1995) 'The social construction of international society', *European Journal of International Relations* 1: 367–89

(1998a) 'International Theory and the mirror of history', *European Journal of International Relations* 4: 347–62

(1998b) *Inventing International Society. A history of the English School*. Basingstoke, London, New York

Dušanić, S. (1979) 'Arkadika', *AM* 94: 97–135

(1994) 'Plato and the two maritime confederacies of Athens', in L. A. Foresti, A. Barzanò, C. Bearzot, L. Prandi & G. Zecchini (edd.) *Federazioni e Federalismo nell'Europa Antica*. Milan: 87–106

(1999) 'Isocrates, the Chian intellectuals, and the political context of the *Euthydemus*', *JHS* 119: 1–16

Dyer, H. C. (1997) *Moral Order/World Order. The role of normative theory in the study of international relations*. Basingstoke, London, New York

Eatough, G. (1971) 'The use of ὅσιος and kindred words in Thucydides', *AJPh* 92: 238–51

Egger, E. (1866) *Études Historiques sur les Traités Publics chez les Grecs et chez les Romains depuis les Temps les Plus Anciens jusqu'aux Premiers Siècles de l'Ère Chrétienne*, 2nd edn Paris (1st edn 1861)

Ehrenberg, V. (1947) 'Polypragmosyne. A study in Greek politics', *JHS* 67: 46–67

Elfstrom, G. (1983) 'On dilemmas of intervention', *Ethics* 93: 709–25

   (1998) *International Ethics. A reference handbook.* Santa Barbara, Denver, Oxford

Ellis, J. R. (1976) *Philip II and Macedonian Imperialism.* London

England, E. B. (ed. and tr.) (1921) *The* Laws *of Plato*, vol. I: *Books I–VI.* Manchester, London and New York

Epp, R. (1996) 'Martin Wight: international relations as a realm of persuasion', in F. A. Beer & R. Hariman (edd.) *Post-Realism. The rhetorical turn in International Relations.* East Lansing: 121–42

   (1998) 'The English School on the frontiers of international society: a hermeneutic recollection', in T. Dunne, M. Cox & K. Booth (edd.) *The 80 Years' Crisis. International Relations 1919–1999.* Cambridge: 47–63 (= *Review of International Studies* 24)

Evans, G. & M. Sahnoun (edd.) (2001) *The Responsibility to Protect. Report of the International Commission on Intervention and State Sovereignty.* Ottawa

Evans, R. J. (1997) *In Defence of History.* London

Everson, S. (1998) 'The incoherence of Thrasymachus', *OSAPh* 16: 99–131

Fairclough, N. (2000) *New Labour, New Language?* London and New York

Falkner, C. (1996) 'Sparta and the Elean War, ca. 401/400 BC: revenge or imperialism?', *Phoenix* 50: 17–25

Faraone, C. A. (1993) 'Molten wax, spilt wine and mutilated animals: sympathetic magic in Near Eastern and early Greek oath ceremonies', *JHS* 113: 60–80

   (1999) 'Curses and social control in the law courts of classical Athens', *Dike* 2: 99–121

Farrar, C. (1988) *The Origins of Democratic Thinking. The invention of politics in classical Athens.* Cambridge

Fauber, C. M. (1998) 'Was Kerkyra a member of the Second Athenian League?', *CQ* ns 48: 110–16

Ferguson, J. (1958) *Moral Values in the Ancient World.* London

Figueira, T. J. (1993) '*Autonomoi kata tas spondas* (Thucydides 1.67.2)', in *Excursions in Epichoric History. Aiginetan essays.* Lanham, Md: 255–92 (orig. pub. in *BICS* 37 (1990): 63–88)

   (1998) *The Power of Money. Coinage and politics in the Athenian Empire.* Philadelphia

Finley, J. H. (1967) *Three Essays on Thucydides.* Cambridge, Ma.

Finley, M. I. (1975a) 'The ancient Greeks and their nation', in *The Use and Abuse of History.* London: 120–33

   (1975b) 'The problem of the unity of Greek law', in *The Use and Abuse of History.* London: 134–52

   (1977) 'Thucydides the moralist', in *Aspects of Antiquity. Discoveries and controversies.* Harmondsworth: 48–59

(1978) 'The fifth-century Athenian empire: a balance sheet', in P. D. A. Garnsey & C. R. Whittaker (edd.) *Imperialism in the Ancient World*. Cambridge: 103–26

(1985a) 'Max Weber and the Greek city-state', in *Ancient History. Evidence and Models*. London: 88–103

(1985b) *Studies in Land and Credit in Ancient Athens, 500–200 BC. The horos inscriptions*, 2nd edn. New Brunswick and Oxford (1st edn New Brunswick 1951)

(1985c) 'War and empire', in *Ancient History. Evidence and models*. London: 67–87

Fischer, M. (1993) 'On context, facts, and norms: response to Hall and Kratochwil', *International Organization* 47: 493–500

Fisher, N. R. E. (1976) '*Hybris* and dishonour: I', *G&R* ns 23: 177–93

(1979) '*Hybris* and dishonour: II', *G&R* ns 26: 32–47

(1990) 'The law of *hubris* in Athens', in P. A. Cartledge, P. C. Millett & S. C. Todd (edd.) *Nomos. Essays in Athenian law, politics and society*. Cambridge: 123–38

(1992) *Hybris. A study in the values of honour and shame in Ancient Greece*. Warminster

(2000) '*Hybris*, revenge and *stasis* in the Greek city-states', in H. Van Wees (ed.) *War and Violence in Ancient Greece*. London: 83–123

Flower, M. A. (2000a) 'Alexander the Great and panhellenism', in A. B. Bosworth & E. J. Baynham (edd.) *Alexander the Great in Fact and Fiction*. Oxford and New York: 96–135

(2000b) 'From Simonides to Isocrates: the fifth-century origins of fourth-century panhellenism', *CA* 19: 65–101

Forde, S. (1992) 'Classical realism', in T. Nardin & D. R. Mapel (edd.) *Traditions of International Ethics*. Cambridge: 62–84

Foucart, P.-F. (1888) 'Décrets athéniens du IVme siècle', *BCH* 12: 153–79

(1898) 'Traité d'alliance de l'année 362', *RA* 33: 313–27

Frank, A. G. & B. Gills (edd.) (1993) *The World System. 500 years or 5000?* London

Freeden, M. (1996) *Ideologies and Political Theory. A conceptual approach*. Oxford

Frost, M. (1996) *Ethics in International Relations. A constitutive theory*. Cambridge (rev. edn of *Towards a Normative Theory of International Relations*. Cambridge 1986)

(1998) 'A turn not taken. Ethics in International Relations at the Millennium', in T. Dunne, M. Cox & K. Booth (edd.) *The 80 Years' Crisis. International Relations 1919–1999*. Cambridge: 119–32 (= *Review of International Studies* 24)

Fuks, A. (1984) 'Patterns and types of social-economic revolution in Greece from the fourth to the second century BC', in *Social Conflict in Ancient Greece*.

Jerusalem and Leiden: 9–39 [orig. pub. in *Proceedings of the Israel Academy of Sciences and Humanities* 5 (1973) 51–81]

Funke, P. (1980) *Homónoia und Arché. Athen und die Griechische Staatenwelt vom Ende des Peloponnesischen Krieges bis zum Königsfrieden (404/3–387/6 v. Chr.)*, *Historia* Einzelschriften 37. Wiesbaden

Gabrielsen, V. (2000) 'The synoikised *polis* of Rhodes', in P. Flensted-Jensen, T. Heine Nielsen & L. Rubinstein (edd.) *Polis and Politics. Studies in Ancient Greek History presented to Mogens Herman Hansen on his sixtieth birthday, August 20, 2000*. Copenhagen: 177–205

Gaddis, J. L. (1992/3) 'International Relations theory and the end of the Cold War', *International Security* 17: 5–58 (repr. in A. Linklater (ed.) *International Relations. Critical concepts in political science*. London and New York 2000, vol. II: 440–98)

Gager, J. G. (1992) *Curse Tablets and Binding Spells from the Ancient World.* New York and Oxford

Garner, R. (1987) *Law and Society in Classical Athens.* London and Sydney

Garnsey, P. D. A. (1996) *Ideas of Slavery from Aristotle to Augustine.* Cambridge

Garst, D. (1989) 'Thucydides and neo-realism', *International Studies Quarterly* 33: 3–27

Gauthier, D. P. (ed.) (1970) *Morality and Rational Self-Interest.* Englewood Cliffs

Gauthier, P. (1972) *Symbola. Les étrangers et la justice dans les cités grecques.* Nancy

Gawantka, W. (1975) *Isopolitie. Ein Beitrag zur Geschichte der zwischenstaatlichen Beziehungen in der griechischen Antike.* Munich

Gehrke, H. J. (1985) *Stasis. Untersuchungen zu den inneren Kriegen in den griechischen Staaten des 5. und 4. Jahrhunderts v. Chr.* Munich

George, J. (1996) 'Understanding International Relations after the Cold War: probing beyond the Realist legacy', in M. J. Shapiro & H. R. Alker (edd.) *Challenging Boundaries. Global flows, territorial identities*. Minneapolis and London: 33–79

Gill, C. (1995) *Greek Thought, Greece and Rome*, New Surveys in the Classics 25. Oxford

    (1998) 'Altruism or reciprocity in Greek ethical philosophy', in C. Gill, N. Postlethwaite & R. Seaford (edd.) *Reciprocity in Ancient Greece*. Oxford: 303–28

Gill, C., N. Postlethwaite & R. Seaford (edd.) (1998) *Reciprocity in Ancient Greece*. Oxford

Gillis, D. (1970) 'The structure of arguments in Isocrates' *De Pace*', *Philologus* 114: 195–210

Gilpin, R. (1986) 'The richness of the tradition of political realism', in R. Keohane (ed.) *Neorealism and its Critics*. New York: 301–21

    (1988) 'The theory of hegemonic war', *Journal of Interdisciplinary History* 18: 591–606 (repr. in W. Blanco & J. T. Roberts (edd. & tr.), *Thucydides The*

Peloponnesian War. A new translation, backgrounds and contexts, interpretations. New York and London 1998: 479–89)

Glotz, G. (1915) 'Le droit des gens dans l'antiquité grecque', *Mémoires Présentés pars Divers Savants à l'Académie des Inscriptions et Belles-Lettres* 13: 91–103

Goertz, G. (1994) *Contexts of International Politics*. Cambridge and New York

Golden, M. (1998) *Sport and Society in Ancient Greece*. Cambridge

(2000) 'Epilogue: some trends in recent work on Athenian law and society', in V. J. Hunter & J. C. Edmondson (edd.) *Law and Social Status in Classical Athens*. Oxford and New York: 175–85

Goldstein, J. S. & J. R. Freeman (1990) *Three-Way Street. Strategic reciprocity in World Politics*. Chicago

Gomme, A. W. (1937) 'The greatest war in Greek History', in *Essays in Greek History and Literature*. Oxford: 116–24

Graham, A. J. (1983) *Colony and Mother City in Ancient Greece*, 2nd edn. Chicago (1st edn Manchester 1964)

Graham, G. (1997) *Ethics and International Relations*. Oxford

Grant, J. R. (1965) 'A note on the tone of Greek diplomacy', *CQ* ns 15: 261–6

Green, P. (1996) 'The metamorphosis of the barbarian. Athenian panhellenism in a changing world', in R. W. Wallace & E. M. Harris (edd.) *Transitions to Empire. Essays in Greco-Roman history, 360–146 BC, in honor of E. Badian*. Norman and London: 5–36

(1999) 'War and morality in fifth-century Athens: the case of Euripides' *Trojan Women*', *AHB* 13: 97–110

Grieser-Schmitz, D. (1999) *Die Seebundpolitik Athens in der Publizistik des Isokrates. Eine quellenkritische Untersuchung vor dem Hintergrund realer historischer Prozesse*. Bonn

Griffith, G. T. (1978) 'Athens in the fourth century', in P. D. A. Garnsey & C. R. Whittaker (edd.) *Imperialism in the Ancient World*. Cambridge: 127–44

Griffiths, M. (1999) *Fifty Key Thinkers in International Relations*. London and New York

Grote, G. (1888) *A History of Greece*, 5th edn, 10 vols. London (1st edn, 12 vols., 1846–56)

Gschnitzer, F. (1958) *Abhängige Orte im Griechischen Altertum*. Munich (1973) 'Proxenos', *RE* Supplement 13: 629–730

Gustafson, L. S. (ed.) (2000) *Thucydides' Theory of International Relations. A lasting possession*. Baton Rouge

Guthrie, W. K. C. (1971) *The Sophists*. Cambridge

Guzzini, S. (1998) *Realism in International Relations and International Political Economy. The continuing story of a death foretold*. London and New York

Habicht, C. (1961) 'Falsche Urkunden zur Geschichte Athens im Zeitalter der Perserkriege', *Hermes* 89: 1–35

Hack, H. M. (1978) 'Thebes and the Spartan hegemony 386–382 BC', *AJPh* 99: 210–27

Hall, E. (1989) *Inventing the Barbarian. Greek self-definition through tragedy.* Oxford

Hall, J. M. (1997) *Ethnic Identity in Greek Antiquity.* Cambridge
  (2002) *Hellenicity. Between ethnicity and culture.* Chicago and London

Hall, R. B. & F. W. Kratochwil (1993) 'Medieval tales: neorealist "science" and the abuse of history', *International Organization* 47: 479–91

Halliwell, S. (1994) 'Popular morality, philosophical ethics, and the *Rhetoric*', in D. J. Furley & A. Nehamas (edd.) *Aristotle's* Rhetoric. *Philosophical essays.* Princeton: 211–30

Hamel, D. (1995) '*Strategoi* on the *bema.* The separation of political and military authority in fourth-century Athens', *AHB* 9: 25–39
  (1998) *Athenian Generals. Military authority in the classical period.* Boston and Leiden

Hamilton, C. D. (1979) *Sparta's Bitter Victories. Politics and diplomacy in the Corinthian War.* Ithaca
  (1980) 'Isocrates, *IG* ii² 43, Greek propaganda and imperialism', *Traditio* 36: 83–109

Hammond, N. G. L. (1972) *A History of Macedonia*, vol. I: *Historical Geography and Prehistory.* Oxford
  (1989) *The Macedonian State. Origins, institutions and history.* Oxford
  (1991) 'The sources of Justin on Macedonia to the death of Philip', *CQ* ns 41: 496–508
  (1994) *Philip of Macedon.* London
  (1997) 'What may Philip have learnt as a hostage at Thebes?', *GRBS* 38: 355–72

Hampl, F. (1938) *Die griechische Staatsverträge des 4. Jhdts. v. Christi Geb.* Leipzig

Hansen, M. H. (1975) *Eisangelia. The sovereignty of the people's court in Athens in the fourth century* BC *and the impeachment of generals and politicians.* Odense
  (1983a) '*Demos, Ecclesia* and *Dicasterion* in Classical Athens', in *The Athenian Ecclesia. A collection of articles 1976–83.* Copenhagen: 139–60 (orig. pub. in *GRBS* 19 (1978) 127–46)
  (1983b) 'Did the Athenian *Ecclesia* legislate after 403/2?', in *The Athenian Ecclesia. A collection of articles 1976–83.* Copenhagen: 179–206 (orig. pub. in *GRBS* 20 (1979): 27–53)
  (1983c) '*Nomos* and *psephisma* in fourth-century Athens', in *The Athenian Ecclesia. A collection of articles 1976–83.* Copenhagen: 161–77 (orig. pub. in *GRBS* 19 (1978): 315–30)
  (1995) 'The "autonomous city-state". Ancient fact or modern fiction?', in M. H. Hansen & K. A. Raaflaub (edd.) *Studies in the Ancient Greek Polis, Historia* Einzelschriften 95; CPC Papers 2. Stuttgart: 21–43
  (1996) 'Were the Boiotian *Poleis* deprived of their *autonomia* during the First and Second Boiotian Federations? A reply', in M. H. Hansen &

K. A. Raaflaub (edd.) *More Studies in the Ancient Greek Polis, Historia Einzelschriften* 108; CPC Papers 3. Stuttgart: 127–36

(1998) *Polis and City State. An ancient concept and its modern equivalent.* Copenhagen

Hansen, M. H & T. H. Nielsen (edd.) (2004) *An Inventory of Archaic and Classical Greek Poleis.* Oxford

Harbour, F. W. (1999) *Thinking About International Ethics. Moral theory and cases from American foreign policy.* Boulder and Oxford

Harding, P. (1973) 'The purpose of Isokrates' *Archidamos* and *On the Peace*', *CSCA* 6: 137–49

(1976) 'Androtion's political career', *Historia* 25: 186–200

(1981) 'In search of a polypragmatist', in G. S. Shrimpton & D. J. McCargar (edd.) *Classical Contributions. Studies in honour of Malcolm Francis McGregor.* Locust Valley: 41–50

(ed. & tr.) (1994) *Androtion and the* Atthis. *The fragments.* Oxford

(1995) 'Athenian foreign policy in the fourth century', *Klio* 77: 105–25

Harris, D. (1995) *The Treasures of the Parthenon and Erechtheion.* Oxford

Harris, E. M. (1995) *Aeschines and Athenian Politics.* New York and Oxford

Hartog, F. (1996) *Mémoire d'Ulysse. Récits sur la frontière en Grèce ancienne.* Paris

Heath, M. (1990) 'Justice in Thucydides' Athenian speeches', *Historia* 39: 385–400

Heatley, D. P. (1919) *Diplomacy and the Study of International Relations.* Oxford

Hedrick, C. W. (1999) 'Democracy and the Athenian epigraphical habit', *Hesperia* 68: 387–439

Henry, A. S. (1983) *Honours and Privileges in Athenian Decrees. The principal formulae of Athenian honorary decrees.* Hildesheim, Zürich and New York

(1996) 'The hortatory intention in Athenian state decrees', *ZPE* 112: 105–19

Herbert, S. (1928) 'The Wilson Chair of International Politics', in I. Morgan (ed.) *The College by the Sea. A record and review.* Aberystwyth: 185–7

Herman, G. (1987) *Ritualised Friendship and the Greek City.* Cambridge

(1990) 'Treaties and alliances in the world of Thucydides', *PCPhS* 36: 83–102

(1993) 'Tribal and civic codes of behaviour in Lysias 1', *CQ* ns 43: 406–19

(1994) 'How violent was Athenian society?', in R. G. Osborne & S. Hornblower (edd.) *Ritual, Finance, Politics. Athenian democratic accounts presented to David Lewis.* Oxford: 99–117

(1995) 'Honour, revenge and the state in fourth-century Athens', in W. Eder (ed.) *Die athenische Demokratie im 4. Jahrhundert v. Chr. Vollendung oder Verfall einer Verfassungsform?* Stuttgart: 43–60

(1996) 'Ancient Athens and the values of Mediterranean society', *Mediterranean Historical Review* 11: 5–36

(1998) 'Reciprocity, altruism and the Prisoner's Dilemma: the special case of Classical Athens', in C. Gill, N. Postlethwaite & R. Seaford (edd.) *Reciprocity in Ancient Greece.* Oxford: 199–225

(2000) 'Athenian beliefs about revenge: problems and methods', *PCPhS* ns 46: 7–27

Hershey, A. S. (1911) 'The history of international relations during Antiquity and the Middle Ages', *American Journal of International Law* 5: 901–33

Hesk, J. P. (2000) *Deception and Democracy in Classical Athens*. Cambridge

Heskel, J. (1997) *The North Aegean Wars, 371–360 BC*, *Historia* Einzelschriften 102. Stuttgart

Heuß, A. (1934) 'Abschluß und Beurkundung des griechischen und römischen Staatsvertrages', *Klio* 27: 14–53, 218–57

Highby, L. I. (1936) *The Erythrae Decree. Contributions to the early history of the Delian League and the Peloponnesian Confederacy*, *Klio* Beiheft 36. Leipzig

Hill, C. (1985) 'History and International Relations', in S. Smith (ed.) *International Relations. British and American perspectives*. Oxford: 126–45

Hinsley, F. H. (1986) *Sovereignty*, 2nd edn. Cambridge (1st edn London 1966)

Hobbes, T. (1996 (1651)) *Leviathan*, rev. edn, ed. R. Tuck. Cambridge (orig. pub. London 1651)

Hobbs, A. (2000) *Plato and the Hero. Courage, manliness and the impersonal good*. Cambridge

Hobson, J. M. (2000) *The State and International Relations*. Cambridge

Hodge, A. T. (1960) *The Woodwork of Greek Roofs*. Cambridge

Hodkinson, H. & S. Hodkinson (1981) 'Mantineia and the Mantinike. Settlement and society in a Greek polis', *ABSA* 76: 239–96

Hodkinson, S. (2000) *Property and Wealth in Classical Sparta*. London

Hölkeskamp, K. J. (1992) 'Written law in archaic Greece', *PCPhS* 38: 87–117

Hoffman, M. (1993) 'Agency, identity and intervention', in I. Forbes & M. Hoffman (edd.) *Political Theory, International Relations and the Ethics of Intervention*. Basingstoke, London, New York: 194–211

Hoffman, S. (1977) 'An American social science: international relations', *Daedalus* 106.3: 41–60 (repr. in J. Der Derian (ed.) *International Theory. Critical investigations*. Basingstoke and London 1995: 212–41; and in A. Linklater (ed.) *International Relations. Critical concepts in political science*. London and New York 2000, vol. I: 77–98)

(1984) 'The problem of intervention', in H. Bull (ed.) *Intervention in World Politics*. Oxford and New York: 7–28

Hollis, M. & S. Smith (1990) *Explaining and Understanding International Relations*. Oxford

Holsti, K. A. J. (1985) *The Dividing Discipline. Hegemony and diversity in International Theory*. London and Sydney

(1995) *International Politics. A framework for analysis*, 7th edn. London and Englewood Cliffs (1st edn 1967)

Hornblower, S. (1982) *Mausolus*. Oxford

(1987) *Thucydides*. London

(1991) *A Commentary on Thucydides*, vol. I: *Books I–III*. Oxford

275

(1992a) 'The religious dimension to the Peloponnesian War, or, what Thucydides does not tell us', *HSPh* 94: 169–97

(1992b) 'Thucydides' use of Herodotus', in J. M. Sanders (ed.) *ΦΙΛΟΛΑΚΩΝ.
Laconian studies in honour of Hector Catling*. Athens: 141–54

(1994) 'Narratology and narrative techniques in Thucydides' in *id*. (ed.), *Greek
Historiography*. Oxford: 131–66

(1995) 'The fourth-century and Hellenistic reception of Thucydides', *JHS* 115:
47–68

(1996) *A Commentary on Thucydides*, vol. II: *Books IV–V.24*. Oxford

(2002) *The Greek World 479–323 B.C.*, 3rd edn. London

(2004) *Thucydides and Pindar. Historical narrative and the world of epinikian
poetry*. Oxford

Hosack, J. (1882) *On the Rise and Growth of the Law of Nations, as Established
by General Usage and by Treaties, from the Earliest Time to the Treaty of
Utrecht*. London

Howard, M. (1983) 'Ethics and power in international policy', in *The Causes of
Wars and Other Essays*, 2nd edn. Hounslow: 49–64 (1st edn 1983)

(1989) *War and the Liberal Conscience*, 2nd edn. Oxford (1st edn London
1978)

Hugill, W. M. (1936) *Panhellenism in Aristophanes*. Chicago

Hunter, V. J. (1994) *Policing Athens. Social control in the Attic lawsuits, 420–320
BC*. Princeton

Hussey, E. L. (1985) 'Thucydidean History and Democritean Theory', in P. A.
Cartledge & F. D. Harvey (edd.) *Crux. Essays in Greek History presented to G. E. M. de Ste. Croix on his 75th birthday*. London and Exeter:
118–38 (= *HPTh* 6)

Hutchings, K. (1999) *International Political Theory. Rethinking ethics in a global
era*. London, Thousand Oaks, New Delhi

Huysmans, J. (1997) 'James Der Derian: the unbearable lightness of theory', in
I. B. Neumanm & O. Wæver (edd.) *The Future of International Relations.
Masters in the making?* London and New York: 337–58

Ilari, V. (1980) *Guerra e Diritto nel Mondo Antico*, pt. 1: *Guerra e Diritto nel
Mondo Greco-Ellenistico fino al III Secolo*. Milan

Irwin, T. H. (1995a) *Plato's Ethics*. New York and Oxford

(1995b) 'Prudence and morality in Greek ethics', *Ethics* 105: 284–95

Jackson, R. (ed.) (1999) *Sovereignty at the Millennium*. Oxford (= *Political Studies* 47.3)

Jacobson, H. (1975) 'The oath of the Delian League', *Philologus* 119: 256–8

Jaeger, W. (1938) *Demosthenes. The origin and growth of his policy*. Cambridge,
Ma.

(1945) *Paideia. The ideals of Greek culture*, vol. III: *The Conflict of Cultural
Ideals in the Age of Plato*, tr. G. Highet. Oxford

Jahn, B. (1999) 'IR and the state of nature: the cultural origins of a ruling ideology',
Review of International Studies 25: 411–34

Janis, M. W. (1984) 'Jeremy Bentham and the fashioning of "International Law"', *American Journal of International Law* 78: 405–18

(ed.) (1991) *The Influence of Religion on the Development of International Law*. Dordrecht, Boston, London

Jansson, P. (1997) 'Identity-defining practices in Thucydides' *History of the Peloponnesian War*', *European Journal of International Relations* 3: 147–65

Jarvis, D. S. L. (2000) *International Relations and the Challenge of Postmodernism. Defending the discipline*. Columbia

Jeffery, L. H. (1990) *The Local Scripts of Archaic Greece. A study of the origin of the Greek alphabet and its development from the eighth to the fifth centuries BC*, rev. edn (with a supplement by A. W. Johnston). Oxford (1st edn 1961)

Jehne, M. (1994) *Koine Eirene. Untersuchungen zu den Befriedungs- und Stabilisierungsbemühungen in der griechischen Poliswelt des 4. Jhdt v. Chr.*, *Hermes* Einzelschriften 63. Stuttgart

Jørgensen, K. E. (2000) 'Continental IR theory: the best kept secret', *European Journal of International Relations* 6: 9–42

John, I., M. Wright & J. Garnett (1972) 'International Politics at Aberystwyth, 1919–1969', in B. Porter (ed.) *The Aberystwyth Papers. International Relations 1919–1969*. London: 86–102

Johnson, L. M. (1993) *Thucydides, Hobbes and the Interpretation of Realism*. DeKalb

Johnstone, S. (1999) *Disputes and Democracy. The consequences of litigation in ancient Athens*. Austin

Jokic, A. (ed.) (2003) *Humanitarian Intervention. Moral and philosophical issues*. Peterborough, Ont. and Ormskirk

Jolowicz, H. F. & B. Nicholas (1972) *Historical Introduction to the Study of Roman Law*, 3rd edn. Cambridge [1st edn 1932]

Jones, C. (1998) *E. H. Carr and International Relations. A duty to lie*. Cambridge

Jones, C. P. (1999) *Kinship Diplomacy in the Ancient World*. Cambridge, Ma. and London

Jones, R. E. (1981) 'The English School of International Relations. A case for closure', *Review of International Studies* 7: 1–13

Jordan, B. (1986) 'Religion in Thucydides', *TAPhA* 116: 119–47

Jüthner, J. (1923) *Hellenen und Barbaren. Aus der Geschichte des Nationalsbewußtseins*, Das Erbe der Altern 8. Leipzig

Kahler, M. (1997) 'Inventing International Relations: International Relations theory after 1945', in M. W. Doyle & G. J. Ikenberry (edd.) *New Thinking in International Relations Theory*. Boulder and Oxford: 20–53

Kahrstedt, U. (1942) 'Zwei Urkunden zur Geschichte von Argos und Kreta in der Pentakontaetia', *Klio* 43: 72–91

Kallet-Marx, L. (1993) *Money, Expense and Naval Power in Thucydides' History 1–5.24*. Berkeley

Kaplan, M. (1966) 'The new Great Debate: traditionalism vs. science in International Relations', *World Politics* 19: 1–20 (repr. in K. Knorr & J. Rosenau (edd.) *Contending Approaches to International Politics*. Princeton 1969: 39–61; and in A. Linklater (ed.) *International Relations. Critical concepts in political science*. London and New York 2000, vol. II: 377–93)

Kapparis, K. (1995) 'The Athenian decree for the naturalisation of the Plataeans', *GRBS* 36: 359–78

Karavites, P. (1980) '"Euergesia" in Herodotus and Thucydides as a factor in interstate relations', *RIDA* 3rd ser. 27: 69–79

    (1982a) '*Eleutheria* and *autonomia* in Greek interstate relations', *RIDA* 29: 145–62

    (1982b) *Capitulations and Greek Interstate Relations. The reflection of humanistic ideals in political events*, Hypomnemata 71. Göttingen

    (1984a) 'Greek interstate relations and moral principles in the fifth century BC', *PP* 26: 161–92

    (1984b) 'The political use of *eleutheria* and *autonomia* in the fourth century among the Greek city-states', *RIDA* 31: 167–91

    (1992) *Promise-Giving and Treaty-Making. Homer and the Near East*, *Mnemosyne* Supplement 119. Leiden, New York and Cologne

Keen, A. G. (1996) 'Were the Boiotian *poleis autonomoi*?', in M. H. Hansen & K. A. Raaflaub (edd.) *More Studies in the Ancient Greek Polis, Historia* Einzelschriften 108; CPC Papers 3. Stuttgart: 113–25

Kelly, D. H. (1970) 'What happened to the Athenians captured in Sicily?', *CR* ns 20: 127–31

Kennedy, G. (1958) 'Isocrates' *Encomium of Helen*. A panhellenic document', *TAPhA* 89: 77–83

    (1959) 'Focusing of arguments in Greek deliberative oratory', *TAPhA* 90: 131–8

Keohane, R. (ed.) (1986) *Neorealism and its Critics*. New York

Kerferd, G. B. (1981) *The Sophistic Movement*. Cambridge

Kiechle, F. (1969) 'Zur Humanität in der Kriegführung der griechischen Staaten', in F. Gschnitzer (ed.) *Zur Griechischen Staatskunde*, Wege der Forschung 96. Darmstadt: 528–77 (orig. pub. in *Historia* 7 (1958): 129–56)

Kleve, K. (1964) '*Apragmosyne* and *Polypragmosyne*: two slogans in Athenian politics', *SO* 39: 83–8

Knoepfler, D. (1984) 'Le décret de Hégésippe d'Athènes pour Érétrie', *MH* 41: 152–61

    (1995) 'Une paix de cent ans et un conflit en permanence: étude sur les relations diplomatiques avec Érétrie et les autres cités de l'Eubée au IVe siècle av. J. C.', in E. Frézouls & A. Jacquemin (edd.) *Les Relations Internationales. Actes du colloque de Strasbourg, 15–17 juin 1993*. Paris: 309–64

    (2001) *Eretria: Fouilles et recherches XI. Décrets érétriens de proxénie et de citoyenneté*. Lausanne

Knutsen, T. L. (1997) *A History of International Relations Theory*, 2nd edn. Manchester and New York (1st edn 1992)

Koehler, U. (1876) 'Über zwei athenische Vertragsurkunden', *AM* 1: 184–205

Koh, H. H. (1997) 'Why do nations obey international law?', *Yale Law Journal* 106: 2599–659

Kokaz, N. (2001) 'Moderating power: a Thucydidean perspective', *Review of International Studies* 27: 27–49

Konstan, D. (1997) *Friendship in the Classical World*. Cambridge
  (2000) 'Altruism', *TAPhA* 130: 1–17

Kratochwil, F. W. (1982) 'On the notion of "interest", in international relations', *International Organization* 36: 1–30
  (1983) 'Is international law "proper" law?', *Archiv für Rechts- und Sozialphilosophie* 69: 13–46
  (1984) 'Thrasymmachos revisited: on the relevance of norms and the study of law for International Relations', *Journal of International Affairs* 37: 343–56
  (1988) 'The Protagorean quest: community, justice and the "oughts" and "musts" of international politics', *International Journal* 43: 205–40
  (1989) *Rules, Norms and Decisions. On the conditions of practical and legal reasoning in international relations and domestic affairs*. Cambridge
  (1993) 'The embarrassment of changes: neo-realism as the science of Realpolitik without politics', *Review of International Studies* 19: 63–80

Kraut, R. (ed. and tr.) (1997) *Aristotle: Politics Books VII and VIII*. Oxford and New York

Krentz, P. (ed. and tr.) (1989) *Xenophon. Hellenika I–II.3.10*. Warminster
  (ed. and tr.) (1995) *Xenophon. Hellenika II.3.11–IV.2.8*. Warminster

Krippendorff, E. (1989) 'The dominance of American approaches in International Relations', in H. Dyer & L. Mangasarian (edd.) *The Study of International Relations. The state of the art*. Basingstoke and London: 28–39

Kunsemüller, O. (1935) *Die Herkunft der platonischen Kardinaltugenden*. Erlangen

Kyparissis, N. (1924/5) 'Αἱ ἀνασκαφαὶ τῶν Βασιλικῶν Στάβλων', *AD* 9: 68–72

Lambert, S. D. (2004) 'Athenian state laws and decrees 352/1–322/1. I. Decrees honouring Athenians', *ZPE* 150: 85–122

Lambrechts, A. (1958) *Tekst en Uitzicht van de Atheense Proxeniedecreten tot 323 v.C.* Brussels

Lane Fox, R. (1997) 'Demosthenes, Dionysius and the dating of six early speeches', *C&M* 48: 167–203

Larsen, J. A. O. (1944) 'Federation for peace in Ancient Greece', *CPh* 39: 145–62
  (1962) 'Freedom and its obstacles in ancient Greece', *CPh* 57: 230–4

Laurent, F. (1862) *Études sur l'Histoire de l'Humanité*, vol. II: *La Grèce*. Brussels and Leipzig (orig. pub. as *Histoire du droit des gens et des relations internationales*. Gand 1850)

Lawton, C. L. (1995) *Attic Document Reliefs. Art and politics in ancient Athens*. Oxford

Lebow, R. N. (1996) 'Play it again Pericles: agents, structures, and the Peloponnesian War', *European Journal of International Relations* 2: 231–58
  (2003) *The Tragic Vision of Politics. Ethics, interests and orders*. Cambridge

279

Lebow, R. N. & B. S. Strauss (edd.) (1991) *Hegemonic Rivalry. From Thucydides to the nuclear age*. Boulder and Oxford

Leech, H. B. (1877) *An Essay on Ancient International Law*. Dublin

(1883a) 'Ancient international law', *Contemporary Review* 43: 260–74

(1883b) 'Ancient international law. Part II', *Contemporary Review* 44: 890–904

Lefèvre, F. (1998) *L'Amphictionie Pyléo-Delphique. Histoire et institutions*. Paris

Legon, R. P. (1967) 'Phliasian politics and policy in the early fourth century BC', *Historia* 16: 324–37

Lehmann, G. A. (1978a) 'Spartas *Arche* und die Vorphase des Korinthischen Krieges in den Hellenica Oxyrhynchia', *ZPE* 28: 109–26

(1978b) 'Spartas *Arche* und die Vorphase des Korinthischen Krieges in den Hellenica Oxyrhynchia, II', *ZPE* 30: 73–93

Lendon, J. E. (2000) 'Homeric vengeance and the outbreak of Greek wars', in H. Van Wees (ed.) *War and Violence in Ancient Greece*. London: 1–30

Leng, R. J. (1993) *Interstate Crisis Behaviour, 1816–1980. Realism versus reciprocity*. Cambridge

Leopold, J. W. (1981) 'Demosthenes on distrust of tyrants', *GRBS* 22: 227–46

Lepard, B. D. (2002) *Rethinking Humanitarian Intervention. A fresh legal approach based on fundamental ethical principles in international law and world religions*. University Park, Pa.

Leppin, H. (1999) *Thukydides und die Verfassung der Polis. Ein Beitrag zur politischen Ideengeschichte des 5. Jahrhunderts v. Chr, Klio* Beihefte n.f. 1, Berlin

Lévy, E. (1983) 'Autonomia et éleuthéria au Ve siècle', *RPh* 57: 249–70

Lewis, D. M. (1997a) 'The Athenian Coinage Decree', in *Selected Papers in Greek and Near Eastern History*, ed. P. J. Rhodes. Cambridge: 116–30

(1997b) 'The Athens Peace of 371', in *Selected Papers in Greek and Near Eastern History*, ed. P. J. Rhodes. Cambridge: 29–31

(1997c) 'Democratic institutions and their diffusion', in *Selected Papers in Greek and Near Eastern History*, ed. P. J. Rhodes. Cambridge: 51–9

(1997d) 'The federal constitution of Keos', in *Selected Papers in Greek and Near Eastern History*, ed. P. J. Rhodes. Cambridge: 22–8 (orig. pub. in *ABSA* 57 (1962): 1–4)

Linklater, A. (1990) *Men and Citizens in the Theory of International Relations*, 2nd edn. London (1st edn 1982)

(1992) 'The question of the next stage in international relations theory: a critical-theoretical point of view', *Millennium* 21: 77–98 (repr. in *id*. (ed.) *International Relations. Critical concepts in political science*. London and New York 2000, vol. IV: 1633–54)

(1995) 'Neo-realism in theory and practice', in K. Booth & S. Smith (edd.) *International Relations Theory Today*. Cambridge and Oxford: 241–62

(1996) 'The achievements of critical theory', in S. Smith, K. Booth & M. Zalewski (edd.) *International Theory. Positivism and beyond*. Cambridge: 279–98

(2000) 'General introduction', in *id.* (ed.) *International Relations. Critical concepts in political science*, 5 vols. London and New York: 1–21

Lintott, A. (1982) *Violence, Civil Strife and Revolution in the Classical City, 750–330 BC*. London and Canberra

Little, R. (1993) 'Recent literature on intervention and non-intervention', in I. Forbes & M. Hoffman (edd.) *Political Theory, International Relations and the Ethics of Intervention*. Basingstoke, London, New York: 13–31

(1995) 'Neorealism and the English School: a methodological, ontological, and theoretical reassessment', *European Journal of International Relations* 1: 9–34

(2000) 'The English School's contribution to the study of international relations', *European Journal of International Relations* 6: 395–422

Livingstone, R. W. (ed.) (1921) *The Legacy of Greece*. Oxford

Lloyd, G. E. R. (1968) *Aristotle. The growth and structure of his thought*. Cambridge

Long, D. & P. Wilson (edd.) (1995) *Thinkers of the Twenty Years' Crisis: Inter-War Idealism Reassessed*. Oxford

Lonis, R. (1977) 'Les otages dans les relations internationales en Grèce antique. Insuffisances et ambiguïtés d'une garantie', in *Mélanges Offerts á Léopold Sédar Senghor. Langues – littérature – histoire anciennes*. Dakar: 215–34

(1980) 'La valeur du serment dans les accords internationaux en Grèce classique', *DHA* 6: 267–86

Loomis, W. T. (1992) *The Spartan War Fund. IG V 1, 1 and a new fragment, Historia* Einzelschrift 74. Stuttgart

Loraux, N. (1978) 'Mourir devant Troie, tomber pour Athènes – de la gloire de l'héros à l'idée de la cité', *Information sur les Sciences Sociales* 17: 801–17

(1986a) *The Invention of Athens. The funeral oration in the classical city*, tr. A. Sheridan. Cambridge, Ma. (orig. pub. as *L'Invention d'Athènes. Histoire de l'oraison funèbre dans la cité classique*. Paris 1981)

(1986b) 'Thucydide a écrit la Guerre du Péloponnèse', *Métis* 1: 139–61

Loriaux, M. (2000) 'Introduction. Law and moral action in International Relations thought', in C. Lynch & M. Loriaux (edd.) *Law and Moral Action in World Politics*. Minneapolis and London: xi–xxiii

Low, P. A. (2005) 'Looking for the language of Athenian imperialism', *JHS* 125: 93–111

Luard, D. E. T. (1976) *Types of International Society*. New York and London

Luccioni, J. (1961) *Démosthène et le Panhellénisme*. Paris

Lücke, S. (2000) *Syngeneia. Epigraphisch-historische Studien zu einem Phänomen der antiken griechischen Diplomatie*. Frankfurt am Main

Luppino, E. (1991) 'Agesilao re di Sparta: immagine e realtà', in M. Sordi (ed.) *L'Immagine dell' Uomo Politico. Vita publica e morale nell'antichità*. Milan: 89–107

Lyons, G. M. & M. Mastanduno (edd.) (1995) *Beyond Westphalia? State sovereignty and international intervention*. Baltimore and London

Ma, J. (2000) *Antiochus III and the Greek Cities of Western Asia Minor.* Oxford

MacDowell, D. M. (1976) '*Hybris* in Athens', *G&R* ns 23: 14–31

Mackay, D. J. (1880) *International Relations. Opening address (Edinburgh 1880).* London

Macleod, C. (1983a) 'Reason and necessity: Thucydides III.9–14, 37–48', in *Collected Essays*, ed. O. Taplin. Oxford: 88–102 (orig. pub. in *JHS* 98 (1978): 64–78)

  (1983b) 'Thucydides and tragedy', in *Collected Essays*, ed. O. Taplin. Oxford: 140–58

  (1983c) 'Thucydides' Plataean debate', in *Collected Essays*, ed. O. Taplin. Oxford: 103–22 (orig. pub. in *GRBS* 18 (1977): 227–46)

MacMullen, R. (1963) 'Foreign policy for the *polis*', *G&R* ns 10: 118–22

Magnetto, A. (1997) *Gli Arbitrati Interstatali Greci*, vol. II: *Dal 337 al 196 a.C.* Pisa

Maine, H. S. (1861) *Ancient Law. Its connection with the early history of society, and its relation to modern ideas.* London

Manning, C. A. W. (1962) *The Nature of International Society.* London

Mapel, D. R. & T. Nardin (edd.) (1998) *International Society. Diverse ethical perspectives.* Princeton

Marek, C. (1984) *Die Proxenie.* Frankfurt am Main, Bern, New York

Markwell, D. J. (1986) 'Sir Alfred Zimmern revisited: 50 years on', *Review of International Studies* 12: 279–92

  (2004) 'Zimmern, Sir Alfred Eckhard (1879–1957)', *Oxford Dictionary of National Biography* (Online) Available: http://www.oxforddnb.com/view/article/37088 (Accessed 21 January 2006)

Martin, A. (1886) *Quomodo Graeci ac Peculiariter Athenienses Foedera Publica Iure Iurando Sanxerint.* Paris

Martin, V. (1940) *La Vie Internationale dans la Grèce des Cités, VIe–IVe S. av. J.-C.* Paris

Masaracchia, A. (1995) *Isocrate. Retorica e politica.* Rome

Mathieu, G. (1925) *Les Idées Politiques d'Isocrate.* Paris

Mattingly, H. B. (1996a) 'The growth of Athenian imperialism', in *The Athenian Empire Restored.* Ann Arbor: 87–106 (orig. pub. in *Historia* 12 (1963): 257–73)

  (1996b) 'The language of Athenian imperialism', in *The Athenian Empire Restored.* Ann Arbor: 361–85 (orig. pub. in *Epigraphica* 36 (1974): 33–56)

  (1996c) 'The protected fund in the Athenian coinage decree (*ATL* D 14, par.7f)', in *The Athenian Empire Restored.* Ann Arbor: 347–51 (orig. pub. in *AJPh* 95 (1974): 280–5)

Mayall, J. (1990) *Nationalism and International Society.* Cambridge

  (ed.) (1996) *The New Interventionism 1991–1994. United Nations experience in Cambodia, Former Yugoslavia and Somalia.* Cambridge

McGlew, J. F. (1993) *Tyranny and Political Culture in Ancient Greece.* Ithaca and London

McKay, K. L. (1953) 'The Oxyrhynchus Historian and the outbreak of the "Corinthian War"', *CR* ns 3: 6–7

McMahan, J. (1986) 'The ethics of international intervention', in A. Ellis (ed.) *Ethics and International Relations*, Fulbright Papers 2. Manchester: 24–51

Meiggs, R. (1943) 'The growth of Athenian imperialism', *JHS* 63: 21–34

(1972) *The Athenian Empire*. Oxford

(1982) *Trees and Timber in the Ancient Mediterranean World*. Oxford

Meritt, B. D. (1970) 'Ransom of the Athenians by Epikerdes', *Hesperia* 39: 111–14

Meyer, M. (1989) *Die Griechische Urkundenreliefs*. Berlin

Michelini, A. N. (1998) 'Isocrates' civic invective: *Acharnians* and *On the Peace*', *TAPhA* 128: 115–33

Mill, J. S. (1984 (1859)) 'A few words on non-intervention', in J. M. Robson (ed.) *The Collected Works of John Stuart Mill*, vol. XXI: *Essays on Equality, Law and Education*. Toronto and London: 110–24 (orig. pub. in *Fraser's Magazine* 90 (1859): 766–76; this repr. from *Dissertations and Discussions* 3. London 1867: 153–78)

Miller, J. D. B. (1979/80) 'The commonwealth and world order: the Zimmern vision and after', *Journal of Imperial and Commonwealth History* 8: 159–74

Miller, J. D. B. & R. J. Vincent (edd.) (1990) *Order and Violence. Hedley Bull and International Relations*. Oxford

Millett, P. C. (1993) 'Warfare, economy and democracy in classical Athens', in J. Rich & G. Shipley (edd.) *War and Society in the Greek World*. London and New York: 177–96

(1998) 'Encounters in the Agora', in P. A. Cartledge, P. C. Millett & S. von Reden (edd.) *Kosmos. Essays in order, conflict and community in Classical Athens*. Cambridge: 203–28

Miltner, F. (1931) 'Seewesen', *RE* Supplement 5: 906–62

Missiou, A. (1987) 'Coercive diplomacy in Greek interstate relations', *CQ* ns 37: 336–45

(1992) *The Subversive Oratory of Andokides. Politics, ideology and decision-making in democratic Athens*. Cambridge

(1998) 'Reciprocal generosity in the foreign affairs of fifth-century Athens and Sparta', in C. Gill, N. Postlethwaite & R. Seaford (edd.) *Reciprocity in Ancient Greece*. Oxford: 181–97

Mitchell, L. G. (1997a) *Greeks Bearing Gifts. The public use of private relationships in the Greek World 435–323 BC*. Cambridge

(1997b) 'Φιλία, εὔνοια and Greek interstate relations', *Antichthon* 31: 28–44

Momigliano, A. (1936) 'Un momento di storia greca: la pace del 375 a.C. e il Plataico di Isocrate', *Athenaeum* ns 14: 3–35

(1966a) 'La κοινὴ εἰρήνη dal 386 al 338 a.C.', in *Terzo Contributo alla Storia degli Studi Classici e del Mondo Antico*. Rome: 393–419 (orig. pub. in *RFIC* ns 12 (1934): 482–514)

283

(1966b) 'George Grote and the study of Greek History (Inaugural Lecture, University College London, 1952)', in *Studies in Historiography*. London: 56–74

(1966c) 'Some observations on causes of war in ancient historiography', in *Studies in Historiography*. London: 112–26 (orig. pub. in *Acta Congressus Madvigiani Hafniae* 1 (1958): 199–211)

Monceaux, P. (1886) *Les Proxénies Grecques*. Paris

Monoson, S. S. & M. Loriaux (1998) 'The illusion of power and the disruption of moral norms: Thucydides' critique of Periclean policy', *American Political Science Review* 92: 285–97

Moore, J. (ed.) (1998) *Hard Choices. Moral dilemmas in humanitarian intervention*. Lanham and Oxford

Morgenthau, H. (1946) *Scientific Man versus Power Politics*. Chicago

(1985) *Politics Among Nations. The struggle for power and for peace*, 7th (brief) edn, ed. K. Thompson. New York (1st edn 1949)

Moritani, K. (1988) '*Koine Eirene*. Control, peace and *autonomia* in fourth-century Greece', in T. Yuge & M. Doi (edd.) *Forms of Control and Subordination in Antiquity*. Tokyo and Leiden: 573–7

Morpeth, N. (1993) 'Autarkeia: notes on its cultural and historical context', in C. Mackie & H. Tarrant (edd.) *Multarum Artium Scientia. A 'chose' for R. Godfrey Tanner, Prudentia* Supplement. Auckland: 126–30

Mosley, D. J. (1961) 'Who "signed" treaties in ancient Greece?', *PCPhS* ns 7: 59–63

(1973) *Envoys and Diplomacy in Ancient Greece, Historia* Einzelschriften 22. Wiesbaden

Mossé, C. (1973) *Athens in Decline, 404–86 BC*, tr. J. Stewart. London and Boston

Moysey, R. A. (1982) 'Isocrates *On the Peace*: rhetorical exercise or political advice?', *AJAH* 7: 118–27

Müllerson, R. (2000) *Ordering Anarchy. International law in international society*. The Hague, Boston, London

Murphy, A. J. (1996) 'The sovereign state system as a political-territorial ideal: historical and contemporary considerations', in T. J. Biersteker & C. Weber (edd.) *State Sovereignty as Social Construct*. Cambridge: 81–120

Murray, G. (1900) 'The exploitation of inferior races in ancient and modern times: an imperial labour question with a historical parallel', in F. W. Hirst, G. Murray & J. L. Hammond *Liberalism and the Empire*. London: 118–57

(1946) 'Theopompus or, the Cynic as historian (Gray Lecture 1928)', in *Greek Studies*. Oxford: 149–70

Murray, O. (1966) "Ὁ ἀρχαῖος δασμός', *Historia* 15: 142–56

(1990) 'The Solonian law of *hubris*', in P. A. Cartledge, P. C. Millett & S. C. Todd (edd.) *Nomos. Essays in Athenian law, politics and society*. Cambridge: 139–45

Nardin, T. (1983) *Law, Morality and the Relations of States*. Princeton

(1992) 'Ethical traditions in international affairs', in T. Nardin & D. R. Mapel (edd.) *Traditions of International Ethics*. Cambridge: 1–22

(1998) 'Legal positivism as a theory of international society', in D. R. Mapel & T. Nardin (edd.) *International Society. Diverse Ethical Perspectives*. Princeton: 17–35

Navari, C. (1993) 'Intervention, non-intervention and the construction of the state', in I. Forbes & M. Hoffman (edd.) *Political Theory, International Relations and the Ethics of Intervention*. Basingstoke, London, New York: 43–59

Nease, A. S. (1949) 'Garrisons in the Athenian Empire', *Phoenix* 3: 102–11

Neil, R. A. (ed.) (1901) *The* Knights *of Aristophanes*. Cambridge

Neufeld, M. A. (1995) *The Restructuring of International Relations Theory*. Cambridge

Neustadt, R. E. & E. R. May (1986) *Thinking in Time. The uses of history for decision-makers*. New York and London

Nicholson, M. (1981) 'The enigma of Martin Wight', *Review of International Studies* 7: 15–22

(2000) 'What's the use of International Relations?', *Review of International Studies* 26: 183–98

Nicholson, P. P. (1974) 'Unravelling Thrasymachus' arguments in "The Republic"', *Phronesis* 19: 210–32

Nielsen, T. H. (1997) 'Triphylia. An experiment in ethnic construction and political organisation', in *id.* (ed.) *Yet More Studies in the Ancient Greek Polis, Historia* Einzelschriften 117; CPC Papers 4. Stuttgart: 129–62

Nincic, M. & J. Lepgold (edd.) (2000) *Being Useful. Policy relevance and International Relations theory*. Ann Arbor

Nixon, L. & S. R. F. Price (1990) 'The sizes and resources of Greek cities', in O. Murray & S. R. F. Price (edd.) *The Greek City from Homer to Alexander*. Oxford: 137–70

Norlin, G. (ed. and tr.) (1929) *Isocrates*, vol. II. London and New York

North, H. (1947) 'A period of opposition to *sophrosyne* in Greek thought', *TAPhA* 73: 1–17

(1966) *Sophrosyne. Self knowledge and self-restraint in Greek literature*. Ithaca

Ober, J. (1978) 'Views of sea power in the fourth-century Attic orators', *AncW* 1: 119–30

(1989) *Mass and Elite in Democratic Athens. Rhetoric, ideology and the power of the people*. Princeton

(2001) 'Thucydides Theoretikos/Thucydides Histor: Realist theory and the challenge of history', in D. R. McCann & B. S. Strauss (edd.) *War and Democracy. A comparative study of the Korean War and the Peloponnesian War*. Armonk and London: 273–306

Ogilvie, R. M. (1964) *Latin and Greek. A history of the influence of the Classics on English life from 1600–1918*. London

Oliver, J. H. (1936) 'Inscriptions from Athens', *AJA* ns 40: 460–5

285

Olson, W. C. (1972) 'The growth of a discipline', in B. Porter (ed.) *The Aberystwyth Papers. International Relations 1919–1969*. London: 3–29

Olson, W. C. & N. G. Onuf (1985) 'The growth of a discipline: reviewed', in S. Smith (ed.) *International Relations. British and American perspectives.* Oxford: 1–28

Onuf, N. G. (1989) *World of Our Making. Rules and rule in social theory and international relations.* Columbia

Oppenheim, F. E. (1987) 'National interest, rationality and morality', *Political Theory* 15: 369–89

Orrieux, C. & P. Schmitt Pantel (1999) *A History of Ancient Greece*, tr. J. Lloyd. Malden & Oxford (orig. pub. as *L'Histoire Grecque*. Paris 1995)

Orwin, C. (1994) *The Humanity of Thucydides*. Princeton

Osborne, M. J. (1981–3) *Naturalization in Athens*, 4 vols. Brussels

Osborne, R. G. (1985) 'Law in action in Classical Athens', *JHS* 105: 40–58
    (1999) 'Archaeology and the Athenian Empire', *TAPhA* 129: 319–32
    (2000a) *The Athenian Empire*, LACTOR 1. Harrow, 4th edn
    (2000b) 'Religion, imperial politics and the offering of freedom to slaves', in V. J. Hunter & J. C. Edmondson (edd.) *Law and Social Status in Classical Athens*. Oxford and New York: 75–92

Osgood, R. E. (1953) *Ideals and Self-Interest in America's Foreign Relations. The great transformation of the twentieth century*. Chicago and London

Osiander, A. (1998) 'Rereading early twentieth-century IR theory: Idealism revisited', *International Studies Quarterly* 42: 409–32 (repr. in A. Linklater (ed.) *International Relations. Critical concepts in political science*. London and New York 2000, vol. 1: 223–51)
    (2001) 'Sovereignty, International Relations, and the Westphalian myth', *International Organization* 55: 251–87

Ostwald, M. (1969) *Nomos and the Beginnings of Athenian Democracy*. Oxford
    (1982) *Autonomia. Its Genesis and Early History*. Chico
    (1986) *From Popular Sovereignty to the Sovereignty of Law. Law, society and politics in fifth-century Athens*. Berkeley, Los Angeles, London
    (1993) '*Stasis* and *autonomia* in Samos: a comment on an ideological fallacy', *SCI* 12: 51–66
    (2002) 'Athens and Chalkis. A study in imperial control', *JHS* 122: 134–43

Pagden, A. (1982) *The Fall of Natural Man. The American Indian and the origins of comparative ethnology*. Cambridge

Panagopoulos, A. (1978) *Captives and Hostages in the Peloponnesian War.* Athens

Panessa, G. (1999) Philiai. *L'amicizia nelle relazioni interstatali dei Greci*, vol. 1: *Dalle origini alla fine della Guerra del Peloponneso*. Pisa

Paradisi, B. (1957) 'Due aspetti fondamentali nella formazione del diritto internazionale antico', *Annali di Storia del Diritto* 1: 169–259

Parekh, B. (1997) 'The dilemmas of humanitarian intervention: introduction', *International Political Science Review* 18: 5–7

Parfit, D. (1979) 'Prudence, morality and the Prisoner's Dilemma', *PBA* 65: 539–64

Parker, R. (1983) *Miasma. Pollution and purification in early Greek religion.* Oxford

(1996) *Athenian Religion. A history.* Oxford

(1998) *Cleomenes on the Acropolis*, Oxford Inaugural Lecture

Parry, A. (1969) 'The language of Thucydides' description of the plague', *BICS* 16: 106–18

Pearson, L. (1952) '*Prophasis* and *aitia*', *TAPhA* 83: 205–23

(1962) *Popular Ethics in Ancient Greece.* Stanford

Pečírka, J. (1966) *The Formula for the Grant of Enktesis in Attic Inscriptions.* Prague

Pelling, C. B. R. (2000) *Literary Texts and the Greek Historian.* London and New York

Perlman, S. (1964) 'The causes and outbreak of the Corinthian War', *CQ* ns 14: 64–81

(1969) 'Isocrates' "Philippus" and panhellenism', *Historia* 18: 370–4

(1976) 'Panhellenism, the polis and imperialism', *Historia* 25: 1–30

(1985) 'Greek diplomatic tradition and the Corinthian League of Philip of Macedon', *Historia* 34: 153–74

(1991) 'Hegemony and *arkhe* in Greece: fourth-century BC views', in R. N. Lebow & B. S. Strauss (edd.) *Hegemonic Rivalry from Thucydides to the Nuclear Age.* Boulder and Oxford: 269–86

Phillipson, C. (1908) *Two Studies in International Law.* London

(1911) *The International Law and Custom of Ancient Greece and Rome*, 2 vols. London

(1915) *International Law and the Great War.* London

(1916) *Termination of War and Treaties of Peace.* London

Photos-Jones, E., A. Cottier, A. J. Hall & L. G. Mendoni (1997) 'Kean miltos: the well-known iron oxides of antiquity', *ABSA* 92: 359–71

Piccirilli, L. (1973) *Gli Arbitrati Interstatali Greci,* vol. 1: *Dalle Origini al 338 a.C.* Pisa

(2001) 'La diplomazia nella Grecia antica: temi del linguaggio e caratteristiche degli ambasciatori', *MH* 58: 1–31

(2002) *L'invenzione della Diplomazia nella Grecia Antica*, Rapporti Interstatali nell'Antichità 1. Rome

Pickard-Cambridge, A. W. (1914) *Demosthenes and the Last Days of Greek Freedom.* London and New York

Pistorius, T. (1985) *Hegemoniestreben und Autonomiesicherung in der griechischen Vertragspolitik klassischer und hellenistischer Zeit.* Frankfurt am Main, Bern, New York

Plescia, J. (1970) *The Oath and Perjury in Ancient Greece.* Tallahassee

Plezia, M. (1982) 'Agesilaos und Timotheos: zwei Staatsmännerporträts aus der Mitte des IV Jhs', *ICS* 7: 49–61

Porciani, L. (1996) 'L'ideologia politica del *Panegirico* di Isocrate', *ANSP* ser. 4, vol. I: 31–9

Porter, B. (ed.) (1972) *The Aberystwyth Papers. International Politics 1919–1969.* London

  (1972) 'Holders of the Woodrow Wilson Chair', in *id.* (ed.) *The Aberystwyth Papers. International politics 1919–1969.* London: 361–9

Pouilloux, J. (1954) *Recherches sur l'Histoire et les Cultes de Thasos*, vol. I: *de la Fondation de la Cité à 196 avant J.-C.*, Études Thasiennes 3. Paris

Pownall, F. S. (1998) 'Condemnation of the impious in Xenophon's *Hellenica*', *Harvard Theological Review* 91: 251–77

Price, J. J. (2001) *Thucydides and Internal War.* Cambridge

Price, S. R. F. (1999) *Religions of the Ancient Greeks.* Cambridge

Prinz, K. (1997) *Epitaphios Logos. Struktur, Funktion und Bedeutung der Bestattungsreden im Athen des 5. und 4. Jahrhunderts.* Frankfurt am Main

Pritchett, W. K. (1971–91) *The Greek State at War*, 5 vols. Berkeley, Los Angeles, London/Oxford

Purnell, R. (1978) 'Theoretical approaches to International Relations: the contribution of the Greco-Roman world', in T. Taylor (ed.) *Approaches and Theory in International Relations.* London and New York: 19–31

Quandt, R. E. (1961) 'On the use of Game Models in theories of International Relations', in K. Knorr & S. Verba (edd.) *The International System. Theoretical essays.* Princeton: 69–76

Raaflaub, K. A. (1979a) 'Beute, Vergeltung, Freiheit'? Zur Zielsetzung des Delisch-Attischen Seebundes', *Chiron*: 1–22

  (1979b) 'Polis Tyrannos: zur Entstehung einer politischen Metapher', in G. W. Bowersock, W. Burkert & M. C. J. Putnam (edd.) *Arktouros. Hellenic studies presented to Bernard M. W. Knox on the occasion of his 65th birthday.* Berlin and New York: 237–52

  (1984) 'Athens "Ideologie der Macht" und die Freiheit des Tyrannen', in W. Schuller (ed.) *Studien zum Attischen Seebund*, Xenia: Konstanzer Althistorische Vorträge und Forschungen 8. Konstanz: 45–86

  (2000) 'Zeus Eleutherios, Dionysos the Liberator, and the Athenian Tyrannicides. Anachronistic uses of fifth-century political concepts', in P. Flensted-Jensen, T. H. Nielsen & L. Rubinstein (edd.) *Polis and Politics. Studies in Ancient Greek History presented to Mogens Herman Hansen on his sixtieth birthday, August 20, 2000.* Copenhagen: 249–75

  (2004) *The Discovery of Freedom in Ancient Greece*, rev. edn, tr. R. Franciscono. Chicago and London (orig. pub. as *Die Entdeckung der Freiheit. Zur historischen Semantik und Gesellschaftsgeschichte eines politischen Grundbegriffes der Griechen.* Munich 1985)

Rademaker, A. (2005) *Sophrosyne and the Rhetoric of Self-Restraint. Polysemy and persuasive use of an ancient Greek value term.* Leiden

Radicke, J. (1995) *Die Rede des Demosthenes für die Freiheit der Rhodier (Or.15).* Stuttgart and Leipzig

Raeder, A. (1912) *L'Arbitrage International chez les Hellènes*. Kristiania and New York

Rahe, P. A. (1995/6) 'Thucydides' Critique of Realpolitik', *Security Studies* 5: 101–39

Ramsbotham, O. (1997) 'Humanitarian intervention 1990–5: a need to reconceptualize?', *Review of International Studies* 23: 445–68

Rawls, J. (1999) *The Law of Peoples: with 'The Idea of Public Reason Revisited'*. Cambridge, Ma. and London

Raymond, G. A. (1997) 'Problems and prospects in the study of international norms', *International Studies Quarterly* 41: 205–45

Redslob, R. (1923) *Histoire des Grands Principes du Droit des Gens, depuis l'Antiquité jusqu'à la Veille de la Grande Guerre*. Paris

Regan, P. M. (1998) 'Choosing to intervene: outside interventions in internal conflicts', *Journal of Politics* 60: 754–79

Reus-Smit, C. (1999) *The Moral Purpose of the State. Culture, social identity, and institutional rationality in International Relations*. Princeton

Rhodes, P. J. (1985) *The Athenian Boule*, rev. edn. Oxford (1st edn 1972)

   (1987) '*Nomothesia* in Classical Athens', in A. Giuliani & N. Picardi (edd.) *L'Educazione Giuridica*, vol. v: *Modelli di Legislatore e Scienza della Legislazione. 2: Modelli storici e comparativi*. Perugia: 5–26

   (1993) 'The Greek *poleis*: demes, cities and leagues', in M. H. Hansen (ed.) *The Ancient Greek City-State*, CPC Acts 1. Copenhagen: 161–82

   (1994) 'The polis and the alternatives', in D. M. Lewis, J. Boardman, S. Hornblower & M. Ostwald (edd.) *The Cambridge Ancient History*, vol. vi: *The Fourth Century BC*, 2nd edn. Cambridge: 565–91

   (1999) 'Sparta, Thebes and *autonomia*', *Eirene* 35: 33–40

Rhodes, P. J. with D. M. Lewis (1997) *The Decrees of the Greek States*. Oxford

Rich, P. (1995) 'Alfred Zimmern's cautious idealism. The League of Nations, international education, and the Commonwealth', in D. Long & P. Wilson (edd.) *Thinkers of the Twenty Years' Crisis*. Oxford: 79–99

Roberson, B. A. (ed.) (1998) *International Society and the Development of International Relations Theory*. London and Washington

Roberts, A. & B. Kingsbury (1993) 'The UN's roles in international society since 1945', in *eid.* (edd.) *United Nations. Divided World. The UN's roles in international relations*, 2nd edn. Oxford: 1–62 (1st edn 1988)

Robertson, N. (1976) 'False documents at Athens: fifth-century history and fourth-century publicists', *Historical Reflections/Réflexions Historiques* 3: 3–24

Robinson, W. I. (1996) *Promoting Polyarchy. Globalization, US intervention, and hegemony*. Cambridge

Roebuck, D. (2001) *Ancient Greek Arbitration*. Oxford

Roisman, J. (2003) 'The rhetoric of courage in the Athenian orators', in R. M. Rosen & I. Sluiter (edd.) *Andreia. Studies in manliness and courage in classical antiquity*. Leiden and Boston: 127–43

Romilly, J. de (1958) '*Eunoia* in Isocrates or the political importance of creating good will', *JHS* 78: 92–101

(1963) *Thucydides and Athenian Imperialism*, tr. P. Thody. Oxford (orig. pub. as *Thucydide et l'imperialisme athénien: la pensée de l'historien et la genèse de l'oeuvre*. Paris 1947)

(1968) 'Guerre et paix entre cités', in J.-P. Vernant (ed.) *Problèmes de la Guerre en Grèce Ancienne*. Paris and The Hague: 207–20

(1971) *La Loi dans la Pensée Grecque, des Origines à Aristote*. Paris

(1972) 'Vocabulaire et propagande ou les premiers emplois du mot *homonoia*', in *Mélanges de Linguistique et de Philologie Grecques Offerts à Pierre Chantraine*. Paris: 199–209

(1977) *The Rise and Fall of States according to Greek Authors*. Ann Arbor

(1979) *La Douceur dans la Pensée Grecque*. Paris

Rood, T. (1998) *Thucydides. Narrative and explanation*. Oxford

(2004) 'Panhellenism and self-presentation: Xenophon's speeches', in R. Lane Fox (ed.) *The Long March. Xenophon and the Ten Thousand*. London and New Haven: 305–29

Rorty, A. O. (1996) 'Structuring rhetoric', in *ead*. (ed.) *Essays on Aristotle's Rhetoric*. Berkeley, Los Angeles, London: 1–33

Rosenau, J. N. (1968) 'The concept of intervention', *Journal of International Affairs* 22: 165–76

(1997) *Along the Domestic-Foreign Frontier. Exploring governance in a turbulent world*. Cambridge

Rostovtseff, M. I. (1922) 'International relations in the ancient world', in E. A. Walsh (ed.) *The History and Nature of International Relations*. New York: 31–65

Roux, G. (1979) *L'Amphictionie, Delphes, et le Temple d'Apollon au IVe Siècle*. Lyon and Paris

Rowe, C. (2000) 'Introduction', in C. Rowe & M. Schofield (edd.) *The Cambridge History of Greek and Roman Political Thought*. Cambridge: 1–6

Rubin, A. P. (1997) *Ethics and Authority in International Law*. Cambridge and New York

Ruschenbusch, E. (1978) *Untersuchungen zu Staat und Politik in Griechenland vom 7–4 Jh. v. Chr.* Bamberg

Rusten, J. S. (1989) *Thucydides. The Peloponnesian War. Book II*. Cambridge

Ryder, T. T. B. (1965) *Koine Eirene. General peace and local independence in Ancient Greece*. London

Ste. Croix, G. E. M. de (1954/5) 'The character of the Athenian Empire', *Historia* 3: 1–41

(1963) 'The alleged secret pact between Athens and Philip II concerning Amphipolis and Pydna', *CQ* ns 13: 110–19 (repr. in S. Perlman (ed.) *Philip and Athens*. Cambridge 1973: 36–45)

(1972) *The Origins of the Peloponnesian War*. London and Ithaca

(1981) *The Class Struggle in the Ancient Greek World. From the archaic age to the Arab conquests.* London and Ithaca

Sanchez, P. (1997) 'Le serment amphictionique [Aeschin. *Legat* (2) 115]: un faux du IVe siècle?', *Historia* 46: 158–71

Saunders, T. J. (1991) *Plato's Penal Code. Tradition, controversy and reform in Greek penology.* Oxford

Schiller, A. K. (1996) 'Political territoriality of the Classical Athenians, 508–338 BC', PhD Wisconsin-Madison

Schmidt, B. C. (1998) *The Political Discourse of Anarchy. A disciplinary history of International Relations.* Albany

Schmidt, G. (1990) 'Fluch und Frevel als Elemente politischer Propaganda im Vor- und Umfeld des Peloponnesischen Krieges', *RSA* 20: 7–30

Schmitz, W. (1988) *Wirtschaftliche Prosperität, soziale Integration und die Seebundpolitik Athens. Die Wirkung der Erfahrungen aus dem Ersten Attischen Seebund auf die athenische Außenpolitik in der ersten Hälfte des 4. Jahrhunderts v. Chr.* Munich

Schneider, J. G. (ed.) (1849) *Xenophontis* Historiae Graecae. *Libri septem.* Leipzig

Schofield, M. (1999) 'Sharing in the Constitution', in *Saving the City. Philosopher Kings and other classical paradigms.* London and New York: 141–59 (orig. pub. in *Review of Metaphysics* 49 (1996): 831–58)

Schroeder, P. (1994) 'Historical reality vs. neo-realist theory', *International Security* 19: 108–48

Schütrumpf, E. (1972) 'Kosmopolitismus oder Panhellenismus? Zur Interpretation des Ausspruchs von Hippias in Platons Protagoras (337c ff)', *Hermes* 100: 5–29

Schultheß, R. (1935) '*Synthêkê*', *RE* Supplement 6: 1158–68

Schwarzenburger, G. (1980) 'Historical models of international law: toward a comparative history of international law', in W. E. Butler (ed.) *International Law in Comparative Perspective.* Alphen aan der Rijn and Germantown: 227–50

Schweigert, E. (1940) 'Greek inscriptions', *Hesperia* 9: 309–57

Schwenk, C. (1985) *Athens in the Age of Alexander. The dated laws and decrees of 'the Lykourgan Era' 338–322 BC.* Chicago

Seaford, R. (1998) 'Introduction', in C. Gill, N. Postlethwaite & R. Seaford (edd.) *Reciprocity in Ancient Greece.* Oxford: 1–11

Seager, R. & C. J. Tuplin (1980) 'The freedom of the Greeks of Asia: on the origins of a concept and the creation of a slogan', *JHS* 100: 141–54

Sealey, R. (1993) *Demosthenes and his Time. A study in defeat.* New York and Oxford

Sheets, G. A. (1994) 'Conceptualising international law in Thucydides', *AJPh* 115: 51–73

Shipley, G. (1993) 'Introduction: the limits of war', in J. Rich & G. Shipley (edd.) *War and Society in the Greek World.* London and New York: 1–24

Shorey, P. (1893) 'On the implicit ethics and psychology of Thucydides', *TAPhA* 24: 66–88

Siewert, P. (1972) *Der Eid von Plataiai*. Munich

Sinclair, T. A. (1952) *A History of Greek Political Thought*. London

Smarczyk, B. (1990) *Untersuchungen zur Religionspolitik und politischen Propaganda Athens im Delisch-Attischen Seebund*. Munich

Smith, S. (1989) 'Paradigm dominance in International Relations. The development of International Relations as a social science', in H. C. Dyer & L. Mangesarian (edd.) *The Study of International Relations. The state of the art*. Basingstoke: 3–27

　(1995) 'The self-images of a discipline: a genealogy of International Relations theory', in K. Booth & S. Smith (edd.) *International Relations Theory Today*. Cambridge and Oxford: 1–37

　(1996) 'Positivism and beyond', in S. Smith, K. Booth & M. Zalewski (edd.) *International Theory. Positivism and beyond*. Cambridge: 11–44 (repr. in A. Linklater (ed.) *International Relations. Critical concepts in political science*. London and New York 2000, vol. II: 568–96)

　(2000) 'Wendt's world', *Review of International Studies* 26: 151–63

Smith, S., K. Booth & M. Zalewski (edd.) (1996) *International Theory. Positivism and beyond*. Cambridge

Smith, T. W. (1999) *History and International Relations*. London and New York

Snell, F. J. (ed.) (1887) *Lysias* Epitaphios. Oxford

Squillace, G. (2000) 'L'ultimo intervento di Filippo II in Tessaglia nella propaganda macedone e antimacedone', *Aevum* 74: 81–94

Stephen, J. K. (1884) *International Law and International Relations. An attempt to ascertain the best method of discussing the topics of international law*. London

Stern, G. (1995) *The Structure of International Society. An introduction to the study of International Relations*. London and New York

Stevenson, L. & D. L. Haberman (1998) *Ten Theories of Human Nature*. New York and Oxford (rev. edn of L. Stevenson, *Seven Theories of Human Nature*. Oxford 1974)

Strasburger, H. (1958) 'Thukydides und die politische Selbstdarstellung der Athener', *Hermes* 86: 17–40

Strauss, B. S. (1997) 'The problem of periodization: the case of the Peloponnesian War', in M. Golden & P. Toohey (edd.) *Inventing Ancient Culture. Historicism, periodization and the ancient world*. New York and London: 165–75

Strauss, B. S. & J. Ober (1990) *The Anatomy of Error. Ancient military disasters and their lessons for modern strategists*. New York

Stray, C. (1998) *Classics Transformed. Schools, universities and society in England, 1830–1960*. Oxford

Suganami, H. (1989) *The Domestic Analogy and World Order Proposals*. Cambridge

(2001) 'C. A. W. Manning and the study of international relations', *Review of International Studies* 27: 91–107

Symonds, R. (1991) *Oxford and Empire. The last lost cause?*, 2nd edn. Oxford (1st edn London 1986)

Taylor, C. C. W. (1990) 'Popular morality and unpopular philosophy', in E. M. Craik (ed.) *Owls to Athens. Essays on classical subjects presented to Sir Kenneth Dover*. Oxford: 233–43

(1998) 'Platonic ethics', in S. Everson (ed.) *Ethics*, Companions to Ancient Thought 4. Cambridge: 49–76

Ténékidès, G. (1931) 'L'amphictyonie de Delphes et la ligue de Corinthe dans leur affinités avec la Société des Nations', *Revue Générale de Droit International Public* 38: 5–20

(1993) 'La notion juridique d'indépendence et la tradition hellénique', in *Les Relations Internationales dans la Grèce Antique*. Athens: 3–226

Thériault, G. (1996) *Le Culte d'Homonoia dans les Cités Grecques*. Lyon and Québec

Thomas, R. (1992) *Literacy and Orality in Ancient Greece*. Cambridge

(1995) 'Written in stone? Liberty, equality, orality and the codification of law', *BICS* ns 2: 59–74 (repr. in L. Foxhall & A. D. E. Lewis (edd.) *Greek Law in its Political Setting. Justifications not justice*. Oxford 1996: 9–31)

(2000) *Herodotus in Context. Ethnography, science and the art of persuasion*. Cambridge

Thompson, K. W. (1985) *Moralism and Morality in Politics and Diplomacy*. Lanham

(1994) *Fathers of International Thought. The legacy of political theory*. Baton Rouge and London

Thompson, W. R. (1995) 'Comparing world systems: systemic leadership succession and the Peloponnesian War case', in C. Chase-Dunn (ed.) *The Historical Evolution of the International Political Economy*, vol. I. Aldershot: 271–86

Thür, G. (1996) 'Oaths and dispute settlement in ancient Greek law', in L. Foxhall & A. D. E. Lewis (edd.) *Greek Law in its Political Setting. Justifications not justice*. Oxford: 57–72

Tillyard, E. M. W. (1914) *The Athenian Empire and the Great Illusion*. Cambridge

Tod, M. N. (1913) *International Arbitration amongst the Greeks*. Oxford

Todd, S. C. (1985) 'Athenian internal politics 403–395 BC, with particular reference to the speeches of Lysias', PhD Cambridge

(1993) *The Shape of Athenian Law*. Oxford

(2000) 'The language of law in Classical Athens', in P. Coss (ed.) *The Moral World of the Law*. Cambridge: 17–36

Todd, S. C. & P. C. Millett (1990) 'Law, society and Athens', in P. A. Cartledge, P. C. Millett & S. C. Todd (edd.) *Nomos. Essays in Athenian law, politics and society*. Cambridge: 1–18

Too, Y. L. (1995) *The Rhetoric of Identity in Isocrates. Text, power, pedagogy*. Cambridge

Tracy, S. V. (1995) *Athenian Democracy in Transition. Attic letter-cutters of 340–290 BC*. Berkeley, Los Angeles, London

Trevett, J. (1992) *Apollodorus the Son of Pasion*. Oxford

Triantaphyllopoulos, I. K. (1985) *Das Rechtsdenken der Griechen*. Munich

Tritle, L. A. (1993) 'Philip, Athens and Euboea', in W. J. Cherf (ed.) *Alpha to Omega. Studies in honor of George John Szemler on his 65th birthday*. Chicago: 227–38

Tuck, R. (1999) *The Rights of War and Peace. Political thought and the international order from Grotius to Kant*. Oxford

Tuplin, C. J. (1984) 'Timotheus and Corcyra: problems in Greek history 375–373 BC', *Athenaeum* 62: 537–68

　(1985) 'Imperial Tyranny: some reflections on a Classical Greek political metaphor', in P. A. Cartledge & F. D. Harvey (edd.) *Crux. Essays in Greek History presented to G. E. M. de Ste. Croix on his 75th birthday*. London and Exeter: 348–75 (= *HPTh* 6)

　(1993) *The Failings of Empire. A reading of Xenophon Hellenica 2.3.11–7.5.27, Historia* Einzelschriften 76. Stuttgart

Tyler, T. R. (1990) *Why People Obey the Law*. New Haven and London

Usher, S. (1994) 'Isocrates: paideia, kingship and the barbarians', in H. A. Khan (ed.) *The Birth of the European Identity. The Europe–Asia contrast in Greek thought, 490–322 BC*. Nottingham: 131–45

Van Effenterre, H. & F. Ruzé (1994–5) *Nomima. Receuil d'inscriptions politiques et juridiques de l'archaïsme grec*, 2 vols. Rome

Van Wees, H. (1998) 'The law of gratitude: reciprocity in anthropological theory', in C. Gill, N. Postlethwaite & R. Seaford (edd.) *Reciprocity in Ancient Greece*. Oxford: 13–49

　(2001) 'War and peace in ancient Greece', in B. Heuser & A. V. Hartmann (edd.) *War, Peace and World Orders in European History*. London and New York 2001: 33–47

　(2004) *Greek Warfare. Myths and realities*. London

Varouxakis, G. (1997) 'John Stuart Mill on intervention and non-intervention', *Millennium* 26: 57–76

Vasquez, J. A. (1995) 'The post-positivist debate: reconstructing scientific enquiry and International Relations theory after Enlightenment's fall', in K. Booth & S. Smith (edd.) *International Relations Theory Today*. Cambridge and Oxford: 217–40

　(1998) *The Power of Power Politics. From Classical Realism to Neotraditionalism*. Cambridge (rev. version of *The Power of Power Politics. A critique*. London and New Brunswick 1983)

Vatin, C. (1983) 'Les Danseurs de Delphes', *CRAI*: 26–40

Vaughn, P. (1991) 'The identification and retrieval of the hoplite battle-dead', in V. D. Hanson (ed.) *Hoplites. The classical Greek battle experience*. London and New York: 38–62

Veligianni-Terzi, C. (1997) *Wertbegriffe in den attischen Ehrendekreten der Klassischen Zeit*. Stuttgart

Verzijl, J. H. W. (1968) *International Law in Historical Perspective*, vol. I: *General Subjects*. Leiden

Vincent, R. J. (1974) *Nonintervention and International Order*. Princeton

Vinogradoff, P. (1922) *Outlines of Historical Jurisprudence*, vol. II: *The Jurisprudence of the Greek City*. Oxford

Virgilio, B. (1969) 'Rassegna di studi sulle prossenie greche', *RFIC* 97: 494–501

Wæver, O. (1996) 'The rise and fall of the inter-paradigm debate', in S. Smith, K. Booth & M. Zalewski (edd.) *International Theory. Positivism and beyond*. Cambridge: 149–85

  (1997) 'Figures of international thought: introducing persons instead of paradigms', in I. B. Neumann & O. Wæver (edd.) *The Future of International Relations. Masters in the making?* London and New York: 1–37

  (1999) 'The sociology of a not so international discipline: American and European development in International Relations', in P. J. Katzenstein, R. O. Keohane & S. D. Krasner (edd.) *Exploration and Contestation in the Study of World Politics*. Cambridge, Ma. and London: 47–87

Walbank, F. W. (1985a) 'Political morality and the friends of Scipio', in *Selected Papers. Studies in Greek and Roman History and Historiography*. Cambridge: 157–80 (orig. pub. in *JRS* 55 (1965): 1–16)

  (1985b) 'The Problem of Greek Nationality', in *Selected Papers. Studies in Greek and Roman History and Historiography*. Cambridge: 1–19 (orig. pub. in *Phoenix* 5 (1951): 41–60)

Walbank, M. (1978) *Athenian Proxenies of the Fifth Century BC*. Toronto and Sarasota

Walker, R. B. J. (1993) *Inside/Outside. International politics as political theory*. Cambridge

Walker, T. A. (1899) *A History of the Law of Nations*, vol. I: *From the Earliest Times to the Peace of Westphalia, 1648*. Cambridge

Wallace, M. B. (1970) 'Early Greek *proxenoi*', *Phoenix* 24: 189–208

Wallace, R. W. (1985) *The Areopagos Council to 307 BC*. Baltimore and London

Walters, K. R. (1980) 'Rhetoric as ritual: the semiotics of the Attic funeral oration', *Florilegium* 2: 1–27

Waltz, K. N. (1959) *Man, the State, and War. A theoretical analysis*. New York

  (1979) *Theory of International Politics*. New York

  (1997) 'Evaluating theories', *American Political Science Review* 91: 913–17

Walz, J. (1936) *Der Lysianische Epitaphios, Philologus* Supplement 29.4. Leipzig

Walzer, M. (1994) *Thick and Thin. Moral argument at home and abroad*. Notre Dame and London

  (2000) *Just and Unjust Wars. A moral argument with historical illustrations*, 3rd edn. New York (1st edn 1977)

Warner, R. (1979) (tr.) *Xenophon: A History of My Times*, rev. edn, ed. G. L. Cawkwell. Harmondsworth (1st edn 1966)

Watson, A. (1990) 'Systems of states', *Review of International Studies* 16: 99–109
(1992) *The Evolution of International Society. A comparative historical analysis*. London and New York
(1998) 'The British Committee for the Theory of International Politics: some historical notes', (Online) Available: http://www.leeds.ac.uk/polis/englishschool/watson98.doc (Accessed 21 January 2006)

Watson, L. C. (1991) *Arae. The curse poetry of antiquity*. Leeds

Watts, A. (2000) 'The importance of international law', in M. Byers (ed.) *The Role of Law in International Politics. Essays in international relations and international law*. Oxford and New York: 5–16

Webb, K. (1994) 'Academics and practitioners: power, knowledge and role', in M. Girard, W.-D. Eberwein & K. Webb (edd.) *Theory and Practice in Foreign Policy-Making. National perspectives on academics and professionals in International Relations*. London and New York: 13–25

Weber, C. (1995) *Simulating Sovereignty. Intervention, the state and symbolic exchange*. Cambridge

Wegner, A. (1936) *Geschichte des Völkerrechts*. Stuttgart

Wehrli, F. (1968) 'Zur politischen Theorie der Griechen: Gewaltherrschaft und Hegemonie', *MH* 25: 214–25

Weinfeld, M. (1990) 'The common heritage of covenantal treaties in the ancient world', in L. Canfora, M. Liverani & C. Zaccagnini (edd.) *I Trattati nel Mondo Antico. Forma, ideologia, funzione*. Rome: 175–91

Welch, D. A. (1994) 'Can we think systematically about ethics and statecraft?', *Ethics and International Affairs* 8: 23–37
(2003) 'Why international relations theorists should stop reading Thucydides', *Review of International Studies* 29: 301–19

Welsh, J. M. (ed.) (2003) *Humanitarian Intervention and International Relations*. Oxford

Welwei, K.-W. (1986) '"Demos" und "Plethos", in Athenischen Volksbeschlüssen um 450 v. Chr.', *Historia* 35: 177–91

Wendt, A. (1992) 'Anarchy is what states make of it: the social construction of power politics', *International Organization* 46: 391–425 (repr. in J. Der Derian (ed.) *International Theory. Critical Investigations*. Basingstoke and London 1995: 129–77; and in A. Linklater (ed.) *International Relations. Critical concepts in political science*. London and New York 2000, vol. II: 615–51)
(1999) *Social Theory of International Politics*. Cambridge

West, W. C. (1995) 'The Decrees of Demosthenes *Against Leptines*', *ZPE* 107: 237–47

Westlake, H D. (1989) 'Diplomacy in Thucydides', in *Studies in Thucydides and Greek History*. Bristol: 19–33

Wheeler, E. L. (1984) 'Sophistic interpretations and Greek treaties', *GRBS* 25: 253–74

Wheeler, N. J. (2000) *Saving Strangers. Humanitarian intervention in international society.* Oxford

(2001) 'Humanitarian intervention after Kosovo: emergent norm, moral duty, or the coming anarchy?', *International Affairs* 77: 113–28

Whelan, F. G. (1983) 'Socrates and the 'meddlesomeness' of the Athenians', *HPTh* 4: 1–29

(1998) 'Legal positivism and international society', in D. R. Mapel & T. Nardin (edd.) *International Society. Diverse ethical perspectives.* Princeton: 36–53

White, N. (2002) *Individual and Conflict in Greek Ethics.* Oxford

Whitehead, D. (1993) 'Cardinal virtues: the language of public approbation in democratic Athens', *C&M* 44: 37–75

(1998) Review of Veligianni-Terzi 1997, (Online) Available: http://ccat.sas. upenn.edu/bmcr/1998/98.1.09.html (Accessed 21 January 2006)

Whitley, J. (1997) 'Cretan Laws and Cretan Literacy', *AJA* ns 101: 635–61

Wickersham, J. (1994) *Hegemony and Greek Historians.* Lanham

Wight, M. (1966a) 'Western values in International Relations', in H. Butterfield & M. Wight (edd.) *Diplomatic Investigations. Essays in the theory of international politics.* London: 89–131

(1966b) 'Why is there no international theory?', in H. Butterfield & M. Wight (edd.) *Diplomatic Investigations. Essays in the theory of international politics.* London: 17–34 (repr. in J. Der Derian (ed.) *International Theory. Critical Investigations.* Basingstoke and London 1995: 15–35; and in A. Linklater (ed.) *International Relations. Critical concepts in political science.* London and New York 2000, vol. I: 27–42)

(1977) *Systems of States*, ed. and intro. H. Bull. Leicester

(1979) *Power Politics*, ed. H. Bull & C. Holbraad. Harmondsworth

(1991) *International Theory: the Three Traditions*, ed. G. Wight & B. Porter. Leicester

Wilhelm, A. (1940) 'Vier Beschlüsse der Athener', in *Abhandlungen der Preussischen Akademie der Wissenschaften, Jg. 1939, phil.-hist. Kl. Nr. 22.* Berlin: 3–29 (repr. in *Akademieschriften zur griechischen Inschriftenkunde (1895–1951)* vol. III: *1939–1951.* Leipzig 1974: 15–41)

(1942) *Attische Urkunden*, vol. v. Vienna and Leipzig

Will, E. (1956) *Doriens et Ioniens. Essai sur la valeur du critère ethnique appliqué à l'étude de l'histoire et de la civilisation grecques.* Paris

Williams, B. A. O. (1981) 'Philosophy', in M. I. Finley (ed.) *The Legacy of Greece. A new appraisal.* Oxford: 202–55

(1993) *Shame and Necessity.* Berkeley, Los Angeles, London

Wilson, D. (1987) *Gilbert Murray OM 1866–1957.* Oxford

Wilson, J. B. (1987) *Athens and Corcyra. Strategy and tactics in the Peloponnesian War.* Bristol

Wilson, P. (1998) 'The myth of the "First Great Debate"', in T. Dunne, M. Cox & K. Booth (edd.) *The 80 Years' Crisis. International Relations 1919–1999*. Cambridge: 1–15 (= *Review of International Studies* 24)

Wilson, W. (1889) *The State. Elements of historical and practical politics. A sketch of institutional history and administration*. Boston, Ma.

(1968) *The Papers of Woodrow Wilson*, vol. v: *1885–1888*, ed. A. S. Link. Princeton

Windsor, P. (1989) 'Foreword', in H. Dyer & L. Mangasarian (edd.) *The Study of International Relations. The state of the art*. Basingstoke and London: viii–xi

Woodhead, A. G. (1970) *Thucydides on the Nature of Power*. Cambridge, Ma.

Yatromanolaki, J. (1997) *Sympheron, Dikaion and Nomoi in Deliberative Rhetoric. Studies in Aristotle's Rhetoric and Demosthenes' deliberative speeches*. Athens

(2000) 'θέματα συμφερόντος και δικαίου στον "Ὑπὲρ Μεγαλοπολιτῶν"(XVI) λόγο του Δημοσθένους', in F. I. Kakridis, G. M. Sifakis, I. Touloumakos & O. Tsagkarakis (edd.) Κτερίσματα. Φιλολογικά μελετήματα αφιερωμένα στον Ιωάννη Σ. Καμπίτση *(1938–1990)*. Heraklion: 11–39

Yunis, H. (ed.) (2001) *Demosthenes* On the Crown. Cambridge

Zahrnt, M. (1971) *Olynth und die Chalkidier. Untersuchungen zur Staatenbildung auf der Chalkidischen Halbinsel im 5. und 4. Jahrhundert v. Chr.* Munich

Ziegler, K.-H. (1994) *Völkerrechtsgeschichte: ein Studienbuch*. Munich

Zimmern, A. E. (1911) *The Greek Commonwealth. Politics and economics in fifth-century Athens*, 1st edn. Oxford (5th edn 1931)

(1921a) *My Impressions of Wales*. London

(1921b) 'Political thought', in R. W. Livingstone (ed.) *The Legacy of Greece*. Oxford: 321–52

(1926a) *The British Commonwealth in the Post-War World*. London

(1926b) *The Third British Empire. Being a course of lectures delivered at Columbia University, New York*, 1st edn. London (3rd edn 1934)

(1928) 'History as an art', in *Solon and Croesus. And other Greek essays*. London: 41–57

(1931) *The Study of International Politics*, Oxford Inaugural Lecture

(1936) *The League of Nations and the Rule of Law 1918–1935*, 1st edn. London (2nd edn 1939)

Ziolkowski, J. E. (1981) *Thucydides and the Tradition of Funeral Speeches at Athens*. New York

(1993) 'National and other contrasts in the Athenian funeral orations', in H. A. Khan (ed.) *The Birth of the European Identity. The Europe-Asia contrast in Greek thought, 490–322 BC*. Nottingham: 1–35

INDEX

Treaties, leagues, and other interstate agreements are listed under the names of the parties involved.

305

INDEX LOCORUM

Inscriptions are listed at the end of this index.

308